THREE FAITHS, ONE GOD

THREE FAITHS, ONE GOD

*The Formative Faith and Practice of Judaism,
Christianity, and Islam*

BY

JACOB NEUSNER
BRUCE CHILTON
WILLIAM GRAHAM

BRILL ACADEMIC PUBLISHERS, INC.
BOSTON • LEIDEN
2002

Library of Congress Cataloging-in-Publication Data

Neusner, Jacob, 1932–
    Three faiths, one God: the formative faith and practice of Judaism, Christianity, and Islam/by Jacob Neusner, Bruce Chilton, and William Graham.
        p. cm.
    Includes bibliographical references and index.
        ISBN 0–391–04146–0
        1. Monotheism—Comparative studies. 2. Judaism. 3. Christianity. 4. Islam. I. Chilton, Bruce. II. Graham, William A. (William Albert), 1943–. III. Title.

BL221 .N45 2002
291.1'4—dc21

2002011456

ISBN 0–391–04146–0
Paperback ISBN 0–391–04180–0

PRINTED IN THE UNITED STATES OF AMERICA

CONTENTS

PREFACE

The three monotheist religious traditions, Judaism, Christianity, and Islam, are here systematically described, side by side. Our concern is how, in the early, or classical sources[1] of each of the three the belief in one unique God, who made heaven and earth and who made himself known to his Creation, works itself out in the three different ways set forth here. We lay stress upon Judaism, Christianity, and Islam not as competing philosophies but as three autonomous religious traditions, each with its own way of telling its unique story, yet all of them addressing a common set of five issues: (1) what we know about God and how we know it; (2) what it means to form God's people; (3) what living the holy way of life requires; (4) how to deal with outsiders to the faith; and (5) what the goal of human history, namely the resurrection and last judgment, is.

That is not to allege that the three traditions share a common structure, only that they intersect at some important points of fundamental concern. Here we spell out the five we perceive to be the most important. This is therefore a work of description. Involved, first of all, are the particularities of the three religions: how each one of them, with its own unique foci and emphases, doctrines, practice, and beliefs, respectively, forms a coherent social system of thought and practice. But readers will observe points of commonality and note similar circles of conviction. The conclusion may be simply put. Although comparable in basic categories, in details each stands on its own. God lives in the details, but it is one and the same God. This we show when the three are set forth in a single, common context. In this way we put the relevant information at peoples' fingertips. The upshot is, while at important points the three religions address the same topic and in some ways overlap, they differ sufficiently so that they cannot claim to be saying the same things, and only to be doing so each in its own idiom. The differences are more than

---

[1] In the citations that follow, each of the authors translated the original Jewish (Neusner), Islamic (Graham), or Christian (Chilton) sources, unless otherwise noted.

verbal. But we aspire to show, too, that the three religions bear in common the potential of mutual understanding despite their variance in their particularities.

That is because of a simple fact. Falling into the genus of religion and forming a single sub-species of theistic religions, the three monotheisms among all theistic religions bear a unique relationship to one another. That is because they concur not only in general, but in particular ways. Specifically, they tell stories of the same type, and some of the stories that they tell turn out to go over much the same ground. Specifically, Judaism, with its focus upon the Hebrew Scriptures of ancient Israel, tells the story of the one God, who created man in his image, and of what happened then within the framework of Israel, the holy people. Christianity takes up that story but gives it a different reading and ending by instantiating the relations between God and his people in the life of a single human being. For its part, in sequence, Islam recapitulates some basic components of the same story, affirming the revelations of Judaism and then Christianity, but drawing the story onward to yet another climax. We cannot point to any three other religions that form so intimate a narrative relationship as do the successive revelations of monotheism. No other set of triplets tells a single, continuous story for themselves as do Islam in relationship to Christianity, and Christianity in relationship to Judaism. What demands close reading is this: within the logic of monotheism, how do Islam, Christianity, and Judaism represent diverse choices among a common set of possibilities?

Here we explore five fundamental, indicative topics on which they concur and differ. The basic categories are congruent; their articulation is not. Our thesis is, if in these matters we understand the relationships among the three different faiths in one God, we may comprehend much about them. By showing the range and potential of a common conviction that God is one and unique, makes demands upon man's social order and the conduct of everyday life, distinguishes those who do his will from the rest of humanity, and will stand in judgment upon all mankind at the end of days, the three religions address a common program. But differing in detail, each affords perspective upon the character of the others. Each sheds light on the choices the others have made from what, we maintain, defines a common agendum, a single menu: the category-formations that they share. Here, then, is the order of exposition.

The Classical Sources and Statements (Chapter One). First, we define the sources upon which we draw for the description, analysis, and interpretation of the normative doctrines of Judaism, Christianity, and Islam. In this way we explain why we rely upon the writings specified. Then we address the five topics that in our view sustain comparison and contrast among the three religious monotheisms.

The Person of God (Chapter Two). Does the interior logic of monotheism require God to be represented as incorporeal and wholly abstract, or can the one, unique God be represented by appeal to analogies supplied by man? In line with Genesis 1:26, which speaks of God's making man "in our image, after our likeness," and the commandment (Ex. 20:4), "You shall not make yourself a graven image or any likeness of anything" in nature, what conclusions are to be drawn? At one end of the continuum, Islam insists that God cannot be represented in any way, shape, or form, not even by man as created in his image, after his likeness. At the other end, Christianity finds that God is both embodied and eternally accessible in the fully divine Son, Jesus Christ. In the middle Judaism represents God in some ways as consubstantial with man, in other ways as wholly other.

The People of God (Chapter Three). God makes himself known to particular persons, who, in the nature of things, form communities among themselves. God addresses a "you" that is not only singular—a Moses or a Jesus or a Muhammad—but plural—all who will believe, act, and obey. Islam, Christianity, and Judaism concur that the faithful form a distinct group, defined by those who accept God's rule and regulation. But, among all humanity, how does that group tell its story, and with what consequence for the definition of the type of group that is constituted? Judaism tells the story of the faithful as an extended family, all of them children of the same ancestors, Abraham and Sarah. It invokes the metaphor of a family, with the result that the faithful adopt for themselves the narrative of a supernatural genealogy, one that finds within the family all who identify themselves as part of it by making its story their genealogy too. Islam dispenses entirely with the analogy of a family, defining God's people instead through the image of a community of the faithful worshippers of God, seeing Muslims as supporters of one another and caretakers of the least fortunate or weakest members of the community.

Where Judaism speaks of a family among the families of humankind or of "Israel" as a nation unlike all others, sui generis, Islam takes the diametrically opposed view. Its "people of God" are ultimately extensible to encompass all humankind within the community of true worshippers of God. Here Christianity takes a middle position. Like Judaism, it views the faithful as a people, but like Islam, it obliterates all prior genealogical distinctions, whether of ethnicity, gender, or politics. So Christians form "a people of the peoples," "a people that is no people," using the familiar metaphor of Israel. At the same time, they underscore, like Islam, a conception of themselves as comprised by mankind without lines of differentiation.

The Holy Way of Life (Chapter Four). God has set forth what he wants from his people, which is the love and devotion of his creatures. This comes to realization in a program of actions to be carried out and to be avoided. These concern acts of prayer, study, contemplation and reflection on divine revelation (in the case of Judaism, study of Torah; in the case of Christianity, the realization and enactment of the image of Christ within the individual believer and the community; in the case of Islam, particular prescribed ritual acts of piety and worship [testimony of faith, ritual prayer, almsgiving, fasting, pilgrimage] as well as recitation of God's word, calling upon him in personal prayer, and obedience to His will). All three also require deeds of philanthropy in charity and acts of loving kindness, above and beyond the requirements of the law. Judaism and Islam share certain food laws, e.g., not to eat carrion but to eat only meat from animals that have been properly slaughtered, and Christianity in its formative age forbade the faithful to eat meat that had been offered to idolatry. Where Islam requires a pilgrimage to Mecca, the observance of the festivals of Judaism encompassed a pilgrimage to the Temple in Jerusalem when it still stood; and Christianity portrayed all the faithful as pilgrims to the new, heavenly Jerusalem that God was preparing for his people. In these and comparable ways, the three religions aim at defining acts that realize God's will and that sanctify God's people.

Believers and Unbelievers (Chapter Five). How are God's people to relate to everybody else? What are the consequences of the conviction that the one and only God has made himself known through one community or person or family to humanity at large? Specifically, what is the task of the believer vis-à-vis the unbeliever? At one side of the continuum, Judaism asks the faithful to avoid participating in, or in any way affirming, the activities of the idolaters in their idolatry. Amiable relationships on ordinary occasions give way to strict isolation from idolatry and all things used in that connection. On the other side of the continuum, Islam, for reasons equally systemic, takes the most active role, undertaking to obliterate idolatry by wiping out its worshippers. Judaism in its classical statement defined its task as passive avoidance, joined with a willingness to accept the sincere convert. Islam called for the active extermination of idolatry, joined with an insistence that, to live, the idolater must renounce his error and acknowledge the one true God as his own. Yet early Islam took a very different position vis-à-vis Jews and Christians and a few other "people of Scripture." These were to be tolerated so long as they did not threaten Muslims or the practice of Islam. Christianity found its position in the middle. On one hand, like Judaism and Islam, Christianity forbade the faithful to utilize anything that could serve idolatry and to refrain, even at the cost of death ("martyrdom"), from all gestures of complicity with idolatry. On the other hand, like Judaism and unlike Islam, Christianity in its formative age contemplated not a holy war of extermination but an ongoing campaign of evangelism, to win over idolaters. True, in due course, Christianity would slide over to the Islamic side of this continuum, but that happened many centuries beyond the classical age. In its formative centuries, Christianity's logic dictated a policy toward unbelievers that placed the religion in the middle, between Judaic passivity and Islamic activity.

The End of Days (Chapter Six). Here is where the interior logic (as well as the articulation) of the three monotheisms both converges and diverges. As told in common, the story finds the resolution of the dialectic of how the one omnipotent and just God can account for a world of manifest injustice. All three religions concur that God will bring the end of days, when all mankind will be raised from the dead and judged, and those found worthy will enter Paradise. At issue is, what do the faithful have to do to advance the end-time? Predictably, Judaism, at its end of the continuum, asks the faithful in one accord to carry out God's will as stated from the beginning, sanctifying the Sabbath of creation one time in accord with the Torah. So Judaism looks inward, within Israel, for the salvation of humanity through Israel's own act of sanctification. Then who is saved at the end, if not all those who acknowledge the one true God? And that will encompass, the prophets say, all of humanity. At the other end of the continuum, Islam holds that no human effort can advance or retard the Last Day. God alone will recall His creation to himself in His own good time. All human beings can do is prepare themselves for the Day of Resurrection by living daily lives of piety and probity. At the Resurrection all who have died before will be called forth with all who are living to face the accounting of their earthly lives and inherit accordingly either Paradise or the Fire as their eternal abode. And Christianity takes a middle position, insisting that the world as we know it, down to the very bodies we inhabit, is to be changed definitively. But in that transformation, a metamorphosis from flesh to spirit and death to life, the identities that we have crafted during the course of our lives are to endure. All people, with or without an explicit knowledge of the Son of God, have known his image in their human experience: so from the point of view of the *eschaton* they have fashioned or have refused to fashion an existence which is commensurate with eternity.

These topics show us similarity and difference: a series of single continua, different positions within each continuum. The interior logic of monotheism raises for the three religions a common set of questions. But then each religion tells the story in its way, and the respective narratives—in character, components, and coherence— shape the distinctive responses spelled out here. That is how the three religions of one God converge and diverge: they converge in their basic structures, which are more symmetrical than asymmetrical, and they diverge in the way their systems work out the implications of monotheism as monotheism is embodied in the continuing narratives, those of Judaism, then Christianity, finally Islam.

We recognize that setting our expositions side by side, without entering into elaborate discussion of comparisons and contrasts but allow the data to speak for themselves, assigns a task to the reader. It is to find a single perspective to encompass the three religions that affirm the unity of God. That is the task that today confronts the entire civilized world. We cannot claim to have accomplished it; we only aver that we have clarified some of the principal issues in common on which all three religious traditions set forth their respective judgments—and therefore differ about a common set of issues. On that basis, there can be a reasoned debate, some day.

JACOB NEUSNER, Bard College
BRUCE CHILTON, Bard College
WILLIAM GRAHAM, Harvard University

CHAPTER ONE

THREE FAITHS, ONE GOD:
THE CLASSICAL STATEMENTS

A. The Issue

When we speak of "Judaism," "Christianity," and "Islam," we refer to large and complex religious traditions, spread over space and time, full of diversity and even conflict. The fundamental difference between Reform and Orthodox Judaism on the authority of the Torah, the centuries-long dispute between Sunni and Shiite Islam, and the tripartite civil war within Christianity among Orthodox (Greek, Russian, and other), Catholic (whether Roman or Anglican), and Evangelical Protestant denominations (not to mention the extraordinary diversity among Evangelicals) manifest the same basic problem. Contemporary debates within Islam on the "true Islam" and the authentic meaning of "Jihad" only underscore the diversity characteristic of all three cognate religions. In defining what we refer to as "Judaism," "Christianity," and "Islam," we have first to ask, which among the Judaisms, Christianities, and Islams, do we compare to which among the others? And further, to what period and definition of those great, complex traditions do we make reference? The question demands attention, because, as everyone knows, "Judaism" encompasses a variety of intersecting, but readily differentiated religious systems, spread over space and time, that concur on some few matters but differ on a great many, and the same is true of Christianity and Islam.

But most Judaisms today and over time make reference to a single corpus of writings, all Christianities privilege the Bible (Old and New Testaments) as the guide to faith in God's Son within the communion of believers, and Islamic communities, however diverse, affirm the divine sanction and authority of the Qur'ān, Sunna, and *hadīth*. For the purpose of comparison, in these pages we form an ideal type out of the evidence, the documents in particular, to which most Judaisms, Christianities, and Islams, make reference. Since we do not make reference to the condition of (an) Islam, Christianity, or

Judaism at some one time and place, for the purposes of comparison and contrast we do not consider borrowings and influences, one
from and upon the other. We deal with large structures of ideas that
the respective families of religions deem convey their fundamental
theological paradigms, e.g., Torah, Christ, Prophet. We compare not
the histories of ideas in the here and now of the social order but
the systems viewed as ideal types.

That is why, when we compare the three great traditions, we
invoke the theologies that emerge from their respective, authoritative writings. For the present purpose, it follows, we do not take
account of variations here and there that later on captured attention. We certainly do not point to the classical formulations to account
for—or even provide background for—contemporary traits of Judaism,
Christianity, or Islam, let alone conflicts between and among them.
Ignoring variables of no consequence for a comparative theology of
foundations, we construct out of the classics an exercise in comparison and contrast between and among those models for Judaism,
Christianity, and Islam that all Judaisms, Christianities, and Islam
affirm. What that means, in actuality, is that the theological systems
of the most influential and norm-setting statements—those of Rabbinic Judaism, Catholic, Orthodox Christianity, and Islam in its purest
form—here meet without regard to the particularities of time or
place. We like to think that if Judaism's Moses or Rabbi, Christianity's
Jesus Christ, and Islam's Prophet Muhammad met as the faithful of
their traditions conceive matters, and if they chose to conduct a conversation on things that count, these are the topics they would choose,
and here are the things they would tell one another.

B. Normative Judaism: The Torah, Written and Oral

I. *The Theology*

"Judaism" here refers to the Judaic religious system set forth by
Scripture (the Hebrew Scriptures of Ancient Israel, also known as,
Christianity's Old Testament or its Hebrew Bible), as mediated in
the Rabbinic writings of the first six centuries of the Common Era
(c.e. = a.d.). Together, Scripture and the Rabbinic Writings call
themselves "the Torah," the one in writing, the other formulated

and transmitted orally and only later written down by the Rabbinic sages of the formative age. Responding to the generative dialectics of monotheism, Rabbinic Judaism systematically reveals the justice of the one and only God of all creation. God is not only God but also good. Appealing to the facts of Scripture, the sages ("our sages of blessed memory") in the first six centuries C.E. constructed a coherent theology, a cogent structure and logical system, to expose the justice of God. When we speak of Rabbinic Judaism, we refer to the religious structure and system that animate the documents produced in that time by those authorities. The theology that systematizes that religion is what is expounded in these pages as Judaism.

The theology of Rabbinic Judaism conveys the picture of world order based on God's justice and equity. The categorical structure of Rabbinic Judaism encompasses three components: God and man, the Torah, Israel and the nations. The working-system of Rabbinic Judaism finds its dynamic in the struggle between God's plan for creation—to create a perfect world of justice—and man's will. That dialectics embodies in a single paradigm the events contained in these sequences: rebellion, sin, punishment, repentance, and atonement; exile and return; or the disruption of world order and its restoration. The following are the four principles of the theology of Rabbinic Judaism:

1. God formed creation in accord with a plan, which the Torah reveals. World order can be shown by the facts of nature and society set forth in that plan to conform to a pattern of reason based upon justice. Those who possess the Torah—Israel—know God, and those who do not—the gentiles—reject him in favor of idols. What happens to each of the two sectors of humanity, respectively, corresponds to their relationship with God. Israel in the present age is subordinate to the nations, because God has designated the gentiles as the medium for penalizing Israel's rebellion, meaning through Israel's subordination and exile to provoke Israel to repent. Private life as much as the public order conforms to the principle that God rules justly in a creation of perfection and stasis.

2. The perfection of creation, realized in the rule of exact justice, is signified by the timelessness of the world of human affairs and their conformity to a few enduring paradigms that transcend change (constituting a theology of history). No present, past, or future marks time, but only the recapitulation of those patterns. Perfection is further

embodied in the unchanging relationships of the social common-
wealth (constituting a theology of political economy), which assure
that scarce resources, once allocated, remain in stasis. A further indication of perfection lies in the complementarity of the components
of creation, on the one side, and, finally, the correspondence between God and man in God's image (theological anthropology), on
the other.

3. Israel's condition, public and personal, marks flaws in creation.
What disrupts perfection is the sole power capable of standing on
its own against God's power, and that is man's will. What man controls and God cannot coerce is man's capacity to form intention and
therefore to choose either arrogantly to defy, or humbly to love,
God. Because man defies God, the sin that results from man's rebellion flaws creation and disrupts world order. The paradigm of the
rebellion of Adam in Eden governs, the act of arrogant rebellion
leading to exile from Eden thus accounting for the condition of
humanity. But, as in the original transaction of alienation and consequent exile, God retains the power to encourage repentance by
punishing man's arrogance. In mercy, moreover, God exercises the
power to respond to repentance with forgiveness—that is, a change
of attitude evoking a counterpart change. Since, commanding his
own will, man also has the power to initiate the process of reconciliation with God—through repentance, an act of humility—man
may restore the perfection of that order that through arrogance he
has marred.

4. God ultimately will restore the perfection that embodied his
plan for creation. In the work of restoration death that comes about
by reason of sin will die, the dead will be raised and judged for
their deeds in this life; and most of them, having been justified, will
go on to eternal life in the world to come. The paradigm of man
restored to Eden is realized in Israel's return to the Land of Israel.
In that world or age to come, however, that sector of humanity that
through the Torah knows God will encompass all of humanity.
Idolaters will perish, and humanity that comprises Israel at the end
will know the one, true God and spend eternity in his light.

In its own behalf, Judaism has always claimed to state the meaning of the revealed Torah of Sinai, written and oral. And, indeed,
recorded in this way, the story told by Rabbinic Judaism proves
remarkably congruent to Scripture's account of matters from Genesis

through Kings. It is wholly familiar, with its stress on God's justice (to which his mercy is integral), man's correspondence with God in his possession of the power of will, man's sin, and God's response.

If we translate into the narrative of Israel, from the beginning to the calamity of the destruction of the (first) Temple, what is set forth in both abstract and concrete ways in Rabbinic Judaism, we turn out to state a reprise of the authorized history laid out in Genesis through Kings and amplified by the principal prophets. Furthermore, the liturgy of synagogue and home recapitulates characteristic modes of thought of Rabbinic Judaism and reworks its distinctive constructions of exemplary figures, events, and conceptions. In defining the religion that the world calls "Judaism" and that calls itself "the Torah," sages have maintained from the very beginning that they possessed the Torah revealed by God to Moses at Mount Sinai ("Moses received Torah at Sinai and handed it on to Joshua, Joshua to elders, and elders to prophets, and prophets handed it on to the men of the great assembly"). That is the Judaic religious system to which most Judaisms later on make reference, and which, to the very present day, defines normative Judaism.

II. *The Documents that Convey the Theology*

In Rabbinic Judaism, the Torah is set forth and preserved in three media:

(1) a book, the Hebrew Scriptures or "Old Testament,"
(2) a memorized oral tradition, first written down in the Mishnah, ca. 200 C.E., and Rabbinic sages' works of Mishnah- and Scripture commentary and amplification, and
(3) the model of a sage who embodies in the here and now the paradigm of Moses, called a rabbi.

Rabbinic literature is the corpus of writing produced in the first six centuries C.E. by sages who claimed to stand in the chain of tradition from Sinai and uniquely to possess the oral part of the Torah, revealed by God to Moses at Sinai for oral formulation and oral transmission, in addition to the written part of the Torah possessed by all Israel. Among the many, diverse documents produced by Jews in late antiquity, the first seven centuries C.E., only a small group cohere and form a distinctive corpus, called "Rabbinic literature."

Three traits together suffice to distinguish Rabbinic literature from all other Jewish (ethnic) and Judaic (religious) writings of that age:

(1) These writings of law and exegesis, revered as holy books, copiously cite the Hebrew Scriptures of ancient Israel ("Written Torah").

(2) They acknowledge neither the authority, nor even the existence, of other Judaic (or gentile) books apart from the ancient Israelite Scriptures.

(3) They promiscuously and ubiquitously cite sayings attributed to named authorities, unique to these writings themselves, most of whom bear the title "rabbi."

Rabbinic literature is divided into two large parts, law and lore. Each part is formed as a commentary to a received part of the Torah, the Mishnah and Scripture, one oral, the other written, respectively. The written part requires no attention here: it is simply Scripture (Hebrew: "the Written Torah," or Tanakh, comprising Torah, Nebi'im, Ketubim, also known as "the Old Testament" part of the Christian Bible). The oral part begins with the Mishnah, a philosophical law code that reached closure at the end of the second century. The written part of course comprises the Pentateuch and other books of ancient Israelite Scripture. Promulgated under the sponsorship of the Roman-appointed Jewish authority of the Land of Israel ("Palestine"), Judah the Patriarch, the Mishnah formed the first document of Rabbinic literature and therefore of the Judaic system, "Rabbinic Judaism," or "the Judaism of the dual Torah," that took shape in this period. The attributed statements of its authorities, sages or rabbis called Tannas ("repeaters," "memorizers," for the form in which the sayings were formulated and transmitted), enjoyed the standing of traditions beginning at Sinai. Numerous anonymous sayings, alongside the attributed ones and bearing upon the same controverted questions, appear as well.

The Mishnah and the Exegetical Tradition of Rabbinic Judaism. Comprising six divisions, dealing with agriculture, holy seasons, women and family affairs, civil law and politics, everyday offerings, and cultic purity, the Mishnah served as the written code of the Patriarch's administration in the Land of Israel, and of that of his counterpart, the exilarch, in Iranian-ruled Babylonia as well. Alongside the Mishnah's compilation of sages' sayings into well-crafted divisions, tractates, and chapters, other sayings of the same authorities circulated, some of them finding their way, marked as deriving from Tannaitic authority, into the Tosefta and the two Talmuds.

Three exegetical documents formed around parts of the Mishnah. These were, specifically:

1. The Tosefta, a compilation of supplementary sayings organized around nearly the whole of the Mishnah as citation and gloss, secondary paraphrase, and freestanding complement thereto, of no determinate date but probably concluded about a century after the closure of the Mishnah, hence ca. 300 C.E.;
   and two Talmuds, or sustained and systematic commentaries to the Mishnah;
2. the Talmud of the Land of Israel, also known as the Palestinian Talmud, which reached closure in ca. 400 C.E., a commentary to most of the tractates of the Mishnah's first four divisions; and
3. the Talmud of Babylonia, concluded in ca. 600 C.E., providing a sustained exegesis to most of the tractates of the Mishnah's second through fifth divisions.

Scripture and the Exegetical Tradition of the Written Torah. Parts of the Written Torah attracted sustained commentary as well, and, altogether, these commentaries, called Midrash-compilations, form the counterpart to the writings of Mishnah-exegesis. It should be noted that both Talmuds, in addition, contain large composites of Midrash exegesis, but they are not organized around books or large selections of Scripture. The part of Rabbinic literature that takes Scripture, rather than the Mishnah, as its organizing structure covers the Pentateuchal books of Genesis, Exodus, Leviticus, Numbers, and Deuteronomy, and some of the writings important in synagogue liturgy, particularly Ruth, Esther, Lamentations, and Song of Songs, all read on special occasions in the sacred calendar. Numbering for late antiquity twelve compilations in all, the earliest compilations of exegesis, called Midrash, were produced in the third century, the latest in the sixth or seventh.

Sages and the Exemplary Torah. There is a third type of writing in Rabbinic literature, which contains teachings of sages on theological and moral questions. This comprises a very small, freestanding corpus, tractate Abot ("the fathers," or founders) and Abot deRabbi Nathan ("the fathers according to Rabbi Nathan"). The former collects sayings of sages, and the latter contributes additional stories about them. But the bulk of Rabbinic literature consists of works of exegesis of the Mishnah and Scripture, which is to say, the principal documents of the Torah, oral and written respectively. Still, throughout the documents of the Orah Torah are also collected compositions and large compilations that are devoted to the sayings and exemplary deeds of named sages.

A Mishnah and Midrash, Halakhah *and* aggadah *(Law and Lore).* Viewed as a whole, therefore, we see that the stream of exegesis of the Mishnah and exploration of its themes of law and philosophy flowed side by side with exegesis of Scripture. Since the Mishnah concerns itself with normative rules of behavior, it and the documents of exegesis flowing from it ordinarily are comprised of discussion of matters of law, or, in Hebrew, *Halakhah.* Much of the exegesis of Scripture in the Midrash compilations concerns itself with norms of belief, right attitude, virtue, and proper motivation. Encased in narrative form, these teachings of an ethical and moral character are called *Aggadah,* or lore.

Midrash exegesis of Israelite Scripture was in no way particular to the Rabbinic literature. To the contrary, the exegesis of the Hebrew Scriptures had defined a convention of all systems of Judaism from before the conclusion of Scripture itself; no one, including the sages who stand behind Rabbinic literature, began anywhere but in the encounter with the Written Torah. But collecting and organizing documents of exegeses of Scripture in a systematic way developed in a quite distinct circumstance.

For Rabbinic literature, the circumstance was defined by the requirement of Mishnah-exegesis. The Mishnah's character itself defined a principal task of Scripture-exegesis. Standing by itself, providing few proof texts to Scripture to back up its rules, the Mishnah bore no explanation as to why Israel should obey its rules. Brought into relationship to Scriptures, by contrast, the Mishnah gained access to the source of authority by definition operative in Israel, the Jewish people. Accordingly, the work of relating the Mishnah's rules to those of Scripture got under way alongside the formation of the Mishnah's rules themselves. It follows that explanations of the sense of the document, including its authority and sources, would draw attention to the written part of the Torah.

We may classify the Midrash compilations in three successive groups: exegetical, propositional, and exegetical-propositional (theological). In our account of Judaism, these are the books that are frequently abstracted.

(1) *Exegetical Discourse and the Pentateuch.* One important dimension, therefore, of the earliest documents of Scripture-exegesis, the Midrash-compilations that deal with Leviticus, Numbers, and Deuteronomy, measures the distance between the Mishnah and Scripture and aims to close it. The question is persistently addressed in analyzing Scripture: Precisely how does a rule of the Mishnah relate to, or rest upon, a rule of Scripture? That question demanded an answer, so that the status of the Mishnah's rules—and, right alongside, of the Mishnah itself—could find a clear definition. Collecting and arranging exegeses of Scripture as these related to passages of the Mishnah first reached literary form in *Sifra*, on Leviticus, and in two books, each called *Sifré*, one on Numbers, the other Deuteronomy (ca. 300 C.E.) All three compositions accomplished much else. For, even at that early stage, exegeses of passages of Scripture in their own context and not only for the sake of Mishnah-exegesis attracted attention. But a principal motif in all three books concerned the issue of Mishnah-Scripture relationships.

A second, still more fruitful path in formulating Midrash-clarifications of Scripture also emerged from the labor of Mishnah-exegesis. As the work of Mishnah-exegesis got under way in the third century, exegetes of the Mishnah and others alongside undertook a parallel labor. They took an interest in reading Scripture in the way in which they were reading the Mishnah itself. That is to say, they began to work through verses of Scripture in exactly the same way—word for word, phrase for phrase, line for line—in which, to begin with, the exegetes of the Mishnah pursued the interpretation and explanation of the Mishnah. Precisely the types of exegesis that dictated the way in which sages read the Mishnah now guided their reading of Scripture as well. And, as people began to collect and organize comments in accord with the order of sentences and paragraphs of the Mishnah, they found the stimulation to collect and organize comments on clauses and verses of Scripture. This kind of verse-by-verse exegetical work got under way in the *Sifra* and the two *Sifrés*, and reached fulfillment in Genesis Rabbah (ca. 400 C.E.) presents a line-for-line reading of the book of Genesis. Characteristic of the narrowly-exegetical phase of Midrash-compilation is the absence of a single, governing proposition, running through the details. It is not possible, for example, to state the main point, expressed through countless cases, in *Sifra* or *Sifré* to Deuteronomy.

(2) *From Exegesis to Proposition.* A further group of Midrash-compilations altogether transcends the limits of formal exegesis. Beyond these two modes of exegesis—search for the sources of the Mishnah in Scripture, line-by-line reading of Scripture as of the Mishnah—lies yet a third, an approach we may call "writing with Scripture," that is, using verses of Scripture in a context established by a propositional program independent of Scripture itself. To understand it, we have to know how the first of the two Talmuds read the Mishnah. The Yerushalmi's authors not only explained phrases or sentences of the Mishnah in the manner of Mishnah- and Scripture-exegetes. They also investigated the principles and large-scale conceptual problems of the document and of the law given only in cases in the Mishnah itself. That is to say, they dealt not only with a given topic, a subject and its rule, and the cases that yield the rule, but with an encompassing problem, a principle and its implications for a number of topics and rules.

This far more discursive and philosophical mode of thought produced for Mishnah-exegesis sustained essays on principles cutting across specific rules. Predictably, this same intellectual work extended from the Mishnah to Scripture. Exegesis of Scripture beyond that focused on words, phrases, and sentences produced discursive essays on great principles or problems of theology and morality. Discursive exegesis is represented, to begin with, in Leviticus Rabbah, a document that reached closure, people generally suppose, sometime after Genesis Rabbah, thus ca. 450 C.E. It marked the shift from verse-by-verse to syllogistic reading of verses of Scripture. It was continued in Pesiqta deRab Kahana, organized around themes pertinent to various holy days through the liturgical year, and Pesiqta Rabbati, a derivative and imitative work.

Typical of discursive exegesis of Scripture, Leviticus Rabbah presents not phrase-by-phrase systematic exegeses of verses in the book of Leviticus, but a set of thirty-seven topical essays. These essays, syllogistic in purpose, take the form of citations and comments on verses of Scripture to be sure. But the compositions range widely over the far reaches of the Hebrew Scriptures while focusing narrowly upon a given theme. They moreover make quite distinctive points about that theme. Their essays constitute compositions, not merely composites. Whether devoted to God's favor to the poor and humble or to the dangers of drunkenness, the essays—exegetical in form, discursive in character—correspond to the equivalent, legal essays, amply represented in the Yerushalmi. The framers of Pesiqta deRab Kahana (ca. 500 C.E.) carried forward a still more abstract and discursive mode of discourse, one in which verses of Scripture play a subordinate role to the framing of an implicit syllogism, which predominates throughout, both formally and in argument.

(3) *Saying One Thing through Many Things.* Writing with Scripture reached its climax in the theological Midrash-compilations formed at the end of the development of Rabbinic literature. A fusion of the two approaches to Midrash-exegesis—the verse-by-verse amplification of successive chapters of Scripture and the syllogistic presentation of propositions, arguments, and proofs deriving from the facts of Scripture—was accomplished in the third body of Midrash-compilations: Ruth Rabbah, Esther Rabbah Part I, Lamentations Rabbah, and Song of Songs Rabbah, all of indeterminate date but possibly of the sixth century. Here we find the verse-by-verse reading of scriptural books. But at the same time, a highly propositional program governs the exegesis, each of the compilations meaning to prove a single, fundamental theological point through the accumulation of detailed comments.

Halakhah and Aggadah, Mishnah and Midrash in a Single Definitive Document. The Talmud of Babylonia, or Bavli, ca. 600 C.E., which was the final document of Rabbinic literature, also formed the climax and conclusion of the entire canon and defined this Judaism from its time to the present. The Talmud of Babylonia forms the conclusion and the summary of Rabbinic literature and is the most important document of the entire collection. One of its principal traits is the fusion of Mishnah- and Scripture-exegesis in a single compilation. The authors of units of discourse collected in the Talmud of Babylonia or Bavli drew together the two, up-to-then distinct, modes of organizing thought, either around the Mishnah or around Scripture. They treated both Torahs, oral and written, as equally available in the work of organizing large-scale exercises of sustained inquiry. So we find in the Bavli a systematic treatment of some tractates of the Mishnah. And within the same aggregates of discourse, we also find (in somewhat smaller proportion to be sure, roughly 60% to roughly 40% in a sample made of three tractates) a second principle of organizing and redaction. That principle dictates that ideas be laid out in line with verses of Scripture, themselves dealt with in cogent sequence, one by one, just as the Mishnah's sentences and paragraphs come under analysis, in cogent order and one by one.

Dating Rabbinic Documents. The dates given above are reliable only for the broad time-frame, ca. 200–600 c.e.—if that. While we have no exact dates for the closure of any of the documents of Rabbinic literature—all the dates we have are mere guesses, we have solid grounds on setting them forth in the ordinal sequence (1) Mishnah, Tosefta, (2) Yerushalmi, (3) Bavli for the exegetical writings on the Mishnah, and the three corresponding, and successive groups—(1) Sifra and the two Sifrés, (2) Genesis Rabbah, Leviticus Rabbah, Pesiqta deRab Kahana, Pesiqta Rabbati, then (3) Ruth Rabbah, Esther Rabbah Part One, Lamentations Rabbah, and Song of Songs Rabbah—for the exegetical writings on Scripture. The basis in the case of the sequence from the Mishnah is citation by one compilation of another, in which case, the cited document is to be dated prior to the document that does the citing. The basis in the case of the sequence from Scripture is less certain; we assign a post-Mishnah date to Sifra and the two Sifrés because of the large-scale citation of the former in the latter. The rest of the sequence given here rests upon presently-accepted and conventional dates and therefore cannot be regarded as final.

C. CLASSICAL CHRISTIANITY: THE BIBLE, OLD AND NEW TESTAMENTS

I. *The Theology*

Christian faith understands itself to be grounded in the Holy Spirit, God's communication of the divine self in all its richness. Access to the Holy Spirit is possible because in Jesus Christ God became human. The incarnation (God's becoming flesh, *caro* in Latin) is what provides the possibility of divine Spirit becoming accessible to the human spirit.

Speaking from the perspective of Christian faith, then, there is a single source of theology: the Holy Spirit that proceeds from the Father and Son. Because God's very nature is love itself, this procession outward to all those he created is the unique and indivisible means of revelation. Human beings are created with the capacity to know Spirit in this sense. Yet the inspiration of the Holy Spirit has been discovered and articulated by means of distinct kinds of literature in the history of the church. By becoming aware of the diversity of those sources, both the variety and the coherence of Christianity may be appreciated.

The Scriptures of Israel have always been valued within the church, primarily in the Greek translation used in the Mediterranean world (the Greek rendering is called the "Septuagint," after the seventy-two translators who were said to have produced it; see *The Letter of Aristeas*). Those were the only Scriptures of the church in its primitive phase, when the New Testament was being composed. In their meetings for prayer and worship, followers of Jesus saw the Scriptures of Israel "fulfilled" by their faith: their conviction was that the same Spirit of God active in the prophets was, through Christ, available to them in a way that realized its power and constituted Israel, God's chosen people, afresh.

The New Testament was produced in primitive communities of Christians to prepare people for baptism, to order worship, to resolve disputes, to encourage faith, and like purposes. As a whole, it is a collective document of primitive Christianity. Its purpose is to call out and order true Israel in response to the triumphant news of Jesus' preaching, activity, death, and resurrection. The New Testament provides the means of accessing the Spirit spoken of in the Scriptures of Israel. Once the New Testament was formed, it was natural to refer to the Scriptures of Israel as the "Old Testament."

The Old Testament is classic for Christians, because it represents the ways in which God's Spirit might be known. At the same time, the New Testament is normative: it sets out how we actually appropriate the Spirit of God, which is also the Spirit of Christ. That is why the Bible as a whole is accorded a place of absolute privilege in the Christian tradition: it is the literary source from which we know both how the Spirit of God has been known and how we can appropriate it.

"Early Christianity" designates the period between the second and fourth centuries C.E. during which the church founded theology on the basis of the Scriptures. Although Christians were under extreme—sometimes violent—pressure from the Roman Empire, the Early Christian era was a time of unique creativity. From thinkers as different from one another as Bishop Irenaeus in second-century France and Origen, the speculative, third-century teacher active first in Egypt and then in Palestine, a common Christian philosophy began to emerge. Early Christianity might also be called a "catholic" phase, in the sense that it was a quest for a "general" or "universal" account of the faith; but that designation may lead to confusion with Roman Catholicism after our period, and is avoided here.

After the Roman Empire itself embraced Christianity in the fourth century, the church was in a position formally to articulate its understanding of the faith by means of common standards. During this period correct norms of worship, baptism, creeds, biblical texts, and doctrines were established. From Augustine in the West to Gregory of Nyssa in the East, Christianity for the first and only time in its history approached being truly ecumenical.

II. The Documents that Convey the Theology

Jesus and his movement clearly recognized the traditional grouping of the Hebrew canon into the Torah, the Prophets (often distinguished between the Former Prophets [Joshua-2 Kings] and the Latter Prophets [Isaiah-Malachi]), and the Writings. That grouping is cited in almost so many words in Luke 24:44. But the Gospels themselves were written in Greek, and the Bible of the church was also Greek in language and Hellenistic in conception. A great deal of work has been done in recent years on the Greek text of the Septuagint;[1] less attention has been given to the actual structure of the rendering, which amounts to a radical revision of the significance of the Hebrew Bible. The Septuagint truly creates an Old Testament by the time of the first extant manuscript of the whole (Codex Vaticanus, dated in the fourth century C.E.).

As Henry Barclay Swete showed long ago, the ordering of books—the sequence and structure of the canon—follows a pattern in the Septuagint significantly different from that of the Hebrew Bible. In the Codex Vaticanus, an order is followed that is as foreign to the Hebrew Bible as it is to the English Bible:

1. Genesis, Exodus, Leviticus, Numbers, Deuteronomy, Joshua, Judges, Ruth, 1–4 Kings, 1–2 Chronicles, 1–2 Ezra;
2. Psalms, Proverbs, Ecclesiastes, Song of Songs, Job, Wisdom of Solomon, Wisdom of Sirach, Esther, Judith, Tobit;
3. Hosea, Amos, Micah, Joel, Obadiah, Jonah, Nahum, Habakkuk, Zephaniah, Haggai, Zechariah, Malachi, Isaiah, Jeremiah, Baruch, Lamentations, Letter of Jeremiah, Ezekiel, Daniel.

This grouping is by no means fixed; and even the content of the Greek Bible famously deviates, not only from the Hebrew canon (producing the academic category of the "Apocrypha," works of the Septuagint without apparent Hebrew originals), but in the text being used as one moves from manuscript to manuscript, ancient commentator to ancient commentator. Still, Swete was able to show that Vaticanus attests to a representative order, in which the first category was "historical," the second "poetical," and the third "prophetic."[2]

Swete argued that this grouping was initially literary, derived from the reception of the Greek Bible in Alexandria, but he also suggested at the close of his discussion that "it may have seemed fitting that the Prophets should immediately precede the Evangelists." That is a remarkable insight, and one which helps us to understand the

[1] See, for example, Eugene Ulrich, "Origen's Old Testament Text: The Transmission History of the Septuagint to the Third Century C.E.," *The Dead Sea Scrolls and the Origins of the Bible* (Grand Rapids and Leiden; Eerdmans and Brill, 1999), 202–223; and (more generally) Julio Trebolle Barrera, *The Jewish Bible and the Christian Bible* (Leiden and Grand Rapids; Brill and Eerdmans, 1998), 301–323.
[2] H. B. Swete, *An Introduction to the Old Testament in Greek* (Cambridge: Cambridge University Press, 1902), 197–230, see especially pp. 201, 217–219.

sequence within the third category, that of prophecy (which also departs signally from the Hebrew Bible). The Septuagintal order, by commencing with the minor Prophets, is able to finish off with the greatest of the literary Prophets: Isaiah, Jeremiah (with the additions of Baruch, Lamentations, and the Letter), and Ezekiel. Even more strikingly, the canon closes with Daniel, now emphatically and climactically one of the *Prophets* (rather than one of the Writings, as in the Hebrew Bible). Its references to the resurrection (12:2) and to the Son of Man (7:13; 9:21; 10:16) make it an ideal transition into the story of Jesus. It is interesting that the canon of the New Testament, which was also solidifying during the fourth century, closes similarly on a strong note of prophecy, with the Revelation of John.

Tertullian in North Africa reflects the strict attachment to divine Spirit, and the imminent expectation of judgment, which characterized much of Christianity during the second century. He addressed his *Apology* to those who might be called upon to judge Christians, but in fact it was intended to counter the common prejudice that Christianity encountered. It is as effective an example of rhetoric as one will find, and at the same time it illustrates the legal situation and the popular reaction to the new religion. The *Apology* was written in 197 C.E., shortly after Tertullian's conversion to Christianity. The uncompromising stance is characteristic of the climate of the movement in Carthage, and may explain why, around 207 C.E., Tertullian himself became a Montanist, attracted by the asceticism which comported with the conviction that each believer was a vessel of the Holy Spirit.

Writers such as Tertullian, who shaped Christian theology out of the raw materials of the Old and New Testaments, the nascent faith in Jesus, and their own attainments in philosophy, are know as the Fathers of the church. These patristic theologians were often boldly experimental, as in the case of Tertullian, even to the point of breaking with their own communities and the church at large. Yet they have left a wealth of intellectual reflection on faith, which has been mined until this day. Not even a representative sample of the Fathers can be noted here, but a few prominent examples must be cited.

Irenaeus, bishop of Lyons during the second century, countered Gnostic understandings of the gospel with what was called by his time a "catholic" faith. Faith as catholic is "through the whole" (*kath holou*) of the church. It is faith such as you would find it in Alexandria,

Antioch, Corinth, Ephesus, Lyons, Rome—wherever. That construction of Christianity is designed to avoid any particular requirement (such as adherence to one of the esoteric myths of Gnosticism) being made upon Christians as such.

Irenaeus' attempt to join in establishing a generic or "catholic" Christianity called attention to four aspects of faith, which have remained constant in classic definitions of Christianity. First, faith was to be expressed by means of the Scriptures as received from Israel; there was no question of eliminating the Old Testament (which was part of the program of many Gnostics). Second, faith was grounded in the preaching of the Apostles, as instanced in their own writings and (derivatively) in the creeds. Third, communities were to practice their faith by means of the sacraments that were universally recognized at that time, Baptism and Eucharist. Fourth, the loyalty of the church to these principles was to be assured by the authority of bishops and priests, understood as successors of the Apostles. Taken together, these were the constituents of "the great and glorious body of Christ." They made the church a divine institution: "Where the Spirit of God is, there is the church and all grace, and the Spirit is truth" (see Irenaeus, *Against Heresies* 4.33.7)

Although Irenaeus's conception was designed to be inclusive, it was purposely at odds with emerging Gnosticism. The issue was not only the authority of the Old Testament (which was typically contested by Gnostics). Gnostics also cherished writings that were not apostolic, sacraments of initiation that were not universal, and leaders who were authorized by private revelation rather than the Spirit moving communally in the church. Irenaeus's concern to establish this fourfold definition of the church is consonant with one of his most vivid observations. Just as there are four quarters of the heavens, four principal winds that circle the world, and four cherubim before the throne of God, he says, so there are four Gospels. Indeed, the number four corresponds to the four universal (or catholic) covenants between God and humanity: those of Noah, Abraham, Moses, and Christ (see Irenaeus, *Against Heresies* 3.9.8). The Gospels belong to the order of the very basics of life, and—what is equally important in Irenaeus's mind—the basics of life belong to the Gospels. The power of God is not to be abstracted from the terms and conditions of the world in which we live. In insisting upon that, teachers such as Clement of Alexandria and Irenaeus opposed the popular dualism

that was a principal appeal of the Gnostics. Resisting the widespread
fashion of abstracting God from this world, catholic Christians insisted
upon the Incarnation as the key to the revelation of God's truth to
humanity.

The incarnational emphasis of catholic Christianity is accurately
conveyed by its most ancient, second-century confession of faith,
which is still in use under the title, the "Apostles' Creed." The form
in which it is currently used, however, was considerably developed
during a time beyond our period of interest. As a guide to its ancient
formulation, the best source is the *Apostolic Tradition* of Hippolytus.[3]
Hippolytus sets out the three questions which candidates for baptism answered, "I believe."

> Do you believe in God the Father Almighty?
> Do you believe in Christ Jesus the Son of God,
>   born by the Holy Spirit of the Virgin Mary,
>   who was crucified under Pontius Pilate and died
>   and rose again on the third day, alive from the dead
>   and ascended into heaven
>   and sat on the right hand of the Father
>   who will come to judge the living and dead?
> Do you believe in the Holy Spirit
>   and the holy church and the resurrection of the flesh?

The division of the creed into three sections, corresponding to Father, Son, and Spirit, is evident. That marks the commitment of the
early Christian church to the Trinity as a means of conceiving God.
Its commitment necessitated a philosophical explanation, which Origen
provided during the third century. Indeed, the Trinity correlates with
the kind of Incarnational faith that is expressed in the creed.

The Incarnation refers principally to Jesus as the embodiment of
God, from the time of the prologue of John's Gospel (1:1–18). In
the creed, however, that view of the Incarnation is developed further. The longest, middle paragraph shows in its focus on Jesus as

---

[3] See Philip Carrington, *The Early Christian Church*, vol. 2, *The Second Christian
Century* (Cambridge: Cambridge University Press, 1957), 330–331; Francis Xavier
Murphy, "Creed," *New Catholic Encyclopedia* (New York: McGraw-Hill, 1967), 432–438;
Joseph Cullen Ayer, *A Source Book for Ancient Church History: From the Apostolic Age to
the Close of the Conciliar Period* (New York: Scribner's, 1913), 123–126; Roger E. Olson,
The Story of Christian Theology: Twenty Centuries of Tradition & Reform (Downers Grove:
InterVarsity, 1999), 128–131.

God's eternal Son that the ancient practice of Christian catechesis is at the heart of the creed, and that paragraph is a fine summary of the Gospels (compare Peter's speech in Acts 10:34–43, where baptism is also at issue). Its level of detail articulates a rigorous alternative to the tendency of Gnosticism towards abstraction. But the statement about Jesus does not stand on its own. His status as Son is rooted in the recognition of the Father, understood as the creator of the heavens and the earth. The creed begins with an embrace of the God of Israel as creator and with an equally emphatic (if indirect) rejection of dualism.

The last paragraph of the creed, devoted to the Holy Spirit, also recollects the catechesis of Christians which climaxed with baptism and reception of the Spirit. That basic understanding was rooted in the catechesis of Peter (again, see Acts 10:34–43, and the sequel in vv. 44–48). But here the common reception of the Spirit is used to assert the communal nature of life in the Spirit. To be baptized is to share the Spirit with the Holy church: that is where communion with God, forgiveness, and the promise of the resurrection are to be found.

Finally, the creed closes on a deeply personal and existential note. "The resurrection" refers, not to Jesus' resurrection (which has already been mentioned), but to the ultimate destiny of all who believe in him. The creed does not spell out its understanding of how God raised Jesus and is to raise believers from the dead, but it is unequivocal that people are all to be raised themselves, as embodied personality. There is no trace here of joining an undifferentiated divine entity, or of some part of us (a soul, an essence) surviving in a disembodied way.

In its assertion of the continuity of the body before and after the resurrection, non-Gnostic Christianity came increasingly to stress the complete (that is, material) identity between what had died and what was raised from the dead. Whether the issue was what God raised in the case of Jesus or would raise in the case of the faithful, material conceptions came to predominate. Resurrection was not only of the spiritual body that Paul refers to in 1 Corinthians 15:44, the identity that figures in the medium of flesh, but of the flesh itself. The Latin version of the creed actually refers to the resurrection of the flesh at its close. Catholic Christianity emerged as orthodox at the moment it became creedal, and regularized faith in terms of certain opinions (*doxai*) which were held to be right (*ortho-*). That emergence came in the context of opposition to Gnostic versions of Christianity, and the result was the greater attachment to literal, material theologies of the resurrection from the second century onward.

During the last decade of the second century, Clement of Alexandria offered instruction to Christians in that great city and intellectual center. He was active there until the persecution that broke out in 202 under Septimus Severus. Clement developed a brilliant philosophy of Christian faith, which he produced in conscious opposition to Gnostic teachings. His greatest works constitute a trilogy. The first is an introduction to Christianity as a superior philosophical teaching (the *Protrepticos*); the second, the *Paidagogos* or "Tutor," is an account of how Christ serves as our moral guide in the quest for true knowledge and perfection. Finally, his "Miscellanies," the *Stromateis* (literally, "Carpet Bags"), is a wide-ranging and complex work. Initially, it was intended as a defense of Clement's thesis that Christian revelation surpasses the achievements of human reason, but its structure and expression are obscure. For that reason, the *Paidagogos* is probably the best introduction to Clement's innovative philosophy of Christianity.

Born in 185, Origen knew the consequences that faith could have in the Roman world: his father died in the persecution of Septimus Severus in 202. Origen accepted the sort of renunciation demanded of apostles in the Gospels, putting aside his possessions to develop what Eusebius in the fourth century calls the philosophical life demanded by Jesus (see Eusebius, *History of the Church* 6.3). His learning resulted in his appointment to the catechetical school in Alexandria, following the great examples of Pantaenus and Clement. Eusebius reports that Origen castrated himself (*History of the Church* 6.8), inspired by Jesus' teaching in Matthew 19:12; but it seems likely he is repeating a calumny by Demetrios, bishop of Alexandria, who objected to Origen's ordination by the bishops of Jerusalem and Caesarea.[4] Origen moved from Alexandria to Caesarea in Palestine, to some extent as a result of bitter dispute with Demetrios, his episcopal nemesis. During the Decian persecution (250 c.e.) Origen was tortured, and he died of ill health in 254.

[4] See Jacob Neusner and Bruce Chilton, *The Intellectual Foundations of Christian and Jewish Discourse: The Philosophy of Religious Argument* (London: Routledge, 1997), 75–86.

Origen was the most powerful Christian thinker of his time. His *Hexapla* pioneered the compared study of texts of the Old Testament, while his commentaries and sermons illustrate the development of a conscious method of interpretation. His most characteristic work, *On First Principles*, is the first comprehensive Christian philosophy extant. It offers a systematic account of God, the world, free will, and Scripture. His *Against Celsus* is a classic work of apologetics, and his contribution to the theory and practice of prayer (represented in the classic source of meditation edited by Basil the Great during the fourth century, the *Philokalia*) is unparalleled. Throughout, Origen remains a creative and challenging thinker. Condemned by later councils of the church for his daring assertion that even fallen angels could theoretically one day repent and be saved (see *Apology* I.6), Origen is perhaps the most fascinating theologian in the Christian tradition.

Eusebius (260–340), bishop of Caesarea (from 314 C.E.), was deeply influenced by the martyr Pamphilus, his teacher and model. Eusebius was imprisoned in 309 at the same time Pamphilus was, although Eusebius himself was released. After Constantine embraced Christianity, Eusebius was prominent in the ecumenical church at various councils from Nicea onward, as well as a friend of the Emperor. His *History of the Church* is the starting point of ecclesiastical history. He expresses better than anyone both the pitiless quality of the persecution under Diocletian, and the inexpressible relief which followed. Constantine for him heralds the new day of Christ's revelation to the world.

Gregory of Nyssa inhabited a very different world from that of Clement or even Eusebius. By his time, Christianity was in fashion within the Empire. He was the brother of Basil of Caesarea in the Cappodocian region of Asia Minor, and Gregory himself was bishop of Nyssa (between 371 and 394). Together with their friend Gregory, son of the bishop of Nazianzus, they are known as the "Cappodocian Fathers." Of these champions of the emerging Trinitarian doctrine of their day, Gregory especially represents the interpenetration of the Hellenistic literary tradition with the orientation of Christianity. Deeply influenced by Origen, he also remained married long into his episcopate, and only took monastic vows after his wife's death.

Augustine was born in 354 in Tagaste in North Africa, the son of a petty administrator and his Christian wife. A benefactor from

Tagaste enabled him to continue his studies in rhetoric in Carthage, where he was deeply influenced by his reading of Cicero, and then accepted the popular philosophy of Manicheanism. Its conception of the struggle between good and evil as two masses opposed to one another appealed to him deeply. Further study in Rome and Milan led to Augustine's conversion to Christianity. Rome brought him into contact with thinkers who showed him that Manicheanism was based upon unproved dogma, while in Milan he heard the sermons of Bishop Ambrose. Ambrose demonstrated to Augustine that the authority of faith did not contradict reason. At the same time, a reading of Neo-Platonism enabled Augustine to conceive of God as immaterial, beyond time and space.

Philosophy was the first expression of Augustine's faith. Even while he was preparing for baptism, he wrote treatises, and he continued doing so in Rome afterwards. Then he returned to Tagaste, living and writing with a few friends. A visit to Hippo Regius proved fateful, however. He was made a priest, and later became bishop of the small town. He continued to write extensively, but in a more pointed way against those who attacked the church. He particularly concerned himself with Manicheanism. In addition, he criticized two viewpoints that demanded perfection of Christians. The Donatists attempted to force from the church those who had cooperated with Roman authorities during the period of persecution, while the Pelagians argued that human effort was sufficient to attain redemption. In those controversies, Augustine's mastery of the concept of grace was brilliantly articulated.

In addition, Augustine wrote about instructing new members of the church and penned homilies which were the basis of his popular fame. Three profoundly innovative works have influenced the world of letters and Christian doctrine ever since. His *Confessions* (finished in 400) are the epitome of his introspective method: the analysis of his own life enables him to lay out the forces at work in the human soul. The *City of God* (413–425), occasioned by the sack of Rome in 410, sets out the pattern of redemption within the patterns of global history. *On the Trinity*—his great synthetic work begun in 400—is a meditation on the imprint of God's image within us and around us. He died in 430, while Hippo was under siege by the Vandals, whose advent presaged the dissolution of the empire.

D. FOUNDATIONAL ISLAM: QUR'ĀN AND PROPHETIC SUNNAH

"Islam" is properly an act not a thing: the Arabic word *islām* denotes the action of "submitting [to God]" rather than some reified—and by implication fixed—entity that we like to label a religion. It has, however, come to be used to designate also the long and historically major tradition of faith and practice that began shortly after the beginning of the seventh century C.E. with the calling of Muhammad ibn 'Abdullāh of Mecca to be a prophet and a messenger or apostle of the One God. Here we shall use "Islam" in a conventional way to refer to that cumulative tradition over the past fourteen centuries, which the community of the Muslim faithful (who have been its transmitters) developed and constantly changed in diverse ways in widely diverse places and contexts. Yet despite the consequent great diversity of Islamic tradition over this long period and across the many cultural divides it has traversed in its development, we shall be trying in what follows to sketch some of the foundational ideas and ideals that have endured across sectarian divisions and ethnic, cultural, and linguistic boundaries. These are the ideas and ideals that have been constant enough and identifiable enough that we can call them in some sense "classical," "traditional," or even "normative," in the eyes of the great majority of Muslims, even for the most part those of differing sectarian orientations. In doing this, we shall draw upon those major literary sources of the tradition that come closest to being universally authoritative for Muslim thought and practice—namely the texts that have been the sources of religious authority and guidance for myriad generations of Muslims down to the present day—the texts that Muslims consider to be the founding documents of their tradition.

These religious texts are potentially manifold, but the most important and most universally revered among all Muslims past and present by any reckoning is the Muslim scriptural text, or Qur'ān (lit., "Reciting"). This is a collection of divine revelations received by Muhammad over approximately twenty-two years according to traditional reckoning, from ca. 610 C.E. until his death in 632. The classical sources further report that the oral revelations were collected during the lifetime of the Apostle of God both in the memories of many of his followers, or "Companions," and in the writing of several of them who served as "scribes of the Revelation." Again according to traditional accounts, the third Caliph, or "Successor," 'Uthmān began to fear the loss of the sacred text through the deaths of the best reciters and memorizers. Consequently, he instituted near the end of his rule (644–656) a redaction effort that brought together the most able former companions of the Prophet who had either written or memorized texts of the revelations. This commission assembled the text that has ever after served as the Qur'ān for the vast majority of Muslims, the so-called codex of 'Uthmān, or 'Uthmānic Codex.

The most important texts after the Qur'ān are the collected reports of the words and actions of Muhammad himself, together with those of his companions. These are known collectively under the rubric *hadīth*, usually rendered "Tradition" when referring to the collective body of thousands of individual traditions, each of which is also called an *hadīth*, or single report/tradition. The *hadīth* are understood by Muslims to be the chief vehicle of the Sunnah, or "tradition" ("traditional practice," lit. "beaten path," "way") of Muhammad and his original community, the pristine *Ummah* of the first generation of Muslims in Mecca and Medina. Although small, personal collections apparently preceded the great compilations of *hadīth* from at least the second Islamic century and perhaps even the decades just after Muhammad's death, the codification and collection of major quantities of *hadīth*s took place largely in the third century A.H./ninth century C.E. at the hands of the developing class of religiously learned scholars, or *'ulamā'*. The question of the authenticity of the thousands of reports in these collections is a vexing one, as both Muslim and non-Muslim scholars have recognized. Some number of them are surely creations by later generations of prophetic dicta that claim to be words of Muhammad but cannot be; but some number of them must also go back to the early days of the Islamic movement and the lifetimes of the Prophet and his companions. What is most difficult is to ascertain which are which. Fortunately, for our purposes we need not trouble ourselves with this question. Why? Because we are interested in the life of these texts and their contents in the minds and hearts of Muslims down through the formative centuries. By this, we mean the period of three or three-and-a-half centuries after the death of Muhammad taken as in some sense defining the "classical" in Islamic religion and culture. Our question is, What did

Muslims of these early Islamic centuries preserve and recognize as legitimate (and legitimating) texts carrying the established practice, or Sunnah, of Muhammad and his companions?

There are also many other important texts from the first three Islamic centuries, including biographies of the Prophet (*sīrah*), historical accounts of the early years of the community and its later development under the caliphate (*maghāzī*, "battle campaigns," and *ta'rīkh*, "history, chronicle"), Qur'ān interpretation (*tafsīr*), early mystical, or *sūfī*, texts, writings from the early stages of the development of jurisprudence (*fiqh*), and various kinds of early texts containing discussion of theological questions (including but not limited to documents belonging more formally to the emerging discipline of theological debate (*kalām*), to name only the most prominent.

Thus it can be plausibly argued that there are sound arguments for utilizing not simply or even primarily Qur'ān and *hadīth*, but also all of the other aforementioned genres of material, if one wishes to cover the full historical range of Muslim religious literature in the early centuries of Islam. The major argument for our approach being largely limited to Qur'ān and *hadīth* is that even across sectarian boundaries, Muslims have universally recognized the ultimate authority of the Qur'ān, and the vast majority of Muslims that of the *hadīth*, albeit clearly as second to the Qur'ān. There is, to be sure, the caveat that the normative Shī'ī collections of *hadīth* differ from those of the Sunnī majority, especially in that they include many traditions from those early imāms who are recognized by Shī'īa as the rightful and authoritative, divinely guided successors to Muhammad in leadership of the community. However, here we shall focus largely on Sunnī *hadīth*, since we are striving to present a picture of basic Muslim positions on major theological issues that transcend sectarian differences; and for the majority of Muslim interpretive traditions certainly the Qur'ān, and to some degree some or most of the *hadīth* of the Prophet, are recognized as the two fundamental sources of authority and guidance.

Nevertheless, while recognizing the ahistorical and essentialist nature of our chosen textual focus, we shall try where appropriate to point out major sectarian divergences even while we are seeking out those points on which the vast majority of Muslims can agree. Our goal remains that of presenting ideas that may be said to form the "essentials" of the Muslim religious worldview insofar as they would be recognizable and affirmable by most Muslims of most times, places, and theological persuasions. While it can be plausibly argued that this idealized Islam, like any other religious ideal, has never been realized and sustained in a concrete historical situation, what is critical for our purposes here is that this ideal, in all of its multifaceted complexity, has had the power to inspire and often to unite Muslims across the centuries and around the globe to aspire to a more perfect realization of their faith, practice, and community. That is, after all, what ideals are for.

I. *The Theology*

When we turn to the question of the basic "theology" that emerges from the normative sources, we have to remember that any description we can muster must needs be an imaginative effort of interpretation that cannot in the final analysis take us back to some imagined "pristine" Islam as practiced in the "original community" of the Prophet's lifetime or the decades thereafter. Our reading of the qur'ānic and *hadīth* texts will be colored inevitably by our reading of later Islamic history and texts. However, we can try to keep especially to, above all, the qur'ānic thought world; then, secondarily and to a lesser degree, the general lines of classical Qur'ān interpretation and the diverse materials of the *hadīth*. Nor can our interpretation claim to describe a "normative" Islam in the sense that it is "truer" or otherwise "better" than variant traditions also calling themselves "Muslim." But it can attempt to describe Islam on the basis of the texts that are most sacred and authoritative for the massive majority of Muslims over time and around the globe. Thus when we speak here of "normative" Islam, we mean essentially Islam in consonance with the Qur'ān and, by extension, with the classical texts, preeminently the *hadīth*, which supplement, interpret, and extend the Qur'ān. This shuts off normative in terms of chronology sometime around the middle of the fourth/tenth century, which is a relatively arbitrary choice; however, it does provide us with a general picture of what Muslims held Islam to have been in the classical world of the early centuries when so many institutions, ideas, and practices began and solidified prior to becoming normative or classical for later generations.

The center of Muslim faith is God alone, and the whole Qur'ān as God's verbatim speech is a revelation of His will and His dealings with His creation. World order is based on God's justice and omnipotent sustenance of the universe: a major message of the Qur'ān is that God is revealed to all human beings not only in His verbal revelations but all around in the natural world, where His signs abound. In the next chapter, we shall see with greater specificity just who Muslims understand God to be and how they understand him to relate to His human creatures.

What we must stress is that Muslims understand God to be above all Creator, Sustainer, and ultimately Judge of creation. He is the God of history, human and cosmic, and the Lord of all beings, human and otherwise. As His creations, human beings owe their lives and their allegiance to Him alone; it is also He alone who can offer them life beyond death, salvation beyond this contingent world in which humans have the opportunity to prepare for the eternity that lies beyond this world.

History itself has direction and goal, or *telos*: what began with creation of the universe at God's hands will end with His reclaiming of time and space, and of all created beings, at the end of time, on the Day of Judgment. All human striving is to be directed towards the final reckoning, when those who have died in every age will be resurrected and brought before the throne of God to be judged according to their actions and intentions in their earthly lives. When the judgment is done, God will reclaim creation and usher in eternal life for his creatures, either in His Garden, or Paradise, or in His fire, or Hell. This eschatological vision of the ultimate reward or punishment for all lives in this world stands as the culminating scene of human history and destiny.

God's merciful and just dealing with His created world, between its creation and the eschaton, is shown, however, in the fact that He has made every effort from His side to prepare humankind for the coming judgment. In the vastness, magnificence, and beneficence of His created natural world, He has offered human beings endless signs of His power and sovereignty, as well as of His bounty, mercy, and care for His creatures in this world. Furthermore, He has sent a long series of prophets and messengers to previous human communities, beginning with His first prophet, Adam, and his offspring, exemplified in the greatest prophetic model of faith, Abraham, and culminating in the last of the long line of prophets and messengers, Muhammad b. 'Abdullāh, whose prophetic career and the divine scripture that he brought as the Qur'ān mark God's last attempt to set forth "the straight way," the path to salvation, the way that God would have human beings walk as His obedient servants and worshippers. This final and consummate guidance is still available to Muslims even long after the death of Muhammad the man—most perfectly in God's word as revealed to Muhammad and codified as Scripture in the Qur'ān, but also in the remembered model of the life, person, and example of Muhammad himself, and in the example that he and the first community of Muslims set long ago.

II. *The Documents that Convey the Theology*

Scripture in Islam is both theoretically and historically a single, relatively short text derived from the revelatory experience of one man in one fairly delimited time period—roughly the last twenty, or, to follow tradition more precisely, the last twenty-two years of Muhammad's life. Even if we take the period when the revelations given during Muhammad's active career as the Messenger of God were probably codified and assembled into one text, we are only talking about an additional twenty years or so after the Prophet's death. Over against, in the Jewish and Christian cases, the long periods of writing, collection, and redaction—not to mention the time involved in agreeing on what was to be included and what excluded from the "scriptures" of the Hebrew Bible and the Christian New Testament—the period in which the Qur'ān came into being and was pulled together and recognized as the very word of God was stunningly short. While a few modern, non-Muslim scholars have tried to question the authenticity of the qur'ānic materials as texts stemming from Muhammad's lifetime and even as texts codified under 'Uthmān, the third Islamic caliph, or "successor," of the Prophet, the preponderance of scholarly opinion, both Muslim and non-Muslim, has been that the Qur'ān is indeed essentially if not entirely the product of Muhammad's experience as God's messenger. Furthermore, there is widespread agreement that its written form ever since, with some minor variations, has been that given it by those men and women who compared their copies of portions of the whole with memorized and written versions preserved by others in order to produce what became known ever after as the afore-mentioned "Codex of ʿUthmān," the consonantal text that has been authoritative down to the present.

The Qurʾān, however, is not first and foremost a written docu-ment, but rather an oral text to be recited. Its very name is a ver-bal noun in form, meaning "reciting," "recitation." *Qurʾān* was apparently a new formation of the Arabic root *q-r-ʾ*, derived most likely from the Syriac Christian *qeryānā* (*lectio*, "reading") and per-haps also influenced by Aramaic *qeraya*ʾ and the Hebrew term of the Jews for a scriptural reading, *miqrāʾ*.[5] All of these words are from the same Semitic root meaning "recite" or "read [aloud]." What Muhammad received from God was an ongoing stream of relatively short, sometimes almost ecstatic and grippingly poetic, sometimes prose-like and didactic, revelations that, once collected, came to form the text of holy scripture for Muslims.

Yet while the Qurʾān has ever been first and foremost an oral text to be recited and memorized—a living text of God's very words, it has also from early on been understood as the latest, and indeed the last, of a long series of revealed texts given to a long line of God's messengers. The Qurʾān itself, unlike the Jewish or Christian scriptures, puts forward a notion of "scripture" (*kitāb*, plur. *kutub*) as a generic category of divinely given texts going back through his-tory to earlier peoples to whom God also sent messengers with a revelation from His heavenly *Kitāb*. The Qurʾān is the name of what is in a real sense the culminating "edition" of God's scriptural mes-sage, his heavenly "Scripture," and therefore a final guidance for human beings who have failed to follow earlier revelations or man-aged to corrupt their revealed texts over time.

This has led to the absolutely unimpeachable and central impor-tance of the Qurʾān as the single verbatim divine authority for human life. It is not possible to reject the authority of the Qurʾān as Scripture (even though it is certainly possible to interpret it in diverse ways), as God's word, without cutting oneself off from the Muslim com-munity. Most Muslims live in intimate contact with this text. Every

---

[5] Cf. Arthur Jeffery, *The Foreign Vocabulary of the Qurʾān* (Baroda, India: Oriental Institute, 1938), 233–234; W. A. Graham, "The Earliest Meaning of *Qurʾān*," *Die Welt des Islams* 23/24:361–377.

Muslim must know at least enough of the text by heart—at a minimum the *Fātihah*, or Opening *sūrah* (chapter) and usually one or two other short sūrahs, in order to perform with validity the worship rite (*salāt*) that is prescribed for five different times of every day for a Muslim. Many Muslims can recite lengthy passages or even the entire text (which is similar in its length to that of the Christian New Testament); internalizing the whole Qur'ān through memorization is a great pious act and earns one the title of *hāfiz* (fem. *hāfizah*), one who "holds" or "protects" the text in one's memory. It is a rare occasion in a Muslim society when an event or any remotely important action is not marked by shorter or longer citation or recitation of the Qur'ān.

The Qur'ān is absolutely central to what it means to be a Muslim; it is the medium of the most direct possible contact with the divine, for in its words the Muslim hears God speaking. It is not, however, as many non-Muslims suppose, primarily or even significantly a law book. Its prime content is paranetic: hortatory, inspirational, and moral in nature. It summons humankind to worship of the One God. It calls upon them to use their God-given intelligence to look around them and recognize the reality of their Creator, God Almighty, in His created world—with its beauties, bounties, and manifold signs for the discerning. It calls upon listeners to heed not only the signs of nature, but also those in the instructive stories of earlier messengers and prophets and their faith, as well as in the stories of earlier peoples who, having been sent guidance from God, rejected Him, or lapsed from the true path of worship and service after they had submitted to Him. It calls upon the Prophet to rise and warn people of the coming judgment at the end of the world, when the righteous shall be resurrected and ushered into God's eternal Garden, while the resurrected evil-doers will be sent to the eternal torment of the fire. It calls on human beings to live righteously and do good works—to take care of the weak, defend the defenseless, support one's fellows, and fight the polytheists who associate partners with God and the unbelievers who oppress or attack Muslims. It speaks often to particular situations of the Prophet and the first community (*ummah*) of the faithful, comforting, chiding, exhorting, encouraging, promising vindication after the sufferings and trials of the difficult days before the Muslims triumphed. And the Qur'ān contains also directions for the new *ummah* and its members: how to deal with social issues such as female infanticide; the difficult plight of widows, orphans, and the poor; commercial dealings and wealth; support of the community as a whole; personal piety and practice; family matters such as marriage and divorce, death and inheritance; transgressors—adulterers, murderers, liars, hypocrites, and apostates; and non-Muslims from Jews and Christians to idolaters. It is not a law book, yet it provides a theological and moral framework within which laws and statutes for personal, ritual, family, commercial, criminal, and state affairs could be developed, and within which a Muslim could live a righteous life.

Thus it is the Qur'ān that stands as the one fixed source for Muslim piety and practice. Yet since it is not a long book or a compendium of law, it was from the outset necessary for its revelations to be interpreted and their intent and principles followed in concrete matters of everyday life. The Qur'ān, like the Torah, calls for its audience to reform their entire lives, to form themselves according to God's will and ordinances, and to make every aspect of their existence, from their inward thoughts, personal habits, and religious faith and practice to their social, political, and commercial life—*muslim*, "submissive" to God's will. It starts from the clear premise that, first, God has called his human creatures to live righteously if they are to be His servants and thus be among the righteous in the Garden for all eternity; and, second, He has given them the necessary guidance about how to be righteous in all aspects of their lives. From this it follows that it is possible to be righteous according to God's will (*shar*ʿ), God's law (*sharīʿah*). And because the Qur'ān offers much general guidance about the spirit that should govern human action under God's law, but does not spell out in great detail the statutes of that law, it has been necessary for human beings to interpret and expand upon its words.

In the first instance, the authoritative interpretation was in effect easily available in the person of the Prophet so long as he was present to lead his people and to translate the qur'ānic norms and ideals into concrete decisions about personal, family, and communal life, as well as the affairs of the city-state of Medina (which after his death soon evolved into an Arabian confederacy under the aegis of Muhammad and Islam). With the death of Muhammad, that guidance and effective law-giving power had to be vested elsewhere: to some degree it devolved upon the early "successors," the caliphs who took over leadership of both the new, growing state organization and its armies and treasury and the allegiance of the core community of the faithful. Ultimately, and to a larger degree, it devolved upon the most pious and respected companions of the Prophet, who advised their caliphal leaders and worked to preserve the Qur'ān and the memory of Muhammad and his activity in their midst. A later tradition ascribed to Muhammad calls these faithful companions the true successors of the Prophet. These were those recognized as the first of the many subsequent generations of the 'ulamā' ("ulema"), those earned persons to whom the community was to look for guidance much as the nascent, post-prophetic, and post-biblical Jewish community looked to the Tannaim and the rabbis in general, or the early Christian community to the apostles, early martyrs, and "fathers" of the church.

What evolved out of the developing recognition and high estimation of the 'ulamā' in the *Ummah* was a second special category of text for guidance and authoritative information of all kinds alongside the Qur'ān itself. This was the aforementioned *hadīth* literature, the collected reports of the sayings and actions and piety of the Messenger of God during his lifetime—what came to be described as the *Sunnah*, or "way," the modus operandi of the Prophet. These reports (*hadīths*) gave the post-prophetic community effective access to the guidance of Muhammad's *Sunnah* in his absence, so long as there were trustworthy and pious persons who had known him, who could give these hadīth reports to others, and who could draw analogies from them to new situations, just as they could do with qur'ānic texts. Only the *hadīth* provided, in great abundance (and their evident post-prophetic proliferation), much greater detail about specific matters than did the exalted Qur'ān. Thus, where Muhammad had been the interpreter of the Qur'ān during his lifetime, the companions (and after them the following generation and after them the next, and so on) and the hadīth reports that they transmitted and used to deal with new situations and their problems became the functional mediators of the Qur'ān's vision for the early *Ummah*. A later major collector of hadīth reports, Ibn Mājā, even went so far as to note (in the form of a hadīth ascribed to Muhammad) that "the Sunnah is judge over the Qur'ān, not the Qur'ān over the Sunnah," which is simply to state the hermeneutical axiom that whatever or whoever interprets another text has in a real sense control over the meanings of that text. Once the *hadīth* and its transmission became important to the practical direction of Muslim personal and communal life, this literature also became the second major source of inspired, authoritative guidance and normative precedent alongside the noble Qur'ān.

In the third Islamic century, the *hadīth* came to be recognized as the second of the "two sources" (*aslān*; sing. *asl*; plur. *usūl*) of guidance according to Islamic norms (and, ultimately, the legal codification of those norms). By this time, the reports of the sayings and actions of the Prophet were being collected with zeal across the much expanded Islamic world, from Spain to Central Asia. Specialists had grown up who memorized prodigious numbers of these *hadīths* and transmitted them to their students and peers. The practice had long since developed whereby each report was accompanied, if it was to be taken seriously as something authentically transmitted across several generations from the Apostle of God, by a chain or "support," *isnād*, of the transmitters back to Muhammad who had passed it on. Every *hadīth* needed its isnād, or, if possible, multiple isnāds in which the individual transmitters were listed and could be checked for their reputations, their temporal overlap with the persons in the chain of transmission before and after them, and their known presence in places where they could have heard *hadīths* from their source and transmitted them to the next-named person in the chain. All knew that many of the *hadīth* collected were spurious, having been created often out of whole cloth, sometimes out of faulty memories or loosely transmitted stories, to meet the needs of Muslim piety and practice in the first three centuries. While, however, Muslims always assumed a certain authority and reliability for the *hadīth* as a whole (despite the difficulty of detecting forgeries), and these texts came to serve as the major source for interpreting and extending the words of the Qur'ān in order to guide the expanding Muslim community, or *Ummah*, the problem of inventions or simply errors threatened the validity of what was transmitted as "sound" traditions from the companions and Prophet. Thus a whole science of *hadīth* criticism soon arose to try to validate those reports that were authentic and discredit those that were forgeries—but that is beyond our scope of concern.

What interests us is the fact of the growing authority of the Sunnah of the Prophet as it could be gleaned from the *hadīth*. The interpretation of Islamic norms through recourse to the *hadīth* and their interpretation, much like that through recourse to the qur'ānic text and its interpretation, meant that ultimately each generation of Muslim interpreters—who rapidly came to be preeminently the *'ulamā'* of the community, those learned in Qur'ān, Sunnah, Arabic language and grammar, and the other tools needed to be taken seriously as one competent to be an interpreter—each generation of these interpreters came to be "judges over" both Qur'ān and Sunnah. They became the arbiters of Islamic norms through their development of a science of jurisprudence as well as Qur'ān interpretation, *hadīth* criticism and interpretation, and the other linguistic and religious disciplines appropriate to a clerical institution. A tradition from the Prophet was often quoted to explain the collective authority of the Muslim community, the *Ummah muslimah*, and its religious leadership: "My people will never agree upon an error." This expresses the fact that a consensus of Muslims—which practically means consensus of those qualified to make interpretive decisions, namely the *'ulamā'*— upon a given interpretation of Qur'ān and Sunnah was the ultimate arbiter of Muslim standards. In this way the imprimatur of the Muslim community of the faithful was assumed to rest upon the greater part of the massive corpus of the *hadīth* and its transmission "according to the sense"—not unlike the way in which its imprimatur was assumed to lie upon the exact and utterly faithful transmission of the verbatim divine word of the Qur'ān because it had been transmitted by too many Muslims in every generation for anyone to have forged additions or tampered with the original text. This concept, known as *tawātur*, or "[uninterrupted,] continuous transmission," has been the measure used to underscore the reliability of those traditions adjudged to have been most accurately passed down.

Here we see the degree to which the authenticity both of the revelations of the Qur'ān and of the traditions of the Prophet rested (and still rests) upon the veracity, faith, and accuracy of many generations of human transmitters.

Finally, as noted above, there are of course other early sources from at least the third and fourth Islamic centuries on which we can rely at many points. These commonly have recourse themselves, however, to citation of proof texts from Qur'ān and *hadīth*, which drives us most commonly back to these latter two copora, the "two sources" par excellence, for our picture of classical Islamic thought and practice in what follows.

CHAPTER TWO

THE PERSON OF GOD

A. THE ISSUE

Whether or not there is a God—the question addressed by philosophy of religion and answered with proofs for the existence of God—does not define the issue of God's personhood for Christianity, Judaism, and Islam. That is because none of these cognate religions asks whether or not there is "a" god. Each founds all knowledge of God on God's own revelation of himself and his will for mankind. All three religions know God through God's self-manifestation, in the person of Jesus Christ, in the Torah, and to the Prophet Muhammad in the Qur'ān, for Christianity, Judaism, and Islam, respectively. So the three religions of monotheism appeal to revelation in their doctrine of, and encounter with, God's person. From the perspective of Christianity and Islam, the knowledge of God is cumulative, while Judaism relies on the dual Torah, written and oral, alone. Christianity appeals to that Written Torah, now called the Old Testament alongside, and as realized in, the New Testament, and Islam calls upon the revelation previously available in the Torah of Moses and the Bible of Christianity, perfecting the whole with the culminating revelations from God to Muhammad in the Qur'ān. That cumulative tradition accounts for the many ways in which the three religions concur about the personhood of God, even as each lays claim to unique, and uniquely true, knowledge of God as God has made himself—above all, his will and purpose—known to humanity.

B. GOD INCARNATE: CHRISTIANITY

How Jesus is regarded as God Incarnate takes us to the heart of the issue called Christology within the Christian tradition. That designation reflects the fact that, although many categories were used to understand Jesus during the period of the New Testament, "Christ" predominated, and was so naturally associated with Jesus (and Jesus alone), that "Christ Jesus" and "Jesus Christ" indistinguishably refer to the church's Lord. So one possible mystery about the messiah in the Hebrew Bible—*who* he might be—is really no mystery for Christianity. His identity may be specified in a way that would satisfy the curiosity of anyone who is not obsessed with nineteenth-century, positivist notions of historical verification.[1]

A second potential uncertainty—what the messiah is to do—is also no mystery, because he is understood already to have performed his work in all its essentials. Specifically, Christ has released divine spirit in baptism, which becomes available to the believer, such that prayer to God as Father is natural (Galatians 4:4–6), behavior in the manner of Jesus is possible (John 13:12–17), and public thanksgiving with other Christians in eucharistic worship becomes a joy (1 Corinthians 11:23–26). He who proclaimed God's kingdom provides access to that kingdom, so we are transferred into that realm which is final in respect of time, transcendent in respect of space, perfect, holy, and inclusive of all those who enter its narrow gate. The entire system of Christian faith presupposes a familiarity with Christ Jesus, at least in narrative terms, and an awareness of the range of what he offers in the practice of the church and in the divine realm.

The question that the New Testament does not fully resolve, but in which it finds itself implicated, is: How can Jesus be Christ? What makes it possible for him, given his historical identity as a rabbi from Galilee during the first century, to provide full access to the power of God's spirit and gracious inclusion within the divine kingdom? That is the systemic question of Christology. Frequently, attempts are made to answer that question by tabulating the titles of Jesus in the New Testament and identifying what is held to be their common denominator. By such a method, the term "prophet" is frequently isolated as the origin of Christology.[2] Such exercises only prove in their results what should have been obvious from the outset: early Christians could agree on no single title which they felt conveyed the identity of Jesus. "Prophet" puts Jesus in a category

---

[1] For a biographical narrative which synthesizes the results of critical inquiry, see Bruce Chilton, *Rabbi Jesus: An Intimate Biography* (New York: Doubleday, 2000).

[2] For a representative discussion, see *Crisis in Christology: Essays in Quest of Resolution* (ed. W. R. Farmer; Livonia: Dove, 1995).

which was not widely used during his period, and which in any case must be redefined in order to be applied to him, just as "Christ" itself, "son of man" (inspired from Daniel 7), "son of God," "lord," "teacher" or "rabbi" must be redefined.

The number of such titles undermines the attempt to identify any one of them as the single, sufficient origin of Christology. Consideration of them each individually reveals that each can in fact be applied misleadingly to Jesus. He is no prophet in the exact manner of Moses or Isaiah, in that Jesus was never a figure of truly national stature. If by "messiah" or "Christ" we have in mind only the wise, forceful ruler of the *Psalms of Solomon* who subdues all comers with the word of his mouth (17:21–46), it is difficult to see how that term should be applied to Jesus at all. "Son of man," as referred to in Daniel 7, is a purely heavenly and angelic figure, whose precise connection with Jesus is not immediately obvious. "Son of God," on the other hand, seems almost too flexible to be informative: it might refer to an angel (Genesis 6:2), to all Israel (Exodus 4:22), or to a righteous person (Wisdom of Solomon 2:18). "Lord," "teacher," and "rabbi" might similarly be taken as titles of relative (and rather conventional) honor, or as allusions to God's own attributes as master, instructor, and judge. If the history of research has shown plainly how much there might be in a name, it has also demonstrated that the welter of titles and allusions makes literal precision regarding Jesus' identity within Christianity confusing.

But that indicates that the literal exercise has been too narrowly conceived. The phenomenon at hand is the aggregation and redefinition of a series of titles, with one of them (Christ) emerging finally as the most widely used, albeit as a virtual synonym for Jesus himself. The best way to investigate the phenomenon is not to tabulate the titles, but to understand how the categories of early Judaism are taken up and framed in order to convey Jesus' identity. Following a generative approach guided by the development of the texts of the New Testament, we will read examples of the catechetical Christology of the Synoptic Gospels (that is, the Christology designed for catechumens seeking baptism), and then of Pauline and Johannine Christologies. On that basis, we will then proceed to the more advanced developments of the Revelation, Colossians, and the stories of Jesus' nativity. By following these generations of meaning, the sense of Jesus as God Incarnate will emerge.

Who Do Men Say That I Am?

The story of Peter's confession of Jesus (Matthew 16:13–20; Mark 8:27–30; Luke 9:18–21) is a classic of primitive Christology. The Petrine account—reflecting the kind of tradition Peter himself handed on to Paul ca. 35 C.E. (see Galatians 1:18–19) has Jesus ask who people say he is. Common identifications are given (John the Baptist, Elijah, one of the prophets). Jesus then asks who the disciples say he is, and Peter answers that he is the Christ.

The direction of the questioning leads away from the notion that a prophetic Christology is adequate; the disciples are implicitly encouraged by Jesus to try another category, which is precisely what Peter attempts. The response of Peter occasions a signal variation within the Synoptic tradition. Mark (8:30) and Luke (9:21) have Jesus admonish his disciples not to speak concerning his identity. Matthew (16:17–19), on the other hand, has Jesus praise Peter as the bearer of special revelation; the admonition to silence then follows (16:20). The peculiarly Matthean narrative makes explicit what the Synoptic Gospels generally presuppose: "Christ" is the designation which will ultimately triumph. Even so, Peter's confession is immediately qualified by Jesus' own prediction, the first in the Synoptics, that— as "the Son of man"—he is about to suffer, be condemned, and executed (Matthew 16:21–23; Mark 8:31–33; Luke 9:22). The pericope as a whole is a magisterial demonstration that no single term, not even "Christ," may be accurately used of Jesus, unless it is redefined in the light of knowledge of Jesus himself. The *person* infuses any designation with meaning, rather than the reverse.

The method of begging the question, of seeking a response to the issue of who Jesus might be, is also evident in the instructional source of Jesus' sayings known to scholarship as Q. One dictum from the Q material in particular has long attracted critical attention (Matthew 11:25b–27; Luke 10:21–22):

> I warrant to you, Father, Lord of heaven and of earth, that you hid these things from wise and understanding people, and uncovered them to infants! Yes, Father, because so it became pleasing before you. Everything has been delivered over to me by my Father, and no one recognizes the Son except the Father, nor does anyone recognize the Father except the Son and one to whom the Son elects to uncover.

The saying is set in the instructional source within a series of denunciations against those who have rejected the message of Jesus and his followers (Matthew 11:20–24; Luke 10:12–15, compare vv. 16–20). Over against those whose arrogance blinds them to a simple truth, the saying contrasts the "infants" (*nepioi*).

The metaphor builds upon the axiom, well established within the Petrine catechesis, which is the foundation of the Synoptic Gospels—that, in order to enter the kingdom, one must receive it as a child receives, without inhibition or restraint, completely absorbed by the vision of what is sought (Matthew 19:13–15 and 18:3; Mark 10:13–16; Luke 18:15–17).[3] What is commended about children in such sayings is not their romantic innocence (a theme that ill accords with the skepticism of antiquity); rather, their naïve, single-minded desire is commended as a good model for how to enter the kingdom. A due sense of proportion is precisely what prevents the wise and intelligent from the revelation which the naïve might enjoy.

The praise of poor, serving classes implied their proximity to Jesus in a letter attributed to Peter (see 1 Peter 2:18–25), but their socioeconomic status in itself was not the point of the call to follow him. Rather, the call to discipleship was more readily heard among underclasses; response to the call itself was to be manifest in selfless love, from whatever class one might derive. There is a certain analogy with the present saying from the instructional source, which is not a summons to undifferentiated naiveté. The "infants" are defined in a specific fashion as those to whom the Son chooses to reveal the Father. The relationship between Father and Son is the generative point of the saying. Each of them is the sole and sufficient criterion of who the other is; within that circle of intimacy, "infants" are only included by incorporation, because the Son reveals the truth to them. By the time we come to the end of the saying, the term "infants" is no longer even a metaphor of human temperament, but a way of speaking about how believers are related to God the Father through Christ.

The whole of the teaching turns, then, around the circular relationship of mutual knowledge between Father and Son. In a man-

---

[3] See the treatment of J. I. H. McDonald, *Jesus and the Ethics of the Kingdom: Biblical Foundations in Theology* (London: SPCK, 1987; Grand Rapids: Eerdmans, 1988), 83–89.

ner even more radical than in the pericope concerning Peter's confession, any established category by which to measure Jesus (however exalted) is refused in this saying from Q. Father and Son are
truly intelligible to one another alone; anyone else is (at best) a
fledgling adopted into the family circle. The pericope underscores
its method by its abstract lack of specification, even as to whether
the "son" referred to is "of God" or "of man." The hearer is left
to decide, and then to see that a decision between the alternatives
is beside the point, because titles are deliberately and self-consciously
transcended here. The instructional source joins the Petrine catechesis in insisting upon *the priority of a way of thinking about Jesus* over
any title that may be used of him. Both passages proceed from an
insight concerning Jesus' relationship with God, which then becomes
the basis upon which categories which might be applied to him are
rejected or qualified. The one option not taken is that of simply
embracing a previous category.

The new radicalism of the instructional source is its insistence
upon the mutuality of the relationship between Father and Son. One
might have predicted, on the basis of the story concerning Peter's
confession, that Jesus might say that no one knows the Son truly
except the Father. God alone can be the valid standard of God's
own emissary. But the instructional source introduces what is not a
corollary, but a statement of equivalent weight: that no one knows
the Father truly except the Son. The Jesus of John's Gospel will say
to his disciples (by way of a response to Thomas's question, 14:6–7):

> I am the way and the truth and the life; no one comes to the Father
> except through me. If you knew me, you will know my Father, and
> from this moment you do know him and have seen him.

The inescapable implication, that seeing Jesus is identical with seeing the Father, is spelled out in an exchange with Philip (vv. 8–9).
Johannine Christology will concern us formally at a later stage; for
now, the issue of note is that the fourth Gospel has picked up and
expanded upon the symmetrical and mutual relationship between
Father and Son that is a feature of Q.

The instructional saying manifests what is commonly regarded as
a "high" Christology, precisely in that the relationship is fully mutual,
and not a matter of the subordination of Jesus to the Father. Commentators for better than a century have come to call the passage

the "Johannine meteorite," as if it were unexpected so early within the traditions behind the Gospels.[4] The terminology betrays the implicit Christology of liberal critics themselves. They suppose that Jesus must originally have thought of himself simply as anointed by God—messiah in the sense of being dispatched for a purpose—and that pious imagination provided the rest.

C. F. D. Moule has summarized the liberal consensus, and goes on to remark:

> And it does, at first sight, look like an easy bridge for the fancy to traverse: starting from a human, messianic Son, it crosses over to a divine, transcendental Son.[5]

There are, however, two big holes in the bridge. The first is that, as we have seen in the instance of Peter's confession, the tradition is especially slippery just when it concerns using "messiah" as an adequate category for Jesus. It could only be used as a title after it had been defined anew; Professor Moule observes that "Jesus could scarcely have been styled Messiah (or Christ) after his crucifixion at all unless his friends had already become convinced that he was Messiah in some unusual and transcendental sense."

Because Professor Moule is both a skilled exegete and a theologian of Anglican doctrine, his terms of reference in this article (and elsewhere) are doctrinal as well as textual. Specifically, he wishes to know whether the earliest of Christologies was "evolutionary," crossing the "easy bridge" he describes, or "transcendental," that is, animated by the conviction that Jesus is "'one in being' with God." His contribution to the study of Christology is one of the most important in the last century, because he demonstrated the reflexive recourse to an evolutionary point of view among interpreters, and he suggested an exegetically viable alternative along ontological lines.[6] Perhaps the greatest tribute to his contribution is that it has been consistently sidestepped in a doctrinal controversy that has proceeded along the party lines of liberals and conservatives.

---

[4] See the discussion in W. D. Davies and Dale C. Allison, *A Critical and Exegetical Commentary on the Gospel according to Saint Matthew*, The International Critical Commentary (Edinburgh: Clark, 1991), 271–297.

[5] C. F. D. Moule, "Incarnation: Paradox That Will Not Go Away," *Times Higher Education Supplement* (23 December 1977), 11.

[6] *The Origin of Christology* (New York: Cambridge University Press, 1979).

This is just one example of what strikes me as the arid debate between liberals and conservatives that has had a reductionist influence on the study of the New Testament. Liberals are so committed to an evolutionary approach that they frequently ignore its exegetical problems. Conservatives are so afraid that critical inquiry will let them down that they often prefer simply to assert scriptural "inerrancy" and leave the connection between scripture and their own beliefs unexplored. In their respective campaigns of programmatic silence, Professor Moule, an interpreter of the first order, had been largely ignored just as he was making a most seminal contribution.

From the perspective of a generative exegesis in search of an understanding of Christianity as a system of religion, Professor Moule's critique of the liberal consensus is of the first importance. His own alternative, however, which he styles the "transcendental" Christology of Christian orthodoxy, is one I hesitate to take up without reservation. The antinomy between the alternatives is, to begin with, typical of the tension between science and orthodoxy which has fixated intellectual observers since the nineteenth century. That antinomy could conceivably prove to be important within the New Testament, and therefore of merit in understanding the development of Christology; or—as seems more likely—it may turn out to be an artifact of a division between faith and reason that has been characteristic of intellectual thought since the Enlightenment.

I would therefore reformulate Professor Moule's criticism of the liberal consensus. Instead of invoking an allegedly transcendental assessment of Jesus among the disciples, I have suggested simply that the Petrine confession insists that no single term, not even "Christ," may be accurately used of Jesus, unless it is redefined in the light of knowledge of Jesus himself. Jesus is the term of reference that determines the propriety of a title, and not the reverse, because Jesus' relationship to God is what makes and unmakes the relevance of the title. For Jesus' relationship, the instructional source goes on to insist, is more *with* God than *to* God: Father and Son constitute a circle of intimacy in comparison with which all else is subsidiary, and into which one may only be included by the grace of revelation. The first hole in the evolutionary bridge is that the term "messiah," the postulated point of departure, offers no easy transition to such a notion. Indeed, we might go a bit farther than Professor Moule, and suggest that it is only possible to appreciate the Petrine

confession and Jesus' acknowledgement of his Father when terms
such as "messiah" are qualified to the point of redefinition.

That brings us to the second hole in the evolutionary bridge,
which is—if anything—even more gaping than the first. There are
simply too many titles applied to Jesus within too short a space of
time to sustain the argument that one title spawned the rest. Moreover,
there is no reason to suppose such titles would have had to have
been manufactured simply because Jesus was effective as a teacher
or reputed for unusual deeds. Several brilliant rabbis taught during
the first century, some of them skilled in healing and a few of them
credited with an ability to influence natural phenomena; they man-
aged to do so without being called "messiah," "son of God," "son
of man," or the like. A few revolutionary figures are styled "false
prophets" by Josephus, and the famous messianic pretender of the
second century, Simon bar Kosiba, styled himself Bar Kokhba ("son
of the star," after Numbers 24:17) in order to proclaim his invinci-
ble might. But the untitled precedents far outweighed the titled, and
insofar as titles are invoked, they signal a political and military power
that Jesus never actually exercised or even pretended to exercise.

A doctrinal approach such as Professor Moule's infers from such
evidence that Jesus himself must have been very different from his
contemporaries, that there was a "transcendental" dimension within
his person that escaped categorization, and yet that resonated—however partially—with the primary categories of how God was expected
definitively to act through a single person on behalf of humanity. A
systemic approach, such as that pursued here within the discipline
of comparison, must eschew reference to the transcendent, except as
such reference might emerge *within* the system at hand. The systemic
impact of Peter's confession and Jesus' acclamation of his Father's
revelation is to make the relationship between Jesus and God the
point from which any assessment of Jesus is to be generated, and at
the same time the only means of access to God.

What Has God made of Humanity with Christ?

We have seen that part of the fundamental understanding of the
primitive catechesis for baptisands is that the intimate and mutual
relationship between Father and Son provides the key, not only to
Jesus' identity, but to the possibility of a believer having an identity

before God. Christians know who they are as God's children in the light of their knowledge of Jesus as God's Son. A corollary of that understanding is that what God makes of his relationship with Jesus is an extension of God's self to us. Christ and church are related, because the Son is related both intimately to the Father and constitutionally—that is, humanly—to believers.

A single confusion produces what is called subordinationism, both ancient and modern. When Christ is described in relation to God *in respect of believers* (as created human beings), the emphasis naturally falls upon a notion of dependence vis-à-vis God. During the fourth century, that led Arius to his claim that Christ was subordinate to the Father, in the sense that there was a time when the Son was not.[7] From the nineteenth century and thereafter, we have had the "evolutionary" Christology described by Professor Moule, according to which there was a time when the Christ was not. In both cases, the connection of Jesus to humanity is used to argue that, like humanity, Jesus Christ, the Son of God, is temporally conditioned in relation to (or, in doctrinal terms, subordinate to) the Father God. But it ought to be obvious that, while Jesus may need to be described in temporal terms, as a figure at the generative point of the literary history of the New Testament, as Christ, his intimate relationship with the Father is such that any temporal reference is meaningless. Jesus Christ's unique status implies that categorical clarity must be preserved: he may be understood in respect of his humanity or in respect of his relationship to the divine, but the two sorts of reference must not be confounded if any insight is to be gained. That, in any case, was the finding of Christian Orthodoxy in what is called the Athanasian Creed.

Paul and John provide good instances of self-conscious clarity in categorical development for the purposes of the kinds of controversy with others and reflection within the community that typified discussion within the earliest churches. An example of Pauline Christology will here illustrate how Christ's identity is held to change the constitution of human beings within controversial discourse, while John's Gospel will be read to suggest how a more purely theological reflection developed.

---

[7] See John Meyendorff, *Christ in Eastern Christian Thought* (New York: St. Vladimir's Seminary Press, 1975).

First Corinthians 15:12–24 demonstrates the importance for Paul of Christ's transfer of the believer (at baptism, and thereafter) from his or her previous condition into the realm of God. It is perfectly consistent with that emphasis that Paul proceeds to posit a formal analogy between Adam and Christ (1 Corinthians 15:45–49):

> So also it is written, "The first man, Adam, became a living psyche"; the last Adam is life-giving spirit. The spiritual is not first, but the psychic is, then the spiritual. The first man was from earth—dust, the second man from Heaven. As is the man of dust, such are those who are dust; as is the heavenly man, such are those who are heavenly. And just as we bore the image of the dust, so shall we bear the image of the heavenly.

Paul often speaks with less clarity than one might wish, but here the matter is put plainly.

Insofar as there has been confusion in regard to the statement, it has stemmed from attempts at translation, not Paul's thought. In particular, he adheres to two conventions that need to be honored in any rendering, if he is to be understood. First, Paul thinks of "Adam" as the primordial human being, which he generally refers to as "man." The meaning of the passage turns on the analogy that, just as the human constitution is laid down in the "first man" (Adam) it is seen to be changed in the "second man" (Christ). Another convention is equally significant. Paul is not demeaning "Adam," or humanity at large, when he calls him "psychic" (*psychikon*): he means simply he was possessed of a "soul" (*psyche*), complete with its animate self-consciousness and reason. Paul really does not dismiss Adam as "physical" (so the Revised Standard Version) or as "natural" (so the King James Version) in order to praise Christ for the mere possession of human rationality. His point is rather that, just as "Adam" represents a genuinely creative act, enabling human life to flow forth thereafter, so "Christ" is a new creation, which makes possible a transition into Spirit, the very world of God.

The transition into the realm of Spirit for believers is envisaged within 1 Corinthians 15 as at the resurrection. Paul also invokes the image of Christ as a second Adam in association with baptism in Romans, written one or two years after the Corinthians' correspondence, ca. 57 C.E. In an extended comparison, Paul contrasts the rule of sin from the transgression of Adam (compounded by the awareness of sin that the law of Moses occasioned) with the grace which flows from Jesus Christ (5:12–21).

His conclusion is as concise as what he wrote to the Corinthians (Romans 5:18–21):

> Therefore as through one person's transgression there was condemnation for all men, so also through one person's justice there was exoneration unto life for all men. For just as through one man's disobedience many were made sinners, so also through the obedience of one many shall be made righteous. And law came in, in order that the transgression might abound: where sin abounds, grace overflows. So that just as sin ruled in death, grace might rule through righteousness unto eternal life through Jesus Christ our lord.

Here, the insistence upon the transference into a new realm by means of grace is as emphatic as in 1 Corinthians 15, but the moment of the transfer is not resurrection, but baptism, which is the subject of pointed exposition in Romans 6:1–11.

The link between the two moments, baptism and resurrection, is effectuated by Paul's conception of Spirit. The very spirit which cries out "Abba!" in baptism (Romans 8:15), after the manner of Jesus Christ himself, is also the principle which is to transform the lives and the existence of believers: "If the Spirit of the one who raised Jesus from the dead dwells in you, the one who raised Christ from the dead will also make alive your mortal bodies through the Spirit dwelling in you" (Romans 8:11). Baptism and resurrection are joined by the single spirit of the Christ, who also teaches us to pray to God as our Father and to follow in his own path. Precisely when Paul may seem to be speaking of Christ within the terms of reference of humanity as we know it, the cutting edge of his Christology becomes apparent: Jesus Christ can be the second Adam, who offers humanity a new constitution of its existence both ethically and eschatologically, precisely as a function of his intimate and unique relation to God's spirit.

The fourth Gospel also develops a distinctive vocabulary in order to articulate Jesus' impact upon humanity, which is largely derived from the theological language of the Targumim, the Aramaic paraphrases of the Hebrew Bible employed within worship in synagogues. Jesus is explained in terms of God's "word," *logos* in Greek, *memra* in Aramaic. *Memra*, a nominal form of the verb "to speak" (*amar*), is the Targumic reference to God's activity of commanding. God might simply be thought of as commanding what is ordered when the term is used, but the emphasis might also fall on how people respond to the order, or on what lies behind the divine order and the human response. *Memra* might convey a range of emphases, both interior to the act of commanding, informing the decision of command, and consequent upon the act, devolving from it. Context alone permits us to make a selection among its various senses. There is no such thing as a *concept* of God's *memra*, certainly not as personal being or hypostasis, nor even a systematic idea that is fully consistent from Targum to Targum. What links the Targumim, in their distinct usages of *memra*, is not a theological thought, but a theological manner of speaking of God in terms of divine commanding. *Memra* is not invoked haphazardly when some verb of speaking happens to be used of God in the Hebrew text that is rendered. The Targums suggest that the usage of the term reflects the ways in which given interpreters conceived of God's intention in the command, or the human response to what is effected (or affected) by the command.

The prologue of John's Gospel presents a particular construal of how Jesus Christ personally might be understood as a part of God's commanding *logos* or *memra*.[8] The first usage of *logos* in the Gospel simply establishes its identity with God (and not—it must be emphasized—with Jesus, 1:1):[9]

> In the beginning was the word, and the word was related to God, and the word was God.

The word is identified as the creative, primordial source of what exists (1:2, 3), in a way quite consistent with the association of *memra* and creation within the Targumim.

The common notion that the *logos* is to be identified willy-nilly with Jesus in the prologue is to some extent based upon a reading

---

[8] See Bruce Chilton, "Typologies of *Memra* and the Fourth Gospel," *Targum Studies* 1 (1992): 89–100.

[9] The preposition *pros* in Greek straightforwardly means "to" or "in relation to." This verse has in the past been rendered, "and the word was *with* God." That translation is a function of later Christian theology, in which *logos* was simply and irreducibly identified with Jesus. The prologue shows us how that identification was effectuated, without simply collating Jesus to *logos*.

of the text in Greek which does not attend adequately to its obviously deliberate sequence. God's *logos* is said to be the place where "life" is, and that life is held to be the "light" of all humanity (v. 4). Insofar as an immediately christological category is developed in the prologue, that category is "light," not "word." It is the "light" which shines in the darkness (v. 5), which enlightens every person (v. 9). Most crucially, the "light," a neuter noun in Greek (*to phos*), is identified as masculine and singular in v. 10:

> In it was the world, and the world came into existence
> through it, and the world did not know *him*.

From that textual moment, the usage of pronouns and the summary reference to Jesus' ministry (vv. 11–13, cf. vv. 6–8) makes it clear we are dealing with a person, not an entity. But, from the present point of view, the telling factor is that Jesus has been presented, precisely and grammatically, as the light which takes its origin in the *logos*, rather than as the *logos* in itself.

We then come to the clause which has dominated the reading of the fourth Gospel, and which has been taken as the cornerstone of a christological construction of the *logos* in Christian theology from the second century (v. 14a):

> And the *logos* became flesh and dwelt among us.

Once *logos* has been identified with Jesus, as it is for Clement of Alexandria and Irenaeus during the second century, the reference of the clause can only be to the incarnation. Indeed, the Latin text of the clause, *et verbum caro factum est*, is conventionally taken in association with the creedal assertion that the "Son," understood as the second person of the Trinity, became incarnate (*incarnatus est*). But all such readings and construals are possible only on the assumption that the *logos* and Jesus are interchangeable; then he is a pre-existent, personal entity come down from heaven. The problem with such an exegesis of the Johannine text is the care with which Jesus is *not* directly associated with the *logos* in vv. 1–13.

But if v. 14 is not read as asserting a christological incarnation, what else can it be saying? An approach to that question which is guided by our observation of the usage of *memra* in the Targumim suggests an answer. *Memra* is essentially God's mighty command, vindicating and warning his people; v. 14 refers to this *logos* as becoming flesh, and then explains that assertion by saying it "dwelt among us" (*eskenosen en hemin*). The verb *skenoo*, it is often observed, relates naturally to *shakhen* in Hebrew and Aramaic, from which *Shekhinah*, the principal term of reference to God's presence in the cult, is derived. To describe the *logos*, understood as *memra*, as dwelling among us such that we might behold its glory, is consistent with Targumic usage.

The "glory" beheld is subjected to a precise qualification at the end of the verse; it is "glory as of an only one with a Father, full of grace and truth" (1:14c). At this point, elementary misreadings have obscured a complex statement. The assertion is *not* "we beheld his glory, glory as of the only Son from the Father," as in the Revised Standard Version; still less is it "we have seen his glory, the glory of the only Son, who came from the Father," as in the New International Version. The definite articles are conspicuously absent from the text in Greek; the glory spoken of is as of *an* only child, not "the only Son." The comparison is straightforwardly metaphorical, not doctrinal: the glory of *logos* was as a child's, reflecting the Father's.

Now, however, comes the element of genuine complexity in the logic of the Greek text: the glory of the *logos* is "as of an only one (*hos monogenous*) with a Father," and we know, as readers of the Gospel, that Jesus is God's Son. Indeed, we know explicitly from the body of the Gospel that Jesus, as God's "Son," speaks His "word,"[10] and that the reaction to the one is congruent with the reaction to the other. The inference that the glory of the logos was "as of" Jesus is therefore precisely consonant with the presentation of the Gospel as a whole. Jesus speaks the word of God; as the Son who was sent by his Father, he permits God's own voice to be heard.

---

[10] In the Gospel, the overarching perspective is established that the *logos* is God's primordially, rather than simply Jesus' (or even Jesus' in God's). It is on that basis that Jesus can claim that the word he speaks will judge anyone who rejects him and does not accept his utterances (John 12:48–50). It is neither Jesus himself nor what he says that will judge such a person on the last day, but the *logos* (here functioning much as the *memra* in the Targumim). The *logos* spoken by Jesus is held to have a dynamic property, as in 15:3, where it is held to have purified those who belong to Jesus. It is Jesus nonetheless, and no other, who is understood to speak the *logos*, and the treatment of the disciples is to reflect people's response to his word (15:20).

The remainder of the prologue reflects the maintenance of the distinction between the *logos* and Jesus and suggests the sense in which we should understand that the *logos* "became flesh." John, we are told, witnessed "concerning it" (*peri autou*, that is, the word), by saying of Jesus, "This was he of whom I said, He that comes after me" (v. 15). Fundamentally, the *logos* is still more the object of the prologue's attention than Jesus himself is, and that continues to be the case in v. 16:

> For from the fullness *autou* we have all received, even grace upon grace.

Autou, whether taken of the *logos* or of Jesus, is a masculine pronoun, but the statement is a resumption of what has been said in vv. 3–5: we live from devolutions of the *logos*, the dynamic structure of word, light and life.

The understanding that God's "word" is still the essential issue in play makes the transition to the next topic straightforward (v. 17):

> For the law was given through Moses, grace and truth came through Jesus Christ.

The connection of *logos*, taken as *memra*, to the revelation through Moses is evident. Moreover, the syntax and logic of v. 17 coheres with that of v. 16; the coordination of God's activity in creation with his dona- tion of the law through Moses is established within Targumic usage.

The link between the verses is literal as well. The "grace" (*he charis*) which came through Jesus Christ (v. 17) is correlative to the "grace upon grace" (*charin anti charitos*) we have all received (v. 16). There is a constant and consistent activity of God's *logos* from the creation and through the revelations to Moses and to Jesus. The *logos* in John develops well established notions of the *memra* in early Judaism. At no point and in no way does the prologue present the revelation through Jesus as disjunctive with the revelation through Moses: any such disjunction is an artifact of imposing an anachro- nistic Christology upon the text. Verse 17 also provides guidance in regard to the reading of v. 14. The statement that grace and truth "came" (*egeneto*) through Jesus Christ is comparable to the assertion that God's word "became" (*egeneto*) flesh; in both cases, the under- lying contention is that Jesus is the person in whom God's word— His activity in creating and revealing, is manifest.

The last verse of the prologue is also the last word of the present reading. Verse 18 makes an assertion which makes any exclusively incarnational reading appear nonsensical:

> No one has at any time seen God; an only begotten, God, who was in the bosom of the Father, that one has made him known.

The first clause makes no sense whatever if the prologue means to say that Jesus simply is the *logos*. If the *logos* is God (v. 1:1), and Jesus is that "word," v. 18 is more than paradoxical. But v. 18 makes eminent sense on just the reading we have here suggested: no one has at any time seen God, provided the reader has followed the logic of his revelation as the prologue outlines it. Jesus, as an only begotten (again, without the article), has made God known (*exegesato*). Jesus is the word made flesh in the fourth Gospel, not the word *simpliciter*. Just as we would expect on the basis of our reading of passages that refer to *logos* in the body of the Gospel, Jesus is presented as the exegesis of God, the one who speaks his word. In that role, the fourth Gospel can refer to Jesus as God (*theos*) just as Philo refers to Moses:[11] not to make an ontological assertion, but to insist that the instrument of God's word is to be taken as divinely valued.

Christ the Redeemer as Lord and God

John's Gospel points beyond the development of its own Christology to the bolder claims of its community in Ephesus. When Thomas, the famous doubter, encounters the risen Jesus he exclaims, "My Lord and my God!" (John 20:28). Jesus replies, "Do you believe because you have seen me? Blessed are those who, without having seen, yet believe" (20:29). In the final analysis, however nuanced the portrayal of Jesus in respect of God's eternal word of command, his *memra* or *logos*, the Gospel concludes its narrative portrayal of Jesus' teaching and acting on God's behalf with the assertion that, substantially, Jesus *is* God. The ontological claim is made only at the close of the Gospel; after Jesus' instrumental representation of God, in the manner of Moses, is explored in the prologue, an entire Gospel

---

[11] See *Legum Allegoria* I.40; *De Sacrificiis Abelis et Caini* 9; *Quod Deterius Potiori insididari soleat* 161–162; *De Migratione Abrahami* 84; *De Mutatione Nominum* 19; *De Vita Moses* 1.158; *Quod Omnis Probus Liber sit* 43.

pursues the matter further, until Jesus is treated, not only instrumentally but functionally, as God.

Within the Johannine circle of literature, imagery of the Gospel itself was taken up in order to convey that claim ontologically, to the point that it becomes unmistakably plain. The Revelation of John is generally dated to around 100 C.E. The document itself is written in a Semitized Greek, with self-consciously bad grammar: the errors of case and tense, for example, are below a rudimentary level. And such approximations of archaism can scarcely be taken as naive when a Jewish congregation is dismissed as a "synagogue of Satan" (2:9; 3:9). A formal distance from Judaism is self-consciously assumed.

Likewise, Jesus as the divine lamb is now explicitly an object of worship. The *amnos* of John 1:29, 36 has become a surreally diminutive "little lamb (*arnion*) standing as slain" (Revelation 5:6). The attribution to the *arnion* of divine status is obvious both in its placement, in the midst of the throne, the living creatures, and the elders, and in its possession of seven eyes "which are the spirits of God sent out into all the earth." Although the term *arnion* in Koine appears unequivocally to connote the helplessness of a lamb, so that the fact of its slaughter is emphasized, the focus of the Revelation is the power that proceeds from the lamb after its slaughter. Indeed, the lamb is worthy of heavenly and human worship (5:8, 13; 7:9–10) precisely as slain (5:12). That is what provides it the authority to open the seals (6:1f.) and exercise judgment with God (6:15–16; cf. 14:10; 17:12–14).

The essential focus of the Synoptic catechesis regarding Eucharist, the solidarity of believers in the witness of a faithful martyr, is also assumed in the Revelation. Indeed, that solidarity is combined with the imagery of Jesus as a sacrifice for sin in the portrayal of Christian martyrs as those who have whitened their robes in the blood of the lamb (7:14): they indeed enjoy the presence of the lamb in their midst, now portrayed as shepherding them (7:17). The notion of whitening in blood is no paradox, once it is understood that the underlying issue is the purification which a sacrifice for sin effects. And the imagery of the lamb's blood is explicitly linked with the theme of Christian witnessing in 12:11.

There is genuine and bold creativity involved, however, in the assertion that the lamb is best regarded as slain from the foundation of the world (13:8). That conviction is expressed in the same verse that regards the book of life as belonging to the lamb. The association of the two ideas is no coincidence. Jesus' death is now viewed as an eternal sacrifice that both gives him access to the divine throne and offers his followers solidarity with his triumphant purity. For that reason, those followers—or at least 144,000 of them, marked especially for purity—are to appear with the lamb on Mount Zion and offer worship in the presence of the throne, the four beasts, and the elders (14:1–5). Ultimately, however, all those who conquer the beast and its image are to join in the song of Moses and of the lamb (15:2–4; cf. 21:22–27).

The festal quality of the solidarity of faithful followers with the lamb leads to the at first sight unlikely imagery of the marriage of the lamb with his bride, an image of the Jerusalem which is to come (21:1–14). The earlier blessing pronounced on those who are called to "the wedding supper of the lamb" (19:9, cf. v. 7 also, and the context from v. 1) locates the occasion which produced the imagery: reference to the parable of the wedding feast (Matthew 22:1–10; Luke 14:16–24) has joined with a conception of the Eucharist in which union with God is effected by participation in Christ. It is a union which even makes the seer, and any faithful Christian, a fellow servant with the angelic host (cf. Revelation 19:9–10), a citizen of the new Jerusalem whose purpose is the worship of God and the lamb (22:1–5).

Perhaps because the idiom of the Revelation is visionary, it is possible for it to express openly and trenchantly what even the Gospel according to John only intimates. The discourse of vision also does not require that the obviously pertinent systematic question be posed: If Jesus is God, are there two Gods? The situation is similar in the exalted language of the letter to the Philippians (ca. 85 C.E.). It closes its praise of Jesus' example (2:5f.) with a doxological conclusion (2:10–11):

> So that at the name of Jesus every knee should bow, in Heaven and earth and in the depths, and every tongue acknowledge that Jesus Christ is Lord, to the glory of God, the Father.

What Thomas can stammer in recognition of the resurrected Jesus, and the Johannine seer can see in a rhapsody of spirit, Timothy's Paul (so identified in Philippians 1:1) can echo in an exaltation of praise.

Stammering, rhapsody, and exaltation, however, may not be dismissed as "merely" emotional outbursts or epiphenomenal exaggeration. Feelings are part of the totality of any religious system of which we are aware, and the affective engagement of diverse documents, at just the moment when Jesus Christ's status as God is asserted, must give us pause. Timothy's Paul enables us to pursue the matter further, in that Colossians (ca. 90 C.E., cf. Colossians 1:1) is taken up largely with the issue of a Christology of Jesus' being as God.

The interface between redemption and such a Christology is clearly signaled: the introduction of the key passage refers to God's transfer of the believer "into the kingdom of the Son of his love" (Colossians 1:13). In him, the text proceeds, "we have redemption, the forgiveness of sins" (v. 14). Colossians then goes on to make a Christological statement comparable to the Johannine prologue, in that Christ is portrayed in terms of the creational imagery of Genesis 1.

But Timothy's Paul directly asserts Jesus' existence *prior* to any historical appearance (Colossians 1:15–20):

> He is the invisible God's image, firstborn of all creation, because everything was created by him, in Heaven and on earth, visible and invisible.
> Be they angelic thrones or lordships or principalities or authorities, everything has been created through him and for him.
> He is before all things, and all things consist in him, and he is the head of the body, the church.
> He is the beginning, firstborn of the dead, that he might personally be precedent in all things.
> For in him all the fullness was pleased to dwell, and through him—and for him—to reconcile all things (whether on earth or in Heaven), as he made peace through the blood of his cross.

The advanced nature of the passage is manifest, not only in its development of the language of John's Gospel, but in its elaboration of typically Pauline expressions. The church as the body of Christ, which had been used by Paul to insist that all Christians belong to one another in Christ (1 Corinthians 12:12–27; Romans 12:4–13), here is applied in the sense of a hierarchy, to insist that Christ is the church's head. And the Pauline emphasis upon the importance of reconciliation between people as a function of their salvation in Christ (2 Corinthians 5:14–21; Romans 5:10) here reaches into the truly cosmic dimensions of the powers behind the visible world (Colossians 1:20, 22; Ephesians 2:16).

Colossians reaches into the treasury of early Christian theology in order to fashion a true Christology: an ontology of Jesus Christ as God. The very person who died on the cross is the origin and the goal of the entire creation; he is the primordial first instance, the inherent principal of order, and the proleptic end point of all things. Early and orthodox Christianity in the centuries after the formation of the New Testament would avail itself of the language and thought of Colossians in order to agree upon creedal confessions of Christology. The length, complication, and violence of the struggle for creedal unity belong to an old story, which cannot be rehearsed here. But the canonical system we are describing does directly indicate why that struggle began, why it endured, and why it is far from over. Jesus, personally and historically, is there identified with God in the creation, maintenance, and redemption of humanity and everything connected with humanity. The canonical system does not explain how that confession is to be reconciled with monotheism; it does not specify how divinity is to be claimed for Jesus, and it does not even concern itself directly with the biography of the person for whom so much is claimed. Although those questions are left to be worked out, the stakes involved in how they are answered are incalculably high. After all, the person of whom we speak is our origin, our destiny, the very face of God. The Christian dispute concerning Christology, no less than the Christian quest for ecumenical unity (see John 17:20–23), is a vital and necessary aspect of its canonized system of religion.

Uncompromising and trenchant though Colossians is in its claim of Jesus' divinity, at one point there is a certain obscurity. Which "fullness" is it that chooses to dwell in him (1:19)? It would seem to be the divine fullness, which also is to reconcile all things in Christ, but there may be a certain ambiguity. If so, Colossians later removes it, in a passage that begins by discussing the ethical implications of baptism (2:6–11a):

> As you, then, received Christ Jesus the Lord, walk in him, rooted and built up in him and established in faith—just as you were taught, abounding in thanksgiving. See to it lest anyone make prey of you by means of philosophy and empty deceit: the tradition of men and the elements of the world, and not Christ. For in him all the fullness of deity dwells bodily, and you are fulfilled in him, who is the head of

every principality and authority. In him also you were circumcised
with a circumcision made without hands.

If there were some ambiguity in the earlier statement about the "fullness," now it is exploited, because it is asserted both that the faithful are fulfilled in Christ Jesus, and—more dramatically—that deity
resides bodily in him.

For all that the claim is plain, it is not without complexity. The
language of "body" has already been deployed to speak of the church
of which Christ is head (see also 1:24; 2:10, and vv. 16–19) so that
believers' endowment with "Christ in you" (1:27) is also an indwelling
of God in their midst. But the "bodily" indwelling of God is not
merely a metaphorical way to speak of the church. The category of
"body" is also meant in its pragmatic sense, as when Colossians states
that Christ has "reconciled [you] by the body of his flesh through
death" (1:22). Deity is first of all resident there and at that moment
"bodily," and on that basis may be said to dwell in the church
as well.

The fundamental response to the issue of Christology, then, is
ontological. Jesus Christ speaks of God, teaches God's way, conveys
divine grace, transforms human life, offers access to the kingdom,
simply because he is God. There is a functionally infinite variety of
ways to speak of Christ's being as God, and the reverse; and—as we
have already remarked—serious differences are bound to emerge as
that variety is realized. But it is characteristic of Christianity that the
range of ways God is reflected in Christ can only be explained fully
by relating Christ and deity substantially—and not simply by representing Christ as correct in certain of his opinions about God.

At the time the Gospels according to Matthew and Luke were
produced (during the final decades of the first century), narrative
versions of the nativity were available in Damascus and Antioch.
There is not sufficient agreement between the two versions to make
them appear to have been part of the generally available catechesis
which the Synoptic Gospels represent, and the divergences between
them make it impossible to construct anything approaching a har-
monized, historical account. Nonetheless, scholarship has doggedly
read the opening chapters of Matthew and Luke as if the self-evidently appropriate aim were to discover what sort of historical information regarding Jesus' birth may have been available in Damascus

and Antioch.[12] An approach more suitable to the interests that produced the texts would see in them both, rather than scraps of reminiscence organized by pious imagination, serious investigations in
narrative form of what it means for deity to dwell bodily in Jesus,
and from that place to shine in the life of believers.

Matthew's story has Joseph told by an angel not to fear to take
Mary as his wife, in that what has been begotten in her is from
holy spirit (1:18–20). The angel goes on to command Joseph to name
the child Jesus, in that he will save his people from their sins, and
the events are said to have fulfilled a passage from Isaiah which
speaks of the child Emanuel, "God with us" (1:21–23). The Matthean
understanding of Joseph's place in the proceedings is ambivalent:
Joseph is troubled in the first place because he knows he is not Jesus'
father (1:18–19), and yet Jesus' Davidic ancestry comes through him
(1:2–17). The only resolution the text offers is at the level of what
results from whatever happened: that which is begotten is from Spirit,
and the child will save his people as God in our midst.

Luke's nativity is framed more from early Christian hymns of
praise than from reflections on specifiable passages of the Hebrew
Bible, and the whole of the narrative is focused on Mary more than
on Joseph. Here the angel Gabriel himself announces to Mary what
is to take place (1:30b–31):

> Fear not, Mary, for you have found favor with God. And behold, you
> will become pregnant and bear a Son, and you will call his name
> Jesus. He shall be great, and will be called Son of the most high, and
> the Lord God will give him the throne of David his father, and he
> will reign over the house of Jacob forever and of his kingdom there
> will be no end.

The perplexity concerning how this could be is Mary's rather than
Joseph's in this case (1:34), and once again the angel explains, in a
canticle which shows some of the formal signs of poetry (v. 35):

> Holy Spirit will come upon you, and [God] most high's power will
> overshadow you: therefore that which is begotten shall be called holy,
> God's Son.

---

[12] See Raymond E. Brown, *The Birth of the Messiah: A Commentary on the Infancy
Narratives in the Gospels of Matthew and Luke* (New York: Doubleday, 1999).

The psalmodic language of Luke gives the appearance of being more explicit than Matthew's, and yet the central assertion is the same: by one means or another, he who is the source of divine Spirit in baptism is himself of God's spirit from the outset. Just that union of physical body and divine presence constitutes the central assertion of the nativity, in either version. In that it occurs within the womb of Mary, her place as the bearer of God (the *theotokos* of later orthodoxy) is implicit, and yet receives its notice.

The mystery of the messiah within Christianity concerns how it is that Jesus Christ, a rabbi from Galilee who came to grief and rose again, can offer us communion with God (by means of baptism in his name, prayer in his manner, ethics after his example, and Eucharist), access into a divine kingdom which is also his, and partnership in a body of believers who contest the finality of race, history, time, and death. The solution of the mystery is a riddle over which the Christian insists upon puzzling, because in the puzzling faith rejoices. Jesus is the Christ because he is God himself, bodily in an instant of human experience which can be located historically, bodily also in an eternal moment of God's own destiny which can be described theologically. He who was born of a woman, within the constraints of humanity, was then and has been forever that divine force which restless human natures seek, the bodily fullness which answers the pangs of human vacancy.

C. One God, Many Forms: Judaism

Judaism concurs with Islam that God cannot be represented by any human form. But, with Christianity, it conceives of man in God's image, therefore of man and God as in some ways comparable. Then the question is, in what ways? The middle position between Islam and Christianity may be characterized as a God who incorporates human traits but not a God in human form: corporeal but not incarnate, so to speak. The issue is, what traits of man and God intersect, in what ways is man like God?

Any account of Judaism on God's personhood begins with God as creator of the world, giver of the Torah, and redeemer of Israel. Israel the holy people meets God in the Torah at Sinai, when God— not Moses—proclaims, "The Lord, the Lord! a God compassionate and gracious, slow to anger, abounding in kindness and faithfulness, extending kindness to the thousandth generation, forgiving iniquity, transgression, and sin" (Ex. 34:6). Only in the revelation of the Torah does Israel attain that certain knowledge about God that holy Israel offers humanity. For those who practice Judaism, the encounter with God takes place in the Torah, hence, in the study of the Torah. The place and time for meeting God is not only at prayer, then, but in the holy circle of sage and disciples, and it is in books that portray God's self-revelation to Moses at the burning bush (Exodus 3) or in the still small voice Elijah heard, that through all time Israel finds God. In more secular language, Judaism knows God through God's self-manifestation in the Torah—and otherwise, so Judaism maintains, there should be no specific, reliable knowledge of God, Creator of heaven and earth, who reveals the Torah and who redeems humanity at the end of days. And knowing God through the Torah means meeting God in many conditions indeed.

Characterization of God

A definitive statement of the proposition that in diverse forms God appears to humanity is in the following:

> A. Another interpretation of *I am the Lord your God [who brought you out of the land of Egypt]* (Ex. 20:2):
> B. Said R. Hinena bar Papa, "The Holy One, blessed be He, had made His appearance to them with a stern face, with a neutral face, with a friendly face, with a happy face.
> C. "with a stern face: in Scripture. When a man teaches his son Torah, he has to teach him in a spirit of awe.
> D. "with a neutral face: in Mishnah.
> E. "with a friendly face: in Talmud.
> F. "with a happy face: in lore.
> G. "Said to them the Holy One, blessed be He, 'Even though you may see all of these diverse faces of mine, nonetheless: *I am the Lord your God who brought you out of the land of Egypt* (Ex. 20:2).'"

So far we deal with attitudes. As to the iconic representation of God, the following is explicit:

> H. Said R. Levi, "The Holy One, blessed be He, had appeared to them like an icon that has faces in all directions, so that if a thousand people look at it, it appears to look at them as well.

I. "So too when the Holy One, blessed be He, when He was speaking, each Israelite would say, 'With me in particular the Word speaks.'

J. "What is written here is not, I am the Lord, your [plural] God, but rather, *I am the Lord your [singular] God who brought you out of the land of Egypt* (Ex. 20:2)."

That God may show diverse faces to various people is now established. The reason for God's variety is made explicit. People differ, and God, in the image of whom all mortals are made, must therefore sustain diverse images—all of them formed in the model of human beings:

I. Said R. Yosé bar Hanina, "And it was in accord with the capacity of each one of them to listen and understand what the Word spoke with him.

J. "And do not be surprised at this matter, for when the manna came down to Israel, all would find its taste appropriate to their circumstance, infants in accord with their capacity, young people in accord with their capacity, old people in accord with their capacity.

K. "infants in accord with their capacity: just as an infant sucks from the teat of his mother, so was its flavor, as it is said, *Its taste was like the taste of rich cream* (Num. 11:8).

L. "young people in accord with their capacity: as it is said, *My bread also which I gave you, bread and oil and honey* (Ez. 16:19).

M. "old people in accord with their capacity: as it is said *the taste of it was like wafers made with honey* (Ex. 16:31).

N. "Now if in the case of manna, each one would find its taste appropriate to his capacity, so in the matter of the Word, each one understood in accord with capacity.

O. "Said David, *The voice of the Lord is [in accord with one's] strength* (Ps. 29:4).

P. "What is written is not, *in accord with his strength in particular*, but rather, *in accord with one's strength*, meaning, in accord with the capacity of each one.

Q. "Said to them the Holy One, blessed be He, 'It is not in accord with the fact that you hear a great many voices, but you should know that it is I who [speaks to all of you individually]: *I am the Lord your God who brought you out of the land of Egypt*' (Ex. 20:2)."

Pesiqta deRab Kahana XII:XXV

The individuality and particularity of God rest upon the diversity of humanity. But, it must follow, the model of humanity—"in our image" dictates how we are to envisage the face of God. And that is the starting point of our inquiry. The Torah defines what we know about God—but the Torah also tells us that we find God in the face of the other: in our image, after our likeness, means, everyone is in God's image, so if we want to know God, we had best look closely into the face of all humanity, one by one, one by one. But let us start at the beginning. The main point then is clear: however we know God, in whatever form or aspect, it is always one and the same God.

God as Premise, Presence, Person, and Personality

The Torah portrays God in four ways: as premise, person, presence, and personality.

God as Premise. Philosophers work by rational steps from premises to propositions, sifting evidence, conducting argument, reaching upward to conclusions. For the philosophers of the Mishnah, God is both the unitary premise of all being and also the unitary goal of all being. In the Mishnah—as in all other writings of Judaism—God is present not merely in details, when actually mentioned, but at the foundations. To characterize the encounter with God, whether intellectual or concrete and everyday, we must therefore pay attention not alone to passages that speak of God in some explicit way, but, even more so, to the fundamental givens on which all particular doctrines or stories of a document depend. What that fact means in the case of the Mishnah is simple. That great philosophical law code demonstrates over and over again that all things are one, complex things yield uniform and similar components, and, rightly understood, there is a hierarchy of being, to be discovered through the proper classification of all things.

What this means is that, for the philosophers who wrote the Mishnah, the most important thing they wished to demonstrate about God is that God is one. And this they proposed to prove by showing, in a vast array of everyday circumstances, (1) the fundamental order and unity of all things, all being and (2) the unity of all things in an ascending hierarchy, ascend upward to God. So all things through their unity and order to one thing, and all being derives from One God.

In the Mishnah many things are placed into sequence and order—

"hierarchized"—and the order of all things is shown to have a purpose, so that the order, or hierarchization, is purposive, or "teleological." The Mishnah time and again demonstrates these two contrary propositions: (1) many things join together by their nature into one thing, and (2) one thing yields many things. These propositions complement each other, because, in forming matched opposites, the two set forth an ontological judgment. It is that all things are not only orderly, but, in their deepest traits of being, are so ordered that many things fall into one classification, and one thing may hold together many things of a single classification. For this philosophy, rationality thus consists in the hierarchy of the order of things, a rationality tested and proved, time and again, by the possibility always of effecting the hierarchical classification of all things. The proposition that is the Mishnah's then is a theory of the right ordering of each thing in its classification (or taxon), all the categories (or taxa) in correct sequence, from least to greatest. And showing that all things can be ordered, and that all orders can be set into relationship with one another, we transform the ontological message into its components of proposition, argument, and demonstration.

God in Person. Had Judaism emerged from the Mishnah, philosophers over the ages will have found themselves with an easy task in setting forth in a systematic and abstract way the doctrine of God and our relationship with God: the first principle, much like the unmoved mover of Greek philosophy, the premise, the presence, above all, the one who made the rules and keeps them in place. But that philosophical God will have puzzled the faithful over time, who found in the Written Torah the commandment to "love the Lord your God with all your heart, with all your soul, and with all your might," a commandment not readily carried out in behalf of the unmoved mover, the principle and premise of being. Such a God as the philosophers set forth is to be affirmed and acknowledged, but by knowledge few are changed, and all one's love is not all that easily lavished on an abstract presence. When we come to the Talmud of the Land of Israel we meet God in both familiar, but also fresh representation.

The context in which the Yerushalmi took shape—the legitimation, then state-sponsorship, of Christianity—requires mention. The symbolic system of Christianity, with Christ triumphant, with the cross as the now-regnant symbol, with the canon of Christianity now defined and recognized as authoritative, called forth from the sages of the Land of Israel a symbolic system strikingly responsive to the crisis. The representation of God in man, God incarnate, in Jesus Christ, as the Christians saw him, found a powerful reply in sages' re-presentation of God as person, individual and active. God is no longer only, or mainly, the premise of all being, nor is God only or mainly the one who makes the rules and enforces them. God is now presented in the additional form of the one who makes decisions in the here and now of everyday life, responding to the individual and his or her actions. Not only so, but the actions of an individual are treated one by one, in the specific context of the person, and not all together, in the general context of the social world overall. And, as we saw in the Mishnah, that is not the primary activity of God at all.

In the following passage, God serves as the origin of all great teachings, but as we have seen, that fact bears no consequences for the description of God as a person or personality:

E. "Given by one shepherd"—

F. Said the Holy One, blessed be He, "If you hear a teaching from an Israelite minor, and the teaching gave pleasure to you, let it not be in your sight as if you have heard it from a minor, but as if you have heard it from an adult,

G. "and let it not be as if you have heard it from an adult, but as if one has heard it from a sage,

H. "and let it not be as if you have heard it from a sage, but as if one has heard it from a prophet,

I. "and let it not be as if you have heard it from a prophet, but as if one has heard it from the shepherd,

J. "and there is as a shepherd only Moses, in line with the following passage: 'Then He remembered the days of old, of Moses His servant. Where is He who brought out of the sea the shepherds of His flock? Where is He who put in the midst of them His holy Spirit?' (Is. 63:11).

K. "It is not as if one has heard it from the shepherd but as if one has heard it from the Almighty."

L. "Given by one Shepherd"—and there is only One who is the Holy One, blessed be He, in line with that which you read in Scripture: "Hear, O Israel: the Lord our God is one Lord" (Deut. 6:4).

Yerushalmi Sanhedrin 10:1.IX

In studying the Torah, sages and disciples clearly meet the living God and have recorded a direct encounter with and experience of

God through the revealed word of God. But in a statement such as this, alluding to, but not clearly describing what it means to hear the word of the Almighty, God at the end of the line simply forms the premise of revelation. There is no further effort at characterization.

God as Presence. God is understood to establish a presence in the world. This is accomplished both through intermediaries, such as a retinue of angels and also through the hypostatization of divine attributes, e.g., the Holy Spirit, the Presence of Shekhinah (the word that refers to God's presence in the world, corresponding roughly in Christian theology to the Holy Spirit), and the like. The Holy Spirit makes its appearance, e.g., "They were delighted that their opinion proved to be the same as that of the Holy Spirit" (Y. Hor. 3:5.III.PP; Y. A.Z. 3:1.II.AA, etc.). God is understood to enjoy a retinue, a court (Y. San. 1:1.IV.Q); God's seal is truth. These and similar statements restate the notion that God forms a living presence in the world. Heaven reaches decisions and conveys them to humankind through the working of chance, e.g., a lottery:

> "To whoever turned up in his hand a slip marked 'Elder,' he said, 'They have indeed chosen you in heaven.' To whoever turned up in his hand a blank slip, he would say, 'What can I do for you? It is from heaven.'"
>
> Yerushalmi Sanhedrin 1:4.V.FF–GG

The notion that the lottery conveys God's will and therefore represents God's presence in the decision-making process will not have surprised the authorship of the book of Esther. It is one way in which God's presence is given concrete form. Another, also supplied by Scripture, posited that God in the very Presence intervened in Israel's history, e.g., at the Sea of Reeds:

> When the All-Merciful came forth to redeem Israel from Egypt, He did not send a messenger or an angel, but the Holy One, blessed be He, Himself came forth, as it is said, "For I will pass through the Land of Egypt that night" (Ex. 12:12)—and not only so, but it was He and His entire retinue.
>
> Yerushalmi Sanhedrin 2:1.III.O

The familiar idea that God's presence went into Exile with Israel recurs (Y. Ta. 1:1.X.Eff.). But not a single passage in the entire Yerushalmi alleges that God's personal presence at a historical event

in the time of sages changed the course of events. The notion that
God's presence remained in Exile leaves God without personality or
even ample description.

Where God does have a presence in the world, it is not uncom-
monly a literary device, with no important narrative implications.
For example, God is assumed to speak through any given verse of
Scripture. Therefore the first person will be introduced in connection with citing such a verse, as at Y. San. 5:1.IV.E, "[God answers,]
"'It was an act of love that I did [citing a verse,] 'for I said, "The
world will be built upon merciful love"' (Ps. 89:2)." Here since the
cited verse has an "I," God is given a presence in the colloquy. But
it is a mere formality. So too we may say that God has made such
and such a statement, which serves not to characterize God but only
to supply an attribution for an opinion:

> It is written, "These are the words of the letter that Jeremiah sent
> from Jerusalem to the rest of the elders of the exiles" (Jer. 29:1).
>   Said the Holy One, blessed be He, "The elders of the exile are
> valuable to Me. Yet more beloved to Me is the smallest circle that is
> located in the Land of Israel than a great sanhedrin located outside
> of the Land."
>   Yerushalmi Nedarim 6:9.III.CCCCf.

All we have here is a paraphrase and restatement of the cited verse.

Where actions are attributed to God, we have to recognize God's
presence in context, e.g., "The Holy One, blessed be He, kept to
Himself [and did not announce] the reward that is coming to those
who carry out their religious duties, so that they should do them in
true faith [without expecting a reward]" (Y. Qid. 1:7.IX.B). But such
a statement hardly constitutes evidence that God is present and active
in a given circumstance. It rather forms into a personal statement
the principle that one should do religious duties for the right motive,
not expecting a reward—a view we found commonplace in tractate
Abot. So too statements of God's action carry slight characterization, e.g., "Even if 999 aspects of the argument of an angel incline
against someone, but a single aspect of the case of that angel argues
in favor. the Holy One . . . still inclines the scales in favor of the
accused" (Y. Qid. i:9.II.S).

God was encountered as a very real presence, actively listening to
prayers, as in the following:

See how high the Holy One, blessed be He, is above His world. Yet a person can enter a synagogue, stand behind a pillar, and pray in an undertone, and the Holy One, blessed be He, hears his prayers, as it says, "Hannah was speaking in her heart; only her lips moved, and her voice was not heard" (1 Sam. 1:13). Yet the Holy One, blessed be He, heard her prayer.

Yerushalmi Berakhot 9:1.VII.E

When, however, we distinguish God as person—"you"—from God as a well-portrayed active personality, liturgical formulas give a fine instance of the one side of the distinction. In the Yerushalmi's sizable corpus of such prayers, individual and community alike, we never find testimony to a material change in God's decision in a case based on setting aside known rules in favor of an episodic act of intervention. Sages, like everyone else in Israel, believed that God hears and answers prayer. But that belief did not require them to preserve stories about specific instances in which the rules of hearing and answering prayer attested to a particular trait of personality or character to be imputed to God. A specific episode or incident never served to highlight the characterization of divinity in one way, rather than in some other, in a manner parallel to the use of stories by the authors of Scripture to portray God as a sharply-etched personality.

God's Personality. For sages, God and humanity are indistinguishable in their physical traits. They are distinguished in other, important ways. The issue of the Talmud of Babylonia is the re-presentation of God in the form of humanity, but as God. Let us begin with the conception that God and the human being are mirror images of one another. Here we find the simple claim that the angels could not discern any physical difference whatever between man—Adam—and God:

A. Said R. Hoshaiah, "When the Holy One, blessed be He, came to create the first man, the ministering angels mistook him [for God, since man was in God's image,] and wanted to say before the latter, 'Holy, [holy, holy is the Lord of hosts].'
B. "To what may the matter be compared? To the case of a king and a governor who were set in a chariot, and the provincials wanted to greet the king, 'Sovereign!' But they did not know which one of them was which. What did the king do? He turned the

governor out and put him away from the chariot, so that people
would know who was king.

C. "So too when the Holy One, blessed be He, created the first man,
the angels mistook him [for God]. What did the Holy One, blessed
be He, do? He put him to sleep, so everyone knew that he was a
mere man.

D. "That is in line with the following verse of Scripture: 'Cease you
from man, in whose nostrils is a breath, for how little is he to be
accounted' (Is. 2:22)."

Genesis Rabbah VIII:X

It was in the Talmud of Babylonia in particular that God is represented as a fully-exposed personality, like a human being. There we
see in a variety of dimensions the single characterization of God as
a personality whom humanity can know and love.

Telling stories provides the particular means by which theological
traits that many generations had affirmed now are portrayed as qualities of the personality of God, who is like a human being. It is one
thing to hypostatize a theological abstraction, e.g., "The quality of
mercy said before the Holy One, blessed be He." It is quite another
to construct a conversation between God and, e.g., David, with a
complete argument and a rich interchange, in which God's merciful character is spelled out as the trait of a specific personality. And
that is what we find in the Bavli, and, so far as my survey suggests,
not in any prior document. Specifically, it is in the Bavli that the
specification of an attribute of God, such as being long-suffering, is
restated in the following by means of narrative. God then emerges
not as an abstract entity with theological traits but as a fully-exposed
personality. God is portrayed as engaged in conversation with human
beings because God and humanity can understand one another within
the same rules of discourse. When we speak of the personality of
God, we shall see, traits of a corporeal, emotional, and social character
form the repertoire of appropriate characteristics. To begin with, we
consider the particular means by which, in the pages of the Talmud
of Babylonia or Bavli, in particular, these traits are set forth.

The following story shows us the movement from the abstract and
theological to the concrete and narrative mode of discourse about
God:

A. "And Moses made haste and bowed his head toward the earth and
worshipped: (Ex. 34:8):

B. What did Moses see?

C. Hanina b. Gamula said, "He saw [God's attribute of] being long-suffering [Ex. 34:7]."

D. Rabbis say, "He saw [the attribute of] truth [Ex. 34:7]." It has been taught on Tannaite authority in accord with him who has said, "He saw God's attribute of being long-suffering."

E. For it has been taught on Tannaite authority:

F. When Moses went up on high, he found the Holy One, blessed be He, sitting and writing, "Long-suffering."

G. He said before him, "Lord of the world, 'Long-suffering for the righteous?'"

H. He said to him, "Also for the wicked."

I. [Moses] said to him, "Let the wicked perish."

J. He said to him, "Now you will see what you want."

K. When the Israelites sinned, he said to him, "Did I not say to you, 'Long-suffering for the righteous?'"

L. [Moses] said to him, "Lord of the world, did I not say to you, 'Also for the wicked?'"

M. That is in line with what is written, "And now I beseech you, let the power of my Lord be great, according as you have spoken, saying" (Num. 14:17). [Freedman, *The Babylonian Talmud. Sanhedrin*, p. 764, n. 7: What called forth Moses' worship of God when Israel sinned through the Golden Calf was his vision of the Almighty as long-suffering.]

Bavli Sanhedrin 111a–b, VI

The statement at the outset is repeated in narrative form at F. Once we are told that God is long-suffering, then it is in particular, narrative form that that trait is given definition. God then emerges as a personality, specifically because Moses engages in argument with God. He reproaches God, questions God's actions and judgments, holds God to a standard of consistency—and receives appropriate responses. God in heaven does not argue with humanity on earth. God in Heaven issues decrees, forms the premise of the earthly rules, constitutes a presence, may even take the form of a "you" for hearing and answering prayers.

When God argues, discusses, defends, and explains actions, emerges as a personality etched in words, then God attains that personality that imparts to Him the status of a being consubstantial with humanity. It is in particular through narrative that that transformation of God from person to personality takes place. Since personality involves physical traits, attitudes of mind, emotion, and intellect consubstantial with those of human beings, and the doing of the deeds people do in the way in which they do them, we shall now see that all three modes of personality come to full expression in the Bavli. This we do in sequence, ending with a clear demonstration that God incarnate takes the particular form of a sage. And that will yield the problem of the difference between God and all (other) sages.

Scripture knows that God has a face, upon which human beings are not permitted to gaze. But was that face understood in a physical way, and did God enjoy other physical characteristics? An affirmative answer emerges in the following, which settles the question:

A. "And he said, 'You cannot see my face'" (Ex. 33:20).
B. It was taught on Tannaite authority in the name of R. Joshua b. Qorha, "This is what the Holy One, blessed be He, said to Moses:
C. "When I wanted [you to see My face], you did not want to; now that you want to see My face, I do not want you to."
D. This differs from what R. Samuel bar Nahmani said R. Jonathan said.
E. For R. Samuel bar Nahmani said R. Jonathan said, "As a reward for three things he received the merit of three things.
F. "As a reward for: 'And Moses hid his face,' (Ex. 3:6), he had the merit of having a glistening face.
G. "As a reward for: 'Because he was afraid to' (Ex. 3:6), he had the merit that 'They were afraid to come near him' (Ex. 34:30).
H. "As a reward for: 'To look upon God' (Ex. 3:6), he had the merit: 'The similitude of the Lord does he behold' (Num. 12:8)."
I. "And I shall remove my hand and you shall see my back" (Ex. 33:23).
J. Said R. Hana bar Bizna said R. Simeon the Pious, "This teaches that the Holy One, blessed be He, showed Moses [how to tie] the knot of the phylacteries."

Bavli Berakhot 7a, LVI

In the Bavli's stories God not only looks like a human being but also does the acts that human beings do. For example, God spends the day much as does a mortal ruler of Israel, at least as sages imagine such a figure. That is, he studies the Torah, makes practical decisions, and sustains the world (meaning, administers public funds for public needs)—just as (in sages' pictures of themselves) sages do. What gives us a deeply human God is that for the final part of the day, God plays with his pet, leviathan, who was like Hydra, the great sea serpent with multiple heads. Some correct that view and hold that God spends the rest of the day teaching youngsters.

The personality of God encompassed not only physical, but also emotional or attitudinal traits. In the final stage of the Judaism of the dual Torah God emerged as a fully-exposed personality. The character of divinity, therefore, encompassed God's virtue, the specific traits of character and personality that God exhibited above and here below. Above all, humility, the virtue sages most often asked of themselves, characterized the divinity. God wanted people to be humble, and God therefore showed humility.

A. Said R. Joshua b. Levi, "When Moses came down from before the Holy One, blessed be He, Satan came and asked [God], 'Lord of the world, Where is the Torah? [What have you done with it? Do you really intend to give it to mortals?]'

B. "He said to him, 'I have given it to the earth . . .' [Satan ultimately was told by God to look for the Torah by finding the son of Amram.]

C. "He went to Moses and asked him, 'Where is the Torah that the Holy One, blessed be He, gave you?'

D. "He said to him, 'Who am I that the Holy One, blessed be He, should give me the Torah?'

E. "Said the Holy One, blessed be He, to Moses, 'Moses, you are a liar!'

F. "He said to him, 'Lord of the world, you have a treasure in store which you have enjoyed everyday. Shall I keep it to myself?'

G. "He said to him, 'Moses, since you have acted with humility, it will bear your name: "Remember the Torah of Moses, my servant" (Mal. 3:22).'"

Bavli Shabbat 89a

God here is represented as favoring humility and rewarding the humble with honor. What is important is that God does not here cite Scripture or merely paraphrase it; the conversation is an exchange between two vivid personalities. True enough, Moses, not God, is the hero. But the personality of God emerges in vivid ways. The subsequent passage shows how traits imputed to God also define proper conduct for sages, not to mention other human beings.

God in Person: The Corporeality of God

Just as Israel glorifies God, so God responds and celebrates Israel. In the passages at hand the complete personality of God, in physical, emotional, and social traits, comes to expression. God wears phylacteries, an indication of a corporeal sort. God further forms the correct attitude toward Israel, which is one of love, an indication of an attitude on the part of divinity corresponding to right attitudes on the part of human beings. Finally, to close the circle, just as there is a "you" to whom humanity prays, so God too says prayers—to God, and the point of these prayers is that God should elicit from himself forgiveness for Israel:

A. Said R. Nahman bar Isaac to R. Hiyya bar Abin, "As to the phylacteries of the Lord of the world, what is written in them?"
B. He said to him, "'And who is like your people Israel, a singular nation on earth' (1 Chr. 17:21)."
C. "And does the Holy One, blessed be He, sing praises for Israel?"
D. "Yes, for it is written, 'You have avouched the Lord this day . . . and the Lord has avouched you this day' (Deut. 26:17, 18).
E. "Said the Holy One, blessed be He, to Israel, 'You have made Me a singular entity in the world, and I shall make you a singular entity in the world.'
F. "'You have made Me a singular entity in the world,' as it is said, 'Hear O Israel, the Lord, our God, the Lord is one' (Deut. 6:4).
G. "'And I shall make you a singular entity in the world,' as it is said, 'And who is like Your people, Israel, a singular nation in the earth' (1 Chr. 17:21)."
H. Said R. Aha, son of Raba to R. Ashi, "That takes care of one of the four subdivisions of the phylactery. What is written in the others?"
I. He said to him, "'For what great nation is there . . . And what great nation is there . . .' (Deut. 4:7, 8), 'Happy are you, O Israel . . .' (Deut. 33:29), 'Or has God tried . . . ,' (Deut. 4:34). And 'To make you high above all nations' (Deut. 26:19)."
J. "If so, there are too many boxes!
K. "But the verses, 'For what great nation is there' and 'And what great nation is there,' which are equivalent, are in one box, and 'Happy are you, O Israel' and 'Who is like Your people Israel' are in one box, and 'Or has God tried . . . ,' in one box, and 'To make you high' in one box.
L. "And all of them are written in the phylactery that is on the arm."
                                    Bavli Berakhot 6a–b XXXIX

A. It has been taught on Tannaite authority:
B. Said R. Ishmael b. Elisha [who is supposed to have been a priest in Temple times], "One time I went in to offer up incense on the innermost altar, and I saw the crown of the Lord, enthroned on the highest throne, and He said to me, 'Ishmael, My son, bless me.'

C. "I said to him, 'May it be Your will that Your mercy overcome Your anger, and that Your mercy prevail over Your attributes, so that You treat Your children in accord with the trait of mercy and in their regard go beyond the strict measure of the law.'

D. "And He nodded His head to me."

E. And from that story we learn that the blessing of a common person [Ishmael's blessing of God] should not be negligible in your view.

Bavli Berakhot 7a

The corporeal side to the personality of God is clear at the outset, God's wearing phylacteries. The consubstantial traits of attitude and feeling—just as humanity feels joy, so does God, just as humanity celebrates God, so does God celebrate Israel—are made explicit. The social transactions of personality are specified as well. Just as Israel declares God to be unique, so God declares Israel to be unique. And just as Israel prays to God, so God says prayers. What God asks of God is that God transcend God—which is what, in prayer, humanity asks for as well. In the end, therefore, to be "in our image, after our likeness," the power of the powerless, the riches of the disinherited, the valuation and valorization of the will of those who have no right to will is to be not the mirror image of God but very much to be like God. That is how, once more, the dimension of *zekhut* enters in. And with zekhut, we come to the category that defines the proper relationship of a human being to God: one in which what a person does not coerce God but invokes in God an attitude of concern and love for the person. We now turn to the single most characteristic and important theological idea in Rabbinic Judaism—and one that is most difficult to grasp and most profound in its theological implications.

The Humanity of God

As in the Written Torah, so in the Oral Torah, the covenant prevails, and God enters into transactions with human beings and accords with the rules that govern those relationships. So God exhibits precisely the social attributes that human beings do. A number of stories, rather protracted and detailed, tell the story of God as a social being, living among and doing business with mortals. These stories provide extended portraits of God's relationships, in particular arguments, with important figures, such as angelic figures, as well as

Moses, David, and Hosea. In them God negotiates, persuades, teaches, argues, exchanges reasons. The personality of God therefore comes to expression in a variety of portraits of how God will engage in arguments with men and angels, and so enters into the existence of ordinary people. These disputes, negotiations, transactions yield a portrait of God who is reasonable and capable of give and take, as in the following:

> Rabbah bar Mari said, "What is the meaning of this verse: 'But they were rebellious at the sea, even at the Red Sea; nonetheless He saved them for His name's sake' (Ps. 106:7)?
> "This teaches that the Israelites were rebellious at that time, saying, 'Just as we will go up on this side, so the Egyptians will go up on the other side.' Said the Holy One, blessed be He, to the angelic prince who reigns over the sea, 'Cast them [the Israelites] out on dry land.'
> "He said before Him, 'Lord of the world, is there any case of a slave [namely, myself] to whom his master [you] gives a gift [the Israelites], and then the master goes and takes [the gift] away again? [You gave me the Israelites, now you want to take them away and place them on dry land.]'
> He said to him, 'I'll give you one-and-a-half times their number.'
> "He said before him, 'Lord of the world, is there a possibility that a slave can claim anything against his master? [How do I know that you will really do it?]'
> "He said to him, 'The Kishon brook will be My pledge [that I shall carry out My word. Nine hundred chariots at the brook were sunk, (Judg. 3:23) while Pharaoh at the sea had only six hundred, thus a pledge one-and-a-half times greater than the sum at issue.]'
> "Forthwith [the angelic prince of the sea] spit them out onto dry land, for it is written, 'And the Israelites saw the Egyptians dead on the seashore' (Ex. 14:30)."
>
> Bavli Arakhin 15a–b

God is willing to give a pledge to guarantee his word. He furthermore sees the right claim of the counterpart actor in the story. Hence we see how God obeys precisely the same social laws of exchange and reason that govern other incarnate beings.

Still more interesting is the picture of God's argument with Abraham. God is represented as accepting accountability, by the standards of humanity, for what God does.

> Said R. Isaac, "When the Temple was destroyed, the Holy One, blessed be He, found Abraham standing in the Temple. He said to him, 'What is My beloved doing in My house?'

"He said to Him, 'I have come because of what is going on with my children.'

"He said to him, 'Your children sinned and have been sent into exile.''

"He said to Him, 'But wasn't it by mistake that they sinned?'

"He said to him, 'She has wrought lewdness' (Jer. 11:15).

"He said to Him, 'But wasn't it just a minority of them that did it?'

"He said to him, 'It was a majority' (Jer. 11:15).

"He said to Him, 'You should at least have taken account of the covenant of circumcision [which should have secured forgiveness despite their sin]!'

"He said to him, 'The holy flesh is passed from you' (Jer. 11:15).

"And if you had waited for them, they might have repented!'

"He said to him, 'When you do evil, then you are happy' (Jer. 11:15).

"He said to Him, 'He put his hands on his head, crying out and weeping, saying to them, 'God forbid! Perhaps they have no remedy at all!'

"A heavenly voice came forth and said, 'The Lord called you "a leafy olive tree, fair with excellent fruit"' (Jer. 11:16).

"'Just as in the case of an olive tree, its future comes only at the end [that is, it is only after a long while that it produces its best fruit], so in the case of Israel, their future comes at the end of their time.'"

Bavli Menahot 53b

God relates to Abraham as to an equal. That is shown by God's implicit agreement that he is answerable to Abraham for what has taken place with the destruction of the Temple. God does not impose silence on Abraham, saying that that is a decree not to be contested but only accepted. God as a social being accepts that he must provide sound reasons for his actions, as must any other reasonable person in a world governed by rules applicable to everyone. Abraham is a fine choice for the protagonist, since he engaged in the argument concerning Sodom. His complaint is expressed: God is now called to explain himself. At each point then Abraham offers arguments in behalf of sinning Israel, and God responds, item by item. The climax has God promising Israel a future worth having. God emerges as both just and merciful, reasonable but sympathetic. The transaction attests to God's conformity to rules of reasoned transactions in a coherent society.

The Divinity of God: God as Wholly Other

Though in the image of the sage, God towers over other sages, disposes of their lives and determines their destinies. Portraying God as sage allowed the storytellers to state in vivid way convictions about the disparity between sages' great intellectual achievements and their this-worldly standing and fate. But God remains within the model of other sages, takes up the rulings, follows the arguments, participates in the sessions that distinguish sages and mark them off from all other people:

> Said R. Judah said Rab, "When Moses went up to the height, he found the Holy One, blessed be He, sitting and tying crowns to the letters [of the Torah].
>
> "He said to Him, 'Lord of the universe, why is this necessary?'
>
> "He said to him, 'There is a certain man who is going to come into being at the end of some generations, by the name of Aqiba b. Joseph. He is going to find expositions to attach mounds and mounds of laws to each point [of a crown].'
>
> "He said to Him, 'Lord of the universe, show him to me.'
>
> "He said to him, 'Turn around.'
>
> "[Moses] went and took his seat at the end of eight rows, but he could not understand what the people were saying. He felt weak. When discourse came to a certain matter, one of [Aqiba's] disciples said to him, 'My Lord, how do you know this?'
>
> "He said to him, 'It is a law revealed by God to Moses at Mount Sinai.'
>
> "Moses' spirits were restored.
>
> "He turned back and returned to the Holy One, blessed be He. He said to Him, 'Lord of the universe, now if you have such a man available, how can you give the Torah through me?'
>
> "He said to him, 'Be silent. That is how I have decided matters.'
>
> "He said to Him, 'Lord of the universe, you have now shown me his mastery of the Torah. Now show me his reward.'
>
> "He said to him, 'Turn around.'
>
> "He turned around and saw people weighing out his flesh in the butcher-shop.
>
> "He said to Him, 'Lord of the universe, such is his mastery of Torah, and such is his reward?'
>
> "He said to him, 'Be silent. That is how I have decided matters.'"
>
> Bavli Menahot 29b

When we notice that we are like God, but we are not confused with God, this story comes to mind. This is the single most important narrative about the personality of God. Here is the point at which humanity cannot imitate God but must relate to God in an attitude of profound humility and obedience. For God in His role in the story finds definition as hero and principal actor. He is no longer the mere interlocutor, nor does he simply answer questions by citing Scripture.

Quite the contrary, God is always God. God makes all the decisions and guides the unfolding of the story. Moses then appears as the straight man. He asks the questions that permit God to make the stunning replies. Moses who is called "our rabbi" and forms the prototype and ideal of the sage does not understand. God then tells him to shut up and accept His decree. God does what He likes, with whom He likes. Perhaps the story-teller had in mind a polemic against rebellious brilliance, as against dumb subservience. But that does not seem to me the urgent message, which rather requires acceptance of God's decrees, whatever they are, when the undeserving receive glory, when the accomplished come to nothing. That God emerges as a fully-formed personality—the model for the sage—hardly requires restatement.

The Imitation of God

What, exactly, does it mean to imitate God as God is portrayed by the Torah? Efforts are made at summarizing the whole Torah in a few words. Here, in the famous saying that follows, we deal with a theological generalization in the setting of a fable, no evidence, no argument, no reasoning being included. All we have is simply how a great sage said things should be seen:

> There was another case of a gentile who came before Shammai. He said to him, "Convert me on the stipulation that you teach me the entire Torah while I am standing on one foot." He drove him off with the building cubit that he had in his hand.
> He came before Hillel: "Convert me."
> He said to him, "'What is hateful to you, to your fellow don't do.' That's the entirety of the Torah; everything else is elaboration. So go, study."
>
> Bavli Shabbat 31a

The framer of this narrative setting for the Golden Rule has given us an allegation, not an argument; we do not know why the ethical principle of reciprocity ("love your neighbor as yourself," Lev.

19:18) takes priority over any of a dozen candidates; we cannot even say how the Oral Torah, represented by Hillel's statement, relates to the written one, Lev. 19:18 not being cited at all!

What, exactly, are we expected to be and to do because we wish to be "like God"? The answer is given at Leviticus 19:1, "You shall be holy, for I the Lord your God am holy." Our sages of blessed memory spell out the meaning of holiness, and that means to be merciful and compassionate:

> "This is my God and I will adorn Him" (Ex. 15:2)—adorn yourself before him by truly elegant fulfillment of the religious duties, for example: A beautiful tabernacle, a beautiful palm branch, a beautiful ram's horn, beautiful show fringes, a beautiful scroll of the Torah, written in fine ink, with a fine reed, by a skilled penman, wrapped with beautiful silks.
>
> Abba Saul says, "'I will adorn Him'—be like Him: Just as He is gracious and compassionate, so you be gracious and compassionate."
>
> Bavli Shabbat 133b

Abba Saul's statement says in a few words the entire knowledge of God that in the end the Torah—meaning Judaism—provides. For all of the truly pious conduct in doing religious duties, the real imitation of God comes about in our capacity to love one another.

To summarize: What we know about God and ourselves we know because God's grace has permitted us to know—that alone. So the proposition is, the facts provided by the Torah themselves comprise an act of grace. This is demonstrated syllogistically, on the basis of three givens, which were listed in the opening sentences. These three fundamental truths govern throughout: humanity is made in the image of God; Israel is the children of God; Israel possesses the most precious of gifts. These are givens. Wherein lies the gift? The act of grace is that we are told that they are God's gifts to us. We are not only in God's image—something we cannot have known on our own—but God has told us so. Israel are not only God's children—it would have been arrogance to have supposed so on their own—but God has so stated in so many words. Israel possesses the greatest gift of all. They know it: God has said so. So the syllogism draws on three facts to make one point that is not stated but that lies at the goal of the argument.

> R. Aqiba says, "Precious is man, who was created in the image [of God].

"It was an act of still greater love that it was made known to him that he was created in the image [of God], as it is said, 'For in the image of God He made man' (Gen. 9:6).

"Precious are Israelites, who are called children to the Omnipresent.

"It was an act of still greater love that they were called children to the Omnipresent, as it is said, 'You are the children of the Lord your God' (Dt. 14:1).

"Precious are Israelites, to whom was given the precious thing.

"It was an act of still greater love that it was made known to them that to them was given that precious thing with which the world was made, as it is said, 'For I give you a good doctrine. Do not forsake my Torah' (Prov. 4:2)."

Mishnah Abot 3:13–14

These six statements form the paradigm of Judaic theology: not truth alone, but truth enhanced because of the Torah's verification and validation. That is what it means to say that Israel knows God through the Torah. God is known because God makes himself known. With that proposition, Islam and Christianity can well concur. But they will differ in a fundamental way. Where Judaism differs from Christianity is that Christianity uses "incarnation" to refer to one man, not to man. Where Judaism differs from Islam (except for Sufi interpretation) is on the possibility of meeting God even in the human imagination: in the human condition of man. To state matters in a perhaps overly simple way, Islam's God is fundamentally transcendent, Christianity's immanent, and Judaism's in-between.

D. One God, Unitary and Transcendent: Islam

There is a tradition reported, on the authority of the great early Muslim scholar and pietist al-Zuhrī, from Abū Hurayrah, which goes as follows in the version given by Ibn Ishāq (d. 151/768), the famous biographer of the Prophet Muhammad:

When the Apostle of God died, 'Umar b. al-Khattāb got up and said: "Some of the hypocrites will claim that the Apostle of God has died, but truly, the Apostle of God is not dead, by God, but has gone away to his Lord as Moses b. 'Imrān went and was hidden from his people for forty days; then he returned to them after it was said he had died. By God, the Apostle of God will return as Moses did; may he cut off the hands and feet of men who claim that the Apostle of God is dead!"

When the news reached Abū Bakr, he drew near until he reached
the door of the mosque while 'Umar was speaking to the people. He
paid no attention to anything until he went in to the Apostle of God
in 'Ā'ishah's chamber, where he was lying in a corner covered by a
cloak of Yemenī cloth. When he uncovered his face, he drew close
and kissed him, saying: "May you be ransomed with my own mother
and father! As for the death that God ordained for you, you have
tasted it; you will never die a second time!" Then he covered the face
of the Apostle of God again with the cloak. He then went out while
'Umar was still speaking to the people and said: "Quiet, 'Umar. But
'Umar refused and kept speaking; when Abū Bakr saw he would not
be quiet, he approached the people. When they heard his words, they
drew near to him, leaving 'Umar. Then he praised and magnified God
and said: "O people, whoever serves Muhammad, truly, Muhammad
is dead. Whoever serves God, truly God is alive and never dies." Then
he recited this verse [Sūrah 3:144]: "Muhammad is only an apostle;
apostles have passed away before him. Will it be that when he dies
or is killed, you will take to your heels? He who takes to his heels
does God no harm; God will reward the grateful."[13]

Whatever its historicity, probably no other anecdote about the
early Muslims makes so vivid the fundamental premise of Islamic
faith—that God and God alone is worthy of worship and service;
he alone is Omnipotent, the transcendent Center, Source, and Ultimate
Goal of everything in the world He has created.

Naming God

But, we may ask, just who is this singular deity? In many contemporary English-language publications, God as worshipped by Muslims
is typically referred to as *Allāh*, the English transliteration of the
Arabic word for "God." *Allāh* is in fact the primary designation of
the One God used throughout the Arabic text of the Qur'ān, the
revealed scripture of the Muslim community. However, this practice
of speaking in English of God in Islamic contexts as *"Allāh,"* but

---

[13] Muhammad b. Ishāq, Al-Sīrah al-nabawīyah (edd. al-, 4:305–6. Arabic translations throughout are by the present author, although I have consulted scholarly
translations—for Ibn Ishāq, A. Guillaume's; for the Qur'ān, those of Sale, Bell,
Arberry, Paret, Blachère, Pickthall, and Cragg. Subsequent qur'ānic references will
be cited often simply by "S.," followed by the *sūrah*/chapter and *āyah*/verse numbers: e.g., S. 56:6–11. I have used the verse numbering of the standard Cairo text
throughout.

"God" in Jewish and Christian contexts as "God," not *Yahweh* or *ho theos*, represents an unfortunate decision by contemporary Muslims and non-Muslims alike that implies that the One God revealed in the Qur'ān is somehow a different God from the One God revealed in Jewish or Christian scriptures. In fact, *Allāh* is quite simply an exact equivalent both in Muslim scripture and in Jewish and Christian Arabic usage for the English use of "God" as worshipped by Jews and Christians. Indeed, *Allāh* can *only* refer in Arabic to the One God, the Supreme Lord of the Universe, the God of Abraham, Isaac, and Jacob (and of Adam, Moses, Jesus, Muhammad and the rest of His messengers or prophets). Any lesser, and therefore false, god or deity is designated by a different, but cognate word, *al-ilāh*, "the god" (there being no lower and upper case distinction in Arabic, so that "God" might be distinguished in writing from "god"), never by *Allāh*. God's name is as unique as He is.

God is, however, known also by many epithets or attributes, both in the Qur'ān and widely among Muslims in every age and place. The most famous are in the combination *al-Rahmān al-Rahīm*, which consists of two different words from the same verbal root that translate as "the [All-] Merciful," the [All-] "Compassionate," or as "the Compassionate All-Merciful [One]," if we read *al-Rahīm* as a modifier to *al-Rahmān* rather than an appositive to it. *Al-Rahmān* seems to have had the status at one point in Muhammad's career of an alternate proper name alongside *Allāh*, the term that in the course of the two decades of Qur'ānic revelations gradually became *the* proper name of God—something Sūrah 17:110 suggests in its admonition, "Invoke God (*Allāh*), or invoke the All-Merciful (*al-Rahmān*)." However, *al-Rahmān* did remain a prime epithet of God, as we see vividly in the most important invocation in the Qur'ān and all subsequent Islamic usage, namely the phrase known as the *Basmalah*: "In the name of God, the compassionate All-Merciful [One]" (*Bismillāh al-Rahmān al-Rahīm*). This invocation precedes every sūrah of the 114 in the Qur'ān but one (S. 9, likely because it was originally joined to the preceding S. 8). It is also used constantly by Muslims as a prayer and blessing before eating, drinking, or undertaking virtually any action of any consequence. This usage seems to be consonant with God's admonitions in the Qur'ān to "mention the name of God" both "over that which He has given them [humankind] of the beasts of the flocks" (22:34) and "over the [camels] when they are

drawn up in lines" [to be sacrificed on the pilgrimage] (22:36). But
the tradition of the importance of the names by which God is known
and addressed goes even beyond pious and ritual mention of *Allāh*
and *al-Rahmān*, most prominently in the ancient Islamic tradition of
the "most beautiful names of God."

"To God belong the most beautiful names, so invoke Him by
them," runs Sūrah 7:180, and similarly, Sūrah 20:8 reads: "God!
There is no God but He, and to Him belong the most beautiful
names." Sūrah 17:110 (cited in part just above) urges Muhammad,
"Say: 'Invoke God (*Allāh*), or invoke the All-Merciful (*al-Rahmān*);
whichever you invoke, to Him belong the most beautiful names.'"
This qur'ānic tradition of God's most beautiful names has endured
and flourished over the centuries.[14] The reflection upon the meanings of the manifold epithets of God in the Qur'ān early became a
fixture of Islamic theological discourse, especially that regarding the
divine attributes and their relation to God's essence and corporeal-
ity, as in the issue of literal versus metaphorical understanding of
the Qur'ān's anthropomorphic language concerning God (for example, that He "sees," "hears," "sits" upon the Throne, etc.).

The paradigmatic qur'ānic example of the multiplicity of the names
of God is the final three verses of Sūrah 59, 22–24, which alone
provide fourteen divine names (in addition to that of *Allāh* at the
outset), most of which typically begin the traditional lists of God's
"most beautiful names":

> He is God (*Allāh*), than whom there is no god but He; Knower (*ʿĀlim*)
> of the hidden and the visible. He is the All-Merciful (*al-Rahmān*), the
> All-Compassionate (*al-Rahīm*).
>   He is God, other than whom there is no God but He; the King
> (*al-Malik*), the Holy One (*al-Quddūs*), the Peace [or: Perfect One] (*al-
> Sālim*), the All-Faithful (*al-Muʾmin*), the Protector (*Muhaymin*), the Majestic
> (*al-ʿAzīz*), the All-Compelling (*al-Jabbār*), the Sublime (*al-Mutakabbir*).
> Glory be to God above all that they associate with Him!
>   He is God, the Creator (*al-Khāliq*), the Maker (*al-Bārī*), the Fashioner
> (*al-Musawwir*). To Him belong the most beautiful names; whatever is
> in the heavens and the earth glorifies Him. He is the Majestic (*al-
> ʿAzīz*), the Wise (*al-Hakīm*).

---

[14] The most comprehensive study of the most beautiful names of God, and of
their usage in Muslim theological thinking, is that of D. Gimaret, *Les noms divins en
Islam* (Paris, 1988).

Collection and organization of the divine epithets into lists of "the ninety-nine most beautiful names of God" has been an ongoing expression of Muslim religious piety through the ages. This preoccupation with counting the most important names of God (there being even in the Qur'ān many more than only ninety-nine divine epithets, or attributes that suggest such epithets) has resulted in the literary genre of collections of "Most Beautiful Names," each giving such a list and commenting on the linguistic, theological, or spiritual (or a combination of all these) meanings of each of the names.[15] The tradition of making such lists of ninety-nine names goes back to a famous *hadīth* from one of the companions of the Prophet, Abū Hurayrah, one version of which reads: "God has ninety-nine names, one hundred less one; whoever reckons [or: knows by heart] all of them will enter the Garden [Paradise]" (al-Bukhārī, *Sahīh* 97:12). To explain the choice of ninety-nine (rather than one hundred, for example), another version of this tradition, which occurs in one of our earliest personal collections of *hadīth*, adds at the end: "Truly, God is odd [in number] and loves the odd[-numbered]."[16] While some of the specific names vary from list to list, the compilation of the divine names and the invocation of God by them has been a constant in Muslim meditation, prayer, and spirituality. The use of rosaries with ninety-nine beads (or thirty-three, or eleven) to count the ninety-nine names has also been a staple of everyday spirituality in Islamic cultures everywhere.

The importance of God's names has been further reinforced in Islamic life since the time of the Prophet through the naming of Muslims with *'abd* ("servant, worshipper"), followed by one of the names of God in possessive form: 'Abd Allāh, 'Abd al-Rahmān, 'Abd al-Malik, 'Abd al-Azīz, 'Abd al-Jabbār, and so on. In proper usage, nothing but a name of God can follow the word *'Abd* in the construction "Servant of . . . [a name of God]," since a person of true faith serves no one and nothing but God.

---

[15] See ibid., esp. pp. 16ff.

[16] *Sahīfat Hammam b. Munabbih 'an Abī Hurayrah*, ed. R. F. 'Abd al-Muttalib (Cairo, 1985), p. 25, no. 34. Cf. Bukhārī 80:69; Muslim, *Sahīh* 48:5; Abū Dāwūd, *Sunan* 8:1, *i.a.* Hammām b. Munabbih was a second-generation "Follower" of the Prophet who died in the year 132 of the Hijrah (749–750 c.e.); his collection is made up of nearly 140 traditions that he claims to have received from the Companion of the Prophet, Abū Hurayrah.

But who is that One God? His names tell us of the wide range of His sublime attributes, and the overwhelming message of these names (and of all Muslim discussion of God) is that He is above all God the Transcendent: the Sovereign Lord, the Abiding, Eternal, Infinite One, beyond the capacity of human categories to imagine or describe. The dominant note in Muslim religious thought, from the Qurʾān forward, has been the affirmation of divine transcendence. From it all other aspects of the Muslim understanding of God proceed.

God the Transcendent Lord

In almost every Muslim statement about God, His transcendence is either alluded to or assumed, since speaking directly about transcendence is inherently difficult. It strains the limits of human imagination to do justice to the overarching fact of God's categorical and essential Otherness to anything in the world of experience. God so transcends all categories of human existence and all capacities of human language that the use of multiple names and expressions of praise or submission is finally the only available, albeit limited and approximate, means that a contingent, limited human being has of approaching the Unconditioned and Infinite, the Lord of the universe.

One of the most obvious, everyday examples of verbal testimony to the deeply ingrained Muslim sense of God's transcendence of everything that is other than He is the ubiquitous affirmation of God's majesty by Muslims everywhere and in all ages, the *Allāhu akbar*. These words, "God is greatest [literally, "greater" (than anything conceivable)]!," punctuate not only every call to ritual worship and every performance of that worship, but also many everyday moments when a Muslim wishes to express gratitude, wonder, or pleasure, or affirm his or her faith. This simple, powerful declaration of the most important fact about reality there is to know is called the *Takbīr*, or "magnification" of God. Used as ejaculation of praise, meditation formula, talisman, war cry, and much else, the *Takbīr* is the paramount expression among Muslims of God's absolute and utter transcendence, the ringing affirmation that He is ever greater even than anything one can imagine, ever transcendent of whatever else there is in creation, and that therefore He alone can be spoken of as the Greatest of all that is.

Divine transcendence assumes divine infinitude and eternality, for it involves above all God's being unbounded in space and time, transcendent of both. Thus the eternal and infinite qualities of the divine are dominant leitmotifs of Muslim piety. Among Muslims, virtually no qur'ānic Sūrah, no book, no sermon, no prayer, no everyday formality of speech, is without some allusion to these transcendent attributes and their contrast to human finitude. Probably the most succinct and eloquent qur'ānic passage conveying the sense of divine eternality is Sūrah 55:26–27: "All who are upon it [this earth] perish. There endures only the face of your Lord, Possessor of majesty and honor." God perdures, and He does so infinitely; everything else except Him is passing, transient, ephemeral.

Of the myriad statements of divine transcendence and infinitude, the eloquent opening lines of the invocation to one of many works by the great Muslim scholar and mystic, Muhammad Abū Hāmid al-Ghazzalī (d. 1111), are typical:

> Praise be to God, the Living, the Subsisting, the essence of Whose subsisting cannot be mastered by the description of a describer; the Glorious, the quality of whose glory cannot be encompassed by the knowledge of a knower. . . ."[17]

The strong sense of God as stretching infinitely beyond whatever may be conceived brings together the divine attribute of infinitude with the overarching idea of divine transcendence of all that is not infinite and eternal.

This overwhelming awareness of divine transcendence and incomparability is evident at every turn in Muslim rhetoric and thought about God's nature. Any naming or discussion of God is finally an attempt to parse His transcendence into terms that contingent human beings can grasp. In what follows, we shall try to enumerate and elucidate three general emphases of the Muslim sources in their treatment of the transcendent Lord of creation. These three themes, while

---

[17] *Fadā'ih al-Bāṭinīyah*, ed. ʿAbd ar-Rahman Badawī (Cairo, 1964), p. 1. Eng. trans., Richard J. McCarthy, *Freedom and Fulfillment: Annotated Translation of al-Ghazālī's ʿAl-Munqidh min ad-Dalāl and Other Relevant Works of Al-Ghazālī* (Boston: Twayne/ G. K. Hall, 1980): 175. Even though Ghazzalī lived and died perhaps two centuries after the time in which the Islamic community's basic worldview was hammered out, his work was such a dominating force in the last formative stage of classical Muslim piety that we may perhaps be excused for turning to this example from his work.

overlapping at various points, provide a more concrete, vivid picture of God as Muslims know Him. They are: first, *God's omnipotence, omniscience, and sovereignty*; second, *God's oneness, uniqueness, and perfection*; and finally, *God as Creator-Sustainer and His relationship to humankind*.

God's Omnipotence, Omniscience, and Sovereignty

The image of God as the sovereign Lord of the entire cosmos is evident throughout the Qur'ān and all subsequent Muslim literature, but it is above all to the qur'ānic testimony that Muslims have always turned to find expression of the humanly unencompassable grandeur, power, and knowledge of God. Of the many qur'ānic passages that point to God's omnipotence, omniscience, and sovereignty, Sūrah 57:1–6 is among the most eloquent:

> In the name of God the All-Merciful All-Compassionate. Whatever is in the Heavens and the earth magnifies God, for He is the Almighty, the All-Wise. His is the sovereignty over the Heavens and the earth; He gives life and He brings death; and He has power over everything. He is the First and the Last, the Outward and the Inward; and He has knowledge of everything. He it is Who created the Heavens and the earth in six days, then sat astride the throne. He knows what enters the earth and what issues from it, what descends from the sky and what ascends to it. He is with you wherever you are. And God sees fully whatever you do. His is the sovereignty over the Heavens and the earth, and to God all affairs return. He makes the night pass into day, and the day pass into night; He knows the depths within the hearts.

This passage points to the most tangible arena in which God's power, knowledge, and lordship are displayed, namely that of the natural world He has created:

> To God belongs sovereignty over the heavens and the earth, and God is powerful over everything. Truly, in the creation of the Heavens and the earth, and in the variation of night and day are signs for those possessed of understanding—those who remember God when standing, sitting, and lying on their sides, and who reflect on the creation of the Heavens and the earth, saying: "Our Lord, not in vain did You create this; praise be to You; preserve us from the doom of the fire." (S. 3:189–191)

Yet the most powerful and beloved expression of God's all-comprehending, all-encompassing majesty and might is the following passage, the famous "Throne Verse" of Sūrah 2:255, which is purely a psalm of direct praise and glorification of God's omnipotent, omniscient sovereignty:

> God! There is no god but He, the Living, the eternally Subsisting! Neither slumber nor sleep seizes Him. To Him belong whatever is in the Heavens and whatever is on earth. Who is there who can intercede with Him, save by His leave? He knows what is before them and what is after them, and they comprehend not one whit of His Knowledge, save what He wills. His throne stretches across the heavens and the earth, and sustaining both wearies Him not at all. He is the Exalted, the Sublime.

God as omniscient and omnipotent sovereign of the universe has final control over what He has created. To Him belongs the "determining," or "measuring out" (*qadar*), of all things, a concept which has raised throughout Islamic history the issue of God's predestination of human and earthly affairs. Many passages in the Qur'ān stress divine omnipotence and omniscience so strongly that human choice and independent action seem to be excluded: "He whom God guides, truly he is rightly guided, while those whom God leads astray, such are they who perish" (S. 7:178). Thus God guides and leads astray whom He will according to many qur'ānic passages (e.g., 2:6–7; 6:125; 9:51; 10:98–103; 11:118–19; 13:27; 16:37, 40; 32:12–14; 76:30; 81:27–29).

In consonance with such scriptural supports as these, the community's consensus over the centuries has always inclined towards affirming divine *qadar* at the expense of absolute human free will and any concept of natural-law justice. Rationally and religiously, this has stemmed largely from a fear of compromising God's omnipotence and transcendence. If foreknowledge and predetermining control of everything were not His, He would not control His own creation. Thus, of the acts and fate of every human being, one tradition attributed to the Prophet says that they are written "in the mother's womb"; another that "truly, the pen has dried regarding that which you will encounter" (al-Bukhārī 82:1:2,3); still another that "Truly, the hearts of the sons of Adam are as a heart [held] between two of the fingers of the Most Merciful [*al-Rahmān*]. He changes them as He will. Then the Apostle of God said, 'O God, the Turner of hearts, turn our hearts to obedience to You.'" (Muslim 46:3).

Where God is held to be as radically transcendent as He typically is in the Muslim tradition, it is perceived as dangerous to admit of any compromise in His absolute command of creation. Some of the most persistent and bitter theological disputes in Islamic history were waged over the issue of divine predestination and human free will. Indeed some of the earliest traditions from the Prophet that we can trace fairly clearly to at least the late first Islamic century (roughly the first quarter of the eighth century C.E.) are those having to do with differences over divine *qadar*.[18]

Still, the ultimately predestinarian bent in Muslim theological thought has not seriously impinged on individual Muslims' strong sense of personal responsibility and accountability for their actions. This latter awareness is evident in a tradition said to have been transmitted by 'Alī, the cousin and son-in-law of Muhammad:

> One day the Apostle of God was sitting with a stick in his hand, scratching on the ground. He raised his head and said: "There is not one of you whose place in the Garden [or] the fire is not known." [Those present] said: "O Apostle of God, should we then not do anything? Should we not then just rely [on what is foreordained]?" He said, "No, act! For everyone finds easy that for which he was created." Then he recited (S. 92:5–10): "As for him who gives, and is pious, and trusts in the good [or the best (of rewards)], surely We shall ease his way to [true] ease. But as for him who is miserly, and [proudly] thinks himself rich [self-sufficient], and calls the good [or the best (of rewards)] a lie—surely We shall ease his way to hardship." (*Muslim* 46:7)

As the verses cited in this hadīth show, the Qur'ān itself witnesses to God's expectation of human choice and action and the concomitant inevitability of every human being being held finally responsible for his or her deeds, especially on the Day of Judgment. Another vivid example of this is the text of Sūrah 36:54: "On that Day, no soul will be wronged at all, nor will you be repaid for aught except what you have done" (cf. 3:161; 4:110–113; 6:59; 7:28; 11:101; 18:29–30; 53:33–41; 99:6–8). Sūrah 99:7–8 echoes this in speaking of the Last Day: "Whoever has done an atom's weight of good will

---

[18] For a treatment of the traditions related to divine *qadar*, see Josef van Ess, *Zwischen Hadīt und Theologie. Studien zum Entstehen prädestinatianischer Überlieferung* (Berlin & New York: de Gruyter, 1975).

see it, and whoever has done an atom's weight of evil will see it."
This emphasis on the necessity of taking action oneself for good or
evil is also evident in the oft-quoted words of Sūrah 8:53, "That is
because God is not one to change the blessing He has bestowed on
a people until they change what is in themselves . . ." (cf. 13:11).
Finally, there is the enigmatic statement in Sūrah 4:79, which points
towards God's creation of the human being for good, but the latter's perverse penchant for evil: "Whatever befalls you in the way
of good, that is from God; and whatever of evil, that is from yourself. . . ."

The theologians, or *mutakallimūn*, found early on in Islamic history
a rationalizing compromise to underscore this responsibility and
accountability while retaining divine omnipotence. This was the doctrine of "acquisition," whereby God is affirmed as the creator of
human acts, but each individual "acquires" his or her actions through
choice.[19] This scholastic position is not without justification in the
hadīth in which Muhammad is quoted as follows:

> "There is no one of you whose place in [either] the fire or Paradise
> has not been written [for him]." Then one of the men of the people
> said, "Can we not [simply] rely on this, O Apostle of God?" [The
> Prophet] said: "No, rather act, for everyone is prepared [for that for
> which he has been created]." (al-Bukhārī 82:3:5)

For the life of faith, both the problem and such a solution as that
of acquiring acts appropriate to one's fate are in large part academic. From a divine or cosmic perspective, the One God of course
controls all things absolutely; but from a human or temporal perspective, the individual must necessarily choose and act in accordance with or against God's commands, earning divine reward or
punishment by his or her own choices and actions.

The popular caricature of Islam as passive fatalism has little to
do with the composure in the face of God's omnipotent will that a

---

[19] This interpretation is primarily associated with the Ash'arite school and its
eponymous "founder," Abū 'l-Ōasan al-Ash'arī (d. 935/). Cf. the sixth article of a
medieval creedal statement (probably Ash'arite, ca. 10th/4th century), the *Fiqh Akbar
II*: "All the acts of man—his moving as well as his resting—are truly his own acquisition (*kasb*), but God creates them and they are caused by His will, His knowledge, His decision, and His decree." (from trans. in A. J. Wensinck, *The Muslim
Creed*. 1932 [Repr. ed. London: Frank Cass, 1965], 19).

faithful Muslim who has valiantly "striven in God's way" finally must have. All outsider stereotypes to the contrary, the Muslim sense that all is ultimately in God's hands has not been a wholesale excuse to shrug off human responsibility. As we shall see in chapter four below, the importance of shaping one's life and affairs according to the divine will (*shar*) as codified in the religious law, or *sharī'ah*, has been central among Muslims in all times and places: humankind has clearly been charged with obedient worship and service (*'ibādah*; see chapter four) of God and sustained struggle and effort (*jihād*; see chapter five) to do good and spurn evil. Indeed, the duty of "exhortation to good and warning against evil" among one's fellows is a long-standing tradition from the early days of Islam that well symbolizes a Muslim's strong sense of urgency about two things: personal righteousness, doing what is right and abstaining from what is wrong; and personal social responsibility, joining in building a society where good prevails over evil, God's way over that of Satan.

Muslim understanding of God's omnipotence thus entails an acute awareness of human accountability to God as Judge of creation (e.g., "Master of the Day of Reckoning," S. 1:4), for it is above all the human indivdual who, alone among created beings, has the ability to choose obedience or disobedience. God encompasses the *telos*, the endpoint of temporality, toward which all creation is moving. His omnipotence will be manifest at the end of history by his role in the final judgment of His creation, when He will "repay each soul what it has earned, for truly, God is swift in reckoning" (S. 14:51). Thus insistence upon divine *qadar* is not seen as in any way compromising divine justice (*'adl*) in judgment any more than as negating divine mercy (*rahmah*) in forgiving sins out of His infinite compassion. Divine predestination and human accountability are finally a mystery to finite beings—one resolvable only from the perspective of transcendent reality. Muslims accept the reality of both through faith; indeed, they *know* their reality because of their overwhelming conviction (as true *muslims*, true "submitters") of God's omnipotence.

God's Oneness, Uniqueness, and Perfection

The God to whom the manifold "most beautiful" names belong has, however, in Muslim view, no multiplicity in Him. In its uncompromising monotheism, Islam is the most radical of the three Semitic traditions of worship of one God. If there is any "given," any absolute presupposition of a Muslim's faith in the transcendent, omnipotent Lord of creation, it is the absolute oneness and uniqueness of the Almighty. So fundamental is this premise to Muslim faith that it is fair to say that whatever their other doctrinal differences, the same basic understanding of God as unitary, unique, and alone worthy of worship has undergirded and sustained all the diverse Islamic sectarian and interpretive traditions through the centuries. This understanding has rarely, if ever, been subject to radical questioning by Muslims of any time, place, culture, or tendency. The unvarying constants of Muslim faith in all its forms are God's lordship over, as well as transcendence of, all creation, and His uniqueness among and incomparability with everything else in the universe.

The *shahādah* is the statement of "witness" or "testimony" to the two essential facts of Muslim faith established in the Qur'ān: first, "there is no god but God," and second, "Muhammad is the Messenger of God."[20] The first of these affirmations, the confession of faith in none but God, signals one's *islām*, or submission to God. It recurs in every call to each of the five prescribed daily performances of worship (*salāt*). It is traditionally the first word whispered into the ear of a Muslim newborn—a practice paralleled in God's first words to Moses in the qur'ānic version of the latter's prophetic career in Egypt at Sūrah 20:14: "I am God! There is no god except Me; so serve Me and perform the rite of worship (*salāt*) in remembrance of Me." It underscores the absolute and unique character of God as the Only God, He who alone is worthy of worship and praise and obedience. It also recalls the absurdity of any other claimant to superhuman status: only God is God—the One God of Abraham, Isaac, Jacob, Moses, and Jesus and all the other "prophets": "there is none other like unto Him" (S. 112:4).

---

[20] The full *Shahādah* reads: "I bear witness that there is no god but God; I bear witness that Muhammad is the Apostle of God" (*Ashhadu anna lā illāha illa 'llāh; ashhadu anna Muhammadan rasūlu 'llāh*). The two parts of the *Shahādah* do not occur together as a single confession of faith in the Qur'ān, but both parts do recur in varying wording in the sacred text: "no God": 3:62; 37:35; 38:65; 47:19; cf. 2:163; 2:255; 3:2, 6, 18; 4:87; 5:73; 6:102, 106; 7:158; 9:31, 129; 10:90; 11:14; 13:30; 16:2; 18:14; 20:8, 14, 98; 21:25, 87; 23:116; 27:26; 28:70, 88; 35:3; 39:6; 40:3, 62, 65; 44:8; 64:13; 73:9; "Muhammad is the Apostle of God": 48:29; cf. 33:40.

This insistence on God's uniqueness and incomparability is as strong as it is in the Qur'ān and all later Muslim tradition in good part because of the largely polytheistic environment in which the Qur'ān was revealed. The conflict of the qur'ānic message with this environment is evident at numerous points in the Qur'ān:

> So turn aside from the filth of idols and turn aside from lying speech, turning to God [alone], not ascribing partners to Him; for whoever ascribes partners to God, it is as if he had fallen from the sky and the birds had seized him or the wind had blown him to a distant place." (S. 22:30–31)

This strain in the Muslim preaching is also pronounced because of the Christian Trinitarian understanding of God, which to the qur'ānic and subsequent Muslim way of thinking is tantamount to, or at least perilously close to, making the One God less than One—a kind of polytheistic understanding of the Godhead that compromises God's unity and oneness. Indeed, much of the Qur'ān's preaching against *shirk*—"association" of partners with God—is directed not only against the pagan polytheists, but against Christian Trinitarian "polytheism," especially the imputation to God of the fatherhood of Jesus ("He is not begotten, nor does he beget," S. 112:3). Jesus, for Muslims is, exactly like Moses or Muhammad, "only a man, one to whom revelation has come" (S. 18:110).[21]

For Muslims, God is not simply a being above other beings, but rather a Being above all multiplicity (He is *ahad*, "one") and without need of anything other than himself. Indeed, He is the absolute standard, the supreme and perfect instance of one who is *ghanī*, "rich," lit.: "able to do without" any other being or thing. He alone is perfect in and of himself, the only completely perfect and independent Being: the One God, Creator, Sustainer of all existence, infinite, omnipotent, unconditioned, and incomparable in His *ipseity*. He is *samad*, utterly compact, unitary, and everlasting—in other words, absolute in and of himself: without partner or need of anyone or

---

[21] For some flavor of early Muslim lore about Jesus, see the recent collection and translation of sayings ascribed to, and stories about, Jesus in early and classical Islamic sources, see Tarif Khalidi, ed. and trans., *The Muslim Jesus: Sayings and Stories in Islamic Literature* (Cambridge, Mass. and London: Harvard University Press, 2001).

anything else.[22] As creator of all that is, His perfection and uniqueness is beyond any reckoning from within creation. This unicity and
perfection are the Qur'ān's (and Islam's) great, transforming insight,
from which proceeds everything else in the Muslim's faith. Thus the
greatest sin for a Muslim is that of succumbing to any kind of polytheism, or association (*shirk*) of partners with the unique, transcendent Lord of the heavens and earth.

> They, the spirits (*jinn*), have ascribed partners to Him even tthough
> He created them; and they in ignorance have falsely attributed to him
> sons and daughters. May He be glorified and exalted above that which
> they falsely claim. The Creator of the Heavens and the earth! How
> could he have a child when He has no consort? when He created
> everything and is aware of all things? (S. 6:100–101)

Because God alone is God, One without division, unparalleled in
His divine perfection, He has no partners, no equals, no one or
thing even remotely susceptible of comparison with Him. He is forever to be isolated from contamination by all that is less than His
perfection—a conviction that is articulated simply and powerfully not
only, as we have seen, in the first half of the Muslim witness of
faith, the *shahādah* but especially in the words of Sūrah 112 that most
Muslims repeat when they perform the five-times-daily act of worship: "Say, He is God, One! God the Absolute (*samad*)! He does not
beget, nor was He begotten. There is nothing like unto Him!"[23] In
repeating these words, the person of faith affirms God's absolute
oneness, His perfect unity and unicity; furthermore, in doing so he
or she proclaims himself or herself to be a true monotheist, a *muwahhid*, or "unitarian," "one who proclaims [and lives under] the oneness of God." This is the central Muslim virtue of *tawhīd*, the
"declaration of [and faith in] divine oneness." (Both *muwahhid*, *tawhīd*,
and *ahad*, "one," derive from the root *w-h-d*, which denotes oneness.)
Tawhīd symbolizes and summarizes both the commitment to worship and serve God alone and also the taking to heart of His injunction, "Take not two gods! Truly, He is one god only" (S. 16:51).

---

[22] On the term *samad*, see Rudi Paret, "Der Ausdruck *samad* in Sure 112,2," *Der
Islam* 56 (1979): 294–295.

[23] Note that the mention here of "begetting" or "giving birth" refers specifically
to the Christian concepts of God's "fatherhood" and Jesus' "sonship," which for
Muslims are tantamount to *shirk* because of the implied multiplicity of the divine.

Tawḥīd and the consequent life it entails mean absolute rejection of association, or *shirk*, of any kind and dedication to worship and service (*'ibādah*) of God alone, the Unique, the perfect One.

God the Creator and His Relationship to Humankind

In the Muslim as in any fully monotheistic worldview, God is the ground of Being itself, for there is nothing at all that has independent existence apart from His creative and sustaining power. This is not, however, a pantheistic concept but rather the recognition that, apart from God, the one Source and Sustainer of whatever exists, all in the universe is created, transient, and utterly dependent upon its Creator. Neither the physical existence of the universe nor temporal, historical process itself is even thinkable independent of the transcendent Being from Whom it came, upon Whom it depends, and to Whom it will return. God alone is self-sufficient; God alone determines the course of time and history and their ultimate end; God alone controls the visible and invisible universe; and God alone looks after the human creatures at the center of both the created world and the cosmic historical process in which He has placed them.

Indeed, divine agency in the sustaining of all that exists is so fundamental to the qur'ānic and subsequent Muslim worldview that the idea of God as Creator goes well beyond that in the biblical context. It has been a central part of Muslim faith that God not only created the world at one point in the distant past, but that God continually creates, or re-creates, everything at every moment: "Do they not see how God brings creation into being and then repeats it? For God that is truly an easy thing!" (S. 29:19). The very structure of reality is sustained by God's ongoing creative activity. This basic idea was elaborated in Islamic theological thought to the point that atomism became a major part of Islamic thinking about the nature of God and the cosmos: ultimately, there is no natural law of cause and effect, for example, except insofar as God continues to will cause to follow effect in each successive moment, each nanosecond, of existence. He is active at every instant in His ongoing willing and sustenance of the natural order of the cosmos. Here again we see the degree to which Muslims have affirmed the absolute omnipotence and sovereignty of God as the Creator of all that exists in every moment, not just One who has fashioned a cosmic machine and set it in motion to run on its own. God as Creator is therefore also God as absolute Sustainer.

Yet alongside this powerful notion of God's omnipotent and transcendent power and ceaseless involvement in the ongoing existence of the entire cosmos, He is also perceived by the Muslim faithful to be directly concerned with and deeply involved in the affairs of humankind in this world. He has called for and expects His creation to worship and serve Him, and of all creatures, humankind alone has been called to do so by choice rather than by nature. Where the birds in the sky or the trees on the ground praise and serve God in their very existence, humankind has the capacity to be disobedient, to turn from God to false gods, to shun the natural path of submission to Him. As we have seen, to be Muslim is to be a true "submitter" (which is what the active participle *muslim* means) to the One God of All, for He alone is worthy of submission: "To Him belongs all that is in the heavens and in the earth; He is the Exalted, the Great" (S. 42:4). We have also seen that God's sovereignty over all that exists is axiomatic to the very concept of the One God. Sovereignty, *mulk*, belongs to Him alone.

This sovereign, transcendent God is also the bountiful Lord whose creation attests in all its parts to Him as Lord and to the bounties which make life possible:

> Any mercy (*rahmah*) that God apportions people, no one can hold back. And that which He holds back, no one can send thereafter. And He is the Sublime, the Wise. O people! Remember God's bountiful blessing [or "grace": *ni'mah*] to you. Is there any Creator other than God who provides for you from the Heavens and the earth? There is no god but He! How then will you be deceived by lies? (S. 35:2–3)

The created cosmos reminds human beings to whom they should be thankful and whom they should worship and serve, for God is the compassionate all-merciful Lord whose blessings are freely given:

> He it is Who causes water to descend from the sky, from which you have drink, and from which come shrubs with which you feed your livestock. With it He makes flourish the crops, and the olive tree, date-palm, grapevine, and all kinds of fruit. Truly, in this is a sign for a people who reflect. And he has caused the night and day and the sun and moon to serve you, and the stars are subject to serve at his command. Truly, in this are signs for a people of intelligence. And whatever he has created for you on earth of varied kinds, truly in that is a sign

for a people who give heed [lit., "remember"]. It is He Who has made the sea of service, so that you eat from it fresh meat and extract from it ornaments to wear. And you see the ships ploughing through it, so that you may seek something of His bounty, [and] perhaps you will be grateful. (S. 16:10–14)

This is further a sovereign Lord who has never left human beings without guidance to the "straight path" of pure submission, and whose forgiveness is always available for those who stray from the path. His guidance has come from a long line of chosen messengers or prophets, beginning with Adam and extending down to His final messenger and prophet, Muhammad ibn 'Abdullāh of the Arab tribe of Quraysh, who died in the year 732 c.e. God sent revelations to many of these chosen guides, whether the Torah to Moses, the Psalms to David, the Gospel to Jesus, or the Qur'ān ("Reciting") to Muhammad. The last is the final "book" or "scripture" (kitāb), the culminating revelation from the Lord, His explicit and perfect word addressed to humankind. It is the Muslim community that has been charged with its scrupulous preservation and dissemination as well as adherence to its ideals and norms. Where God himself is utterly transcendent, the immanence of His revealed word provides the one point of direct, palpable contact between the Absolute and the contingent, the Eternal and the mortal, God and humankind.

Beyond human life and beyond the created world of space and time, the truth holds that "unto your Lord is the [ultimate] return" (S. 96:8, and a frequent theme in the Qur'ān). Just as God is Creator and Sustainer of the cosmos, so too is He the One who will bring it to an end and receive his creatures once more, rewarding them in His Eternal realm according to what they have done with their time in His created world. God is Master of the Day of Judgment at the end of time, when all human beings shall be resurrected to have their earthly records reviewed and judged by God (see chapter six).

Thus we find that this Wholly Other, this utterly transcendent and eternal Lord, is neither isolated from nor uninvolved with His temporal and transient creation, and its culminating members, human beings. "We are never neglectful of creation" is how S. 23:17 puts it. While it is God the infinite and transcendent Lord to whom Muslims and their most sacred texts, both the Qur'ān and later tradition, testify prominently and persistently, there is also constant testimony to the deep and sustained involvement of the Almighty in this world and especially in the guidance and potential salvation of human beings. This is the aspect of God most fully expressed in the notion of God as the All-Merciful, All-Compassionate who is "nearer than one's own neck vein" (S. 50:16) and whose attribute of mercy triumphs over His anger at human beings' evil acts, as one famous tradition reports:

> The Apostle of God said: "When God finished the creation, He wrote in His book, which is above the Throne: "My mercy overcomes My wrath." (al-Bukhārī 59:1:4)[24]

Thus God emerges from the traditional sources as One who cares about His creatures, One whose key divine attributes are not only cosmic qualities of infinite power and majesty, nor only ones of justice and judgment, but rather qualities of infinite bountifulness, mercy, and love. The former two of these three are everywhere of central importance to Muslim piety and to Muslims' understanding of their Lord's ways with His creatures; the third is not stressed so strongly throughout Muslim tradition as in the Christian tradition. However, the classical Sufi, or "mystical" tradition of heightened personal piety and intensified experience of the divine did build prominently on the qur'ānic base to produce a long tradition of love-piety that has been both elitist and widely popular in its appeal to Muslims over the centuries. In this tradition, the emphasis has been upon the nearness to and intimacy with God, upon experience of and discourse with Him. Here God as Love brings God as omnipotent Other into close proximity to His human creatures. In the Qur'ān itself we find clear statements of God's love and His expectation that his creatures will return that love. In Sūrah 3:31 He addresses His messenger, Muhammad, as follows: "Say, 'If you love God, follow me; God loves you and forgives you your sins. God is forgiving, merciful.'" And in His admonition to the Muslims about turning back from Islam, He says:

> O you who are faithful! Whoever of you goes back on his faith (dīn), [know that] God will bring [instead] a people whom He loves and who love Him, humble towards the faithful, firm towards those who

---

[24] Cf. 97:22:5; 97:28:1; and *Sahīfat Hammām*, p. 22; Muslim 49:14, 15; inter alii.

reject [God], and striving on God's path without fear of blamer's
blame. (S. 5:54)

Nowhere is this more clearly stated than in 3:76: "God loves those
who fear Him." Thus the theme of the love of God and God's love
for His creatures is one deeply rooted in the Qur'ān and especially
tied to the major theme of divine mercy.

This love of God is not, however, to be seen as in any way incon-
sonant with with His justice, which constitutes another major theme
of classical Muslim thought. The Lord of the universe is above all
a just God, and in the end He will requite human actions as they
deserve—tempered always by His endless mercy, but always based
on His standards of justice and right: "And We set a just balance
for the Day of Resurrection, so that no soul is wronged in any way"
(S. 2:165). As early at the second Islamic century, some Muslim
thinkers, the Muʿtazilah, tried to assert that God is *necessarily* just—
an effort to preserve the essential goodness of God. The opponents
of these thinkers won the day, however, for they saw in this formulation a compromising of God's omnipotence, a limitation of God
in that, if justice is elevated over God, God is no longer supreme,
no longer the omnipotent, transcendent Lord of creation. From the
cosmic standpoint, justice must be what God has determined it to
be, nothing more, nothing less. But from the human and ethical
side, God is perfectly just, with a justice that can be relied upon.

The ultimate exercise of His justice will come when God ushers
in the end of this world and the subsequent Day of Judgment. As
we shall note in Chapter 6, the Day of Judgment will see the just
requital of human works, good and bad. With the end of the world
as we know it, all souls will rest in God's eternity and there taste
the fruits of their worldly lives—"eternity, without death, eternity,
without death," as one tradition about the end of both good- and
evil-doers puts it.[25] Thus all will again be gathered again to Him
Who created them in the first place: God the One, the Transcendent,
the Creator, the Sustainer, the Judge, Him to whom is the ultimate
return.

---

[25] al-Bukhārī 81:53:1; *Muslim* 51:40; inter alii.

CHAPTER THREE

GOD'S PEOPLE

A. THE ISSUE

Viewed as a whole, Islam and Christianity exemplify universal religions, deeply particular to various nations and peoples, yet possessed of a transforming vision of humanity under God's rule, in God's image. Both Christianity and Islam concur that Judaism is an ethnic religion, and to be a Jew is to belong to an ethnic group. While in modern times some Jews have concurred, in classic Judaism Israel stands for God's people, formed at Sinai to receive the Torah in behalf of all of humanity. But that theological conviction does not entirely solve the problem of the interplay of the national or the ethnic with the religious and the theological. To be God's people and to address all of humanity with a message possessed, uniquely, by God's people are convictions that define the Judaic tradition as much as (or as little as) the Christian and Islamic.

Then how are we to distinguish a religious tradition from an ethnic affiliation? An ethnic religion shapes a community that is closed to others and sets forth a vision only of itself for itself. No other group counts on its scale of things. A universal religion takes the particular and transforms it into an example of the general. Everyone matters; the stakes encompass all of humanity. An ethnic religion invokes as object of God's concern only the this-worldly and the local; a universal religion encompasses the whole world in its vision of what is at stake in God's relationship to the whole of creation. Only when we know how each of the three great traditions of faith in one God identifies those, within humanity, who form the community of the faithful, God's people, do we grasp how profoundly all three concur that religion is public, political—a collective act that recognizes God's claim upon humanity. Judaism, Christianity, and Islam all constitute religious communities that address all of humanity. In local circumstances each may take on a national or an ethnic coloration. But at their foundations all three transcend the immediate and the particular and deliver a universal message.

B. THE COMMUNITY OF THE FAITHFUL: ISLAM

The understanding of human history both in the Qur'ān and *hadīth* and in the later Muslim community is straightforward: God created the world and humankind in the person of Adam and placed human beings in the world of creation as His vicegerents. They are charged with obedience to their Lord. Those who are faithful and do good in this world are promised eternal life beyond the life of this world in the eternal garden, or paradise, that God has prepared for the righteous. The evildoers here are promised eternal life also, but a life of punishment in the Fire God has prepared for the wicked. Thus the creation of this world began a process that will end in the Day of Judgment and the end of this world, and in Muslim view this process is one in which human individuals and communities play central roles.

In the beginning it was the first man, Adam, to whom God taught the names of all things and before whom he commanded the angels to bow down (S. 2:31–34). All obeyed except Iblīs, who refused and was punished. This signaled the special status of humankind in creation. We find also in the Qur'ān the idea of a covenant between God and His human creatures in passages such as Sūrah 13:20, 25; 57:8, and especially 7:172:

> And [recall] when your Lord brought forth from the loins of the children of Adam their seed/progeny and made them witness to themselves: "Am I not your Lord?" They said: "Assuredly, we bear witness to it," lest you say on the Day of Resurrection, "Truly, of this we were ignorant."

Above all, human beings were created to serve God by their active choice and effort, whereas all other created beings by nature automatically praise God and perform their appropriate God-given functions without willing their obedience or being able to choose to disobey. Thus the human race occupies a special place in creation, one that places it in a unique position of responsibility for choice and action, bringing it thus squarely center stage in the drama of contingent existence.

The assumption in the Qur'ān and in subsequent tradition is that the ideal culmination of history would be the eventual growth of humanity into a single *Ummah muslimah*, or "submissive community," whose members serve and worship God in pure faith:

> And let there be [formed] of you a community (*Ummah*) that invites [people] to the good, demands what is right, and condemns what is reprehensible—such are the ones who flourish. And do not be like those who split away and disputed [even] after there had come to them clear evidence; for them is a mighty punishment. (S. 3:104–105)

Even though the qur'ānic message is aimed clearly at the Arabs in the first instance (as a people who, like earlier peoples, have been given their own revelation by God), its message is also clearly preached in the context of a universalist understanding of human history and destiny. There is a clear sense in the Qur'ān and early tradition that the new Ummah will, or should, be based on faith, not blood affiliation, and that it should embrace all human beings willing to obey and worship God alone, regardless of their race, language, or circumstances. In this regard, the concept of *Ummah* is to some degree analogous to that of "church," or *ekklesia*, in Christian tradition, and to that of Israel in Jewish tradition.

The usual term in the classical sources for the *Ummah* is "the people of the *Sunnah* [tradition, or established practice] and the *Jamāʿah*." The word *jamāʿah*, "community," "collectivity," is a frequent alternative to *Ummah*, "community," which underscores the solidarity and commonality of the faithful as a collective whole. This ideal of human community under God is the vision to which Muhammad and the Qur'ān called human beings. Embodied first in the historical Muslim society founded in the Arabian city of Medina between 622 C.E. and the death of the Prophet in 632, the *Ummah* has continued as an ideal paradigm until the present day, when it has become a worldwide spiritual community embracing one-seventh or more of humanity. The perceived continuity between the Medinan model and the current, highly diverse, and global reality of the Muslim faithful today is symbolic but also crucial for understanding Muslims' feelings about their solidarity with other Muslims worldwide.

The religious faith and practice, or *dīn* [usually rendered "religion" in English], that defines the *Ummah* is understood in Muslim view, however, not as something that began only with Muhammad and the revelation of the Qur'ān. Rather, *Islām* as "the [true] religion (dīn) in God's eyes" (S. 3:19) is held to be identical with the true monotheism to which humankind was called again and again ever since Adam was created as the first of God's human creatures and the first of His messengers. It is the religion of Abraham, Moses, Jesus, and all the Prophets. Thus the faith of those who responded to Muhammad's message was not understood by the Qur'ān or the Prophet as a "new religion" or "latecomer" on the monotheistic scene. Instead, it was, and for Muslims remains, a reformation of the (over time) diluted monotheism of the Judaic and Christian traditions, a restoration of true worship and service of the One God— something as old as humanity itself. It especially is identified with, and taken as a resumption of, the faith and practice of Abraham, the paradigmatic person of faith for all three monotheistic traditions. Thus the Qur'ān speaks of him as the paradigmatic prophetic figure who came before Moses or Jesus (or, of course, Muhammad):

> Abraham was not a Jew, nor a Christian. Rather, he was one of pure faith (hanīf), one who submitted to God (muslim), and not one of the polytheists (lit., those who associate partners with God). (S. 3:67)

Abraham's pure monotheistic faith has been the model for what it means to be muslim in all ages and all sectors of the Islamic community, and just as the Hebrew scriptures speak of "the religion of Abraham, Isaac, and Jacob," so too does the Qur'ān, although its focus is so strongly on the faith of Abraham that it can rightly be said to be, both in the view of the Qur'ān and of later tradition, "the religion of Abraham"—the appropriate worship and service of the Almighty, the Living God, most perfectly exemplified in the life and faith of Abraham.

This notion of the historical antiquity of true islām, true submission to the will of God, is echoed in an important concept regarding the natural propensity of human beings at birth to be disposed to worship and service of God. This is the concept of fitrah, or "way of being created," "natural disposition."[1] In the Qur'ān, its key occurrence for later interpretation is in Sūrah 30:30, in which God addresses His prophet, "Therefore fix your countenance towards dīn (religious practice, or "religion") as a hanīf (one of pure faith in God)—the

---

[1] On fitrah, see D. B. MacDonald, "Fitra," EI² 2:931–32.

fitrah of God, in which He created humanity. . . ." The understanding of *fitrah* here as a natural state of monotheistic piety has been defined for Muslims in particular by a famous hadīth:

> Abū Hurayrah . . . said: "The Apostle of God said: 'No one is born except according to the *fitrah* [taken here as "the natural human state (of faith)"]; then one's parents make one a Jew or Christian or Magian, just as beasts produce their offspring whole [perfect]: Do you see any defect in them?'" Then Abū Hurayrah said, "Recite if you wish [S. 30:30]: '[That is] the natural state (*fitrah*) of God according to which He created (*fatara*) humankind: there is no changing what God has created. That is true religion, but most people do not know [it].'"
> (Muslim, *Saḥīḥ* 46:22; cf. 46:23–26)

This has always been taken to mean "with the innate predisposition [to be submissive to God]." In other words, it is the upbringing of a child that turns him or her to less complete or even pernicious (as in the case of polytheist) religious ways; the natural state of the individual is one of true submission to God, which is what the Qur'ān calls for throughout. This idea of a kind of natural monotheism, which has had a significant place in Muslim thinking over the centuries, does pose problems for the strict logic of predestinarian doctrine in particular. Nevertheless, it has remained a powerful figurative way of saying that "the true *dīn* (religious service/worship, "religion") with God is *islām* (i.e. true "submission")" (S. 3:19) as opposed to any other of the many "religions" that have competed with it over the centuries.

Already in the concept of *fitrah*, we can see the notion that although there are many communities that claim to be the true followers of God or of the true path of righteousness, once the Qur'ān was revealed and Muhammad's mission completed, the best religious way, the most perfect path of worship and service of God, was made manifest in clear terms for the rest of history. The community of true worshippers of the One God was reestablished once and for all time. This is the *Ummah muslimah*. In juxtaposition to the traditions of Jews, Christians and others, it understands itself to be the object of God's words in Sūrah 3:110:

> You are the best community (*ummah*) brought forth for humanity; you enjoin what is reputable and prohibit what is reprehensible, and you have faith in God.

What Muslims believe firmly is that where previous peoples had rejected God's emissaries and become pagan idolaters, or (as in the case of Jews and Christians) not remained true over time to the revelations originally given them by their founding prophets, the Muslims have managed in their collective existence over nearly fourteen centuries to keep the perfection of the revealed divine word of the "Arabic Reciting" (*Qur'ān 'arabī*) uncorrupted and to preserve the words and example of God's final prophet in the *hadīth*. This has been possible because of the earnest efforts of so many faithful persons in every generation, from that of Muhammad to the present one, to transmit faithfully the verbatim word of the Qur'ān and the accurate sense of the traditions ascribed to Muhammad. Thus Muslims hold that any error in such a tradition of transmission (where so many persons in so many linked generations of transmitters have provided cross-checks on forgery and error) would be unthinkable. This is the concept of *tawātur*, or multiple personal transmission involving so many pious transmitters that it does not admit of error; it is based on the strong conviction that reliability does not lie in texts per se but in the authenticity and multiplicity of individual faithful tradents of texts. In other words, personal connectedness and personal integrity within a community of faithful Muslims are the essentials of authenticity and reliability. A key importance of the Ummah lies in its unbroken multiple chains of faithful transmitters who have conveyed the key documents, above all the Qur'ān and the Hadīth, and the original faith of the founding generations of Muslims across the centuries from Muhammad's time to the present day.

If we move from this understanding of the cohesiveness and faithfulness of the *Ummah* of true Muslims to the Muslim understanding of the wider history of religion, we can see at once that the latter involves the fundamental notion that the history of humankind since creation has been marked by its division into different peoples or communities (*umam*, plur. of *ummah*) of varying times, customs, and histories. Another term that is already used in the Qur'ān for these communities is *millah*, which refers to a "religion" or "religious group" such as the Christians, Jews, or one of the heathen peoples (The term is also frequently used in the phrase "the religion of Abraham"; later Islamic usage with the definite article, *al-millah*, refers to Islamic religion, and both as an indefinite singular and in the plural, to "sect[s]"). In the qur'ānic and later Islamic view, all previous peoples or communities have been called to proper submission to the One God; but most of these have either rejected the call or responded only for a time, even if a few generations. Then eventually they have allowed their tradition of faith to become corrupted. Human history consists in the histories of various previous peoples, or "nations" (*umam*) distinguished by their languages, customs, and religious faith and practice. With the coming of Muhammad and the Qur'ān, that history can now be seen as one culminating in what is really a "last call" to righteousness, repentance, and true monotheistic faith: the call to submission, *islām*.

This call is not just a call to personal faith. It is also a call to be part of the universal and pluralistic community, or *Ummah*, of true faith, to be brothers and sisters of those of all backgrounds who have already responded and "submitted" to God and His will as revealed in the Qur'ān and the mission of Muhammad. The Muslim *Ummah* began as an Arab community—made up of those Arabic speakers who responded to Muhammad's preaching and the qur'ānic message at the heart of his preaching. Its Arabic impress has persisted in the necessity of the faithful to learn at least a minimum part of the Arabic Qur'ān sufficient to be able to perform the daily rituals of *salāt*. But the religious and ethnic diversity of the first Muslims before they submitted to the One God was considerable—from pagan tribesmen or city traders and merchants to Arab Jews, Christians, and immigrants from Iran, Yemen, or elsewhere. What may well have started out, possibly in the Prophet's own mind, as a call to Arabs only—a prophetic mission and an Arabic revelation directed at this one people who had not had a prophet or "book" before—rapidly became universalized, so that the non-Arabic speakers encountered in the rapid conquest by Arab-Islamic armies in the two or three decades following Muhammad's death were also offered affiliation and at least a kind of membership in the growing and diversifying *Ummah*. (This affiliation required for some time that non-Arabs be made formally "clients" [*mawālī*] of an Arab tribe or clan group in order for their *islām* to be recognized and for them to receive the rights accorded to Muslims. Eventually, and not without strife and conflict, this practice ceased, and Islam became in fact a "universal" religious tradition in which the faithful of any race, culture, or language group might participate. But this took time.) This ultimately led the *Ummah* to become a cosmopolitan, multiethnic Muslim community that cultivated Arabic as its shared medium of expression because it is the sacred language of God's revealed word. In other words, it was not a homogeneous community of Muslim Arabs that happened to include affiliated but not fully assimilated Arabic-speaking foreigners in it. Furthermore, in those regions where Islam became the majority tradition or the tradition of the ruling elites, the polity was further diversified and made more cosmopolitan by the fact that it included necessarily many non-Muslims. These were primarily Christians and Jews, but eventually even Hindus and other religious adherents who were accorded tolerated status in Islamic states as "people of Scripture," communities who have a sacred book (see chapter five below).

Islamic history has not been without divisive struggles and internal disputes. In the first two to three centuries, caliphal administration joined with the evolution of legal theory and practice and the consolidation of religious norms to give stability to the emerging Islamic society. So powerful was the Muslim vision of the *Ummah* that, upon the demise of a given caliph, or even a caliphal dynasty such as the Umayyads, the community and the caliphal office continued. There were, however, conflicting notions of that vision. In the first three Islamic centuries, two pivotal interpretations with very early origins in events after Muhammad's death reflected idealistic interpretations of the *Ummah*, its leadership and membership. When neither proved viable in the practical world of society and politics, they became minority visions that continued to fire the imaginations of some and to stimulate important theological debates but failed to win broad-based support. A third, "centrist," vision found favor with the majority because it spoke to the widest spectrum of the faithful and accommodated inevitable compromises in the higher cause of Islamic unity and stability.

The most radical idealists traced their political origin to the first civil war (656–661). They were the *Khārijites*, or "seceders" from the camp of the fourth caliph, 'Alī, because, in their view, the latter compromised with the groups who challenged his claim on the caliphate and refused to accept his right to leadership as the best-qualified Muslim. The Khārijites' position was that the Muslim polity must be based on strict qur'ānic principles. They espoused total equality of the faithful and held that the leader of the *Ummah* should be the best Muslim, whoever that might be, of whatever background or station. They took a moralistic, rigorist view of membership in the *Ummah*: anyone who committed a major sin was no longer a Muslim. They were prepared to deny the faith of Muslims whom they felt to be grave sinners. Extreme Khārijites called on true Muslims to join them in rebellion against the morally compromised authority of the reigning caliph; those who did not join them were also considered no longer to be Muslims and were to be fought. These attitudes may well have elicited a well-known tradition ascribed to Muhammad himself: "When one of you calls his fellow an infidel, this name could be applied to either of you."[2] The extremist Khārijite groups became and remained constant rallying points for opposition to the Umayyads and, to a lesser degree, the Abbasids. More moderate Khārijites tempered their aversion to tolerating less-than-pious Muslims and the rule of less-than-ideal caliphs, yet they retained a strong sense of the moral imperatives of Muslim personal and collective duty. Their ideals proved attractive and influenced wider Muslim pietism and theology in the long run. Although the movement declined in Abbasid times (from the late eighth/second century), even today moderate Khārijite groups survive in Oman and North Africa.

A second position was defined largely in terms of a strong view on the rightful leadership of the *Ummah*. Muhammad had no surviving sons, and his son-in-law and cousin ʿAlī claimed the caliphate in 656, partly on the basis of his blood tie to the Prophet. His claim was contested by Muʿāwiya, the Muslim governor of Syria and relative of ʿUthmān, in the first Islamic civil war. When Muʿāwiya took over by default after a Khārijite murdered ʿAlī in 661, many of ʿAlī's followers felt that Islamic affairs had gone awry. Although it is difficult to date the crystallization of the developed ideology of the "partisans of ʿAlī" (*Shiʿat ʿAlī*, or simply the *Shiʿa*, or "Shīʿites"), their roots go back to ʿAlī's murder and especially to that of his son Husayn at Karbala, in Iraq, at the hands of Umayyad troops (680 C.E.).

Whereas all Muslims esteem ʿAlī for his closeness to Muhammad, Shīʿites believe him to be the Prophet's appointed successor. ʿAlī's blood tie with Muhammad was augmented in Shīʿite thinking by belief in the Prophet's designation of him as the true imam, or

---

[2] Ahmad b. Hanbal, *Musnad* (6 vols., Būlāq, 18), 2:18.

Muslim leader, after him. Numerous rebellions in Umayyad times rallied around persons claiming to be such a true successor, whether as an ʿAlīd or merely a member of Muhammad's clan of Hashim. Even the ʿAbbāsids based their right to the caliphate on their Hashimite ancestry. The major Shīʿite pretenders who emerged in the eighth and ninth centuries based their claims on both the Prophet's designation and their descent from ʿAlī and Fatima, Muhammad's daughter. They also stressed the idea of a divinely inspired knowledge passed on by Muhammad to his designated heirs. Thus the true Muslim was the faithful follower of the imams, who carried Muhammad's blood and spiritual authority.

When Shīʿites failed to place a true imam at the head of the imperial state, they interpreted this failure theologically. They saw ʿAlī's assassination by a Khārijite, and especially the brutal massacre of al-Husayn and his family, as proofs of the evil nature of this world's rulers and as rallying points for true Muslims. The martyrdom of ʿAlī and Husayn was extended to a line of ʿAlīd imams that varied among different groups of Shīʿites. True Muslims, like their imams, must suffer. But they would be vindicated in the end by an expected *mahdi*, or "guided one," who would usher in a messianic age and a judgment day that would see the faithful rewarded. (Similar mahdist movements also arose as well throughout Islamic history among the Sunnīs). On several occasions in later history Shīʿite rulers did head some Islamic states. But only after 1500, in Iran, did Shīʿism prevail as the majority faith in a major Muslim state. The Shīʿite vision of the true *Ummah* has been a powerful one, but not one that has been able to muster sufficient consensus to dominate the larger Islamic world.

Khārijite and Shīʿite causes were repeatedly espoused by disaffected groups in the early and later Islamic empire. But it was a third, less sharply defined position on the nature of leadership, membership in the *Ummah*, and status as a Muslim that most Muslims ultimately accepted. In some ways a compromise, it proved acceptable not only to lukewarm Muslims or simple pragmatists, but also to persons of piety as intense as that of any Khārijite or Shīʿite. We may term the proponents of this position centrists. To emphasize the correctness of their views, once they had become a majority, they eventually called themselves *Sunnīs*—followers of the tradition (*sunnah*) established by the Prophet and Qurʾān. Neither they, nor the Shīʿites, nor the Khārijites, have ever been a single sectarian group but have always encompassed a wide range of reconcilable, if not always truly compatible, ideas and groups. They have made up the broad middle spectrum of Muslims who tend to put communal solidarity and maintenance of the overall unity of the *Ummah* above purist adherence to particular theological tenets or insistence upon a narrow interpretation of qualifications for legitimate Muslim leadership. They have been inclusivist rather than exclusivist, a trait that has typified the Islamic (unlike the Jewish or Christian) community through most of its history.

The centrist position on various of the early questions in the community can probably best be seen in what is generally held to be our earliest "creed" (*aqīdah*), which has been dated to the mid-eighth century C.E. Six of its first seven articles are as follows:

> 1. We do not consider anyone to be an infidel on account of sin; nor do we deny his faith; 2. We enjoin what is just and prohibit what is evil; 3. What reaches you could not possibly have missed you; and what misses you could not possibly have reached you; 4. We disavow none of the Companions of the Messenger of God, nor do we adhere to any of them exclusively; 5. We leave the question of 'Uthmān and 'Alī to God, who knows the secret and the hidden. . . . 7. Difference of opinion in the Community is a token of divine mercy." (from the Fiqh Akbar I, 1–5, 7)[3]

In these articles of faith, we see reflexes of the early disputes mentioned above, and of the centrist attempt to reject the radical positions of the Khārijites on sin, piety, predestination, and communal leadership, and those of the Shī'ites on leadership in particular.

The centrist position was simply the most workable general framework for the new Islamic state and, ultimately, the community of the faithful. Naturally much of what we know of its early development has been filtered through the historical and other texts of the third and later centuries of Islam, when the centrist position had solidified as the dominant "traditional" (*sunnī*) group. The basic ideas that emerged in this solidification of the middle were: (1) The *Ummah* is a religiously defined community under divine authority. (2) This

---

[3] Taken from the Fiqh Akbar I, as cited in A. J. Wensinck, *The Muslim Creed* (London: Frank Cass, 1932), pp. 103–104.

translates in terms of political organization into a nomocracy, or society under the authority of God's law, the Shari'a (which is mediated through religious/legal scholars who are the interpreters of the Qur'ān and Tradition). (3) The caliph is the absolute temporal ruler, charged with administering and defending the realm of Islam and protecting Muslim norms and practice; he possesses no greater authority than other Muslims in matters of faith (a position contrary to that of the next largest tradition, that of the Shī'īs). (4) A person who professes to be Muslim by witnessing that "There is no god but God, and Muhammad is His Messenger" should be considered a Muslim (because "only God knows what is in the heart"), and not even a mortal sin excludes such a person automatically from the Ummah (a position directly opposed to that of the early Khārijī, or "Seceder," movement). Under increasingly influential ulema leadership, these and other basic premises of Muslim community came to serve as the theological underpinnings of both the caliphal state and the emerging international Islamic social and religious order.

The universalist *Ummah muslimah* has now been in existence for between twelve and fourteen solar centuries, depending upon when in the first one or two Islamic centuries one dates the final tilt towards a multiethnic, multilingual concept of Muslim society. The most common era identified as the time of that shift is the early 'Abbāsid caliphate—the last half of the eighth and early ninth century C.E., when the major Islamic political capital moved to Baghdad, and Persianate culture began to figure more and more prominently alongside, or sometimes even over, the Arab elements in Islamic culture and Muslim religious life and thought. But the essential religious and theological underpinnings had been there from the time of Qur'ān and Prophet for understanding the Muslim *Ummah* as a supra-national, supra-ethnic, and even supra-sectarian entity that is at once an ideal to be striven for and a perceived present reality. The rhetoric of the equality of all faithful Muslims before God was firmly fixed in Qur'ān and Sunnah, and even while the political and social realities of rank and privilege and power were never absent from early, let alone later, Muslim societies, the explicit ideal of the equality of Muslims was always present. This coexistence of recognition of older (and sometimes newer) standards of rank and nobility within Islamic society and insistence upon religious piety as the only true measure of merit or nobility of spirit among Muslims is demonstrated in a well-known ḥadīth of the Prophet: "the most noble persons are the most pious . . . [but] the best of them in the Jāhilīyah [i.e., before Islam] are the best in Islām, if they are discerning [in religion]."[4] Even though genetic nobility counts still in Islamic societies, real excellence lies at least theoretically in religious knowledge and is necessary to confirm inherited nobility.

The *Ummah* has long extended beyond any one Islamic society or even one caliphal state encompassing numerous Islamic societies. To the present moment, Muslims and non-Muslims speak about the "Muslim world" in a way that no one does about any other religiously defined international group. On the political level, it is largely a fiction, but when one examines the degree of shared religious practice and sensibilities, historical consciousness, and shared religious worldview, it is striking how readily identifiable the fundamentally "Muslim" character of these communal dimensions are, whether one is looking in villages in Malaysia, cities in Iran or the Middle East, the countryside in North or East Africa, or minority communities in Europe and America. This is by no means to argue that Islamic communities within the global *Ummah muslimah* are not infinitely varied and visibly different in practice, thought, and consciousness. It is rather to argue that amidst the obvious diversity and heterogeneity there are also unmistakable strands of a shared common or "classical" Islamic tradition. These are most notably the "five pillars" of religious faith (profession of faith, daily worship, almsgiving, fasting, and pilgrimage); the veneration for the norms of the *sharīʿah*; the rock-solid commitment to monotheism; identifiably Islamic institutions such as family law, Islamic education, or pious endowments (*awqāf*, pl. of *waqf*); and the shared traditions of popular piety—from veneration of the Prophet to celebration of the birthdays (*mawālid*, pl. of *mawlūd*, or *moulid*) of esteemed Muslim saints.

Therefore, it is not facile, reductionist, or essentialist to speak about a shared Muslim "world" of the *Ummah*, so long as we do not glibly imagine that we can reduce Islam as a worldwide tradition of infinite variety to a fixed set of essential norms that must always be prominent for an individual person's faith or a local community's practice to be deemed Muslim. The worldwide *Ummah* lives in the

4 *Muslim*, 43:168; 44:199; al-Bukhārī 60:8:5,14; 60:19:1; 61:1:5,6.

imaginations and hearts of Muslims of every type and place, and
this concept allows Muslims of all sectarian persuasions or cultural
traditions to recognize their often radically different brethren and
sisters in distant places and cultures and even different sectarian traditions as belonging, whatever their many differences, to the single,
inclusive, ideal *Ummah*.

What began in roughly the first two centuries of Islamic communal existence as a concrete ideal that shaped (and of course was
shaped by) the development of Islamic religious, social, and political institutions became later, and remains, a more generalized and
idealized entity that has in today's immense global diffusion and
diversity of local Muslim communities perhaps less concrete reality
but no less symbolic or spiritual validity for Muslims than it did in
the eighth century C.E. The true *Ummah* was never (at least after the
death of the Prophet or perhaps the first few caliphs) a functioning
political entity (and it is not one today nor likely to be one in the
future). But it was and is a powerful religious sodality or spiritual
fellowship—a religious *community*—that has always loomed large in
the consciousness of Muslims everywhere. Not wholly unlike Israel
in Jewish consciousness, the *Ummah* is not the social order of Muslims
as a factual reality, nor is it a discrete social or organized religious
system. It is rather an imaginary construct that encapsulates Muslims'
awareness of there being a brotherhood and sisterhood of the faithful who give allegiance to God's norms. These norms are those out-
lined in Qur'ān and Sunnah and then developed and codified by
subsequent generations (even if differently in different schools of legal
interpretation, sectarian traditions, and geographic locales) under the
rubric "*sharī'ah*" (see chapter four). In this sense, much as the construct Israel does for Jews, the *Ummah* symbolizes the longed-for destiny of the aggregate of faithful submitters to God's will as a collective
community of submission—the community intended for humankind
by their Maker. Those who call themselves Muslim have already
made the commitment to be a part of that community; those who
have not are all potential members who have up to now not heeded
God's call to pure worship and service of their Lord. Thus there is
always an existing *Ummah muslimah* comprising all current Muslims,
and also an unrealized, future one that might encompass all of
humankind. However, as we shall see in chapter six below, the

assumption of the Qur'ān as well as of Islamic tradition is that there will always be deniers of God and His sovereignty even up to the Day of Resurrection and God's final judgment, when those who have submitted to God will be rewarded and those who have rejected God will be punished. Thus in one sense the Muslim understanding of the community of the faithful embraces the fundamental, realistic fact that it will never become coterminous with the human family as a whole but will have to remain finally an unrealized ideal in that regard.

What, then, does the *Ummah* mean to Muslims? In the first instance it means a system of mutual support and caring among the faithful. A saying of the Prophet reported by 'Abd Allāh ibn 'Umar says:

> The Muslim is brother of the Muslim, and he shall not wrong him nor give him over [to be wronged]. If he responds to his brother's need, God will respond to his need; if he relieves him from distress, God will relieve him from part of his distress on the Day of Resurrection, and if he protects a Muslim, God will protect him at the Resurrection.[5]

In the second instance, it represents the egalitarian spiritual community of the faithful that admits of no distinctions of rank among the faithful in the sight of God, except that of piety before God:

> O humankind! We have created you male and female and made you nations and tribes that you may know one another [only]; Truly, the noblest of you in God's eyes is the most pious among you. (S. 49:13)

In the third instance, the *Ummah* as the community defined by allegiance to God's will is the context in which Muslims find support in their struggles to be true submitters to God. It is the realm in which the *sharī'ah*, derived as it is from the Qur'ān and prophetic Sunnah, obtains as the codification of God's ordinances for the pursuit of righteousness. As we shall see in the next chapter, for the Muslim as for the Jew, having God's law to love and to live by is not a burden but rather an immense comfort and support for the faithful. The *Ummah* is conceived as a social reality within which submitting human beings can find the circumstances conducive to the good life desired for his worshippers by God.

---

[5] al-Bukhārī 46:3.

Finally, at another level, the *Ummah* is in a real sense not unlike the ideal of the church (or true Israel: see below) in Christianity, the eschatological community of the promise. The promise is of course the assurance repeated in many places in the Qur'ān that "those who have faith and do righteous works" will be the company admitted on the Day of Judgment to the Garden—the Paradise promised in the Qur'ān. This is not a doctrine of "election" of the Muslims, but one of confirmation through eternal salvation of the good deeds and pure faith of true submitters to God. Simply being a Muslim and member of the *Ummah* does not guarantee salvation; but being a faithful member of the true *Ummah* carries the assurance of being among that group of followers of Muhammad who will be called forth on the Day of Judgment to inherit the promise with him. As the spiritual progeny of Abraham, the Muslims can aspire and strive to be inheritors of the promise, but the Qur'ān reminds them that God's response to Abraham's inquiry about his progeny was "My promise extends not to those who are unjust" (S. 2:124). Individual righteousness and not nominal membership of any group, even the *Ummah*, brings salvation in the end. Still, there is no denying that those who form the true *Ummah muslimah* have a special place in God's plan: "Thus have we made you a median community [between Jews and Christians] so that you may be witnesses to humankind" (S. 2:143). Here the *Ummah* comprises not nominal members of an earthly "religion" but those who have followed God's paths as He would have them do. Historical and eschatological communities are virtually one here; how could it ultimately be otherwise if one is speaking of the ideal of *Ummah*?

C. ALL ARE ONE IN CHRIST JESUS: CHRISTIANITY

Throughout its primitive period, Christianity confronted a consistent challenge both from within and from without: to define itself in regard to Israel. Out of that struggle, for all the volatility involved, a sense of the church emerged which endures to this day.

Israel within Jesus' activity is not a matter of definition, but an imperative of transformation. Those who offer of their own, forgiving and being forgiven, join in that eschatological Israel which benefits even non-Jews (Matthew 8:11; Luke 13:28–29). Jesus' position is difficult to compare with other definitions of Israel current in his period because he provided for no clear social structure. How are we to determine the difference between Jews and non-Jews, between those who are to engage in that eschatological transformation which constitutes Israel and those who are indirectly to benefit from it? And who knows whether a given non-Israelite is to be classed with the centurion (Luke 7:1–10; Matthew 8:5–13) and the Syrophoenician (Mark 7:24–30; Matthew 15:21–28), or with the demons and the pigs (Mark 5:1–20; Matthew 8:28–34; Luke 8:26–39)?

Jesus' focus on non-urban settlements of Jews assured that, as a theoretical or conceptual matter, the difference between Jews and others did not arise as a regularly important issue. Such lines of demarcation had already been drawn by the time he or his follow-ers contacted a village or town. He could proceed—for example in his commissioning of apostles to represent him—on the assumption of a collective understanding of communal identity. The same assump-tion resulted in his acceptance of local practices of purity as valid.

When generic purity was grossly violated, as in the case of the story of the legion (Mark 5:1–20; Matthew 8:28–34; Luke 8:26–39), it was simply assumed that such impurity was inconsistent with Jesus' presence; and the story insists that in any such confrontation, impu-rity will be eliminated. Within that generic concern with purity, col-lective agreement regarding who was marginal within the communal identity was validated, so that the centurion in Capernaum could be embraced without being touched. The Syrophoenician woman, how-ever, signals the extension of the benefits of Israel beyond the realm of any purely local definition of what Israel is. Jesus' occupation of the Temple, especially within the context of his continuity with the book of Zechariah (see chapter 14 especially), confirms the force of his conviction of Israel's fitness for worship, and of the benefit of such worship beyond the limits of Jerusalem, Judah, even Israel as usually understood.[6]

The position of Jesus' followers after his crucifixion differed sig-nally from his own. Jerusalem had become a focus of the move-ment; it became the first Christian urban center among many. The

---

[6] See Bruce Chilton, *The Temple of Jesus: His Sacrificial Program within a Cultural History of Sacrifice* (University Park: Pennsylvania State University Press, 1992).

new environment involved a greater variety of people who claimed
to represent Israel and also non-Jews (including Roman citizens) who
were at odds with any conventional definition of Israel. A conceptual, social definition of what Israel was and should be became necessary for Jesus' movement to negotiate its way among the options
which groups such as priests, Pharisees, and Essenes offered, and to
find a way to express the association within redefined Israel of Gentiles
who accepted baptism in Jesus' name. At the same time, because
the movement was frequently under pressure from the definitions of
other groups, Jesus' followers needed to define themselves in relation to those competing definitions of Israel.

In what follows, we will consider three different policies within
earliest Christianity which attempt a definition of Israel: beginning
with the circle of James, moving through the community of "Q,"
and ending with the circle of Peter. That order is not chronologi-
cal from the point of view of the documents cited; indeed, from the
perspective of textual dating, we should move in the opposite sequence.
Because our concern is with the definition of Israel, we move from
the strictest model of Israel as centered on the Temple (in the circle of James), through the reflection of severe tension within Israel
as a result of Jesus' movement (in "Q"), and on to the conviction
that God's spirit is available through Christ to those outside Israel
as well as to those within (in the circle of Peter).

The Circle of James

The central importance of James to a Temple-loyal dedication to
Jesus as offering access into the mysteries of heaven has been well
established in recent research.[7] A passage within the Gospels will be
the focus of attention here, in order to elucidate James's conception
of Israel itself, which was a function of his attitude toward the Temple.
In order to lay the groundwork for a consideration of James's concern for the Temple, we begin with the description of James provided by Hegesippus, a Christian writer from the second century.

Hegesippus—as cited by Eusebius (see *Ecclesiastical History* II.23.1–
18)—characterizes James, Jesus' brother, as the person who exer-

---

[7] See *James the Just and Christian Origins*: Supplements to *Novum Testamentum* 98 (ed.
B. D. Chilton and C. A. Evans; Leiden: Brill, 1999).

cised immediate control over the church in Jerusalem. Although Peter had initially gathered a group of Jesus' followers in Jerusalem, his interests and activities further afield left the way open for James to become the natural head of the community there. That change, and political changes in Jerusalem itself (some of which are detailed in the next section on the community of "Q"), made the Temple the effective center of the local community of Jesus' followers. James practiced a careful and idiosyncratic purity in the interests of worship in the Temple. He abstained from wine and animal flesh, did not cut his hair or beard, and forsook oil and bathing. According to Hegesippus, those special practices gave him access even to the sanctuary. Josephus reports he was killed in the Temple ca. 62 at the instigation of the high priest Ananus during the interregnum of the Roman governors Festus and Albinus (*Antiquities* 20§§197–203). Hegesippus gives a more circumstantial, less politically informed, account of the martyrdom.

In addition to the sort of close association with the Temple which could and did result in conflict with the authorities there, the circle of James is expressly claimed in Acts to have exerted authority as far away as Antioch, by means of emissaries who spoke Greek (Acts 15:13–35). James alone determines the outcome of apostolic policy. James in Acts agrees that Gentiles who turn to God are not be encumbered with regulations (15:19), and yet he insists they be instructed by letter to abstain "from the pollutions of idols, and from fornication, and from what is strangled, and from blood" (v. 20).

The grounds given for the Jacobean policy are that the law of Moses is commonly acknowledged (Acts 15:21); the implication is that to disregard such elemental considerations of purity as James specifies would be to dishonor Moses. Judas Barsabbas and Silas are then dispatched with Paul and Barnabas to deliver the letter in Antioch along with their personal testimony (vv. 22–29), and are said particularly to continue their instruction as prophets (vv. 32, 33). They refer to the regulations of purity as necessities (v. 28), and no amount of Lukan gloss can conceal that what they insist upon is a serious challenge of Paul's position (compare 1 Corinthians 8).

James's devotion to the Temple is also reflected in Acts 21. When Paul arrives in Jerusalem, James and the presbyters with him express concern at the rumor that Paul is telling Jews who live among the Gentiles not to circumcise. Their advice is for Paul to demonstrate his piety by purifying himself, paying the expenses of four men under a vow, and entering the Temple with them (Acts 21:17–26). The result is a disastrous misunderstanding. Paul is accused of introducing "Greeks" into the Temple, a riot ensues, and Paul himself is arrested (21:27–36). James is not mentioned again in Acts, but Hegesippus' description shows his devotion to the Temple did not wane.

Within the Gospels, certain passages reflect the exceptional devotion of James's circle to the Temple. Perhaps the best example is Mark 7:6–13 (and, with an inverted structure, Matthew 15:3–9); although the topic of the chapter overall is purity, the issue addressed in the passage itself is the sanctity of the Temple in particular (Mark 7:6–13). The issue is spelled out in terms of a dispute concerning *Qorban*, the Aramaic term for a cultic gift (Mark 7:11).

The dispute probably reflects Jesus' own stance, that what is owed to one's parents cannot be sheltered by declaring it dedicated to the Temple. The crucial point of such a gambit of sheltering is that one might continue to use the property after its dedication to the Temple, while what was given to a person would be transferred forthwith.[8] The basic complaint about the practice, especially as stated in the simple epigram of Mark 7:11–12, derives from Jesus. The complaint is characteristic of him; quite aside from his occupation of the Temple, he criticized commercial arrangements there (see Matthew 17:24–27; Mark 12:41–44; Luke 21:1–4).

The dominical epigram has here been enveloped in a much more elaborate argument, crafted within the circle of James. Mark 7:6–13 is a syllogism, developed by means of scriptural terms of reference. Isaiah's complaint (29:13) frames the entire argument: the people claim to honor God, but their heart is as far from him as their vain worship, rooted in human commandments (Mark 7:6b–7). That statement is related in Mark 7:10–12 to the tradition of *Qorban*, taken as an invalidation of the Mosaic prescription to honor parents. The simple and unavoidable conclusion is that the tradition violates the command of God (Mark 7:8–9, 13).

The argument as it stands insists upon the integrity of the Temple

---

[8] See Zeev W. Falk, "Notes and Observations on Talmudic Vows," *Harvard Theological Review* 159 (1966): 309–312.

and the strict regulation of conduct there; it attacks opponents for too little concern for the Temple, not too much. At the same time, the passage presents Jesus as maintaining a literal loyalty to the Scriptures that the Pharisees did not. (The actual form of citation, however, is derived from the Greek translation of the Hebrew Bible, the Septuagint. That is a sign of the Hellenistic phase of the cycle of tradition that James inspired.) Those aspects of the presentation of Jesus' saying are typical of the circle of James.

Regular worship in the Temple only became a characteristic feature of Jesus' movement after the crucifixion and resurrection. Before then, Jesus' conflict with the cultic authorities over the most basic issues of how offerings should be brought to the Temple resulted in deadly opposition to him. But one of the most surprising developments of the period after that time is that a group of Jesus' followers continued to reside in Jerusalem, and that worship in the Temple was one of their primary purposes there. The removal of Caiaphas from the high priesthood (in the year 37; see Josephus, *Antiquities* 18§§88–95), and the consequent reversal of his reforms (to which Jesus himself had objected), fed the conviction of Jesus' followers that he who had been crucified had also been vindicated.

Acts pictures Peter as the first leader of a tightly knit group, which broke bread at home and held property in common (see Acts 1:12–26; 2:46; 3:1–26; 4:1–37). But Peter is also represented as active much further afield. A shift in leadership of the community in Jerusalem, from Peter to James, became necessary, and Acts clearly attests that (see Acts 12:17).

The syllogism in regard to *Qorban* also assumes that devotion to Jesus' teaching is consistent with loyalty to the Temple. Indeed, the entire scene of his martyrdom unfolds in the context of the Temple at the time of Passover, and reflects the particular devotion of James's circle both to that feast and to the conduct of sacrificial worship in the Temple.

Finally, the circle of James applied the Scriptures directly to the situation of Jesus' followers, on the understanding of their regulative authority. As James develops the meaning of Amos 9:11–12 in Acts 15:16–21, the Gentiles are to recognize the triumph of David, and that implies that they are to remain Gentiles. They are not a part of Israel, although they are to keep basic rules of purity in order to honor the law of Israel.

James's focus was on Jesus' role as the ultimate arbiter within the Davidic line, and there was never any question in his mind but that the Temple was the natural place to worship God and acknowledge Jesus. Embracing the Temple as central meant for James, as it meant for everyone associated with worship there, maintaining the purity which it was understood that God required in his house, and keeping it better than many of those associated with the priesthood. That is the point of the scriptural syllogism regarding *Qorban*. According to James, Jesus' purity involved excluding Gentiles, even those who acknowledged some rudiments of purity out of loyalty to the Mosaic law, from the interior courts of the Temple. There, only Israel was to be involved in sacrifice, and followers of Jesus were to accept particular responsibility for such sacrifice (so Acts 21:17–36). The line of demarcation between Israel and non-Israel was no invention within the circle of James, but a natural result of seeing Jesus as the triumphant scion of the house of David.

When Judas Barsabbas and Silas were sent by the council to deliver its judgment (which was originally James's opinion) in Antioch, it authorized James's version of the gospel to be delivered in Greek. When Acts 15:32–33 refers to Judas and Silas as prolonging their visit in Antioch after they had read the letter from the council, we are given a glimpse into the process by which materials originally framed in Aramaic were rendered into Greek. At that moment, the importance of non-Jewish testimony to Jesus within its own environment (rather than within Israel) was emphasized. The sequel to the story of the legion, in which the restored maniac is portrayed as preaching among his own people (Mark 5:18–20), is an example of that development.

At the same time, we are shown how James's classic understanding of Israel was considered authoritative, even for the largely non-Jewish congregation in Antioch. Here, in the place where Jesus' followers were first called "Christians" (so Acts 11:26),[9] it is accepted after a considerable controversy that, although Gentiles may not be required to circumcise, neither may they be considered one with Israel. James's Israel consisted of those who recognized Jesus, the

---

[9] See C. K. Barrett, *The Acts of the Apostles*: International Critical Commentary (Edinburgh: Clark, 1994), 592.

scion of the Davidic line, as the guardian of true, non-commercial purity in the Temple.

The Community of Q

The source called Q, which might be described as the mishnah of Jesus, presents its earliest material in a way which makes it possible to understand Jesus' own preaching topically.[10] The compilation of that mishnah in Aramaic ca. 35 C.E. occurred in circumstances which were generally favorable to the preservation of Jesus' message within an oral environment. There is no reason to suppose Jesus' followers could not have circulated freely in Judea and Galilee, as Q presupposes.

But the composition of Q in its Syrian phase, a decade later, presupposes a significant rejection of the message of Jesus. The eschatological woes pronounced against Chorazin, Bethsaida, and Capernaum (Luke 10:13–15), for example, reflect the refusal of Jesus' emissaries as well as his own hardship. During Jesus' own ministry, Capernaum had provided a model of success (see Luke 4:23); its later resistance—along with more prominent cities such as Bethsaida— provoked a bitter reaction from Jesus himself, which then was articulated as definitive rejection within the community of Q. Deprived of the hospitality which would have been a mark of the acceptance of their message, the community of Q wore their poverty as a badge of honor. Out of this situation there arose the virtual equation between poverty and the kingdom which is such a strong feature of several sayings, especially the first beatitude, "Blessed are the poor, because the kingdom of God is yours" (Luke 6:20).

The blessing of the poor is linked to a scenario in which the rich are to suffer. Moreover, the poor are associated with those who are abused "for the sake of the son of man" and the rich are associated with those who embraced the false prophets of old (Luke 6:20–26). The social situation could hardly be plainer, as David Catchpole has observed:[11]

---

[10] See David Catchpole, *The Quest for Q* (Edinburgh: Clark, 1993).
[11] Catchpole, 94.

> Here, then, by employing the language of opposition which, however,
> falls short of separation, and by building on earlier use of the Deutero-
> nomic pattern of perpetually persecuted prophets, which had been
> employed (as it were) domestically within Israel, the editor allows us
> a glimpse of a situation within the community of Israel.

Tension is rising in Israel, as a result of the attempt after the resurrection to implement Jesus' commission of twelve disciples to represent him. Jesus is now understood as "the son of man," a phrase
that in Catchpole's words "conveys the heavenly status and future
coming in judgment of the Jesus who had been known on earth."
That keen sense of what the future is to bring, the reversal in standing of oppressor and oppressed, developed into the apocalyptic assurance which also characterizes Q. They know they are the "little
flock" to whom the kingdom has been given; only a brief interval
separates them from their reward (Luke 12:32). The judgment of the
kingdom is to be as severe as Q's parable of the returning king (Luke
19:11–27).

The presentation in the mishnaic source of Jesus' promise of the
inclusion of many from east and west in the patriarchal feast of the
kingdom (Matthew 8:11–12; Luke 13:28–29) is marked by a tendency towards polemic against the Jewish opponents of the movement. In the Matthean version, the saying appears as an addendum
to the healing of the servant of the Roman centurion, and with an
explicit warning against "the sons of the kingdom" (v. 12). In the
Lukan version, the saying is presented as part of a discourse concerning salvation, in which hearers are warned that merely having
enjoyed Jesus' company during his lifetime is no guarantee of fellowship with the patriarchs in the eschatological feast (13:22–30).
The differences between the two versions make the supposition of a
fixed, written "Q" appear implausible at this point, and to commend
the model of an instructional source for those who wished to teach
in Jesus' name which was susceptible of local variation. "Q" is best
seen as a mishnah for those who wished to follow the pattern of the
twelve disciples whom Jesus had commissioned as his representatives.

Despite the differences between the versions of Q represented by
Matthew and by Luke respectively, the two Gospels commonly reflect
how the saying was developed between the time of Jesus and the
composition of the source of instructions. Jesus' teaching in this saying focused on those who would come from east and west, marginal

in relation to Israel or even outside Israel, in order to join in the benefits of the feast of the kingdom with Abraham, Isaac, and Jacob. That would have been how his position was remembered around the year 35 C.E., when what we call Q, a mishnah in Jesus' name, began to circulate among Jesus' more prominent followers. Then, however, the experience of resistance to the message that Jesus had commissioned the Twelve to deliver to Israel caused a new note of bitterness to be sounded. "Weeping and gnashing of teeth" was promised to those in Israel who refused to accept the message of the kingdom, and their place at the table of the kingdom was understood to be handed over to those who had been marginal or excluded.

In order to appreciate the position of the community that composed Q, it is vital to understand that the punishment of those in Israel who rejected Jesus was part of an apocalyptic expectation of judgment. What was threatened to particular places that should have embraced the message of Jesus and did not (such as Chorazin and Bethsaida; see Luke 10:13) was also said to be in store for "this generation" of unresponsive Jews as a whole (see Luke 11:31–32, 47–51). "The twelve tribes of Israel" were themselves to be judged by those faithful to Jesus (Luke 22:28–30); descent from Abraham could not be claimed as an unconditional privilege in the eschatological accounting (Luke 3:7–9).

The apocalyptic imagination of Q takes it to the very limit of a classic definition of Israel, such as is represented by the circle of James. The experience of rejection entailed hardship, because the practice mandated by Jesus involved living in communities of Jews on the basis of their hospitality. An inhospitable Israel was to have the very dust of its streets shaken off the disciples' feet (see Luke 10:11), but widespread or persistent inhospitality would obviously constitute a serious challenge to the very existence of Jesus' movement. Q represents a response to that challenge. Those who preached in the name of Jesus around the year 45 C.E. could count on the support of only certain communities, some of them in Syria, and their attitude towards Israel as usually understood was ambivalent.

On the one hand, as a result of the experience of the rejection of Jesus' message, some in Israel are threatened with eschatological judgment. On the other hand, the assumption that Israel is truly the focus of the kingdom's disclosure means that the message must still be directed there, whether it is accepted or not. The usurpation by outsiders of the place of those in Israel who have rejected the message of Jesus' representatives is here a matter of the judgment which is to come, not an accomplished fact in the life of the community. Q is interested less in social constitution that in final justice. The result is that it comes to the brink of replacing Israel with a new model, the church, without actually doing so.

The Circle of Peter

Peter shared with Jesus the hope of a climactic disclosure of divine power, signaled in the willingness of nations to worship on Mount Zion. That hope is certainly attested within sources attested as influential by the first century c.e. Chief among them, from the point of view of its influence upon the New Testament, is the book of Zechariah. Zechariah provided the point of departure for Jesus' inclusive program of purity and forgiveness as the occasions of the kingdom. Jesus is said to have mentioned the prophet by name (see Matthew 23:34–36; Luke 11:49–51).

The book programmatically concerns the establishment of restored worship in the Temple, especially at the feast of Sukkoth (14:16–19). "All the nations" are to go up to Jerusalem annually for worship (v. 16), and the transformation of which that worship is part involves the provision of "living waters" from the city (v. 8, cf. John 4:10, 14). That image is related to an earlier "fountain opened for the house of David and the inhabitants of Jerusalem in view of sin and uncleanness" (13:1). Here we see the association of forgiveness and purity which is a feature of Jesus' program, as well as the notion of an immediate release, without any mention of sacrifice, from what keeps Israel from God. God himself is held to arrange the purity he requires, so that the sacrifice he desires might take place.

Zechariah features the commissioning of a priest (3; see Matthew 16:18, 19), an oracle against swearing (5:3, 4; see Matthew 5:33–37), a vision of a king humbly riding an ass (9:9; see Matthew 21:1–9; Mark 11:1–10; Luke 19:28–40; John 12:12–19), the prophetic receipt of thirty shekels of silver in witness against the owners of sheep (11:4–17; see Matthew 26:14–16; 27:3–10; cf. Mark 14:10, 11; Luke 22:3–6). It is obvious that the connections between Jesus' ministry and Zechariah do not amount to a precise agenda, and Matthew clearly reflects a tendency to increase the fit between the two. But the similarities are suggestive of Jesus' appropriation of Zechariah's prophecy of eschatological purity, as a final, more fundamental connection would indicate. The climactic vision of Zechariah insists that every vessel in Jerusalem will belong to the Lord, and become a fit vessel for sacrifice. As part of that insistence, the text asserts that no trader will be allowed in the Temple (14:20, 21). In the light of Zechariah, Jesus' occupation of the Temple appears an enactment of prophetic purity in the face of a commercial innovation, a vigorous insistence that God would prepare his own people and vessels for eschatological worship.

Peter perpetuated that vision by means of his fidelity both to breaking bread at home with the disciples and in worship within the Temple (see Acts 2:42–47). The common ownership of possessions in Jerusalem, which is emphasized in the description of Petrine practice (in addition to Acts 2:44–45, see 4:32–5:11), also has its roots in the Zecharian vision. Commonality of goods in the vicinity of the Temple implied that no buying or selling would be at issue; it was an extension of just the principle that Jesus had died defending. At the same time, Acts portrays Peter's activity much further afield; he is active in Samaria (8:14–25), Lydda (9:32–35), Joppa (9:36–43), and Caesarea (10:1–48; 12:19). Paul refers, as if as a matter of course, to Peter's presence personally in Antioch (see Galatians 2:11–14), and by the time of the pseudepigraphic 1 Peter (written around 90 C.E.) he is pictured as writing from Rome with Silvanus (see 1 Peter 5:12–13) to churches in the north of Asia Minor (1:1, 2). If, then, Jerusalem was a center for Peter in the way it was not for Jesus, it was certainly not the boundary of his operations. Rather, the Temple appears to have featured as the hub of a much wider network of contacts which linked Jews from abroad and even Gentiles (see Acts 10:1–48; 11:1–18, 15:1–11 with Galatians 2:1–14) in common recognition of a new, eschatological fellowship defined by the teaching of Jesus.

The key to connection between Peter's residence in Jerusalem and his activity in Syria and beyond is provided by the vision related in his name as the warrant for his visit to the house of Cornelius, a Roman centurion (Acts 10:1–48). Peter is praying on a rooftop in Joppa around noon. His vision occurs while he is hungry, and concerns a linen lowering from heaven, filled with four-footed animals, reptiles, and birds. A voice says, "Arise, Peter, slaughter and eat," and he refuses (in words reminiscent of Ezekiel 4:14). But a voice again says, "What God has cleansed, you will not defile" (see Acts 10:9–16).

Peter defends his baptisms in the house of Cornelius on the basis of his vision in the course of a dispute with those who argued that circumcision was a requirement of adherence to the movement (Acts 11:1–18). He also cites his activity among non-Jews at a later point, in the context of what has come to be called the Apostolic Council (Acts 15:7–11). Throughout, the position of Peter appears to have been consistent: God may make, and has made, eschatological exceptions to the usual practice of purity. Those exceptions include the extension of baptism to uncircumcised men, and fellowship with them. From the point of view of both Paul and James, Peter's behavior in Antioch was inconsistent. His commitment to fellowship caused him at first to join in Paul's habit of eating together with non-Jews, but the arrival of some people from James's group caused him then to withdraw from such fellowship (Galatians 2:12). Neither James nor Paul, however, did Peter justice.

James, as we have seen, urged a classic definition upon the followers of Jesus. Paul (as we shall see) experimented with a radically new definition: Israel consists of those who believe in Christ Jesus (Galatians 3:7–14). But Peter appears not to have engaged in questions of conceptual definition. Israel might remain Israel, under the normal understanding, but God's Spirit could also extend to non-Jews and justify their baptism (Acts 10:47). The same sort of conceptual silence in regard to Israel which is characteristic of Jesus' theology is also evident within Peter's.

Peter's emphasis upon the importance of Spirit determined his attitude toward the Scriptures of Israel. In the Transfiguration (Matthew 16:28–17:9; Mark 9:1–10; Luke 9:27–36), for example, Jesus stands side by side with Moses and Elijah; the Son of God and the prophetic covenant together mediate God's own Spirit. But social policy is left largely undefined under Peter's approach. According to Acts 15, Peter concluded on the basis of God's gift of the Spirit to Gentiles that they could not be required to be circumcised (Acts 15:6–11). Yet Paul shows in Galatians 2 that Peter was not willing to make a general principle for or against Mosaic requirements; rather than follow a routine policy, Paul charged that Peter changed his mind when confronted with differing interpretations and practices. His apparent ambivalence reflects a commitment to the twin loyalties of a single son and a single law, together mediating the same spirit.

Despite the continuity of Peter's position with that of Jesus, it could not serve as a practical guide in framing a social identity for the followers of Jesus after the resurrection. The policy of Israel as you found it was wise in the case of Jesus, owing to the cultural and geographical limitation of his ministry. But as soon as his movement extended beyond the land—and more especially beyond the culture—of what was commonly agreed to be Israel, that policy could be portrayed as intellectually bankrupt and morally inconsistent. Was a group of non-Jewish believers who accepted baptism an example of Israel or not? The strength of James's position and Paul's also was that they provided a clear answer to that question, whereas Peter did not.

The Synoptic Gospels and Paul: Practicing the Body of Christ

The circles we have already considered contributed the principal cycles of tradition that stand behind the Synoptic Gospels: groups defined by their loyalty to Peter, or to James, or to the Mishnaic authority of Q. In addition, there was a revision of the Jacobean cycle, promulgated in Greek by Joseph Barsabbas and Silas in Antioch after the council ca. 49 C.E. (see Acts 15:22–33). After 70 C.E., "the little apocalypse" (reflected in Mark 13 and its parallels), a Syrian addition to the Jacobean revision, was composed; it is a response to James's martyrdom and the Temple's destruction.

These cycles were amalgamated into a curriculum for those preparing for baptism in Jesus' name within the many Hellenistic cities where churches emerged. The very name for "church," *ekklesia*, reflects the consciousness of a people who see themselves as "called out" from their surroundings. The term is used in ordinary, secular Greek to refer to an assembly of people summoned for a purpose, and it is applied in the book of Acts both to the congregation of the Israelites whom Moses led out to the wilderness (Acts 7:38) and to the congregation of Jesus' followers in Jerusalem who were subject to persecution (Acts 8:1). The term appears some 114 times in the New Testament and is by far the most common designation of Christian groups, whether considered as the local assembly or as a single movement.

Those who were called out from their usual style of life for baptism required a concentrated education in the life of faith; after all, many of those who were attracted to the teaching of Jesus had had no prior background in Judaism, and no specific information in regard to Jesus himself. The first ecumenical catechesis of the primitive church, developed originally in Antioch, is reflected in the Synoptic Gospels. The most likely exponent of the unified catechesis is Barnabas. His standing is quite consistent with the wide acceptance of the Synoptic tradition. The greater accommodation to Jacobean influence in the Synoptics as compared to Paul is also explained by the influence of Barnabas (see Galatians 2:13).

The Synoptic catechesis was a paradigm that was then developed and published in Rome (Mark, ca. 73 c.e.), Damascus (Matthew, ca. 80 c.e.), and Antioch itself (Luke, ca. 90 c.e.). The spine of each Gospel is the narrative catechesis of the Petrine cycle, supplemented by the mishnah of the Twelve (Q), the Jacobean revision of material, and the apocalyptic addendum of Joseph Barsabbas and Silas. Similarities and differences among the Synoptic Gospels are best understood as functions of the particular sort of catechesis—systematic preparation of catechumens—that was current in each community. No Gospel is simply a copy of another; rather, each represents the choices among varying traditions, written and/or oral, and the development of those traditions that had taken place in a given locality.[12]

Barnabas is blamed by Paul in Galatians for being taken up in the "hypocrisy" of Peter and the "rest of the Jews," because Peter had separated from the company of gentiles he had formally eaten with (Galatians 2:11–13). Peter's position, as we have seen, was in fact a function of his conviction that God's Spirit in baptism overcame the impurity of non-Jews, without abrogating God's choice of Israel. Barnabas can be expected to have been more rigorous than Peter in regard to questions of purity and impurity. As a Levite from Cyprus (Acts 4:36), he had an awareness of what it meant to live with priestly concerns in a Hellenistic environment. His devotion to the Petrine understanding of pure worship is marked by his willingness to sell off his property in order to join the group in Jerusalem (Acts 4:37).

---

[12] See Bruce Chilton, *Profiles of a Rabbi: Synoptic Opportunities in Reading about Jesus*, Brown Judaic Studies 177 (Atlanta: Scholars Press, 1989).

Barnabas, then, was associated with Peter before he was associated with Paul, so that Paul's attempt (as reflected in Galatians) to claim Barnabas's loyalty in opposition to Peter had little chance of success. After all, it was Barnabas's introduction which brought Paul into contact with the apostles in Jerusalem, despite Paul's well deserved reputation as an enemy of the movement (Acts 9:27–30). Whatever disagreements might have stood between James and Barnabas, Barnabas enjoyed the implicit trust of the church in Jerusalem. When followers of Jesus from Cyprus and Cyrene preached to non-Jews in Antioch and enjoyed success, Barnabas was commissioned to investigate (see Acts 11:19–26). It was during the course of a sojourn which lasted over a year that Barnabas introduced Paul to Antioch.

Acts describes Barnabas in the context of his visit in Antioch as "a good man, full of holy spirit and faith" (Acts 11:24). The reference to the Spirit attests his connection with the Petrine understanding of discipleship which he had fully accepted. Given Barnabas's status as a Levite, and the confidence invested in him by the church in Jerusalem when an issue of purity arose (Acts 11:22), it is natural to infer that Barnabas was discrete in his social contacts with non-Jewish believers. Even Paul does not say of Barnabas, as he does of Peter, that he ate commonly with non-Jews, and then separated when emissaries from James arrived (see Galatians 2:11–13). Barnabas's policy was probably consistent, accepting non-Jews in baptism, and continuing to treat them as non-Jews after baptism.

Barnabas represents a committed attempt to convert Peter's dual loyalty, to the Spirit in baptism and to circumcision and purity within Israel, into a coherent social policy. Paul calls the attempt hypocritical because he did not agree with it; in fact it was a brilliant effort to combine inclusiveness with integrity. Acts attempts to minimize the difference between Barnabas and Paul, turning it into a limited matter of who should accompany them in a visit of churches they had preached to previously (see Acts 15:36–41). In fact, their dispute after the council turned around what had always divided them: Barnabas's commitment to separate fellowship in order to preserve the purity of Israel. The person Barnabas wanted to come with them, John called Mark, had been associated with the circle of Peter and was well received in Jerusalem (see Acts 12:12–17, 25; 13:5, 15). (Paul no doubt feared that John Mark would further extend the influence of James.) Barnabas stood by the policy that fellowship among non-Jewish Christians was authorized by their baptism and to be endorsed, but that the fellowship of Israel was also to be maintained.

The social policy of the community as envisaged by Barnabas is instanced in the two signs of feeding, of the 5,000 and the 4,000. Both stories reflect a eucharistic fellowship with Jesus, one for Israel and one for non-Jews. That crucial meaning is the key to what has long perplexed commentators, the significance of the numerological symbols which are embedded in each story and which function in contrast to one another.[13]

In the first story (Matthew 14:13–21; Mark 6:32–44; Luke 9:10b–17), the eucharistic associations are plain: Jesus blesses and breaks the bread prior to distribution (Matthew 14:19; Mark 6:41; Luke 9:16). That emphasis so consumes the story that the fish—characteristic among Christian eucharistic symbols[14]—are of subsidiary significance by the end of the passage (compare Mark 6:43 with Matthew 14:20 and Luke 9:17). Whatever the pericope represented originally, it becomes a eucharistic narrative in the Barnaban presentation. Jesus gathers people in an orderly way (see Matthew 14:18; Mark 6:39, 40; Luke 9:14, 15), by "symposia" as Mark literally has it (6:39); without that order, they might be described as sheep without a shepherd (Mark 6:34).

The Didache 9:4 relates the prayer that, just as bread is scattered on the mountains (in the form of wheat) and yet may be gathered into one, so the church might be gathered into the Father's kingdom. The 5,000 congregate in such a manner, their very number a multiple of the prophetic gathering in 2 Kings 4:42–44. There, Elishah feeds 100 men with twenty loaves of barley, so that the multitude in Mark 6 (and its Synoptic parallels) has been increased by factors of ten and of five, while the amount of food has been quartered. The number ten is of symbolic significance within the biblical tradition, most famously in the case of the ten "words" or commandments of Exodus 34:28. The number five, although it derives from

---

[13] See Bruce Chilton, *A Feast of Meanings. Eucharistic Theologies from Jesus through Johannine Circles*; Supplements to *Novum Testamentum* 72 (Leiden: Brill, 1994).

[14] See C. H. Dodd, *Historical Tradition in the Fourth Gospel* (Cambridge: Cambridge University Press, 1965), 200–201; W. D. Davies and Dale C. Allison, *A Critical and Exegetical Commentary on the Gospel according to Saint Matthew*: International Critical Commentary (Edinburgh: Clark, 1991), 2:481, 493, 494, citing 2 Baruch 29:3–8 and 4 Ezra 6:52.

the story of Elijah itself, also corresponds to the Pythagorean number of man, in that the outline of four limbs and a head approximating to a pentagram.[15]

The authority of the Twelve is a marked concern within the story. Their return in Matthew 14:12b, 13; Mark 6:30, 31; Luke 9:10a after their commission (see Matthew 10:1–42; Mark 6:7–13; Luke 9:1–6) is what occasions the feeding, and their function in the proceedings is definite: Jesus gives them the bread, to give it to others (Matthew 14:19; Mark 6:41; Luke 9:16). Their place here is cognate with their position within another pericope (from the Jacobean cycle) which features the twelve, the parable of the sower, its interpretation, and the assertion that only the twelve possess the mystery of the kingdom (Matthew 13:1–17; Mark 4:1–12; Luke 8:4–10). Such a mystery is also conveyed here, in the assertion that twelve baskets of fragments were gathered after the 5,000 ate. The lesson is evident: the Twelve, the counterparts of the twelve tribes of Israel, will always have enough to feed the church, which is understood to realize the identity of Israel in the wilderness.

The story of the feeding of the 4,000 (Matthew 15:32–39; Mark 8:1–10) follows so exactly that of the 5,000, its omission by Luke may seem understandable, simply as a redundant doublet. But there are distinctive elements in the second feeding story. The 4,000 are a multiple of the four points of the compass, the story follows that of the Canaanite or Syrophoenician woman (Matthew 15:21–28; Mark 7:24–30), and it concerns a throng from a number of different areas and backgrounds (see Matthew 15:21, 29; Mark 7:24, 31). The issue of non-Jewish contact with Jesus is therefore marked here, in a way it is not in the case of the feeding of the 5,000.[16] Likewise, the number 7, the number of bushels of fragments here collected, corresponds to the deacons of the Hellenists in the church of Jerusalem (cf. Acts 6:1–6), and is related to the traditional number of the seventy nations within Judaism. Moreover, the reference to Jesus as giving thanks (*eucharistesas*) over the bread in Matthew 15:36; Mark 8:6 better corresponds to the Hellenistic version of the Petrine Eucharist

---

[15] See Annemarie Schimmel, "Numbers: An Overview," *The Encyclopedia of Religion* (ed. M. Eliade; New York: Macmillan, 1987), 13–19.

[16] See John W. Bowman, *The Gospel of Mark: The New Christian Passover Haggadah*: Studia Postbiblica (Leiden: Brill, 1965), 176–178.

in Luke 22:17, 19; and 1 Corinthians 11:24 than does "he blessed" (*eulogesen*) in Matthew 14:19; Mark 6:39, which better corresponds to the earlier Petrine formula in Matthew 26:26; Mark 14:22.

The Lukan omission of such stories, in fact of the whole of what corresponds to Mark 6:45–8:26 (conventionally designated as "the great omission" of Mark by Luke) seems natural, once their meaning is appreciated: they concern the sense of Jesus in an environment characterized by a mixture of Jews and gentiles. Luke takes up that theme in Acts, and regards its reversion into the ministry of Jesus as anachronism.

After the second feeding, Jesus rebukes his disciples for a failure to understand when he warns them about the leaven of the Pharisees and Sadducees, and asks whether they truly grasp the relationship between the number 12 and the 5,000 and the number 7 and the 4,000 (Matthew 16:5–12; Mark 8:14–21). In the mind of the Hellenistic catechesis, the meaning is clear, and its implications for eucharistic discipline are evident. Celebration of Eucharist in its truest sense is neither to be limited to Jews, as the Jacobean program would have it, nor forced upon communities in a way that would require Jews to accept reduced standards of purity, as the Pauline program would have it. There is for the Hellenistic catechesis of which the Synoptic transformation is a monument, an ongoing apostolate for Jews and gentiles, prepared to feed as many of the church that gather.

For all the careful power of the Barnaban symbolism within the stories of the 5,000 and the 4,000, a largely inadvertent development of meaning was even more widely influential. When Jesus distributed bread during the course of his last meals in Jerusalem, he referred to it as his "flesh." He meant that his fellowship in meals took over from the practice of sacrifice in the Temple; similarly, the celebratory wine took over the function of blood. But by the year 50 C.E., when the Barnaban catechesis emerged within an elaborate narrative of Jesus' passion, a shift in meaning had occurred.

From the time that the narrative of the passion provided the governing context of Jesus' words during his eucharistic celebrations, the bread and the wine were related to Jesus' body and blood in a personal sense. The constant focus on Jesus' own fate within the passion narrative made that development inevitable. The flesh and blood of sacrifice were transformed into means of solidarity with the noble martyr. That transformation was not merely a function of the linguistic decision to render "flesh" (*bisra'*) in Aramaic with "body" (*soma*) in Greek, although that decision fed a deeper, cultural process of transformation. There was no possibility of preventing at least some Hellenistic Christians who followed the eucharistic practice of Synoptics from conceiving of Jesus himself as consumed in the bread and wine.

Jesus' last supper was naturally compared to initiation into mystery within Hellenistic Christianity. He was a new Dionysos, historical rather than mythical, who gave himself, flesh and blood, in the meals that were held in his name. After all, he had said "This is my body," and "This is my blood." For many Hellenistic Christians, that could only mean that Jesus referred to himself: bread and wine were tokens of Jesus, which became his body and blood when believers consumed them.

The Johannine discourse concerning the bread of life, following upon a paschal reading of the feeding of the 5,000, addressed the challenges of a Hellenistic understanding of Eucharist as mystery. By means of a nuanced tension between "flesh" in its ordinary sense (6:63), as alien from God, and Jesus' "flesh" as the medium through which the son of man was sent by God to offer life (6:53–59), the Johannine discourse avoided any crude reduction of Eucharist to the consumption of a god. Jesus' flesh is that bread which he gives (6:51), the true manna, a miracle which animates the world (6:32, 33), because he is himself the bread of life (6:35, 48, 51). The essential nuance, apart from which the discourse is not understandable, is that Jesus' "flesh" as consumed in Eucharist is not flesh in the usual understanding, but the means by which he offers spirit and life (6:63). Yet however sophisticated the discourse may be, it implicitly accepts that the language of mystery is appropriate, suitably refined, for the description of Eucharist. For that reason, the fourth Gospel marks the point at which the Christian practice of Eucharist self-consciously and definitively parted from Judaism, even as imagery of Exodus and Passover was embraced and developed.

John's theology held that personal solidarity with Jesus was effected in eucharistic practice. That overarching meaning could be developed, because the Barnaban cycle had already associated Jesus' "body" and "blood" with the passion and had established the eucharistic meanings of the feeding stories. But unlike John, the Barnaban cycle held to the integrity of Israel as well as the inclusion of non-Jews.

John presents no analog of the feeding of the 4,000, because the scope of the feeding of the 5,000 is already held to include "All that the father gives me" (6:37). Moreover, John places Philip within the episode (6:5, 7), and Philip is understood to be Jesus' contact with "Greeks" (so John 12:20–50).

Contrast with the Johannine presentation of the eucharistic feeding of the 5,000 makes the Barnaban framing of both feeding stories all the more striking by comparison. The twelve baskets are available for Israel; the seven baskets are available for non-Jews who are baptized. Both groups, each belonging to the church of all those who are called out by God and who accept to bear the name of Christ, enjoy solidarity with Christ himself by partaking of his body and blood. The body of Christ had become an identity which all could share within the church, whatever else might divide them.

As a consequence of his association with Barnabas in the leadership of Hellenistic congregations (in Antioch preeminently), Paul was well familiar with the eucharistic meaning of the phrase "the body of Christ." As John A. T. Robinson pointed out in a study that remains valuable, "the words of institution of the Last Supper, 'This is my body,' contain the only instance of a quasi-theological use of the word that is certainly pre-Pauline."[17]

For Paul, Eucharist involved an active recollection of the passion: "For as many times as you eat this bread and drink the cup, you announce the Lord's death, until he comes" (1 Corinthians 11:26). Paul repeats a key terms of reference within the eucharistic tradition in his own voice and draws his conclusion ("for," *gar*), which is that the significance of the Eucharist is to be found in the death of Jesus. Drinking the cup is an act that declares that Jesus died and awaits his *parousia* at one and the same time.

Paul's assumption is that Jesus' last meal, the paradigm of the Lord's Supper, was of covenantal significance, a sacrificial "memorial" which was associated with the death of Jesus in particular. His wording, which refers to Jesus' cup as a new covenant in his blood (1 Corinthians 11:25), agrees with the later version of Petrine tradition which is reflected in Luke (22:20), the Synoptic Gospel that has

---

[17] *The Body, A Study in Pauline Theology*: Studies in Biblical Theology 5 (London: SCM, 1961), 56.

the strongest associations with Antioch. It is likely that Paul's version of the Petrine tradition derived from his period in Antioch, his primary base by his own testimony (in Galatians 2) until his break with Barnabas.

Paul's development of the concept of "the body of Christ" was just that: a development, rather than an original contribution. His commitment to the traditional theology was fierce, as he goes on in 1 Corinthians to indicate (11:27–30):

> So whoever eats the bread and drinks the cup of the Lord unworthily will be answerable to the body and blood of the Lord. Let a man examine himself, and then eat from the bread and drink from the cup. For one who eats and drinks without discerning the body, eats and drinks judgment against himself. For this reason, many are weak and ill among you, and quite a number have died.

Paul's last statement, which associates disease with unworthy participation in the Eucharist, shows how near the symbolic association of the bread and wine with Jesus' body and blood came to being an overt claim for the miraculous power of that food.

Long before the Johannine comparison of Jesus' flesh with the manna God gave his people in the wilderness, Paul had arrived at the same thought. The analogy is developed in the material immediately preceding Paul's presentation of eucharistic tradition (1 Corinthians 10). Christ himself is presented as the typological meaning of Passover, as the entire complex of the exodus—including crossing the sea and eating miraculous food (Exodus 13–17)—in 1 Corinthians 10:6. The cloud which led Israel, and the sea they crossed, correspond to baptism (vv. 1, 2), while the food they ate and the water provided from the rock correspond to Eucharist (vv. 3–4). Typology also enables Paul to make the connection between the idolatry in the wilderness and the fornication in Corinth which is one of his preoccupations (vv. 6–14), but the initial correspondence, between exodus and both baptism and Eucharist, is essential to his argument, and he belabors the point with the introduction, "I would not have you ignorant, brethren" (v. 1).

Within the order of exposition Paul follows, the imagery begins with the cloud and the sea, proceeds through the food in the wilderness, and ends with the water from the rock; the correspondence is to the water (and Spirit) of baptism, the bread of Eucharist, and the

wine of Eucharist respectively (1 Corinthians 10:1–4). The typological key to the sequence is provided by the Pauline exposition of the
rock from which drink flowed: "and the rock was Christ" (10:4). He
demonstrates how, in the setting of Hellenistic Christianity, a paschal
reading of the Eucharist was an important element within a typology of Jesus himself as Passover.

It has frequently been objected that the eucharistic meaning of
"the body of Christ" does not explain Paul's usage overall, because
the concept of eating the body is quite different from being the
body.[18] But the transition from the eucharistic meaning of the phrase
to the corporate meaning of the phrase is not strained, as Paul himself indicates (1 Corinthians 10:16–17):

> The cup of blessing which we bless, is it not fellowship in the blood
> of Christ? The bread which we break, is it not fellowship in the body
> of Christ? Because there is one bread, we are one body, although we
> are many, because we all share from the one bread.

Paul goes on in his letters to develop that insight in many ways, and
later writings in his name were to articulate the motif even further.
But in the passage just cited, Paul shows us both the origin and the
direction of his understanding of "the body of Christ." It begins with
the Hellenistic theology of Eucharist, in which consuming the bread
identifies the believer with Christ's death, and it consummates in the
declaration that all who share that bread are incorporated into Christ,
as into a single body.

The transition is natural for Paul, because he was familiar with
the Hellenistic conception of corporate "body," which was especially
popularized by Stoic writers. The evidence is neatly summarized by
Jürgen Becker:[19]

> Agrippa M. Lanatus, for example, exhorted the plebeians not to break
> off fellowship with the city of Rome because, as in a human organ-
> ism, all members need each other (Livy, *Ab urbe condita* 2.32–33). Plato
> also compares the state with an organism and, as in 1 Cor. 12:26,
> emphasizes the suffering and rejoicing of the members together (Plato,

---

[18] See Oscar Cullman's article in the *Theological Dictionary of the New Testament* (ed.
G. Friedrich, trans. G. W. Bromiley; Grand Rapids: Eerdmans, 1979), 6:95–99, 97.

[19] *Paul: Apostle to the Gentiles* (trans. O. C. Dean; Louisville: Westminster/John
Knox, 1993), 428.

Republic 462C–D). Seneca can see the state as the body of the emperor, who is the soul of the body (Seneca, *De clementia* 1.5.1).

Becker claims that Paul "was probably the first to transfer this idea to a religious communion," but that is an incautious generalization. Philo, after all, observes that the high priest's sacrifice welds Israel together "into one and the same family as though it were a single body" (Philo, *De specialibus legibus* 3.131).

Becker is on firmer ground in his observation that, for Paul, "the body of Christ" is no mere metaphor, but describes the living solidarity of those who share the Spirit of God by means of baptism and Eucharist. Again, Paul is the best commentator on his own thought. He explains in a fairly predictable way how diverse members belong to a single body in 1 Corinthians 12, just after he has treated of the Eucharist. In the midst of that discussion, he puts forward the "body of Christ" as the principal definition of the church (1 Corinthians 12:12–13):

> For just as the body is one and has many members, and all the members of the body (being many) are one body, so is Christ. For in one spirit we were all baptized into one body—whether Jews or Greeks, slave or free—and we all were given to drink of one spirit.

By focusing on the "body" as the medium of eucharistic solidarity and then developing its corporate meaning, Paul turns the traditional, Petrine understanding of Spirit (as received in baptism) into the single principle of Christian identity. His reply to any attempt to form discrete fellowships within the church will now always be, "Is Christ divided?" (so 1 Corinthians 1:13).

The further articulation of "the body of Christ" by Paul and his successors is easily traced. As in the case of 1 Corinthians 12 (and, by way of anticipation, 1 Corinthians 6:15), the point in Romans 12:4–8 is that the society of those who are joined in Christ's body is itself a body which finds its unity in diversity and its diversity in unity. Two deutero-Pauline letters, Colossians and Ephesians, shift the application of the image of the body. Because the identification of the church as Christ's body is taken as found in Colossians (see Colossians 1:18, 24), Christ himself is portrayed as the head of that body (Colossians 1:18; 2:19), in order to stress his preeminence. That portrayal is pursued in Ephesians (1:22–23; 4:15–16), to the point that Christ as "head" of the church can be thought of as distinct

from her, along the lines of a husband from a wife (Ephesians
5:21–33).

The startling quality of the Pauline conception of "the body of
Christ" does not derive from how it is developed within the letters
written by Paul or later attributed to Paul. That trajectory is a relatively consistent product of the interaction between the eucharistic
theology of solidarity with Christ, which was common within Hellenistic
Christianity, and the quasi-Stoic language of incorporation into Christ
which Paul himself had learned in Tarsus, his home. The radical
feature of Pauline usage is not to be found in the development of
the concept itself, but rather in the claim that the church is defined
solely in respect of this "body." Whether Jew or Greek, only incorporation into Christ mattered to Paul (so 1 Corinthians 12:12–13).
The consequence of that univocal definition is spelled out in Ephesians
(after the motif of the body has been invoked): the dividing line
between Jews and non-Jews had been set aside definitively in Christ
(Ephesians 2:11–22). That immediately implied, however, that the
reality of unbelievers in Israel, as well as of non-Jews who refused
to join the "Israel of God" (Galatians 6:13) which was defined by
faith in Christ, had to be confronted, not only as a painful condition, but as a theological challenge. What Christianity made of that
challenge is addressed in chapter five.

D. "Hear, Israel, the Lord Our God, the Lord Is One": Judaism

Beginning with the present: Israel today commonly refers to "the
state of Israel," "the Jewish state." It is a category of contemporary
politics, not of classical theology. Not only so, but when, within
Judaism, people use the word Israel, they tell a story that concerns
a singular group, sharing a common genealogy and culture and history (in contemporary language: "consciousness" and "ethnicity" and
"soul"). Told in the secular framework of nationality, the ethnic-
historical story of Israel obscures the true meaning of Israel in classical Judaism. And Judaism's continuators in Christianity, for their
own reasons, from the very beginning viewed Israel as "the Jews,"
and "the Jews" as an ethnic entity, not a supernatural gathering of

God's people. The upshot is, to understand Israel as the social metaphor of Judaism, we have to set aside familiar definitions and consider an unconventional conception, one that is authentic to the definitive sources of Judaism.

When, in its creed, Judaism proclaims "our God is one," it means, "one for all mankind," the only God. That is the premise of monotheism. But its continuators in Christianity and Islam describe Judaism as a particularistic religion, maintaining that "the one and only God is ours alone," with that "us" standing for an ethnic group, formed by birth and not by faith. Islam describes itself as universal and inclusive, bringing knowledge of God to all mankind, taking up the work of all prior revelations vouchsafed by God and providing the final and definitive one. Christianity explicitly aims to eliminate the boundaries that separate Greek from Israelite, slave from freeborn, male from female, and all the rest. And Judaism speaks of Israel, a most particular term indeed. The ethnicity of Judaism is supposed to derive from its emphasis upon genealogy: birth into the people of Israel via a Jewish mother. A religion one gains by endowment at birth then contrasts with a religion one enters by adoption through conversion or baptism; the one is ethnic, the other universal. The one makes distinctions by reason of birth, the other makes no distinctions among peoples or races or classes at all. That is the basis for the classification of Judaism as ethnic and of Islam and Christianity as universal.

But in normative Judaism, ethnicity played no role of consequence. That is because Judaism in its normative sources speaks not often of "the Jew" (an ethnic term) but very often of Israel. To be Israel in that Judaism meant to live the Godly life in accord with the divinely revealed Torah of Sinai; welcome to join in that holy way of life was any human being that cared to come "under the wing's of God's presence in the world," as the appropriate language framed matters. The Judaism that predominated from the early centuries of the Common Era to our own day forms a religious system that is universal in focus, transnational in location and loyalty, surpassing considerations of ethnic origin alone and receiving as equals all who undertake to accept "the yoke of Heaven" and "the yoke of the Torah," in the language of theology. A gentile enters that "holy Israel" of Judaism by a profession of faith, inclusive of baptism, for women and men, and circumcision in the covenant of Abraham, for men. This person was not meant to suffer discrimination or diminished status by reason of his or her origin elsewhere than in the communion of holy Israel.

To be sure, the home-born belonged by birth, not by a rite of entry, for the conception of Israel as an enduring social entity, deriving as it does from the scriptures of ancient Israel, encompasses an ongoing social entity formed by appeal to common origin with Abraham and Sarah and their children through time. But that social entity, beginning to end, is supernatural, formed by God's command and act, and whether joined by birth or by choice, is uniform and one. Any confusion between that transcendental Israel defined by the Torah and this-worldly social entities formed of persons of common origin, any conception that Judaism is not a religion but (merely) a genealogy, any notion that to be a Jew is innate and instinctual and racial—these contradict the explicit theology of the Torah. But for Judaism, that theology defines the norms and establishes the truth.

In the religion of Judaism, Israel stands for the holy people, whom God has called into being through Abraham and Sarah and their descendants, to whom the prophetic promises were made, and with whom the covenants were entered. In every form of Judaism based on Scripture, Israel is a theological category, not a fact of sociology or ethnic culture or secular politics. The Israel of Judaism forms a supernatural social entity, "chosen," "holy," subject to God's special love and concern. That Israel is not to be confused with the Jewish people, an ethnic group, the people of Israel in a this-worldly framework, let alone the state of Israel, a modern nation-state. Israel in Judaism compares to the Torah, in that, just as the latter is not just another book, so the former is not just another social entity. Just as the story of the Torah speaks of transcendent matters, so the tale of Israel, in Judaism, tells of God's relationship with humanity through the instrument God has chosen for self-manifestation: "You alone have I singled out of all the families of the earth—that is why I will call you to account for all your iniquities," as the prophet Amos put it (Amos 3:2).

Every Judaism uses the word Israel to refer to the social entity that it proposes to establish or define, and all Judaisms deem their Israels to be in continuity with the Israel of whom the Hebrew

Scriptures speak. Some deem the connection to be genealogical and fundamentally ethnic, putting forth a secular definition of their Israel. Rabbinic Judaism defines its Israel in supernatural terms, deeming the social entity to form a transcendental community, by faith. To Rabbinic Judaism Israel does not speak of a merely-ethnic, this-worldly people, but rather a social entity defined by matters of supernatural genealogy, on the one side, and religious conversion, on the other. That is shown by the simple fact that a gentile of any origin or status, slave or free, Greek or barbarian, may enter its Israel on equal terms with those born into the community, becoming thereby children of Abraham and Sarah. The children of converts become Israelite without qualification. No distinction is made between the child of a convert and the child of a native-born Israelite. Since that fact bears concrete and material consequences, e.g., in the right to marry any other Israelite without distinction by reason of familial origin, it follows that the Israel of Rabbinic Judaism must be understood in a wholly theological framework. This Judaism knows no distinction between children of the flesh and children of the promise and therefore cannot address a merely-ethnic Israel, because for Rabbinic Judaism, Israel is always and only defined by the Torah received and represented by "our sages of blessed memory" as the word of God, and never by the happenstance of secular history.

That does not mean that Rabbinic Judaism's Israel ignored this-worldly facts of the life of everyday Israel after the flesh. The fundamental social unit in Israelite society was the household, encompassing the large-scale economic unit of the farmer, his wife and children, slaves, dependent craftsmen and artisans, and reaching outward to other such households to form a neatly-composed social unit, the village—and like villages. But Rabbinic Judaism's systemic social entity transformed the extended family into a representation, in the here-and-now, of mythic Israel. In that way, the social unit adopted for itself and adapted for its purposes the social entity of Scripture and identified itself with the whole life and destiny of that entity. Clearly, therefore, Rabbinic Judaism set forth a theory of the ethnic entity that invoked a metaphor in order to explain the group and identify it. That fundamental act of metaphorization, from which all else follows, was the comparison of persons—Jews—of the here-and-now to the Israel of which the Hebrew Scriptures—the Torah—

speak, and the consequent identification of those Jews with that Israel. Treating the social group—two or more persons—as other than they actually are in the present, as more than a (mere) given, means that the group is something else than what it appears to be.

To explain what is at stake in the category, Israel, we have to recognize that the raw materials of definition are not the facts of the social order—how things are in practical terms—but the imagination of the system-builders. An Israel—that is, a theory of what Israel is and who is counted as part of Israel or as himself or herself Israel—in any Judaic system finds its shape and structure within that system. That Israel takes shape out of materials selected by the systemic framers from a miscellaneous, received or invented repertoire of possibilities. It goes without saying that, in the context of the description of the structure of a Judaism, its Israel is the sole Israel (whether social group, whether caste, whether family, whether class or "population," and whether any of the many social entities admirably identified by sociology) defined by that Judaism. The best systemic indicator is a system's definition of its Israel, and Judaisms, or Judaic systems, from the priests' Pentateuchal system onward, made their statement principally through their response to the question framed in contemporary Judaic and Jewish-ethnic discourse as: "who is a Jew?"

But the systemic component, Israel, finds its definition within the systemic imagination, not in the raw materials of the social world beyond the system. For a system never accommodates the givens of politics and a sheltering society. The notion that society gives birth to religion is systemically beside the point. Systems do not recapitulate a given social order, they define one; and their framers, if they can, then go about realizing their fantasy. An Israel within a given Judaic system is the invention of the system's builders and presents traits that they deem self-evidently true. That is quite without regard to realities beyond the range of systemic control. All that the context presents is a repertoire of possibilities. The framers of the contents then make their choices among those possibilities, and, outside of the framework of the system, there is no predicting the shape and structure of those choices. The system unfolds within its own inner logic, making things up as it goes along—because it knows precisely how to do so.

Israel is the locus of the kingdom of God, since to Israel the Torah is given. Israel is a supernatural category, for Israel consists of all those who are born in Israel, *except for those who deny the principles of the faith*. The categories are defined in terms of belief: affirming a given doctrine, denying another. That fact bears in its wake the implication that Israel as a social entity, encompassing each of its members, is defined by reference to matters of correct doctrine. All "Israelites"—persons who hold the correct opinion—then constitute Israel. Here is an Israel that, at first glance, is defined not in relationships but intransitively and intrinsically. What this means, therefore, is that Israel is not a social entity at all like other social entities but an entity that finds definition, as to genus and not species, elsewhere.

A. All Israelites have a share in the world to come,
B. As it is said, "your people also shall be all righteous, they shall inherit the land forever; the branch of My planting, the work of My hands, that I may be glorified" (Is. 60:21).
C. And these are the ones who have no portion in the world to come:
D. He who says, the resurrection of the dead is a teaching which does not derive from the Torah, and the Torah does not come from Heaven; and an Epicurean.
E. R. Aqiba says, "Also: he who reads in heretical books,
F. "and he who whispers over a wound and says, 'I will put none of the diseases upon you which I have put on the Egyptians, for I am the Lord who heals you' (Ex. 15:26)."
G. Abba Saul says, "Also: He who pronounces the divine Name as it is spelled out."

Mishnah Sanhedrin 10.1

Israel is defined inclusively: to be Israel is to have a share in the world to come. Israel then is a social entity that is made up of those who share a common conviction, and that Israel therefore bears an other-worldly destiny.

Other social entities are not so defined within the Mishnah—and that by definition!—and it must follow that (an) Israel in the conception of the authorship of the Mishnah is sui generis, in that other social entities do not find their definition within the range of supernatural facts pertinent to Israel; an Israel is a social group that endows its individual members with life in the world to come; an Israel[ite] is one who enjoys the world to come. Excluded from this Israel are Israel[ite]s who within the established criteria of social identification exclude themselves. The power to define by relationships does not run out, however, since in this supernatural context of an Israel that is sui generis, we still know who is Israel because we are told who is "not-Israel," now, specific non-believers or sinners. These are, as we should expect, persons who reject the stated belief. We shall return to this matter in chapter five.

That Israel becomes Israel at Sinai through accepting the Torah is formulated in the following language:

A. "The Lord spoke to Moses saying, Speak to the Israelite people and say to them, I am the Lord your God":

B. R. Simeon b. Yohai says, "That is in line with what is said elsewhere: 'I am the Lord your God [who brought you out of the land of Egypt, out of the house of bondage]' (Ex. 20:2).

C. "'Am I the Lord, whose sovereignty you took upon yourself in Egypt?'

D. "They said to him, 'Indeed.'

E. "'Indeed you have accepted My dominion.'

F. "'They accepted My decrees: "You will have no other gods before me."'

G. "That is what is said here: 'I am the Lord your God,' meaning, 'Am I the one whose dominion you accepted at Sinai?'

H. "They said to him, 'Indeed.'

I. "'Indeed you have accepted My dominion.'

J. "'They accepted My decrees: "You shall not copy the practices of the land of Egypt where you dwelt, or of the land of Canaan to which I am taking you; nor shall you follow their laws."'"

Sifra to Ahare Mot CXCIV:II.1

But theories of divine origin of ethnic groups surely circulate broadly; so the claim that, because the Torah brings Israel into being, Israel therefore forms a supernatural social entity, not an ethnic group, need not be fully exposed in the statement just now given.

That gentiles belong on equal terms when they accept that same Torah that makes Israel the people of God changes the ethnic into the universal. In what follows we find the opposite of the view that "God is our God and not yours, God of our way of life and not yours." Rather, we find the conception that God should be your God, not only ours; when God becomes your God, you become part of us; and the way of life that we follow is not "ours," but the one that God demands of everyone. God's people comprises all who accept God's commandments; "we" are not "exclusive channels of divine grace," because God opens the way to everyone who wishes to accept that same grace that now we have. Proof that that is not an ethnic but a purely religious formulation of matters derives from the status of the gentile who accepts the Torah, the covenant, the commandments. The gentile is transformed, no longer what he or she had been, but now become utterly a new creation.

Accepting the Torah makes an ordinary human being into an Israelite. Then the proselyte becomes fully an Israelite. That is not a matter of mere theory. We recall how critical to the formation of Israel genealogy is, with Israel defined as wholly the descendants of the same couple, Abraham and Sarah. It must follow that if the gentile enters Israel, it must be either as a second class Israelite, the gentile possessing no physical genealogy at all; or as a first-class Israelite, the gentile deemed fully a child of Abraham and Sarah. That obviously is no matter of theory. Can the gentile's child marry a home-born Israelite? If so, then Israel is not ethnic at all; if not, then it is. And, as a matter of fact, the gentile's daughter may marry into the priesthood, if he studies the Torah and otherwise attains merit, like any other Israelite. It follows that the gentile is no longer a gentile upon entering Israel, and that can only mean, Israel forms not an ethnic category but a supernatural one. A concrete example suffices. Gentiles are not eligible to bring a sin offering, even if they inadvertently violate the religious duties that pertain to the children of Noah; but Israelites, including proselytes and slaves (purchased as gentiles and converted), do have to do so:

1. A. ["And the Lord said to Moses, 'Say to the people of Israel, "If anyone sins unwittingly in any of the things which the Lord has commanded not to be done, and does any one of them"'" (Lev. 4:1–12)].
   B. Israelites bring a sin-offering, but gentiles do not bring a sin-offering.
   C. It is not necessary to say that [they do not have to bring a sin-offering for inadvertently violating] religious duties that were not assigned to the children of Noah, but even for violating religious duties concerning which the children of Noah were commanded, they do not have to bring a sin-offering on that account.
2. A. "Say to the people of Israel": I know that the sin-offering is owing only from Israelites.
   B. How do I know that it is owing also from proselytes and bondmen?
   C. Scripture says, "If any one [sins unwittingly]."

Sifra to Vayyiqra Dibura Dehobah

It follows that the gentile stands on one side of the line, the convert or slave (one and the same thing) on the other, and there is no distinguishing converts from home-born Israelites. That is the force of the proof before us. One final point concludes the demonstration. The gentile not only enters first-class citizenship in Israel; a gentile who keeps the Torah is in the status of the high priest:

15. A. "by the pursuit of which man shall live":
    B. R. Jeremiah says, "How do I know that even a gentile who keeps the Torah, lo, he is like the high priest?
    C. "Scripture says, 'by the pursuit of which man shall live.'"
    D. And so he says, "'And this is the Torah of the priests, Levites, and Israelites,' is not what is said here, but rather, 'This is the Torah of the man, O Lord God' (2 Sam. 7:19)."
    E. And so he says, "'Open the gates and let priests, Levites, and Israelites will enter it' is not what is said, but rather, 'Open the gates and let the righteous nation, who keeps faith, enter it' (Is. 26:2)."
    F. And so he says, "'This is the gate of the Lord. Priests, Levites, and Israelites . . .' is not what is said, but rather, 'the righteous shall enter into it' (Ps. 118:20).
    G. And so he says, "'What is said is not, 'Rejoice, priests, Levites, and Israelites,' but rather, 'Rejoice, O righteous, in the Lord' (Ps. 33:1)."
    H. And so he says, "It is not, 'Do good, O Lord, to the priests, Levites, and Israelites,' but rather, 'Do good, O Lord, to the good, to the upright in heart' (Ps. 125:4)."
    I. "Thus, even a gentile who keeps the Torah, lo, he is like the high priest."

Sifra to Ahare Mot CXCIV:II

These statements, which exemplify a broad variety of formulations throughout the Rabbinic literature, suffice to demonstrate that Rabbinic Judaism in no way defined Israel in ethnic terms. One could not enter its Israel through ethnic-territorial assimilation, e.g., by marrying a Jew and following Jewish customs and ceremonies. One entered Israel only through an act that we must call religious conversion, but, when one did (or does), that person becomes fully and completely Israel, as though his or her ancestors had stood at Sinai. The reason, of course, is that by accepting the Torah, the convert personally takes up a position at Sinai.

Israel in the Mishnah

While in first century Christianity, Christians claimed to form the "Israel after the spirit," while Jews who did not adopt Christianity were merely "Israel after the flesh," and while Christianity would deny to the Jewish people the status of the Israel of whom Scriptures spoke and to whom the prophets prophesied, these views did not play a role in the thinking of the earlier Rabbinic writings about Israel. The Mishnah took shape at a time at which Christianity formed a minor irritant, perhaps in some places a competing Judaism, but not a formative component of the social order, and certainly not the political power that it was to become. Hence the Mishnah's framers' thinking about Israel in no way took account of the competing claim to form the true Israel put forth by Christianity; Israel remained intransitive, bearing no relationships to any other distinct social entity. The opposite of Israel in the Mishnah is the nations, on the one side, or "Levite, priest," on the other: always taxonomic, never defined out of relationship to others within the same theoretical structure. As we shall see, the opposite of Israel in the Yerushalmi— which came to closure after Christianity had become the state religion of the Roman Empire—became Rome, and Israel found itself defined as a family, with good and bad seed. Now the nations were differentiated, and a different world-order conceived; Israel entered into relationships of comparison and contrast, not merely hierarchy, because Christianity, sharing the same Scriptures, now called into question the very status of the Jews to constitute Israel.

As the Mishnah defines Israel, the category bears two identical meanings: the Israel of (all) the Jews now and here, but also the Israel of which Scripture—the Torah—spoke. And that encompassed both the individual and the group, without linguistic differentiation of any kind. Thus in the Mishnah Israel may refer to an individual Jew (always male) or to all Jews, that is, the collectivity of Jews. The individual woman is nearly always called *bat yisrael*, daughter of (an) Israel(ite). The sages in the Mishnah did not merely assemble facts and define the social entity as a matter of mere description of the given. Rather, they portrayed it as they wished to. They imputed to the social group, Jews, the status of a systemic entity, Israel. To others within Jewry it was not at all self-evident that all Jews constituted one Israel, and that that one Israel formed the direct and

immediate continuation, in the here-and-now, of the Israel of holy
writ and revelation. The Essene community at Qumran did not come
to that conclusion, and the sense and meaning of Israel proposed
by the authorships of the Mishnah and related writings did not strike
Philo as the main point at all. Paul, for his part, reflected on Israel
within categories not at all symmetrical with those of the Mishnah.

The Mishnaic identification of Jewry in the here-and-now with
the Israel of Scripture therefore constituted an act of metaphor, comparison, contrast, identification and analogy. It is that Judaism's most
daring social metaphor. Implicitly, moreover, the metaphor excluded
a broad range of candidates from the status of (an) Israel, the
Samaritans for one example, the scheduled castes of Mishnah-tractate
Qiddushin Chapter Four, for another. Calling (some) Jews Israel
established the comprehensive and generative metaphor that gives
the Mishnaic system its energy. From that metaphor all else derived
momentum.

The Mishnah defines Israel in antonymic relationships of two sorts,
first, Israel as against "not-Israel," gentile; and second, Israel as
against "priest," or "Levite." "Israel" serves as a taxonomic indicator, specifically part of a more encompassing system of hierarchization; Israel defined the frontiers, on the outer side of society, and
the social boundaries within, on the other. To understand the meaning of Israel as the Mishnah and its associated documents of the second and third centuries sort matters out, we need to consider the
sense of "gentile." The authorship of the Mishnah does not differentiate
among gentiles, who represent an undifferentiated mass. To the system of the Mishnah, whether or not a gentile is a Roman or an
Aramean or a Syrian or a Briton does not matter. That is to say,
differentiation among gentiles rarely, if ever, makes a difference in
systemic decision-making.

And, it is also the fact, in the system of the Mishnah, that in the
relationship at hand, Israel is not differentiated either. The upshot
is that just as "gentile" is an abstract category, so is Israel. "Kohen"
is a category, and so is Israel. For the purposes for which Israel/priest
are defined, no further differentiation is undertaken. That is where
for the Mishnaic system matters end. But to the Judaic system represented by the Yerushalmi and its associated writings, "gentile" (in
the collective) may be Rome or other-than-Rome, for instance,

Babylonia, Media, or Greece. That act of further differentiation—
we may call it "speciation"—makes a considerable difference in the
identification of gentile. In the Israel of the Mishnah's authorship,
therefore, we confront an abstraction in a system of philosophy.

If we measure the definition against the social facts in the world
beyond, we see a curious contrast. The Mishnah's systemic categories within Israel did not encompass the social facts that required
explanation. The Mishnah could explain the smallest community of
Jews and "all Israel," just as its system used the word Israel for individual and entire social entity. But the region and its counterparts,
the "we" composed of regions, the corporate society of the Jews of
a given country, language-group, and the like, the real-life world of
communities that transcended particular locations—these social facts
of the middle distance did not constitute subdivisions of the Israel
that knew all and each, but nothing in between. The omitted entity
was the family itself, which played no important role in the Mishnah's
system, except as one of the taxonomic indicators. By contrast, Israel
as family imparted to the details an autonomy and a meaning of
their own, so that each complex component formed a microcosm of
the whole: family to village to Israel as one large family.

The village then comprised Israel, as much as did the region, the
neighborhood, the corporate society people could empirically identify, the theoretical social entity they could only imagine—all formed
"all Israel," viewed under the aspect of Heaven. And, of still greater
consequence, each household—that is, each building block of the village community—constituted in itself a model of, the model for,
Israel. The utter abstraction of the Mishnah had left Israel as individual or as "all Israel," thus without articulated linkage to the concrete middle range of the Jews' everyday social life. Dealing with
exquisite detail and the intangible whole, the Mishnah's system had
left that realm of the society of Jews in the workaday household and
village outside the metaphorical frame of Israel, and Israel viewed
in the image, after the likeness of family made up that omitted middle range. In the Mishnah's Israel we confront an abstraction in a
system of philosophy, one centered upon issues of sanctification.

Israel in the Yerushalmi

Two metaphors, rarely present and scarcely explored in the writings
of the first stage (ca. 70–300 C.E.) in the formation of the Judaism
of the dual Torah came to prominence in the second stage (ca.
400–600 C.E.). That stage is represented by the Talmud of the Land
of Israel and Midrash-compilations put together at the same period.
These were, first, the view of Israel as a family, the children and
heirs of the man, Israel; second, the conception of Israel as sui
generis. While Israel in the first phase of the formation of Judaism
perpetually finds definition in relationship to its opposite, Israel in
the second phase constituted an intransitive entity, defined in its own
terms and not solely or mainly in relationship to other comparable
entities. The enormous investment in the conception of Israel as sui
generis makes that point blatantly. But Israel as family bears that
same trait of autonomy and self-evident definition.

The Israel in the second stratum of the canon of the Judaism of
the dual Torah bears a socially vivid sense. Now Israel forms a family, and an encompassing theory of society, built upon that conception of Israel, permits us to describe the proportions and balances
of the social entity at hand, showing how each component both is
an Israel and contributes to the larger composite as well. Israel as
sui generis carried in its wake a substantial doctrine of definition, a
weighty collection of general laws of social history governing the particular traits and events of the social group. In comparing transitive
to intransitive Israel, we move from Israel as not-gentile and Israel
as not-priest to powerful statements of what Israel is. Now we need
to specify in concrete terms the reasons adduced to explain the rather
striking shift before us. Two important changes account for the
metaphorical revolution at hand, one out at the borders of, the other
within, the Jews' group.

By claiming that Israel constituted "Israel after the flesh," the
actual, living, present family of Abraham and Sarah, Isaac and
Rebecca, Jacob and Leah and Rachel, the sages met head-on the
Christian claim that there was—or could ever be—some other Israel,
of a lineage not defined by the family connection at all, and that
the existing Jews no longer constituted Israel. By representing Israel
as sui generis, the sages moreover focused upon the systemic teleol-

ogy, with its definition of salvation, in response to the Christian claim
that salvation is not of Israel but of the church, now enthroned in
this world as in Heaven. The sage, model for Israel, in the model
of Moses, our rabbi, represented on earth the Torah that had come
from Heaven. Like Christ, in earth as in Heaven, like the church,
the body of Christ, ruler of earth (through the emperor) as of Heaven,
the sage embodied what Israel was and was to be. So Israel as family in the model of the sage, like Moses our rabbi, corresponded in
its social definition to the church of Jesus Christ, the New Israel, of
salvation of humanity. The metaphors given prominence in the late
fourth- and fifth-century writings of "our sages of blessed memory"
then formed a remarkable counterpoint to the social metaphors
important in the mind of significant Christian theologians, as both
parties reflected on the political revolution that had taken place.

In response to the challenge of Christianity, the sages' thought
about Israel centered on the issues of history and salvation, issues
made not merely chronic but acute by the Christian political triumph. That accounts for the unprecedented reading of the outsider
as differentiated, a reading contained in the two propositions concerning Rome: first, as Esau or Edom or Ishmael, that is, as part
of the family; second, of Rome as the pig. Differentiating Rome from
other gentiles represented a striking concession indeed, without counterpart in the Mishnah. Rome is represented as only Christian Rome
can have been represented: it looks kosher but it is unkosher. Pagan
Rome cannot ever have looked kosher, but Christian Rome, with
its appeal to ancient Israel, could and did and moreover claimed to.
It bore some traits that validate, but lacked others that validate.

The metaphor of the family proved equally pointed. The sages
framed their political ideas within the metaphor of genealogy, because
to begin with they appealed to the fleshly connection, the family, as
the rationale for Israel's social existence. A family beginning with
Abraham, Isaac, and Jacob, Israel could best sort out its relationships by drawing into the family other social entities with which it
found it had to relate. So Rome became the brother. That affinity
came to light only when Rome had turned Christian, and that point
marked the need for the extension of the genealogical net. But the
conversion to Christianity also justified the sages' extending membership in the family to Rome, for Christian Rome shared with Israel

the common patrimony of Scripture—and said so. The character of the sages' thought on Israel therefore proved remarkably congruent to the conditions of public discourse that confronted them.

The Metaphor of the Family, "Israel's Children"

When the sages wished to know what (an) Israel was, in the fourth century they reread the scriptural story of Israel's origins for the answer. To begin with, as Scripture told them the story, Israel was a man, Jacob, and his children are "the children of Jacob." That man's name was also Israel, and, it followed, "the children of Israel" comprised the extended family of that man. By extension, Israel formed the family of Abraham and Sarah, Isaac and Rebecca, Jacob and Leah and Rachel. Israel therefore invoked the metaphor of genealogy to explain the bonds that linked persons unseen into a single social entity; the shared traits were imputed, not empirical. That social metaphor of Israel—a simple one and easily grasped— bore consequences in two ways.

First, children in general are admonished to follow the good example of their parents. The deeds of the patriarchs and matriarchs therefore taught lessons on how the children were to act. Of greater interest in an account of Israel as a social metaphor, Israel lived twice, once in the patriarchs and matriarchs, a second time in the life of the heirs as the descendants relived those earlier lives. The stories of the family were carefully reread to provide a picture of the meaning of the latter-day events of the descendants of that same family. Accordingly, the lives of the patriarchs signaled the history of Israel.

The polemical purpose of the claim that the abstraction, Israel, was to be compared to the family of the mythic ancestor lies right at the surface. With another Israel, the Christian church, now claiming to constitute the true one, the sages found it possible to confront that claim and to turn it against the other side. "You claim to form 'Israel after the spirit.' Fine, and we are Israel after the flesh—and genealogy forms the link, that alone." (Converts did not present an anomaly since they were held to be children of Abraham and Sarah, who had "made souls," that is, converts, in Haran, a point repeated in the documents of the period.) That fleshly continuity formed of all of "us" a single family, rendering spurious the notion that Israel could be other than genealogically defined. But that polemic seems to me adventitious and not primary, for the metaphor provided a quite separate component to the sages' larger system.

The metaphor of Israel as family supplied an encompassing theory of society. It not only explained who Israel as a whole was but also set forth the responsibilities of Israel's social entity, its society. The metaphor defined the character of that entity; it explained who owes what to whom and why, and it accounted for the inner structure and interplay of relationship within the community, here-and-now, constituted by Jews in their villages and neighborhoods of towns. Accordingly, Israel as family bridged the gap between an account of the entirety of the social group, Israel, and a picture of the components of that social group as they lived out their lives in their households and villages. An encompassing theory of society, covering all components from least to greatest, holding the whole together in correct order and proportion, derived from Israel viewed as extended family.

That theory of Israel as a society made up of persons who because they constituted a family stood in a clear relationship of obligation and responsibility to one another corresponded to what people much later would call the social contract, a kind of compact that in palpable ways told families and households how in the aggregate they formed something larger and tangible. The web of interaction spun out of concrete interchange now was formed not of the gossamer thread of abstraction and theory but by the tough hemp of family ties. Israel formed a society because Israel was compared to an extended family. That, sum and substance, supplied to the Jews in their households (themselves a made-up category which, in the end, transformed the relationship of the nuclear family into an abstraction capable of holding together quite unrelated persons) an account of the tie from household to household, from village to village, encompassing ultimately "all Israel."

The power of the metaphor of Israel as family hardly requires specification. If "we" form a family, then we know full well what links us, the common ancestry, the obligations imposed by common ancestry upon the cousins who make up the family today. The link between the commonplace interactions and relationships that make "us" into a community, on the one side, and that encompassing entity, Israel, "all Israel," now is drawn. The large comprehends the little, the abstraction of "us" overall gains concrete reality in the "us" of the here-and-now of home and village, all together, all forming a "family." In that fundamental way, the metaphor of Israel as family therefore provided the field theory of Israel linking the most abstract component, the entirety of the social group, to the most mundane, the specificity of the household. One theory, framed in that metaphor of such surpassing simplicity, now held the whole together. That is how the metaphor of family provided an encompassing theory of society, an account of the social contract encompassing all social entities, Jews' and gentiles' as well, that no other metaphor accomplished.

Israel as family comes to expression in, among other writings of the fifth century, the document that makes the most sustained and systematic statement of the matter, Genesis Rabbah. In this theory we should not miss the extraordinary polemic utility, of which, in passing, we have already taken note. Israel as family also understood itself to form a nation or people. That nation-people held a land, a rather peculiar, enchanted or holy land, one that, in its imputed traits, was as sui generis as in the metaphorical thought of the system, Israel also was. Competing for the same territory, Israel's claim to what it called the Land of Israel—thus, of Israel in particular— now rested on right of inheritance such as a family enjoyed, and this was made explicit. The following passage shows how high the stakes were in the claim to constitute the genealogical descendant of the ancestors.

1. A. "But to the sons of his concubines, Abraham gave gifts, and while he was still living, he sent them away from his son Isaac, eastward to the east country" (Gen. 25:6)
   B. In the time of Alexander of Macedonia the sons of Ishmael came to dispute with Israel about the birthright, and with them came two wicked families, the Canaanites and the Egyptians.
   C. They said, "Who will go and engage in a disputation with them."
   D. Gebiah b. Qosem [the enchanter] said, "I shall go and engage in a disputation with them."
   E. They said to him, "Be careful not to let the Land of Israel fall into their possession."
   F. He said to them, "I shall go and engage in a disputation with them. If I win over them, well and good. And if not, you may say, 'Who is this hunchback to represent us?'"

G. He went and engaged in a disputation with them. Said to them Alexander of Macedonia, "Who lays claim against whom?"
H. The Ishmaelites said, "We lay claim, and we bring our evidence from their own Torah: 'But he shall acknowledge the first-born, the son of the hated' (Deut. 21:17). Now Ishmael was the first-born. [We therefore claim the land as heirs of the first-born of Abraham.]"
I. Said to him Gebiah b. Qosem, "My royal lord, does a man not do whatever he likes with his sons?"
J. He said to him, "Indeed so."
K. "And lo, it is written, 'Abraham gave all that he had to Isaac' (Gen. 25:2)."
L. [Alexander asked,] "Then where is the deed of gift to the other sons?"
M. He said to him, "'But to the sons of his concubines, Abraham gave gifts, [and while he was still living, he sent them away from his son Isaac, eastward to the east country]' (Gen. 25:6)."
N. [The Ishmaelites had no claim on the land.] They abandoned the field in shame.

Genesis Rabbah LXI:VII

The metaphor as refined, with the notion of Israel today as the family of Abraham, as against the Ishmaelites, also of the same family, gives way. But the theme of family records persists. The power of the metaphor of family is that it can explain not only the social entity formed by Jews, but the social entities confronted by them. All fell into the same genus, making up diverse species. The theory of society before us thus accounts for all societies, and, as we shall see when we deal with Rome, does so with extraordinary force.

O. The Canaanites said, "We lay claim, and we bring our evidence from their own Torah. Throughout their Torah it is written, 'the land of Canaan.' So let them give us back our land."
P. Said to him Gebiah b. Qosem, "My royal lord, does a man not do whatever he likes with his slave?"
Q. He said to him, "Indeed so."
R. He said to him, "And lo, it is written, 'A slave of slaves shall Canaan be to his brothers' (Gen. 9:25). So they are really our slaves."
S. [The Canaanites had no claim to the land and in fact should be serving Israel.] They abandoned the field in shame.
T. The Egyptians said, "We lay claim, and we bring our evidence from their own Torah. Six hundred thousand of them left us, taking away our silver and gold utensils: 'They despoiled the Egyptians' (Ex. 12:36). Let them give them back to us."

U. Gebiah b. Qosem said, "My royal lord, six hundred thousand men worked for them for two hundred and ten years, some as silversmiths and some as goldsmiths. Let them pay us our salary at the rate of a denar a day."

V. The mathematicians went and added up what was owing, and they had not reached the sum covering a century before the Egyptians had to forfeit what they had claimed. They abandoned the field in shame.

W. [Alexander] wanted to go up to Jerusalem. The Samaritans said to him, "Be careful. They will not permit you to enter their most holy sanctuary."

X. When Gebiah b. Qosem found out about this, he went and made for himself two felt shoes, with two precious stones worth twenty-thousand pieces of silver set in them. When he got to the mountain of the house [of the Temple], he said to him, "My royal lord, take off your shoes and put on these two felt slippers, for the floor is slippery, and you should not slip and fall."

Y. When they came to the most holy sanctuary, he said to him, "Up to this point, we have the right to enter. From this point onward, we do not have the right to enter."

Z. He said to him, "When we get out of here, I'm going to even out your hump."

AA. He said to him, "You will be called a great surgeon and get a big fee."

Genesis Rabbah LXI:VII

The same metaphor serves both Israel and "Canaan." Each formed the latter-day heir of the earliest family, and both lived out the original paradigm. The mode of thought imputes the same species to both social entities, and then makes its possible to distinguish between the two species. We shall see the same mode of thought—the family (but which wing of the family?)—when we consider the confrontation with Christianity and with Rome, in each case conceived in the same personal way. The metaphor applies to both and yields its own meanings for each. The final claim in the passage before us moves away from the metaphor of family. But the notion of a continuous, physical descent is implicit here as well. Israel has inherited the wealth of Egypt. Since the notion of inheritance forms a component of the metaphor of family (a conception critical, as we shall see in the next section, in the supernatural patrimony of the "children of Israel" in the merit of the ancestors), we survey the conclusion of the passage.

Israel as Sui Generis: The Rules of Nature, the Rules of History,
and Supernatural Governance of Israel in Leviticus Rabbah

The definition of Israel comes to us not only in what people expressly
mean by the word, but also in the implicit terms in which they dis-
cuss the social entity. In Leviticus Rabbah the conception of Israel
as sui generis is expressed in an implicit statement that Israel is subject to its own laws, which are distinct from the laws governing all
other social entities. These laws may be discerned in the factual,
scriptural record of Israel's past, and that past, by definition, belonged
to Israel alone. It followed, therefore, that by discerning the regu-
larities in Israel's history, implicitly understood as unique to Israel,
the sages recorded the view that Israel like God was not subject to
analogy or comparison. Accordingly, while not labeled a species unto
itself, Israel is treated in that way sui generis.

To understand how this view of Israel comes to expression, we
have to trace the principal mode of thought characteristic of the
authorship of Leviticus Rabbah. It is an exercise in proving hypotheses by tests of concrete facts. The hypotheses derive from the theology of Israel. The tests are worked out by reference to those given
facts of social history that Scripture, for its part, contributes. As with
the whole range of ancient exegetes of Scripture, Rabbinic authors
treated Scripture as a set of facts. These facts concerned history, not
nature, but they served, much as the facts of nature availed the
Greek natural philosophers, to prove or disprove hypotheses. The
hypotheses concerned the social rules to which Israel was subjected,
and the upshot was that Israel was subject to its own rules, revealed
by the historical facts of Scripture.

The single most common way in which the sages made the implicit
statement that Israel is sui generis derives from their "as-if" mode
of seeing Israel's reality. The sages read Israel's history not as it
seems—that is, not as it would appear when treated in accord with
the same norms as the histories of other social entities—but as a
series of mysteries. The facts are not what appearances suggest. The
deeper truth is not revealed in those events that happen, in common, to Israel and to (other) nations over the face of the earth.
What is happening to Israel is wholly other, different from what
seems to be happening and what is happening to ordinary groups.
The fundamental proposition pertinent to Israel in Leviticus Rabbah

is that things are not what they seem. Israel's reality does not correspond to the perceived facts of this world.

Now if we ask ourselves the source of this particular mode of
thinking about Israel, we find no difficulty in identifying the point
of origin. The beginning of seeing Israel as if it were other than the
here-and-now social group people saw lay in the original metaphorization of the social group. When people looked at themselves, their
households and villages, their regions and language-group, and
thought to themselves, "What more are we? What else are we?" they
began that process of abstraction that took the form of an intellectual labor of comparison, contrast, analogy, and, as is clear, consequent metaphorization. The group is compared to something else
(or to nothing else) and hence is treated as not fully represented by
the here-and-now but as representative, itself, of something else
beyond. And that very mode of seeing things, lying in the foundations of the thought of the Mishnah's authorship, implicit in the
identification of the survivors as the present avatar of Scripture's
Israel, yielded an ongoing process of metaphorization.

The original use of the metaphor, Israel, to serve as the explanation of who the surviving groups were made it natural, from that
time forward, to see Israel under the aspect of the "as-if." How this
mode of thought worked itself out in the documents is clear. The
exegetes maintained that a given statement of Scripture, in the case
of Leviticus, stood for and signified something other than that to
which the verse openly referred. If—as was a given for these exegetes—
water stands for Torah, the skin disease mentioned in Leviticus 13,
in Hebrew called *sara'at* and translated as leprosy, stands for, is caused
by, evil speech, the reference to some thing to mean some other
thing entirely, then the mode of thought is simple.

And what is decisive for our inquiry is that that mode of thought
pertained to Israel alone. Solely in the case of Israel did one thing
symbolize another, speak not of itself but of some other thing entirely.
When other social entities, e.g., Babylonia, Persia, or Rome, stood
for something else, it was in relationship to Israel, and in the context of the metaphorization of Israel. When treated in a neutral context, by contrast, we find no metaphors, e.g., Alexander of Macedonia
is a person, and no symbol stands for that person. When Greece
appears in the sequence of empires leading finally to the rule of
Israel, then Greece may be symbolized by the hare. And there is

another side of the matter too. Other things—the bear, the eagle— could stand for the empires, but—in that metaphorical context— then Israel stands only for itself. Whichever way we have it, therefore, implicit in that view and mode of thought is the notion of Israel as sui generis, lacking all counterpart or parallel entity for purposes of comparison and contrast. The importance of the mode of reading Scripture "as if" it meant something else than what it said, in the case of the exegesis of Leviticus Rabbah, should not be missed. What lies beneath or beyond the surface—there is the true reality, the world of truth and meaning, discerned through metaphorical thinking.

Supernatural Israel

There is a difference between a group defined as ethnic and one framed as religious, and the difference lies in the contrast between cultural and territorial assimilation into an ethnic group, on the one side, and religious conversion, on the other. One cannot become a Bulgarian or a Finn by a profession of faith or an act of allegiance alone. But one can become part of Israel (or the mystical body of Christ or *Ummah muslimah*, "the Muslim community") anywhere in the world. A place in Israel so far as the Torah is concerned is reserved for every gentile who accepts the unity of God and the yoke of the Torah; God's revealed will for humanity. Gentiles become Israel—and so enter into the promise of resurrection from the grave, judgment, and entry into the world to come—wherever they live, so long as how they live accords with the requirements of the Torah, and whatever language they speak, so long as what they say are the professions of Sinai. With the rite of baptism and circumcision for men, baptism for women, the gentile becomes wholly Israel, with no past whatsoever, not even a genealogy, but only a future in Israel. And then gentiles' genealogy becomes the story that the Torah tells. Language, accent, tastes in cuisine or clothing or housing or occupation or way of life or world view (apart from specifics deriving from the Torah)—these give way to a supernatural transformation. All persons may find their way under the wings of God's presence; everyone is welcome to assume the yoke of the Torah and the commandments that stand for the kingdom of God or (in sages' language) of Heaven.

The rabbis of the Mishnah, Midrash, and Talmuds understand

Israel to refer to all those who share the inheritance of Abraham and Sarah, who are called to the Torah, who dwell under the wings of the *shekhinah*—the Hebrew word for God's presence. Israel stands for the Judaism of the dual Torah,—a supernatural entity, not an ethnic one. The distinction is critical when we consider the appropriate category for this Israel. Is Israel a this-worldly people, with customs and ceremonies and exotic ethnic foods, songs, and dances, or is it a supernatural social entity, people called to form a holy community by God at Sinai, that is, comparable to a church? This Israel in Judaism forms the counterpart to church or Muslim *Ummah* in Christianity and Islam, respectively; but not to the Albanians or the Italians or the Algerians or the Swedes. To become part of Israel one affirms a faith, one need not undertake a long process of territorial, cultural, or ethnic assimilation; and such a process, by itself, will not serve.

The entire corpus of the law of the Mishnah attests to the supernatural character of "Israel"—the very "Israel after the flesh"—of which the New Testament speaks as well. Not only so, but, as a matter of fact, the supernatural character of the social entity, Israel, counterpart to the supernatural character of that this-worldly, mystical body of Christ we know as the church, is attested on every page of the Prayer-book of Judaism and in every pertinent line of the Mishnah, Midrash-compilations, and Talmuds. The Judaism of the dual Torah-Israel is no more a merely-ethnic category than "Christ" is a political one ("king of the Jews" indeed!) or than "the church" is a sociological (e.g., an institutional) one. For Rabbinic Torah's Judaism Israel formed a category that was sui generis, supernatural, and entering Israel by coming under the wings of the *shekhinah* bears nothing in common with joining an ethnic group. Israel, "the Body of Christ," and "the Abode of Islam" bear more in common than people ordinarily recognize.

CHAPTER FOUR

THE HOLY WAY OF LIFE

A. The Issue

The three monotheist religions concur that God concerns himself with righteousness and justice. Abraham engages God in a debate with the climax, "Will not the Judge of all the earth do justice?" The prophet, Moses, admonishes Israel to form a kingdom of priests and a holy people. Israel's social order is subject to God's dominion, and so too Christianity and Islam teach not only theological doctrines but God's will for his dominion, God's kingdom, or in secular language: public policy. The upshot is, all three religions concern themselves with how theology is realized in the political order of the godly community.

The Hebrew Scriptures of ancient Israel contain numerous laws aimed at establishing a just and righteous community, and these are framed not only in general terms but in detailed instructions on all manner of transactions and behavioral matters. The Halakhah, or law, of Judaism then carried forward and fulfilled these instructions. Christianity legislated for church order, for the life of the Christian community, in concrete rules governing the way of life so as to anticipate the full realization of Christ's celestial kingdom. Islam required of its faithful the performance of concrete deeds of worship and justice, and Muslim scholars worked out also in detailed and concrete terms what God requires of his creatures, namely conformity with His way, His *sharī'ah*. Thus all three traditions of monotheist religion produced law codes and commentaries to set forth in rich detail norms of conduct and conscience alike.

B. "You Shall be Holy, for I the Lord Your God am Holy": Judaism

The normative law, or *Halakhah*, of the Oral Torah defines the principal medium by which the Rabbinic sages who in antiquity founded

Judaism set forth their message. Norms of conduct, more than norms of conviction, served to convey the sages' statement. The theology of the Written and Oral Torah—that is, Judaism—conveys the picture of world order based on God's justice and equity. The Halakhah embodies the extension of God's design for world order into the inner-facing relationships of (1) God and Israel, (2) Israel's inner order in its own terms, and (3) the Israelite's household viewed on its own in time and space and social circumstance.

1. *Between God and Israel*

The interior dimensions of Israel's relationships with God are treated in the division of Agriculture and the division of Holy Things. The division of Agriculture defines what Israel in the Land of Israel owes God as his share of the produce of the Holy Land, encompassing also Israel's conformity to God's regulation on how that produce is to be garnered. The anomalous tractate, Berakhot, concerns exactly the relationships between God and the individual Israelite in respect to reciting the Shema, saying the prayer, blessings before eating food, and comparable matters. The division of Holy Things corresponds by specifying the way in which the gifts of the Land—meat, grain, oil, wine—are to be offered to Heaven, inclusive of the priesthood, as well as the manner in which the Temple and its staff are supported and the offerings paid for. Two tractates in particular describe the Temple and its rite, and one of them sets forth special problems in connection with the same. The anomalous tractate, *Hullin*, which takes up the correct slaughter of animals for secular purposes, belongs, because its rules pertain also to the conduct of the cult.

2. *Within Israel's Social Order*

The social order that is realized by Israelites' relationships with one another is the subject of the division of Damages. That division spells out the civil law that maintains justice and equity in the social order, the institutions of government and the sanctions they legitimately impose.

3. *Inside the Israelite Household: Interior Time and Space and Circumstance; Sustaining Life*

The inner life of the household, encompassing the individual Israelite, with God is treated in the division of Women, the division of Appointed Times, and the division of Purities, as well as some singleton-tractates such as Hullin. The division of Women deals with the way in which relationships of man and woman are governed by the rules of sanctification enforced by Heaven. These texts take an interest in how family relationships are formed, maintained, and dissolved, and the effects upon the family of invoking Heaven's name in vows. The division of Appointed Times addresses the effect of the advent of holy time upon the conduct of ordinary life, with special reference to the Sabbath and the pilgrim festivals (Passover, Tabernacles), the pilgrimage, and the intermediate days of festivals, the New Year and Day of Atonement, fast days, and Purim. While parts of some of these tractates, and nearly the whole of a few of them, concern conduct in the Temple, the main point of the tractates is to explore the impact upon the household and village of the Appointed times. The same interstitial position—between household and village, on the one side, and Temple and cult, on the other—serves the division of Purity. The laws of the tractates concern mainly the household, since the cleanness-rules spelled out in those tractates concern purity at home. Still, it goes without saying that the same uncleanness that prevents eating at home food that is to be preserved in conditions of cultic cleanness also prevents the Israelite from entering the restricted space of the Temple. But in the balance, the division concerns primarily cleanness in that private domain that is occupied by the Israelite household.

The Holy Way of Life: The Rhythm of the Year, the Rhythm of the Week, the Rhythm of the Individual's Life

The Judaic way of life joins three separate cycles, one in the rhythm of the year, the second in the rhythm of the week, the third in the rhythm of a person's life. The Judaic year follows the lunar calendar, so the appearance of the new moon marks the beginning of a month, and that is celebrated. There are two critical moments in the unfolding of the year: the first full moon after the autumnal equinox, and the first full moon after the vernal equinox. These mark times of heightened celebration. To understand how the rhythm of the year unfolds, however, we begin with the new moon of the month of Tishré, corresponding to September. That marks the New Year, Rosh Hashanah. Ten days later comes the Day of Atonement, commemorating the rite described in Leviticus 16, and marking God's judgment and forgiveness of humanity. Five days afterward is the full moon, which is the beginning of the festival of Tabernacles, in Hebrew, *Sukkot*; that festival lasts for eight days and ends with a day of solemn assembly, Shemini Asseret, and of rejoicing of the Torah, Simhat Torah. So nearly the whole month of Tishré is spent in celebration: eating, drinking, praying, studying, enjoying and celebrating God's sovereignty, creation, revelation, redemption, as the themes of the festivals and solemn celebrations of the season work themselves out. The next major sequence of celebration, as we realize, follows the first new moon after the vernal equinox, which begins the month of Nisan and culminates, at its full moon, with Passover, in Hebrew, *Pessah*, which commemorates the exodus of Israel from Egypt and celebrates Israel's freedom, bestowed by God. Fifty days thereafter comes the festival of Pentecost, in Hebrew, *Shabuot*, which commemorates the giving of the Torah at Mount Sinai. Other occasions for celebration exist, but, apart from the weekly Sabbath, the main holy days are the New Year, Day of Atonement, Tabernacles, Passover, and Pentecost.

Just as the Days of Awe, the New Year and the Day of Atonement, and the festivals of Tabernacles, Passover, and Pentecost mark the passage of the lunar year, so the Sabbath marks the movement of time through the week. The sanctification of the Sabbath, observed on the seventh day, Saturday, is one of the Ten Commandments. It is the single happiest moment in Judaism, and, coming as it does every week, the Sabbath sheds its light on every day. On it people do no servile labor, and they devote themselves to sacred activities, including both synagogue worship and study of the Torah, as well as to eating, drinking, relaxing, and enjoying themselves. The song for the Sabbath day, Psalm 92, expresses the spirit of this observance: it is good to give thanks to the Lord. Faithful Jews find in the Sabbath the meaning of their everyday lives.

The passage of the individual's life, from birth to death, marks out the third of the three cycles in the way of Torah, the cycles that convey the spirit of the Torah, or law as the word is translated. The principal points are birth, puberty, marriage, and death. These events of celebration, which one might call "rites of passage," define life under the law and explain how Judaists seek to live in accord with God's will, which is that Israel live the holy life in the here and now and await salvation at the end of time.

Rites for the private person, as distinct from those for the celebration of the holy people as a community, tend to be simple; they ordinarily take place at home and not in the synagogue. The Torah marks these rites of passage and treats them as critical to the formation of the holy people. The individual, not only holy Israel, stands in a covenanted relationship with God. For males that is concrete and physical. The covenant between God and Israel is not a mere theological abstraction, nor is it effected only through laws of community and family life. It is quite literally engraved on the flesh of every male Jewish child through the rite of circumcision, *brit milah* (the covenant of circumcision).

Circumcision must take place on the eighth day after birth, normally in the presence of a quorum of ten adult males. Elijah, the prophet of scriptural record, is believed to be present. A chair is set for him, based upon the legend that Elijah complained to God that Israel neglected the covenant (1 Kings 19:10–14). God therefore ordered him to come to every circumcision so as to witness the loyalty of the Jews to the covenant. The *mohel*, or circumciser, is expert at the operation. The traditional blessing is said: "Praised are You . . . who sanctified us with Your commandments and commanded us to bring the son into the covenant of Abraham our father." The wine is blessed: "Praised are You, Lord our God, who sanctified the beloved from the womb and set a statute into his very flesh, and his parts sealed with the sign of the holy covenant. On this account, Living God, our portion and rock, save the beloved of our flesh from destruction, for the sake of his covenant placed in our flesh. Blessed are You . . . who makes the covenant."

The advent of puberty is marked by the *bar mitzvah* rite for a young man, and a *bat mitzvah* rite for a young woman, at which a young person becomes obligated to keep the commandments; *bar* means son and *bat* means daughter, with the sense that one is subject to, and *mitzvah* means commandment. The young person is called to pronounce the benediction over a portion of the Torah lection in the synagogue and is given the honor of reading the prophetic passage as well. In olden times it was not so important an occasion as it has become in modern America.

Only when a Jew achieves intelligence and self-consciousness, normally at puberty, is he or she expected to accept the full privilege of *mitzvah* (commandment) and to regard himself or herself as *commanded* by God. Judaism perceives the commandments as expressions of one's acceptance of the yoke of the kingdom of Heaven and submission to God's will. That acceptance cannot be coerced, but requires thoughtful and complete affirmation. The *bar* or *bat mitzvah* thus represents the moment that the young Jew first assumes full responsibility before God to keep the commandments.

Rites of death are simple and brief. The natural process of death is treated as a normal chapter of life. At the onset of death, the dying Jew says a confession:

> My God and God of my fathers, accept my prayer. . . .
> Forgive me for all the sins which I have committed in my lifetime. . . .
> Accept my pain and suffering as atonement and forgive my wrongdoing for against You alone have I sinned. . . .
> I acknowledge that my life and recovery depend on You.
> May it be Your will to heal me.
> Yet if You have decreed that I shall die of this affliction,
> May my death atone for all sins and transgressions which I have committed before You.
> Shelter me in the shadow of Your wings.
> Grant me a share in the world to come.
> Father of orphans and Guardian of widows, protect my beloved family. . . .
> Into Your hand I commit my soul. You redeem me, O Lord God of truth.
> Hear O Israel, the Lord is our God, the Lord alone.
> The Lord He is God.
> The Lord He is God.[1]

The corpse is carefully washed and always protected. The body is covered in a white shroud, then laid in a coffin and buried. Normally burial takes place on the day of death or on the following day. Once the body has been placed in the grave, three pieces of broken pot-

---

[1] *A Rabbi's Manual*, ed. Jules Harlow (New York: The Rabbinical Assembly, 1965), 96.

tery are laid on eyes and mouth as signs of their vanity. A handful of dirt from the Land of Israel is laid under the head.[2] The family recites the *Qaddish*, an eschatological prayer of sanctification of God's name that looks forward to the messianic age and the resurrection of the dead. The prayer expresses the hope that the Messiah will soon come, "speedily, in our days," and that "he who brings harmony to the Heavens will make peace on earth." The mourners remain at home for a period of seven days and continue to recite the memorial *Qaddish* for eleven months. The life-cycle for the private individual is simple, but for the individual as part of Israel, God's holy people, it is rich, absorbing, and encompassing.

The word for concrete instruction concerning one's duty, the proper way of doing things, is *Halakhah*, and when we speak of life under the law, we mean life in accord with the *Halakhah*, the rules and regulations of the holy life. The mythic structure built upon the themes of creation, revelation, and redemption finds expression, not only in synagogue liturgy, but especially in concrete, everyday actions or action-symbols—that is, deeds that embody and express the fundamental mythic life of the classical Judaic tradition.

Halakhah. These action-symbols are set forth in *Halakhah*. This word, as is clear, is normally translated as "law," for the *Halakhah* is full of normative, prescriptive rules about what one must do and refrain from doing in every situation of life and at every moment of the day. But *Halakhah* derives from the root *halakh*, which means "go," and a better translation would be "way." The *Halakhah* is "the way": *the way* man lives his life; *the way* man shapes his daily routine into a pattern of sanctity; *the way* man follows the revelation of the Torah and attains redemption.

For the Judaic tradition, this *way* is absolutely central. Belief without the expression of belief in the workaday world is of limited consequence. The purpose of revelation is to create a kingdom of priests and a holy people. The foundation of that kingdom, or sovereignty, is the rule of God over the lives of humanity. For the Judaic tradition, God rules much as people do, by guiding others on the path

---

[2] A. Z. Idelsohn, *The Ceremonies of Judaism* (Cincinnati: National Federation of Temple Brotherhoods, 1930), 133.

of life, not by removing them from the land of living; creation lies behind; redemption, in the future; Torah is for here and now. To the classical Jew, Torah means revealed law or commandment, accepted by Israel and obeyed from Sinai to the end of days.

The spirit of the Jewish way (*Halakhah*) is conveyed in many modes, for law is not divorced from values, but rather concretizes human beliefs and ideals. The purpose of the commandments is to show the road to sanctity, the way to God. In a more mundane sense, the following provides a valuable insight:

> Raba [a fourth-century rabbi] said, "When a man is brought in for judgment in the world to come, he is asked, 'Did you deal in good faith? Did you set aside time for study of Torah? Did you engage in procreation? Did you look forward to salvation? Did you engage in the dialectics of wisdom? Did you look deeply into matters?'"
>
> Bavli Shabbat, 31(A)

Raba's interpretation of the Scripture, "and there shall be faith in thy times, strength, salvation, wisdom and knowledge" (Isaiah 33:6), provides one glimpse into the life of the classical Jew who followed the way of Torah. The first consideration was ethical: did the man conduct himself faithfully? The second was study of Torah, not at random but every day, systematically, as a discipline of life. Third came the raising of a family, for celibacy and abstinence from sexual life were regarded as sinful; the full use of man's creative powers for the procreation of life was a commandment. Nothing God made was evil. Wholesome conjugal life was a blessing. But, fourth, merely living day-by-day according to an upright ethic was not sufficient. It is true that people must live by a holy discipline, but the discipline itself was only a means. The end was salvation. Hence the pious people were asked to look forward to salvation, aiming their deeds and directing their hearts toward a higher goal. Wisdom and insight—these completed the list, for without them, the way of Torah was a life of mere routine, rather than a constant search for deeper understanding.

How does Judaism spell out the holy way of life that the Torah requires? It is through laws organized in a kind of law code, the Mishnah, which is amplified and extended in a series of secondary documents. The Mishnah covers six principal topics: (1) sanctification of the economy and support of the priesthood, the holy caste; (2)

sanctification of time, with reference to special occasions, appointed times and the Sabbath; (3) sanctification of the family and the individual; (4) the proper conduct of points of social conflict, the political life of the people; (5) the sanctification of the Temple and its offerings, with special emphasis on the everyday and the routine occasions; and, finally, (6) the protection of the Temple from uncleanness and the preservation of cultic cleanness. These six principal subjects form the center of the Mishnah's six divisions and, all together, cover the everyday life of the holy people in the here and now. The rules are phrased in the present tense, people do this, people do not do that, and, overall, they provide an account of an ideal world. For at issue was not merely the everyday, but the sacred—and holiness persisted even though the everyday did not yield such evidence as it had used to. So the message is clear: the established sanctification of Israel endured, events changing nothing.

The Mishnah's Judaism of Sanctification

The topical program of the document, as distinct from the deep issues worked out through discussion of the topics, therefore focuses upon the sanctification of the life of Israel, the Jewish people. The question taken up by the Mishnah, in the aftermath of the destruction of the Temple, is whether and how Israel is still holy. And the self-evidently valid answer is that Israel indeed is holy, and so far as the media of sanctification persist beyond the destruction of the holy place—and they do endure—the task of holy Israel is to continue to conduct that life of sanctification that had centered upon the Temple. Where now does holiness reside? It is in the life of the people, Israel—there above all. So the Mishnah may speak of the holiness of the Temple, but the premise is that the people—that kingdom of priests and holy people of Leviticus—constitute the center and focus of the sacred. The land retains its holiness too, and in raising the crops, the farmer is expected to adhere to the rules of order and structure laid down in Leviticus, keeping each thing in its proper classification, observing the laws of the sabbatical year, for instance. The priesthood retains its holiness, even without the task of carrying out the sacrificial cult. Therefore priests must continue to observe the caste rules governing marriage, such as are specified in Leviticus.

The relationship of man and wife forms a focus of sanctification, and that too retains its validity even now. The passage of time, from day to day with the climax at the Sabbath, from week to week with the climax at the sanctification of the new month, from season to season with the climax at the holy seasons, in particular the first new moon after the autumnal equinox, marked by Tabernacles, and the first new moon after the vernal equinox, marked by Passover—these too continue to indicate the fundamental state and condition of Israel the people: all these modes of sanctification endure, surviving the destruction of the holy Temple. In these and other foci of interest, the Mishnah lays forth a Judaic system of sanctification, joining discourse on the foci of sanctification that no longer survived with discussion on those that flourished even beyond the disaster. If, therefore, we had to specify the single urgent and critical question and the single self evident answer, it would be the following colloquy:

> The compelling question: Is Israel yet holy?
> The self-evident answer: Sanctification inheres in the life of the people.

That is why four of the six principal parts of the Mishnah deal with the cult and its officers. These are, first, Holy Things, which addresses the everyday conduct of the sacrificial cult; second, Purities, which takes up the protection of the cult from sources of uncleanness specified in the book of Leviticus (particularly Leviticus 12–15); third, Agriculture, which centers on the designation of portions of the crop for the use of the priesthood (and others in the same classification of a holy caste, such as the poor), and so provides for the support of the Temple staff; and, fourth, Appointed Times, the larger part of which concerns the conduct of the cult on such special occasions as the Day of Atonement, Passover, Tabernacles, and the like (and the rest of which concerns the conduct in the village on those same days, with the basic conception that what you do in the cult forms the mirror image of what you do in the village). Two further divisions of the document as a whole deal with everyday affairs, with, Damages concerning civil law and government, and, women taking up issues of family, home, and personal status. That, sum and substance, is the program of the Mishnah.

Attitudes, Not only Actions

But the Halakhah extended not only to actions but to attitudes. The sages taught what Israel is supposed to feel. They made a virtue of humility, accommodation, acceptance, good will. What Judaism teaches the private person to feel links her or his heart to what Judaism states about the condition of Israel in history and of God in the cosmos. All form one reality, in supernatural world and nature, in time and in eternity. In the innermost chambers of deepest feelings, the Israelite therefore lives out the public history and destiny of the people, Israel. The notion of the centrality of human feelings in the religious life of Israel presents no surprises. Scripture is explicit on both sides of the matter. The human being is commanded to love God. In the biblical biography of God, the tragic hero, God, will despair, love, hope, feel disappointment or exultation. The biblical record of God's feelings and God's will concerning the feelings of humanity— wanting human love, for example—leaves no room for doubt. Nor does the Judaism that emerges from late antiquity ignore or propose to obliterate the datum that "the merciful God wants the heart." God commands that humanity love God with full heart, soul, mind and might. That is the principal duty of humanity.

Tractate *Abot* presents the single most comprehensive account of religious affections. The reason is that, in that document above all, how we feel defines a critical aspect of virtue. The issue proves central, not peripheral. The doctrine emerges fully exposed. A simple catalogue of permissible feelings comprises humility, generosity, self-abnegation, love, a spirit of conciliation of the other, and eagerness to please. A list of impermissible emotions is made up of envy, ambition, jealousy, arrogance, sticking to one's opinion, self-centeredness, a grudging spirit, vengefulness, and the like. People should aim at eliciting from others acceptance and good will and should avoid confrontation, rejection, and humiliation of the other. This they do through conciliation and giving up their own claims and rights. So both catalogues form a harmonious and uniform whole, aiming at the cultivation of the humble and malleable person, one who accepts everything and resents nothing. True, these virtues, in this tractate as in the system as a whole, derive from knowledge of what really counts, which is what God wants. But God favors those who please others. The virtues appreciated by human beings prove identical to

the ones to which God responds as well. And what single virtue of
the heart encompasses the rest? Restraint, the source of self-abnegation
and humility, serves as the antidote for ambition, vengefulness, and,
above all, for arrogance. It is restraint of our own interest that enables
us to deal generously with others, humility about ourselves that gen-
erates a liberal spirit towards others.

So the emotions prescribed in tractate *Abot* turn out to provide
variations of a single feeling, which is the sentiment of the disci-
plined heart, whatever affective form it may take. And where does
the heart learn its lessons, if not in relationship to God? So: "Make
his wishes yours, so that he will make your wishes his" (*Abot* 2:4).
Applied to the relationships between human beings, this inner discipline of the emotional life will yield exactly those virtues of conciliation and self-abnegation, humility and generosity of spirit, that
the framers of tractate *Abot* spell out in one example after another.
Imputing to Heaven exactly those responses felt on earth, e.g.,
"Anyone from whom people take pleasure, God takes pleasure" (*Abot*
3:10), makes the point at the most general level.

The strikingly fresh medium for traditional doctrines in the Bavli
takes the form of prayers composed by sages. Here the values of the
system came to eloquent expression. Sages prayed that their souls
may be as dust for everyone to tread upon. They asked for humility in spirit, congenial colleagues, good will, good impulses. They
asked God to take cognizance of their humiliation, to spare them
from disgrace. The familiar affective virtues and sins, self-abnegation
as against arrogance, made their appearance in liturgical form as
well. Another noteworthy type of material, also not new, in which
the pages of the Bavli prove rich, portrayed the deaths of sages. One
dominant motif is uncertainty in face of death, a sign of humility
and self-abnegation. The basic motif—theological as much as affective—
encompassing all materials is simple. Israel is estranged from God,
therefore should exhibit the traits of humility and uncertainty, acceptance and conciliation. When God recognizes in Israel's heart, as
much as in its deeds and deliberation, the proper feelings, God will
respond by ending that estrangement that marks the present age. So
the single word encompassing the entire affective doctrine of the
canon of Judaism is alienation.

The Commandments

The religious duties that define the holy way of life are regarded as God's own instructions or commandments: deeds one must do, deeds one must refrain from doing. These range from minor matters of clothing to fundamental issues of sustaining life, in foods one may or may not eat, and propagating life, in sexual relations that are forbidden or permitted. The commandments that comprise holy Israel's way of life are deemed marks of God's love for Israel; so states a rabbi in the Mishnah: R. Hananiah b. Aqashia says, "The Holy One, blessed be he, wanted to give merit to Israel. Therefore he gave them abundant Torah and numerous commandments, as it is said, 'It pleased the Lord for his righteousness' sake to magnify the Torah and give honor to it' (Is. 42:21)."

The Talmud on this matter proposes to reduce the vast number of religious obligations—613, comprised of 365 to correspond to the days of the solar year and 248 to correspond to the bones of the body. In this way the commandments are placed into proportion and context and the main point is identified. That is the point of Rabbi Simlai's exposition attached to Hananiah's statement:

> II.1 A. Therefore he gave them abundant Torah and numerous commandments:
>
> B. R. Simlai expounded, "Six hundred and thirteen commandments were given to Moses, three hundred and sixty-five negative ones, corresponding to the number of the days of the solar year, and two hundred forty-eight positive commandments, corresponding to the parts of man's body."
>
> D. "David came and reduced them to eleven: 'A Psalm of David: Lord, who shall sojourn in thy tabernacle, and who shall dwell in thy holy mountain? (i) He who walks uprightly and (ii) works righteousness and (iii) speaks truth in his heart and (iv) has no slander on his tongue and (v) does no evil to his fellow and (vi) does not take up a reproach against his neighbor, (vii) in whose eyes a vile person is despised but (viii) honors those who fear the Lord. (ix) He swears to his own hurt and changes not. (x) He does not lend on interest. (xi) He does not take a bribe against the innocent' (Psalm 15)."
>
> V. "Isaiah came and reduced them to six: '(i) He who walks righteously and (ii) speaks uprightly, (iii) he who despises the gain of oppressions, (iv) shakes his hand from holding bribes, (v) stops his ear from hearing of blood (vi) and shuts his eyes

from looking upon evil, he shall dwell on high' (Isaiah 33:25–26)."

FF.   ' "Micah came and reduced them to three: 'It has been told you, man, what is good, and what the Lord demands from you, (i) only to do justly and (ii) to love mercy, and (iii) to walk humbly before God' (Micah 6:8)."

GG.   "only to do justly": this refers to justice.

HH.   "to love mercy": this refers to doing acts of loving kindness.

II.   "to walk humbly before God": this refers to accompanying a corpse to the grave and welcoming the bread.

JJ.   And does this not yield a conclusion a fortiori: if matters that are not ordinarily done in private are referred to by the Torah as "walking humbly before God," all the more so matters that ordinarily are done in private.

KK.   ' "Isaiah again came and reduced them to two: 'Thus says the Lord, (i) Keep justice and (ii) do righteousness' (Isaiah 56:1).

LL.   "Amos came and reduced them to a single one, as it is said, 'For thus says the Lord to the house of Israel. Seek Me and live.' "

MM. *Objected R. Nahman bar Isaac, "Maybe the sense is, 'seek me' through the whole of the Torah?"*

NN.   Rather, ' "Habakkuk further came and based them on one, as it is said, 'But the righteous shall live by his faith' (Habakkuk 2:4)."

Bavli Makkot 23b–24a

The purpose of the commandments, that is, the point of the holy way of life, then is to express one's acceptance of the kingship of God; to purify the heart of man; and, above all, to form of the Israelite a human being who loves God and values his creatures. This is best expressed by Hillel, a rabbi of the first century B.C.E.:

A. There was a case of a gentile who came before Shammai. He said to him, "Convert me on the stipulation that you teach me the entire Torah while I am standing on one foot." He drove him off with the building cubit that he had in his hand.

B. He came before Hillel: "Convert me."

C. He said to him, "What is hateful to you, to your fellow don't do.' That's the entirety of the Torah; everything else is elaboration. So go, study."

Bavli Shabbat 2:5 I;12/31a

That story defines the holy way of life of Judaism. All the rest is elaboration, and requires a lifetime of study and performance.

C. "Take up Your Cross, and Follow Me": Christianity

Christianity conceives of people as having a deep affinity with God, and at the same time it acknowledges that between God and humanity an unbridgeable chasm sometimes intrudes. Paul is the preeminent theologian of the ambivalence of this relationship. He wrote extensively to a Christian community in Rome around 57 C.E. His letter to the Romans is the result, the fullest explanation of Paul's theology. In an opening section, Paul concerns himself with the issue of how God may be conceived of as judging people, when they do not even know Him. His response is much the same as that given centuries later in the Qur'ān: God's power and divinity is primordially evident to people from the world around them (Romans 1:19–20):

> What is known of God is evident to them, because He has manifested it to them. His invisible qualities, his eternal power and divinity, have been demonstrated perceptibly from the creation of the world by the things that have been made.

The issue of judgment illuminates how Paul understands God to be known to humanity at large. To Paul the particular qualities of God, because they are behind the world rather than in it, are invisible. God's being God means that He is transcendent in His divinity, beyond the terms of reference of time and space. But His power is also evident, demonstrated by our perception of things made in the world around us. The world is not just an accident of our environment, but that which is created by God. Paul's conviction is consonant with the story of the creation in Genesis 1, and with much else in the Scriptures of Israel.

When Paul refers to God separating him from his mother's womb in Galatians 1:15, there is nothing abstract or theoretical about the imagery of creation. The emphasis rather falls on the immediate and personal link between God and Paul's own being. The imagery is not original with Paul: he is picking up the language of the Old Testament. For example, Psalms 22:9 and 71:6 offer praise to God for taking the speaker from the womb and keeping him safe from childhood. The image is also used in the prophetic literature, when the prophet is said to have been taken from the womb for the purpose of giving his prophecy (see Isaiah 49:1 and Jeremiah 1:5). In all these cases, as in Paul's usage, the imagery expresses not only a sense of being in an ordered creation, but of experiencing God's care within that creation. The prophetic usage enhances the emphasis on one's personal sense of purpose by applying the image to a particular mission one is to accomplish. Paul shares that emphasis, as well.

The prophetic dimension of Paul's reference to God comes out again in his description of God "calling" him. "Calling" is understood to establish a link between God and the person he calls, so that God's word may be delivered. Who is called? It might be a prophet, or all Israel, or Jesus himself. Matthew 2:15 presents the infant Jesus as called from Egypt for his vocation in Israel, in citing the prophetic book of Hosea (11:1). Hosea applies "Out of Egypt I called my Son" to the people Israel, liberated at the time of the exodus. That wording is then interpreted afresh in Matthew to refer to Jesus. That is possible because much of the language of the Old Testament, including reference to God's calling and God's separating a person from the womb, is deliberately developed in the New Testament. The usage of the Old Testament is the point of departure for new applications and unusual developments, designed to convey a sense of intimacy with God.

God initiates the biblical call, but the call must be answered for it to be productive of the communication that is the purpose of the calling. Indeed, the fact of God's call can be the basis upon which people take it upon themselves to call upon God. "Answer me when I call, O God of my righteousness" (Psalm 4:1) is an appeal which is predicated on the previous response to God's call on the part of the psalmist and the psalmist's community.

Paul particularly develops the reciprocity of call and response in his teaching in regard to the Spirit of God. 1 Corinthians 2 shows how, in a letter written a year or two before Romans, Paul sees Spirit at work. If one asks how we can know what God has prepared for us, the answer is that Spirit alone is able to communicate divine purposes. So powerful is the force of Spirit, we will take up this theme only in chapter six, when we come to the discussion of the end of days. For the moment, we observe simply that the initial terms of Paul's knowledge of God, then, are his awareness of God's power and care, and his access to the Spirit of God (see 1 Corinthians 2:9 above all).

But that is by no means the whole of Paul's conception of knowledge of God. Its distinctive feature is that God was pleased "to reveal his Son in me" (Galatians 1:15): that is how Paul knows in the first place that he has been separated from the womb and called by God. The revelation of God's Son in the midst of one's being is the distinctive basis of Christian knowledge of God. In fact, Paul conceives of the moment of receiving God's Spirit in a highly specific manner, linked inextricably to Jesus (Galatians 4:6, treated in chapter six): Baptism is the moment at which, by accepting the revelation of the Son, one can accept that Spirit which is truly divine. Only what has come from God can acknowledge and respond to God: that is the revelation of God's Son within.

Paul brings us, then, to the most characteristic aspect of the Christian understanding of the knowledge of God—its emphasis upon Jesus, the Son of God, as the central mediator of that knowledge. One's own acknowledgement of and response to God remain vital, but they are understood to be possible only because God has already been at work within, shaping a spiritual eye to see him at work and a spiritual ear to hear his call. As Paul conceives of Jesus, he is first of all the Son of God revealed within us. Of course, Paul is aware of the primitive teaching concerning Jesus' deeds and teaching, including a graphic account of his crucifixion (see Galatians 3:1). But his interest in Jesus is not historical. Rather, his attention is taken up by how the revelation of the Son of God might shape our minds and hearts to know God.

The most famous expression of this theme occurs in the letter to the Philippians, which was probably composed after Paul's death, by his follower Timothy (ca. 85 C.E.). It represents a mature Pauline theology, much of it on the basis of what Paul personally had thought. It was composed at a time at which Christians in the Greco-Roman world were largely of the servant class, so that its appeal to the form of Jesus as a servant is especially poignant (Philippians 2:5–8):

> Let this thought prevail among you, which was also in Jesus Christ: Who, being in God's form, did not consider the presumption of equality with God, but emptied himself, taking a servant's form; existing in men's likeness, and found as a man in shape, he humbled himself, becoming obedient unto death, death on a cross.

The point of Paul and Timothy together (see Philippians 1:1) is that it is possible, on the basis of the revelation of the Son of God within

one, to think as Jesus did, although in one's own circumstances. Here
is an example of the imperative to imitate Christ within the New
Testament. Its object is not a slavish mimicry of the historical person, but an embrace of that humble disposition of Christ which
makes the knowledge of God possible, proceeding as it does from
God's own loving nature.

Knowledge of God, then, involves the capacity to acknowledge
God as the source of one's being, the ability to respond to God's
call and to hear him, and an acceptance within oneself of Christ's
own loving disposition—his humility unto death. Christianity's anthropology directly reflects its call to humanity to enter into the vision
of God and to be transformed by the divine Spirit.

This literally other-worldly perspective results in a paradoxical
acceptance of the institutions of this world. That acceptance is
qualified, however, by the observation that all forms of human government are provisional. The same Paul who would die in Roman
during Nero's pogrom against Christians could insist in Romans
(13:1–2):

> Let every person be subject to the governing authorities. For there is
> no authority except from God, and those that exist have been instated
> by God. Therefore one who resists the authorities resists what God
> has appointed, and those who resist will incur judgment.

Peter is said to have died in the same pogrom (crucified, rather than
beheaded, as it is said Paul was),[3] and yet the letter called 1 Peter
(composed around 90 C.E., during another period of persecution)
attributes the following advice to him (4:19): "Therefore let those
who suffer according to God's will do right and entrust their souls
to a faithful Creator." There is every intellectual and practical reason to deny that current experience comes from God. Yet that is
exactly what early Christianity did *not* do.

There is a particularly poignant passage from what is called "The
Acts of the Scillitan Martyrs," in which a Roman judge attempts to
reason with some people who have been denounced for their
Christianity, but are not guilty of any other crime. He explains to
them, very patiently, that they can easily walk away from the court,

---

[3] See Eusebius, *The History of the Church from Christ to Constantine* (tr. G. A. Williamson;
Baltimore: Penguin, 1967), 2.25.

simply by burning some incense before an image of the Emperor, and swearing an oath of allegiance to him as God's son. His patience extends to a conscientious recognition that the act does not actually require belief: only conformity to the due form is required. Many Gnostic Christians would have had no difficulty complying with the judge's request, and no doubt there were other early Christians, loyal to the creed, who nonetheless went along with such friendly advice. But, to the judge's exasperation, the Scillitan martyrs oblige the judge to condemn them to death, which he eventually does. To his mind (as to that of Marcus Aurelius: *Meditations* 11:3), they were obstinate. Christians were proud of such behavior in their ranks and produced an entire literature of martyrdom.

The insistence in 1 Peter 4:19 provides the key to this Christian persistence (or obstinacy, depending upon one's point of view). The fact of God's creation of this world seals it as ultimately good, no matter what our immediate experience of it might make it seem. The beginning of the passage makes its perspective clear (1 Peter 4:12–13):

> Beloved, do not be surprised at the fiery ordeal that is taking place among you to test you, as though something strange were happening to you. But rejoice insofar as you are sharing Christ's sufferings, so that you may also be glad and shout for joy when his glory is revealed.

God's creation of this world in 1 Peter, in the New Testament as a whole and in the rule of faith as articulated in the creed, is not to be understood simply as a theoretical expression of where things originally came from. Of course, Christians do and always have understood that God is good and that what he made (and makes) is very good, in the unmistakable assertion of Genesis 1:31. But they do not say on that basis that what seems bad is really good, or that evil is merely illusory or the work of some other power. Instead, they see present experience as in the process of a transformation, sometimes a painful transformation, in which all goodness (including God's) will be vindicated. Christian faith in creation is more eschatological than anything else: it is concerned with what will happen at the end (*ho eschaton* in Greek) of all things.

Because Christianity is committed to eschatology as the single perspective which makes sense of human experience, it has been obliged to spell out for itself what its eschatology means, how the anticipated transformation of the world is to be worked out. Three types of eschatology have characterized Christianity over time, and they are closely related to one another. All three of them, at any one time, have been represented, although given periods usually represent a commitment to one of the three more than the others. Which of the types is emphasized has a profound impact on how a person and a community deal with suffering, and with how they actually perceive pain. For that reason, the distinctions among the three—and their relationship to one another—are quite important to understand.

Temporal Eschatology. By its very nature, eschatology must involve the end of time as we know and conceive of time. But there is no actual necessity that eschatological expectation should develop into what is defined as an apocalyptic expectation. After all, Jesus instructed his disciples to pray, "Your kingdom will come,"[4] without giving a precise indication of when that moment was to come. Apocalyptic thought involves the claim to understand the sequence and timing of the ultimate events in human affairs, up until and including the end.

Jesus does not appear to have taught any single apocalyptic scheme, and it is even said that, after his resurrection, he explicitly told his followers that "It is not yours to know the times and periods which the Father has set by his own authority" (Acts 1:7). But the fact is that, even without Jesus' encouragement, apocalyptic calendars thrived in primitive Christianity, as evidenced in books in the New Testament such as the Revelation of John, 2 Thessalonians, 2 Peter, and Jude, all of which were produced near the end of the first century. There is no single such calendar, so it seems obvious that Jesus did not endorse any single apocalyptic scheme. But then, the variety of the calendars shows how vibrant and diverse apocalyptic expectation was.

Although other forms of eschatology have tended to dominate over temporal eschatology in the subsequent history of the church, there have been notable examples of renewed apocalyptic fervor, especially during times of extreme social change. Examples include the Anabaptists during the Reformation in Europe, and groups such as the Shakers in the United States during the nineteenth century.

---

[4] For the emphatic wording of the prayer of Jesus, and its Aramaic original, see Bruce Chilton, *Jesus' Prayer and Jesus' Eucharist: His Personal Practice of Spirituality* (Valley Forge, Penn.: Trinity Press International, 1997).

Transcendent Eschatology. Because thought in the modern (and the so-called post-modern) world is, on the whole, not eschatological, it is easy to dismiss eschatology as a primitive and outdated view of the world. The scientific thought of ancient Greece, which has deeply influenced our own view of science, often conceived of physical reality as static and unchanging, and that has inclined us to prefer views of the world which are also static. Now, however, science itself shows us just how conditional human existence is. Physically, not even the universe appears permanent; solid matter seems to be a myth; the very survival of human beings is called into question by the rapid extinction of many other animal and plant species.

Just as our own world has started to seem less stable and unchanging to us, the world of ancient eschatology has proven to be much less simplistic and "primitive" than was once thought to be the case. It was fashionable a century ago to depict eschatology as a strictly temporal teaching, as if time was its only concern. We have just seen that some eschatology is indeed temporal in its emphasis. But to see God as final in human affairs also involves seeing God's kingdom as working now, transforming the very environment in which we live. As Jesus put it, the kingdom of God "is like yeast, which a woman takes, hides in three measures of dough, until the whole is yeasted" (Luke 13:21; Matthew 13:33). Because space, as well as time, is a dimension of God's activity, eschatology also involves seeing God at work now in his final revelation, and it involves the possibility of joining God in his kingdom.

The point of the revelation of the kingdom within our world is that it points beyond our world. The kingdom is transcendent: it comes from outside us, transforms us, and directs us outside ourselves. No theologian more forcefully or influentially emphasized this aspect of eschatology than Origen. In order to explain the value of the promises which are ours in Christ, Origen cites John 17:14, when Jesus asserts that neither he nor his disciples are of the world; and Origen then goes on to explain (*On First Principles* 2.3.6):

> But there is no doubt that the Savior refers to something more glorious and splendid than this present world, and invites and incites all who believe in him to direct their course towards it. But whether that world, which he wishes us to know of, is one that stands apart and separate from this world in space and quality and glory, or whether, as seems more likely to me, it excels in quality and glory but is nevertheless

contained within the limits of this world, is uncertain, and in my opinion an unsuitable subject for the mind and thoughts of human beings.

Origen here expresses a characteristic feature of Christian teaching
concerning transcendence. The point is not to speak of something
so different that we have no inkling what God would do with us.
Rather, God may be perceived to be immanent in the world, and
in His immanence to direct our course towards that which He would
have us be. ("Immanence" is the usual category used to refer to the
divine as existing within the universe as people may perceive it.)
Because Christian teaching of divine transcendence is eschatological,
it links this world with the world to come in the expectation and
the experience of the believer.

Juridical Eschatology. Jesus' well-known parable of a feast to which the
host makes surprising, insistent invitations—and equally categorical
exclusions—voices another emphatic dimension of his own eschatology (see Matthew 22:1–14; Luke 14:16–24). God is portrayed as celebrating in his kingdom with those who would join him, and as
refusing to include those who have rejected the appointed way of
entering his kingdom. Because Jesus was and is rightly known as the
supreme teacher of divine love, this aspect of his teaching is frequently (and all too conveniently) ignored. But there is finally no
compromise in love: it supersedes what would resist it. As the book
of Psalms puts it, God's being king puts an end to everything wicked
and those who represent wickedness, whether individuals or nations
(see Psalm 10:15–16).

The lively sense of the judgment which is involved in God's final
disclosure is a typical, sometimes a dominant, feature of Christianity.
In this, Augustine of Hippo delineates the sort of practice which
would emerge during the Middle Ages. Speaking during the season
of Lent, when the congregation prepares for the celebration of Easter
and Christ's temptation in the wilderness is recalled, Augustine
preached as follows (*Sermon* 206.1):

> Life in this world is certainly the time of our humiliation. These days
> show—by the recurrence of this holy season—how the sufferings of
> the Lord Christ, who once suffered for us by death, are renewed each
> year. For what was done once and for all time so that our life might
> be renewed is solemnized each year so that the memory may be kept
> fresh. If, therefore, we ought to be humble of heart with sentiments

of most sincere reverence throughout the entire period of our earthly sojourn when we live in the midst of temptations, how much more necessary is humility during these days, when we not only pass the time of our humiliation by living, but call attention to it by special devotion! The humility of Christ has taught us to be humble because he yielded to the wicked in his death; the exaltation of Christ lifts us up because by rising again he cleared the way for his devoted followers. Because, "if we have died with him, we shall also live with him; if we endure, we shall also reign with him" (2 Timothy 2:11–12). One of these conditions we now celebrate with due observance in view of his approaching passion; the other we shall celebrate after Easter when his resurrection is, in like manner, accomplished again.

What Augustine is here signaling to us, in the clearest of terms, is the link between devotion to Christ and eschatology. Devotion to him, the imitation of Christ, is not merely encouraged because of Jesus' goodness, but because his life, death, and resurrection maps the path into God's kingdom. Jesus' example charts the single course for passing through the divine judgment which is necessarily a part of the coming of the kingdom.

These three types of eschatology are particularly mentioned here because they correspond to major movements in the formative centuries of Christianity. *Temporal eschatology* typified the first two centuries; *transcendent eschatology* characterized the emergence of Christianity's philosophical dominance between the third century and the seventh century; *juridical eschatology*, of which Augustine is an early example, became the hallmark of Christianity from the Middle Ages onward. Although it may seem confusing to think of eschatology in these different ways, they are all a part of conceiving God as truly final. His finality is such that he will definitively change time, but also space and the nature of justice in human relations. Time and space and ethics are not totally different categories, but are essential dimensions of human experience, so that eschatology rightly involves them all.[5]

---

[5] In fact, Jesus' own eschatology included two further dimensions. His definition of the kingdom provided for a distinctive view of what made for the purity acceptable to God and for an emphasis on the outward, inclusive range of the kingdom. See Bruce Chilton, *Pure Kingdom: Jesus' Vision of God.* Studying the Historical Jesus 1 (Eerdmans: Grand Rapids, 1996). Those dimensions are not included here because they did not amount to distinctive types of eschatology within the formative periods of Christianity. Still, emphasis upon the purity and upon the outward extension of God's kingdom are characteristic of Christianity in most periods.

Eschatology in all of its rich nuances constitutes the fundamental perspective from which Christianity addresses the problem of suffering and urges a positive engagement with the world. The God who makes the world also redeems the world, and he redeems the world that we know, as it is. That may involve waiting over time (temporal eschatology), transforming the place where we stand (transcendent eschatology), and/or entering into a judgment which will change us (juridical eschatology); but in any and all cases, suffering is not the last word, but the transitional word before glory.

The type of eschatology Christianity embraces has determined its portrayal of how we encounter our world and how a holy life may be led. That portrayal, in turn, relates to the anticipation of how God in Christ is to transform the world. The virtue which arises from each eschatology is understood as "power": *virtus* in the Latin sense of the word.

Once time is perceived as the principal dimension within which God acts definitively, the obvious question becomes: Just when will that be? We have already seen above that 1 Peter urges its readers to treat their current persecution as a "fiery ordeal," a test whose end would be glory for those who were proven (1 Peter 4:12–13). But how long was the ordeal to last? Does faith involve the simple assurance that in the end God will triumph, without knowledge of his plan for his people? Or does faith appropriately include a more precise insight into one's own redemption and the redemption of one's fellows? It is no coincidence that the letter called 2 Peter addresses just these questions.

Second Peter is a second-century work attributed to Peter, who (as we have seen) probably died under Nero in Rome in 64 C.E. It takes up the trait of apocalyptic literature as being attributed to a great visionary from the past. (That trait is also represented in the book of Daniel in the Old Testament and 2 Esdras in the Apocrypha.) Here, 2 Peter beautifully and classically sets out an account of how the pain of eschatological delay is experienced within apocalyptic Christianity, and how it might be addressed (2 Peter 3:1–10):

> This is already, beloved, a second letter I write to you; in them I arouse by reminder your sincere intent, to remember the sayings told in advance by the holy prophets and the commandment of your apostles of the Lord and Savior. First, know this: There will come at the

last days scoffers with scoffing, going according to their own desires, and saying,

Where is the promise of his coming? Because although the patriarchs perished, everything remains the same from the beginning of creation! This escapes those who like to think this way: Heavens existed from of old and earth from water and through water subsisted by the word of God. Through them the world then was destroyed, deluged with water. But the present Heavens and the earth by the same word are stored for Fire, kept for the day of judgment and the destruction of the godless. Do not let this one thing escape you, beloved: one day with the Lord is as a thousand years, and a thousand years as one day (Psalm 90:4). The Lord does not delay his promise, as some people suppose delay, but he is generous to you, not wishing you to be destroyed, but that all might attain to repentance.

The pain of time, that it remains unfulfilled by the presence of God, is dealt with through the understanding that it provides an interim for the purpose of repentance. That pain becomes an opportunity, to the extent that it is used as a preparation. Patient penitence is part of the power that transforms the world.

Just as Origen believed that God through Christ had prepared "something more glorious and splendid than this present world," as we have seen, so he pondered what it means to conceive of God and of divine reward as beyond our ordinary terms of reference. His discussion appears within his use of the imagery of light to understand God (*On First Principles* 1.1.5):[6]

Having then refuted, to the best of our ability, every interpretation which suggests that we should attribute to God any material characteristics, we assert that he is in truth incomprehensible and immeasurable. For whatever may be the knowledge which we have been able to obtain about God, whether by perception or reflection, we must of necessity believe that he is far and away better than our thoughts about him. For if we see a man who can scarcely look at a glimmer of the light of the smallest lamp, and if we wish to teach such a one, whose eyesight is not strong enough to receive more light than we have said, about the brightness and splendor of the sun, shall we not

---

[6] For the examples and their elucidation, we are indebted to John Dillon, "Looking on the Light: Some Remarks on the Imagery of Light in the first chapter of the *Peri Archon*," *The Golden Chain: Studies in the Development of Platonism and Christianity* (Aldershot: Variorum, 1990), 215–230 (essay 22).

have to tell him that the splendor of the sun is unspeakably and immeasurably better and more glorious than all this light he can see?

Here the imagery of pain is more than a matter of the discomfort one might feel in the ordinary course of living. The point is rather that our lives at their best do not prepare us to come in contact with God, and the little we know already is itself not something we can sustain. As in the myth of the cave in Plato's *Republic*, a person living in the dark will not readily be accustomed to light.

The difference between Origen and Plato is that, while in the myth of the cave, the person can come into the sun's light, for Origen we cannot know God as God truly is in this life.[7] For that reason, pain is experienced in two directions at once. First, we are not naturally prepared to discover as much of God's light as we do, and that is a painful condition, as in Plato's myth. But second, we are also intrinsically unable to proceed from the intimations of God to the reality they point to, so that we can not be completely fulfilled even after we have prepared ourselves for the light. So the pain of this life is both that it offers too much of the reality of God, and too little of it. The dilemma can only be resolved when we are in a different place, when the transcendence of God, which presently impinges on our lives, becomes the whole of life as we know it. And because that can only occur beyond our world, present experience is not merely painful, but is itself a kind of pain. That is the reason for which Origen emphasizes the irreducible importance for every Christian of the vision of God. Only that vision enables us both to understand and to endure our present predicament, because it anticipates the full reality that is to come.

In *Sermon* 205.1, preceding the sermon in which he explains the eschatological link between humility and exaltation, Augustine portrays the Christian life as inherently painful, and yet as inherently hopeful for that reason. What he says at the start of the season of Lent is a classic exposition, which charts a course for the development of spirituality during the Middle Ages:

> Today we commence the observance of Lent, the season now encountering us in the course of the liturgical year. You are owed an appro-

---

[7] This is Dillon's main point (see p. 225), and his citation of *On First Principles* 1.1.6 demonstrates it admirably.

priately solemn sermon, so that the word of God, brought to you
through my ministry, may sustain you in spirit while you fast in body,
and so that the inner man, thus refreshed by suitable food, may be
able to accomplish and to persevere bravely in the disciplining of the
outer man. For to my spirit of devotion it seems right that we, who
are going to revere the Passion of our crucified Lord in the very near
future, should construct for ourselves a cross of the bodily pleasures
in need of restraint, as the Apostle says, "And they who belong to
Christ have crucified their flesh with its passions and desires" (Galatians 5:24).

Pain here is actually a gate to the promise of transformation. The
fact of our selfish desires, which we experience in our flesh, is what
keeps us from appreciating and joining ourselves to the love of God
in Augustine's thought (see especially his magisterial work, *The City
of God*). So the willing experience of pain actually permits us to know
our true selves, to form a cross of what alienates us from God, and
so through the death of selfishness to understand who we truly are
before God.

Juridical eschatology is the source of Christianity's profound skepticism about the value of human life in the flesh. The problem is
not so much the material of which we are made, as what has become
of it by means of human selfishness. Flesh is where we try to make
gods of ourselves, and in so doing dishonor each other as much as
we dishonor God in our abuse of passion. For Augustine, war, crime,
exploitation, and the violent results of all three are not happen-
stances. His is not a sudden realization that life as he knows it (in
the flesh) is beset by evil. Rather, it is a recognition that these evils
must be overcome by a realization of our truer selves, selves not
subservient to that selfishness. That became the most predominant
virtue in Christianity from the time of the Middle Ages.

Gregory of Nyssa inhabited a very different world from Paul's. By
his time, Christianity was in fashion within the Empire. He was the
brother of Basil of Caesarea in the Cappodocian region of Asia
Minor, and Gregory himself was bishop of Nyssa (between 371 and
394). Together with their friend Gregory, son of the bishop of
Nazianzus, they are known as the "Cappodocian Fathers." Champions
of the emerging Trinitarian doctrine of their day, Gregory especially
represents the interpenetration of the Hellenistic literary tradition
with the orientation of Christianity. Deeply influenced by Origen,
he also remained married long into his episcopate, and only took

monastic vows after his wife's death. More eloquently than any other
Christian teacher, he identified the problem of the sincerity of believers, which obviously needed to be questioned as soon as the Christian
faith became fashionable. Gregory confronted this issue directly in
"On What Is Meant by the Profession 'Christian'":

> Let us, then, consider, first of all, from the term itself what Christianity
> means. From those who are wiser it is, of course, possible for us to
> discover a significance more profound and more noble in every way,
> more in keeping with the dignity of the word. However, what we begin
> with is this: the word "Christ," exchanged for a clearer and more
> familiar word, means "the king," and Holy Scripture, in accordance
> with proper usage, indicates royal dignity with such a word. But since,
> as Scripture says, the divine is inexpressible, incomprehensible, exceed-
> ing all comprehensible thought, the Holy Spirit must inspire prophets
> and apostles, and they contribute with many words and insights to our
> understanding of the incorruptible nature, one setting us right about
> one divine idea and another about another. His dominion over all is
> suggested by the name of Kingdom, and his purity and freedom from
> every passion and every evil is indicated by the names of the virtues,
> each being understood as referring to higher signification. Such expres-
> sions are used as "justice itself" and "wisdom and power" and "truth"
> and "goodness" and "life" and "salvation" and "incorruptibility" and
> "permanence" and "lack of change" and whatever elevated concept
> there is, and Christ is and is said to be all of them. If, therefore, the
> comprehension of every lofty idea is conceived of in the name of Christ
> (for the other qualities mentioned are included under the higher des-
> ignation, each of them being implied in the notion of kingdom), per-
> haps some understanding of the interpretation Christianity will follow.
> If we, who are joined to him by faith in him, are called by his name
> whose incorruptible nature is beyond verbal interpretation, it is alto-
> gether necessary for us to become what is contemplated in connection
> with that incorruptible nature and to achieve an identity which fol-
> lows along with it. For just as by participating in Christ we are given
> the title "Christian," so also are we drawn into a share in the lofty
> ideas which it implies. Just as in a chain, what draws the loop at the
> top also draws the next loops, in like manner, since the rest of the
> words interpreting his ineffable and multiform blessedness are joined
> to the word "Christ," it is necessary for the person drawn along with
> him to share these qualities with him.

The power of Gregory's analysis is that he identifies precisely the
primary engine of Christian ethics: the imitation of Christ. The prosperity of a Christianized Roman Empire put followers of Jesus in
the odd position of being prominent and acceptable. It became con-

ceivable and practicable to become a Christian out of convenience. Gregory reflects the response of exchanging the inquisition which once came from outside, from Roman magistrates, for a searching inquiry within, to test one's own motivations and sincerity.

Engagement with the world, always a duty within Christianity, brings with it suffering in distinct ways. There is the suffering of time, the suffering of place, the suffering of self. Temporal eschatology longs for a different time, transcendent eschatology for a difference place, juridical eschatology for a different self. (What is striking is that these anxieties—of time, place, and self—are precisely the most persistent troubles of modernity.) Yet just where one might expect that these distinct kinds of suffering would develop into distinct responses, Christianity in fact teaches a single, unambiguous strategy, grounded in the teaching of Jesus, best expressed in the famous advice (Matthew 5:38–42):

> You have heard that it was said, An eye for an eye and a tooth for a tooth. But I say to you not to resist the evil one. But to someone who strikes you on the right cheek, turn also the other. And to one who wants to enter judgment with you to take your shirt, give your cloak, too! And with someone who compels a mile's journey from you, travel with him two. Give to the one who asks of you, and do not turn away from one who wants to borrow from you.

Of all the teachings of Jesus, none is more straightforward, and none more challenging. Evil is to be overcome by means of what is usually called non-resistance.

What follows in Matthew states the principle of Jesus' teaching, that we are to love in the way that God does (Matthew 5:43–48; see Luke 6:36). The fundamental quality of that teaching within Christianity is unquestionable (see Matthew 22:34–40; Mark 12:28–34; Luke 10:25–28; Romans 13:8–10). But in the teaching about turning the other cheek, giving the cloak, going the extra mile, offering the money, everything comes down to particular conditions that prevailed during the Roman occupation of the Near East. The fact that this formulation only appears in Matthew (written around 80 c.e.) has given rise to the legitimate question whether it should be attributed to Jesus in its present form. The imagery corresponds to the conditions of the Roman occupation in an urban area, where a soldier of the Empire might well demand provisions and service and money, and all with the threat of force. But even if we acknowledge (as seems only reasonable) that Matthew's Gospel has pitched Jesus' policy in the idiom of its own experience, the policy itself should be attributed to Jesus.

Why should what is usually called non-resistance to evil be recommended? It needs to be stressed that non-resistance is not the same as acquiescence. The injustice that is done is never accepted as if it were just. The acts of turning the other cheek, giving the cloak, going the additional mile, offering the money, are all designed to be excessive, so that the fact of the injustice of what is demanded is underlined. Indeed, it is not really accurate to call the behavior "non-resistance." The point is for the person who makes demands that are unjust to realize they are unjust. Just that policy served Christians and their faith well during the centuries of persecution under the Roman Empire. It was effective because it brought about an awareness within the Empire, even among the enemies of Christianity, that the policy of violent persecution was unjust (and, for that matter, ineffective). Rather than a teaching of non-resistance, this is a version of the advice of how to retaliate. Instead of an eye for an eye, it suggests a cheek after a cheek. This is not non-resistance; it is exemplary response. That is, it is a form of retaliation: not to harm, but to show another way.

The hope that the other way—God's way—will be seen by means of exemplary response, and that once it has been seen it will be followed, is basic to Jesus' policy of exemplary response. That hope is articulated by the three types of eschatology we have seen, in each of which God's ultimate vindication is what awaits the believer at the end. But in every case, the same basic policy of exemplary response is urged as the only authentically Christian response to suffering in the present.

D. "In the Way of God": Muslim Practice

The practice of Islam is ideally exactly what the Arabic word *islām* implies: the practice of "submission" (*islām*) to the one God of all creation. It involves the faithful in the day-to-day work of living life in all its aspects according to God's will rather than their own. And for the Muslim, what God requires is neither asceticism nor any other demanding extreme of religious observance and practice, but rather the living of a full and normal life as an individual person of faith in God, a member of a family, a citizen of both a given social and political order and also a wider Islamic Community, or *Ummah*.

The vision of such a *muslim* life—one of submission to God's will—involves moral and cultic norms that were hammered out and elucidated by the early Muslims in ever-changing circumstances during the first two to four centuries after the Prophet's death. This was the time when Islamic political hegemony and its attendant social and religious order expanded, developed, and solidified with what is, in historical perspective, remarkable rapidity and extent for a new religious and cultural tradition. The development and definition of generally recognized norms for Islamic practice came primarily through the application of God's Word in the Qur'ān and His Messenger's guidance and example (the *Sunnah* of the Prophet Muhammad) regarding righteousness and the moral life to the realities of existing norms and customs of diverse pre-Islamic Mediterranean and southwest Asian societies. This was a dynamic, varied, and complex process that we can only try to reconstruct with hindsight and a great deal of simplification and generalization. Nonetheless, it was a process through which there crystallized a new, ultimately global tradition of faith and practice and culture. This tradition incorporated and developed many local and regional differences but also cultivated many fundamental values and practices that were shared by Muslims from Spain to Central Asia. We need to try to conceptualize and to articulate this reality in some coherent, general way if we are to do justice to the formative development of Islamic faith and culture and their identifiable continuities as well as their obvious internal disparities.

As the world of Islamic political power and religio-cultural influence expanded, especially in the first two or three Islamic centuries, the shared norms, values, and institutions of the many different regional cultures of the early *Ummah* gradually came to characterize what might be called an "Islamic way of life." This *modus vivendi* has remained identifiable in its general outlines even to the present day across the manifold variations of cultural, racial, geographical, linguistic, and socio-political realities encompassed by the ultimately global Islamic tradition. This "Islamic way of life" was articulated and maintained ultimately through the *Ummah*'s consensual interpretation and codification of both Qur'ān and Sunnah. It can best be described as a system of both religious and social norms and the functional means of interpreting and applying them in the various spheres of personal, familial, and communal existence. This system came to be identified under the rubric of *sharīʿah* (literally, "watering place, way to water"; hence, the way to salvation).

Properly understood, the *sharīʿah* is not, however, a human creation; nor is it the human faith and attendant practice that it calls for—which is rather what the Qurʾān calls *dīn*, often translated "religion" (in the sense of "religious practice or observance"). Instead, the *sharīʿah* is the transcendent ideal or divine "Law" established by God for human life. In its developed usage, the *sharīʿah* is, of course, at the concrete level of Muslim experience, represented in the total system of "law" worked out over time by the *Ummah*. This system delineates the practices and norms a person should follow in order to make his or her life, both individually and as a part of the larger Ummah, conform to God's will (*sharʿ*). However, in larger perspective, it is the clearly demarcated path of obedience that leads one to the *dīn* ("religion," worship and service of God) that God has ordained (*sharaʿa*, "to mark out, make manifest a path [to water]"; hence, "to ordain, establish, prescribe"):

> He has ordained (*sharaʿa*) for you the religion (*dīn*) with which He charged Noah, and with which We [God] charged Abraham, Moses, and Jesus. (S. 42:13)

Thus the *sharīʿah* is not (as it is commonly described in the popular press) a legal code or codex of legal practice, but the comprehensive pattern of rights and duties in all facets of life that reflects God's will and as a whole constitutes for human beings the path of true obedience to Him. It involves both religious observances (worship of God and fulfillment of the basic duties of Muslim practice) and just and moral conduct of one's life in all its various spheres (including family life, sexual relations, personal hygiene and diet, business life, political life, and social and communal life). Not unlike Torah, *sharīʿah* is a transcendent ideal that by human effort and struggle in understanding and interpretation can be translated into specific norms for everyday living. In this sense, Islamic jurisprudence, *fiqh* (lit., "understanding," commonly rendered as "jurisprudence"), is the science of discerning both how to know the *sharīʿah* and what its specific implications are for the concrete situations of everyday life in which it should be implemented. Muslim practice in any and every sphere of life is ideally to be based on *sharīʿah; fiqh* is the functional system of jurisprudential reasoning through which this ideal ought to be realized.

The viability of such a system of jurisprudential inquiry based on both revelation and reason derives from the fact that Muslims have faith that God has both sent revelation and prophetic guidance to human beings and also given every human being the power of reason with which to interpret that revelation and prophetic guidance in the specific situations that arise all the time in life. As a result, they live with the comforting conviction that it is possible to do God's will; that God's law is (as it is in the Jewish tradition) a blessing and not a burden. To Muslims, God has not ordained anything in the way of obligations that a person cannot manage, and He has made sure that it is possible for a person to discover what his or her obligations are and then to fulfill them. Thus the existence of the *sharīʿah* is fraught with promise and inspiration, not fear of failure nor any sense of the impossibility of fulfilling God's will. This is not to say that Muslims do not recognize the imperfection of the human condition; but God repeatedly promises in the Qurʾān that if one strives with righteous intention to "urge what is right and denounce what is evil," to do good and avoid what is bad, one can count on God's mercy when one falls short of the mark, as one inevitably will.

Muslims believe that the *Ummah* has been able, as the true community of the faithful, to preserve God's revelation and records of the exemplary life and interpretations of the Apostle of God and his Companions. In addition, Muslims believe that the community has been able through the intellectual efforts of early and later Muslim religious scholars to codify and elucidate specific norms, duties, and limits in all spheres of life. Thus Muslims have not only the guidance of the revealed word of the Qurʾān and the wisdom of the Prophet and earliest generations of Muslims (usually referred to as the *salaf*, the pious "forebears"), but also the ongoing guidance of new generations of learned persons, the ulema (*ʿulamāʾ*, plur. of *ʿālim*, lit., "one who knows"), to turn to when they need to know what to do or how to do it in order to be obedient servants of the Living God.

There has, however, never been in the Islamic community an organized authority analogous to the Christian church hierarchies, Catholic, Orthodox, or Protestant, or even to the Jewish Sanhedrin of Roman times. Priesthood has no equivalent Islamic institution involving any formal induction or "ordination" into a closed professional religious establishment (nor are the ulema even vested as clearly with their status as are rabbis, except where individual temporal states and governments have institutionalized the certification and appointment of ulema under their bureaucratic control). Instead, the ulema have been in the main, both theoretically and practically, an institutionally unofficial but societally recognized and, increasingly with the passage of time, a socially and politically entrenched and powerful infrastructure in Islamic societies. The ulema and the story of their development as a major institution and the key arbiters of *sharīʿah* in the *Ummah* deserve therefore some attention as crucial factors in Muslim practice.

Muhammad's political leadership of the new Arab Islamic *Ummah* devolved upon the "caliphs" ("successors," "vicegerents"), who followed him. However, in the socio-religious sphere, the functional "successors" were those Muslims generally recognized for piety and learning and sought after as informal (or, as in the case of state-appointed judges, even formal) authorities on what is involved in being a *muslim*. Initially they were the Companions (male and female) of Muhammad with greatest stature in the old Medinan *Ummah* (including the first four caliphs). This generation was replaced by those younger (and more and more exclusively male) followers who were most concerned with preserving, interpreting, and applying the Qurʾān, and with maintaining the norms of the Prophet's original *Ummah*. By the time of the fifth caliph in the 660s, this ill-defined but growing group were no longer (or at least rarely) political or military leaders as well as socio-religious ones. Yet they and their successors were the persons who had to meet the needs of a nascent legal religious system that was emerging to implement the *sharīʿah* as a baseline of personal and public norms for the new society.

Because the Qurʾān contained relatively few explicit legal prescriptions, these religious scholars had to draw on precedents from Meccan and Medinan practice, as well as on oral traditions from and about the Prophet and Companions. These they had to reconcile with existing custom and law that preceded the advent of Islam in every city and region of the world Muslim leaders now ruled. They also had to develop and standardize grammatical rules for a common Arabic language based on the Qur'ān and pre-Islamic poetry. Furthermore, they had to improve the phonetic Arabic consonantal script, a task done so well that in time it was applied as the standard written medium for unrelated languages wherever Islamic religion and culture became dominant. Along with these and other religious, intellectual, and cultural achievements, the ulema developed over a period of less than five centuries an enduring pattern of education in Arabic language and the foundational texts of the tradition (beginning with Qur'ān and *hadīth*). This educational system was based on study under those persons who could demonstrably claim a place in an unbroken chain of learning and transmission through generations of trustworthy and knowledgeable Muslims back to the earliest *Ummah* of Companions and Prophet.

As early as Umayyad times (660–750), the ulema emerged in reality as well as name as the guardians of the Muslim conscience, often criticizing caliphal rule when it strayed too far from Muslim norms. As an unofficial but generally recognized infrastructure, these ulema were at once needed and used by the Umayyads and later political leaders to help in the many tasks of running and regulating an expanding society at least nominally expected to be organized and governed by Islamic norms. However, some of the most pious ulema refused to be judges for rulers they considered corrupt or irreligious. The potential and actual conflict of authority between the caliphal institution of governance and the ulema institution of socio-religious authority is epitomized in traditions ascribed to the Prophet which exalt the status of the scholars, such as the following: "Truly, the *'ulamā'* are the heirs of the *anbiyā'* (Prophets)" (al-Bukhārī 3:10).

In time, the ulema became a new elite, a socio-religious leadership eventually identified with the upper class of each regional society under Islamic rule; they even exercised in some areas an hereditary hold on learning and the offices that required it (from imams of mosques to local or higher judges). Rulers and their governors regularly sought their advice, but often only for moral and legal sanction of a contemplated (or accomplished) action. Some ulema gave dubious sanctions, whether freely or under duress, and compromised themselves. Yet incorruptible ulema were seldom persecuted by rulers for their opinions (except when they supported sectarian rebellions), mostly because of their status and influence among rank-and-file Muslims.

The personal legal opinions of the ulema and their collective discussions of issues from theological doctrines to criminal punishments established a basis for religious and social order that gradually became a legal (and theological) system. By the ninth or, at latest, tenth century they had largely defined the understanding of the *sharī'ah* that Muslims ever after have held to be definitive for legal, social, commercial, political, ritual, and moral concerns. This understanding and the methods by which it was derived together became the dual basis of the Muslim science of jurisprudence, or *fiqh*, the core discipline of Islamic learning. Ulema who were recognized for their jurisprudential learning and skills were accordingly known as *fuqahā'* (plur. of *faqīh*, "jurist," "legal scholar").

Thus, without building a hierarchy of "ordained" clergy or any "church" organization, Muslims developed a workable moral-legal system. It was based on a formally trained if informally organized religious and scholarly elite, membership in which was largely a matter of peer and public acceptance and recognition. It also assumed a tradition of concern with moral and religious ideals in matters of public affairs and social order. As a result, if the caliphs, the sultans, and their deputies were seldom paragons of piety, and instead rather often ruthless and sometimes despotic, they had at least to act publicly with some modicum of circumspection and give compensating support for pious standards in public if they wanted to retain any popular support. Thus the ulema shared de facto leadership in Muslim societies with the rulers, even if unequally—a pattern that has endured in Islamic states and provided both a system of authority for the practice of individual Muslims in all periods everywhere and sometimes a counterbalance against the total misuse of political power by oppressive rulers.

The development of jurisprudential thought by the ulema/*fuqahā'* involved many individuals and a number of early schools of religious and legal thought that developed around particular regional groups of scholars or individual teachers and their students. But early on, apparently by sometime in the second century of Islam, an at least generally workable approach to the available resources for interpreting God's will—and hence for discerning what the *sharī'ah* norms require in a given situation—was hammered out and gradually adopted as a formal method for such interpretation. Its most famous codification and articulation was by the great legist and religious scholar, al-Shāfiʿī (d. 204/820). This approach involved a recognition of four fundamental bases for human judgment in legal decision-making (or, in fact, in any decision-making by a Muslim): first and second, the "two [prime] sources [or "roots"]" (*aslān*) of authority, namely Qurʾān and Sunnah; third, the "consensus" (*ijmāʿ*) of the faithful collectively (ideally; more practically, the agreement of the majority of the ulema); and fourth, inferential or analogical reasoning (*qiyās*).

Proof texts for the widespread use of these "sources" as the four formal bases of legal judgment in Islam can be found in the Word of God and the Hadīth of the Prophet. Examples are: (for the Qurʾān:) "And We have sent down to you the Scripture as an explanation of all things, a guidance, a mercy, and good news for the Muslims" (S. 16:89); (for the prophetic Sunnah) "Whosoever obeys the Apostle, obeys thereby God (S. 4:82), or "Obey God and the Apostle" (S. 3:29); (for consensus:)

> Whoever breaks with the Apostle of God after the guidance has been shown clearly to him and follows other than the way of the faithful, him We shall turn over to that to which he has turned and roast him in Gehenna—an evil end! (S. 4:115);

and (for analogical or inferential reasoning) "We have in truth sent down to you [Muhammad] the Scripture with the truth, so that you may judge among humankind according to that which God has shown you" (S. 4:105), or the words of the Prophet, "If a judge reaches a correct decision through exercise of reason, he will be doubly repaid; if he errs, he will [still] be repaid once" (Muslim 30:15; cf. Ibn Hanbal 2:187).

There have been small groups that have striven to use "Qurʾān only" and reject not only Hadīth but also consensus and independent reasoning as formal sources of interpretive certainty, but the de facto use of Scripture, prophetic tradition, reason, and communal consensus has been the most enduring and widely accepted legal norm. This general system for the derivation of legal and moral decisions and norms from a combination of the sources of the tradition and the reasoning of qualified ulema has continued to prevail to the present day, even though numerous Muslim-majority countries today have adopted civil codes that limit formal *sharīʿah* legal jurisdiction to the cultic and sometimes personal and family-law spheres.

The more pressing question, however, for our interest in the development of norms for the practice of Islam is about the content of Islamic law, since this is what will give us the best picture of what the actual practices and usages were that came in the formative centuries of Islamic history to define the *muslim* way of doing things according to the *sharīʿah*. For this we must turn to the textual evidence.

The most general division in the Islamic law books is that between cultic and social duties and actions, that is between interactions with God—namely, "acts of worship/service" (*ʿibādāt*)—and interactions with other human beings—"social interrelations" (*muʿāmalāt*). While this twofold division is not explicit in the major Hadīth compendia, the subcategories appropriate to each of the two are typically given separate chapters in those Hadīth compendia (e.g., the "two Authentic [collections]" of al-Bukhārī and Muslim b. al-Hajjāj) that are arranged according to subjects treated in *fiqh*, or jurisprudence. Thus it is not unreasonable for us to use these two categories to help give a conspectus of Muslim practice.

The *ʿibādāt* come first in the sources—both in the Hadīth collections organized by topic and in the later legal manuals. ʿIbādāt break down into the following major categories: ritual purity or purification, worship (*salāt*), almsgiving (*zakāt*), fasting (*sawm*), and pilgrimage (*Hajj*), although typically other related categories are also added: funerary and burial rites, sacrifice, and so on. Ritual purity is a prerequisite for performing the principal acts of worship in Islam, perhaps most importantly for the *salāt*. *Salāt*, *zakāt*, fasting, and pilgrimage constitute the Muslim ritual obligations that, along with the profession of faith ("I bear witness that there is no god but God and Muhammad is the Messenger of God"), make up the five "pillars" (or "limbs, members," *arkān*)—i.e., the essentials of religious faith and practice, *dīn*, according to God's *sharīʿah*.

Sūrah 9:108 says, "God loves those who purify themselves." Ritual purity is both physical and symbolic. The ablutions that one must make before performing the *salāt* do cleanse one for entering the presence of God in prayer, but they also symbolize more importantly the purification of the spirit and mind that must take place in order for one's worship act to be performed in sincerity and mindfulness. The symbolic nature of this act is made clear from the prophetic traditions that approve of the practice called *tayammum*—using clean sand or dirt as the cleansing agent when water is not available. The object is spiritual purity, which physical cleanliness powerfully symbolizes. Ritual purity is essential if the ritual act of *salāt* is to be valid, and an oft-quoted *hadīth* goes so far as to say that cultivation of proper ritual purity in *salāt* has the power to move God to forgive a worshipper's sins following the performance of that *salāt*:

> ['Uthmān ibn 'Affān] said: "I heard the Apostle of God say, "No Muslim performs ablution, does it well, and performs the *salāt* without his sins between the one *salāt* and the next being forgiven" (Muslim, *Sahīh* 2.6).

The performance of the ritual worship itself is everywhere probably the most visible marker of one's being a Muslim. It is repeatedly paired in the Qur'ān with the giving of alms (*zakāt*) as the twin duties that the Qur'ān holds up as essential to *dīn*, as for example in Sūrah 31:4, where the righteous are described as "those who perform the *salāt* and give *zakāt*, and who are certain in their faith in the Hereafter," or in Sūrah 2:42–43, where the faithful are urged, "Do not confuse truth with falsehood, nor conceal the truth knowingly; perform the *salāt* and give the *zakāt*, and bow [in worship] with those who [also] bow."

Ideally, every Muslim should perform the *salāt* five times each day, each time within the temporal limits laid down for it (e.g. sunset to dark for the magrib, or sunset prayer) in the Hadīth reports and accepted as legally valid. While the Qur'ān has very little specific about the details of *salāt*, including even the specific number required each day, the Hadīth collections devote some of their longest chapters to the general principles, precise details, and practical implementation of the *salāt*—as in the following example urging the prayer leader not to over-extend its performance too zealously:

> [Abū Hurayrah reported]: "The Apostle of God said: 'When one of you leads people in worship, he should keep it short, for among you are the feeble, the sick, and the aged. But when one of you worships by himself, he may extend it as long as he likes.'" (al-Bukhārī, *Sahīh* 10.62.1)

How to hold one's hands and body in the various parts of the ritual performance of *salāt*, what and how to recite from the Qur'ān in it, how to dress for it, when to do it, how to alter it when travelling or in other difficult circumstances, what are acceptable supererogatory performances of it, where it can be performed, what voids its validity—all such issues and many more are dealt with in the *hadīth* compendia and codified in Islamic jurisprudential traditions.

Zakāt has also its own chapters in the *hadīth* compendia and the law books, and it was these two genres that moved the *zakāt* from being a moral obligation inherent in the Islamic ethos to becoming a more formalized and specified system of taxation of wealth for public welfare purposes. The Qur'ān itself has much to say about this tangible expression of a major pious attitude that the Qur'ān makes clear is central to true religiousness, namely the constant attentiveness to the suffering and misfortune of one's fellows and their needs. The "social gospel" preaching of the Qur'ān and the Prophet could not be clearer or more insistent: those who have been blessed with God's bounty are morally bound to share of their wealth with those of their fellows less fortunate than they. The legal expression of this in Islamic societies has been the claim upon a small percentage of a person's wealth each year, usually to be given after the end of the month of fasting and distributed or otherwise used for the good of the less fortunate in the community.

The Qur'ān is insistent about the need to be generous in one's giving for the welfare of others in the *Ummah*. Not only are *salāt* and *zakāt* the pair of practices always named as a shorthand for the core duties of true religious practice, whether that of previous prophets or of Muhammad's *Ummah*; almsgiving also stands as a symbol of the general attitude of caring for others that the Qur'ān enjoins:

> So give to kinsfolk and to the needy and the wayfarer what they are rightly due; that is best for those who desire the face of God and they are the ones who flourish. What you give from [profits from] usury on people's wealth is no profit in God's eyes; but what you give as *zakāt*, desiring the face of God, that will mean double recompense. (S. 30:38–9)

Fasting in the month of Ramadan is also one of the central pious practices expected of observant Muslims. Originally, Muhammad apparently had the early Muslim community in Medina fast, like the Jews, on the day of 'Āshūrā', until the revelation of Sūrah 2:183–5 in 624 abolished this as obligatory and instituting in its stead the month-long daytime fast in

The month of Ramaḍān, in which the Qurʾān was revealed as a guidance for humankind, and clear proofs of guidance and the criterion. Whoever of you is present, let him fast this month, and whoever is sick or travelling, [let him fast] for another [equal] period of days (2:185).[8]

While other times of fasting are mentioned in the Qurʾān and recognized as praiseworthy, only the fast of Ramaḍān is obligatory. Its importance as a time of introspection, prayer, recommitment to God, and greatly heightened sense of belonging to the *Ummah* of fellow Muslims cannot be overestimated as a central ritual in the life of every adult Muslim. A pious tradition from the Prophet proclaims that "God says, 'Fasting is Mine, and I reward it'." The Prophet then goes on to say, "The smell of the mouth of one who is fasting is more delectable to God than the scent of musk." (Muslim 13:165, *Musnad* 3:5; cf. *Muwatta* 18:58, al-Bukhārī 30:2). The spirit of this accords with the immense emotional attachment of Muslims to Ramaḍān practices and the intense feelings of oneness with one's fellows who are undergoing the same suffering each day of the fast that one is undergoing oneself. The joyous rituals of breaking the fast each evening and the celebration of the festival of fast-breaking (*ʿId al-Fiṭr*) at the end of the month are among the best loved ritual observances of the Muslim year.

Pilgrimage to Mecca (*hajj*) at least once in a lifetime is another of the basic religious observances prescribed for every Muslim so long as he or she is physically and financially able: "Pilgrimage to the [Holy] House is a duty to God incumbent upon all persons so long as they can manage a way to do it" (S. 3:97). It is considered a great and important achievement even once in a lifetime to accomplish the often arduous trip so that one arrives early in the month of pilgrimage in the holy environs of Mecca. Every Muslim longs to be able to do this. The rituals of the Hajj emphasize coming into the most holy sanctuary of God; visiting the sites of the origins of the faith going back to Abraham (and, in popular tradition, even to Adam); commemorating the events of the lifetimes of Abraham and Muhammad; and praying shoulder to shoulder with other Muslim persons of faith from around the globe. It is a powerful symbolic

---

[8] On fasting, see the article "Law," *EI*[2], s.v.

statement both of personal piety and devotion and of Muslim unity and solidarity—a graphic reminder of the equality of all the faithful before God.

As we noted above, the discussions of *ʿibādāt* in the law books as well as in the *hadīth* collections include also chapters on things in addition to the "pillars" themselves. The most common of these are funeral rites and burial, pious retreats to a mosque, oaths and vows, sacrifices and sacrificial animals, hunting, food and drink, and the *ʿaqīqah*, or animal sacrifice in thanks for a new-born child.

With regard to the "normative" practices covered under *ʿibādāt* in Islamic legal literature, it is also important to emphasize that in the preceding we have been speaking about only the "classical" ritual practices shared by virtually all Muslims. This means that we are consciously omitting here numerous other ritual or ceremonial events that have been for centuries typical either of most Islamic societies or significant minority or sectarian portions of those societies. First, there are ritual events and commemorations that for many centuries have been widespread observances found in many parts of the Muslim world. For the most part, these are only documented for eras several centuries after than the time of the Prophet (typically from the fifth or later Islamic centuries only), and cannot usually claim to be practices of the early generations of Muslim life. These observances include celebrations of the Prophet's Birthday (*Mawlid*), his "heavenly journey" or "ascent" (*Miʿrāj*), the Day of Recompense (15 Shaʿbān), the birthdays of saints, visitation (*ziyārah*) of saints' tombs, and circumcision (*khitān*). All such observances tend to vary somewhat by region but can be found almost everywhere Islam has prevailed; they are not counted among the obligations of the *ʿibādāt*, even though many of them are deeply ingrained in local Islamic traditions. As widespread as they are, nowhere in the Qurʾān, *hadīth*, or other early sources are they or their observance mandated, nor even discussed as belonging to the religious duties of the *sharīʿah*. Some are evidently very recent: even a major Shīʿī ritual such as the *taʿziyeh*, or passion play, associated with the 10th of Muharram and the martyrdom on that date in 680 C.E. of the second Imām al-Husayn ibn ʿAlī, is not clearly documented before the end of the eighteenth century C.E.

A further, major dimension of Muslim life that does not show up clearly in the "normative" practice and thought treated in the present book is that of popular Sūfī practice. The Sufis, or "mystics" (perhaps better, the "spiritual pietists") of Islam, have, probably from the late first century, but as a developed strand of Islamic piety demonstrably only from the third century onward, provided both some Muslim elites and even more the great mass of the Muslim faithful with norms of spirituality and heightened practice of the *'ibādāt* and other acts of piety that have been tremendously influential, especially in folk religious usage. Qur'ān- and prayer-recitation, and chanting (*dhikr*), both in mosques and notably at tombs; visitation of the tombs of Muslim saints and celebration of their births or deaths; initiation into one or another Sufi "order" (*tarīqah*); and even ascetic practices such as extra fasting or additional performances of *salāt* have been for centuries typical of popular piety in Islamic societies. It must, however, suffice for our brief treatment here to note that these practices, associated most closely with the piety of popular Sufism, have been and remain major facts of everyday Islamic piety and faith around the world, even though they do not fall under the formal rubric of a Muslim's obligatory duty to perform the *'ibādāt* and are not treated explicitly in the early sources (and because they are not, they have often been the targets of literalist and conservative reformers who see such practices as types of "innovation" [*bid'ah*] that have no proper place in "true" Islamic practice). In very real ways the more internalized piety of the Sufis has been a constant reality of Muslim religious life and sensibility since an early, if not the earliest, period of Islamic history.

The *mu'amalāt*, or "social relations," form a much larger legal category of Muslim practice distinct from the religious or cultic observances of the *'ibādāt* and other, "non-canonical" rituals and practices of popular Islam and/or Sufi practice. The *mu'āmalāt* are of considerable importance to the daily life of observant Muslims and to the life of the community in which they live. They involve the full range of everyday activities, from personal issues of hygiene, food, sex, ethics, inheritance, and marriage to business dealings involving land-holding, interest, contracts, and the like, as well as other social or political concerns. The constraints of the current work do not allow treating even a fraction of these in any detail. What we can do is indicate some of the topics that receive attention in the sources and trace where possible the ethos behind them and their regulation in those sources.

The largest category of social relations is that of family matters, and here the Qur'ān offers clear moral guidance and even many specific directives for appropriate personal behavior in diverse aspects of living. A good example of the diversity of these admonitions is found in the varied pronouncements of Sūrah 17:23ff.:

> Your Lord had decreed that you should serve no one but Him and show kindness to parents, whether one or both of them reaches old age with you. Do not rebuke or scold them, but speak kindly to them. Lower to them gently the wing of humility out of compassion and say: "My Lord, have mercy upon them as they nurtured me when I was little." Your Lord knows best what is in your hearts, whether you are upright, and He is forgiving to those who turn to Him.
>
> Give the kinsman his due, and to the poor and the wayfarer, and do not squander (wealth) wantonly—truly, the squanderers are the brothers of the satans, and Satan is ungrateful to your Lord.
>
> Do not kill your children [referring to the pagan practice of female infanticide] from fear of poverty; We shall provide for them and you. Truly, killing them is a grave sin.
>
> Do not approach adultery, for it is surely repugnant and an evil path.
>
> Do not kill a person whose killing God has forbidden except for just cause; if any person is wrongfully killed, We have given his next-of-kin authority [to retaliate]; but let him not be excessive in retaliation, for he has been helped [by the right to retaliate].
>
> Do not touch the property of the orphan except for its improvement, until he comes of age. And keep your covenant; a covenant you will be accountable for.
>
> Give full measure when you measure, and weigh with just scales; that is best and a better interpretation. (S. 17:23–27, 31–35)

As one can see from this passage, even in those relatively limited cases wherein the Qur'ān is prescriptive, more specificity is required for the injunctions involved to be functionally useful. Some of the injunctions above are specified more precisely even in the Qur'ān itself, one example being the case of the *diyah*, or blood-money due for a person killed, which is treated in Sūrah 4:92:

> A believer should not kill a believer other than by mistake. Whoever kills a believer by mistake must free a believing slave and pay blood-money (*diyah*) to the family, unless they remit it [as charity]. If the victim belonged to a people who are your enemies, and was a believer, then freeing a believing slave [is required]. If he belonged to a people with whom yours were allied, then the *diyah* must be paid to them and a believing slave freed. Whoever cannot afford to do this must

fast for two consecutive months in repentance to God. God is All-knowing, All-wise.

More often, the *hadīth* and then the law books of the various schools of legal interpretation provide the needed further interpretation, elaboration, and specification of the qur'ānic injunctions and moral exhortations. One finds, for example, with regard to retribution for fornication by an unmarried person, the following *hadīth* in al-Bukhārī (81:18):

> Said b. Khālid al-Juhānī said: "I heard the Prophet decree with regard to the unmarried person committing adultery that he be flogged with a hundred lashes and exiled for a year. 'Umar b. al-Khattāb exiled [such a person], and this tradition (*sunnah*) still holds."

The range of subjects covered, especially in the *hadīth*, is very broad, encompassing day-to-day activities such as buying and selling, renting, loans, mortgages, partnership, slaves, gifts, wills and testaments, food and eating, hunting and slaughtering, medicines, dress, and so forth. An example from commerce is the chapter devoted in Bukhārī's and other collections to the *salām*, the practice of paying for goods to be delivered at a later date:

> Ibn 'Umar said: "There is no harm in purchasing foodstuff to be delivered within a specified period at a specified price, as long as it is not a growing crop which has not yet ripened free of blight." (al-Bukhārī 35:7)

One of the most extensive areas of qur'ānic and *hadīth* regulation of personal and communal life is that of family relations, from treatment of spouses or widows to the division of inheritances. For example, there is a clear concern for just treatment of all relatives, much of which is directed in the Qur'ān at previous impious practices from female infanticide to treatment of women as chattel rather than partners (even if not in every regard equal partners) in marriage. Another strong theme is the compassionate treatment of orphans, widows, and the poor—the weakest members of society. Several of these are evident in the beginning verses of Sūrah 4:

> Give to orphans their possessions; do not substitute worthless things for good things nor consume their possessions as your own—that would be a great crime. If you fear that you cannot deal equitably with the orphans, marry those of the women who seem good to you—two or

three or four; and if you fear that you cannot be equitable [to more than one], then [only] one, or those [slaves] in your possession; then it is more likely you will not be unjust. Give to the women their dowries as gifts; then if they of their own accord give back some of it to you, use it happily and in good conscience. Do not give to the feebleminded the property that God put in your care, but give them food and clothing from it and speak kind words to them. (S. 4:2–5)

The general emphasis upon the moral imperative to protect those who most need it is evident later in the same Sūrah (4:36):

Serve and worship God; do not associate anything with Him. [Show] kindness to parents and to relatives, orphans, the poor, the person under your protection—whether kin to you or not, your Companion, the wayfarer, and those [slaves/captives] whom your right hands possess.

There are also many qur'ānic and *hadīth* texts that enjoin upon the Muslim fair dealing in all sectors of life. One example of this comes in the chapter on "gifts" in Muslim's *hadīth* collection:

Nu'mān b. Bashīr related: "My father donated to me some of his property. My mother 'Amra bint Rawāhah said, 'I shall not be happy [about this] until you make the Apostle of God witness it.' So my father went to the Apostle of God to have him witness the gift to me. The Apostle of God said to him, 'Have you done the same with all of your sons?' He said, 'No.' Whereupon he [the Prophet] said: 'Fear God and be evenhanded with respect to your children.' My father came back and retrieved the gift." (*Muslim* 3:5)

Finally, in speaking of the practice of Islam, it is crucial to note one important prerequisite for the efficacy and validity of every act of devotion to God and compliance with His *sharī'ah*, namely intention (*nīyah*). Every ritual action, including ablution, must be attended by a conscious expression of the worshipper's intention to perform the duty well and in purity of heart and mindfulness of what is being done. And well beyond ritual obligations, any action a person takes is understood to be validated by the intention of the actor. Thus it is no accident that the great *hadīth* compendium of al-Bukhārī has as the first hadīth in the very first chapter the famous words of Muhammad:

Actions are [judged] according to [their] intentions, and every man gets what he has intended: thus he who emigrated [from Mecca to Medina] for the sake of world[ly things] or for a woman [to marry], his emigration (*hijrah*) was for that for which he emigrated.

This attitude is sustained throughout Islamic jurisprudence and generally in Islamic life: even a good deed is lessened or nullified by wrong intention and a bad deed also is mitigated by good intention and worsened by evil intent. The clear Muslim understanding is that God looks into the heart and judges by what is there, not simply by the external acts that a person performs: "Gods knows what is in your hearts" (S. 33:51). This is both a terrible burden of responsibility and a great gift to the pious, for it means that what counts is purity of spirit, not purity of conformity to external standards of good actions. Here is where Sufi piety begins also, for it places always a premium on the internal rather than the external and underscores the centrality of personal sincerity to true faith rather than mere conformity to external practice of the faithful.

This emphasis on the inner intent and quality of faith has also meant that Muslims have been generally (even though not always, to be sure) much more capable than their Christian counterparts of tolerating rather than persecuting as heretics other Muslims with whom they disagree: it is often argued that if a person says he or she is *muslim* in truth, other Muslims should take them at their word, for only God knows the true, inmost state of their faith and obedience and it is His part, not the Muslims', to sit in judgment on the sincerity of their faith.

The clear thrust of all of the foregoing is that *islām* consists both in overt practices and in inner faithfulness. It is thus appropriate to close the discussion of the practice of Muslims with the words of Sūrah 2:177, the most famous qur'ānic statement of what true *islām* entails:

> There is no virtue in turning your faces to the east and to the west [in worship]; rather the virtuous person is one who has faith in God, in the Last Day, in angels, in scripture, and in the prophets; who, in spite of one's love of it, gives of one's wealth to relatives, orphans, the poor, travelers, and supplicants, and to free slaves; who performs the *salāt* and gives alms; and those who keep their pacts when they make them, who are steadfast in adversities, hardships, and evil times—these are those who are true, and these are the God-fearing.

CHAPTER FIVE

THE BELIEVERS AND THE UNBELIEVERS

A. The Issue

One God, revealing himself to the faithful, divides humanity between those that know Him and those that do not know Him. Judaism, Christianity, and Islam in common faced the question, how are we to think about, and deal with, idolaters, meaning, those who do not know God? Judaism managed without answering that question; in its classical Rabbinic writings, it did not come to grips with the anomaly represented by either Christianity (sharing Scriptures with Judaism but drawing other conclusions from them) or, it goes without saying, Islam. Christianity and Islam had, however, to frame doctrines to come to terms with Judaism, and Islam with Christianity as well.

Since monotheism maintains there is, and can be, only one, unique God, all humanity divides into those who know or respond to God and those who do not. On a single continuum, Judaism framed the policy of avoiding idolaters while Islam, because of the context in which it arose, had actively to engage them. Judaism prayed that at the end of days God would draw all mankind to knowledge of him. Islam assigned to the believers in the here and now the task of replacing idolatry with monotheistic faith and worship. These represent the extreme: a passive Judaism depending upon God to resolve the anomaly of idolatry, an active Islam attempting to win human beings away from idolatry to submission to the one true Lord of creation. Christianity defined itself as the true Israel from the moment of its consciousness of itself, and for that reason took up, as a systemic aspect of its self-definition, an ongoing dialogue with Judaism. Christ came to be understood as the central truth of the Torah and the Prophets, and that model, which traced the influence of the incarnation in the wisdom of Israel's Scriptures, was also applied to the truths of other religious and philosophical systems.

B. Avoid Idolaters at All Costs: Judaism

In the classical sources of Judaism, persons beyond holy Israel are classified as idolaters and so are unclean. For idolatry is unclean; the idol stands for death: to be avoided at all costs. Gentiles are idolaters, and Israelites worship the one, true God, the source of life, who has made himself known in the Torah. In the Oral Torah, that is the difference—the only consequential distinction—between Israel and the gentiles. Then how does the distinction in theory make a difference in the practice, the conduct, of everyday affairs? What is at stake is that Israel stands for life, and the gentiles, like their idols, for death. An asherah-tree, which serves like an idol, like a corpse, conveys uncleanness to those who pass underneath it. That is stated explicitly by the Mishnah at Abodah Zarah 3:8: "And he should not pass underneath it, but if he passed underneath it, he is unclean." Idolatry then conveys uncleanness the way a corpse does, and idolaters are to be avoided.

Why idolatry defines the boundary between Israel and everybody else is simple to understand. The reason is that idolatry—rebellious arrogance against God—encompasses the entire Torah. The religious duty to avoid idolatry is primary; if one violates the religious duties, he breaks the yoke of commandments, and if he violates that single religious duty, he violates the entire Torah. Violating the prohibition against idolatry is equivalent to transgressing all Ten Commandments. How does Judaism explain the fact of life, that at this time only a minority of mankind knows God? It is mankind's own decision. Here is a protracted account of the way in which the Torah represents the gentiles in relationship to Israel. The story portrays the last judgment, when the nations complain that God has shown favoritism to Israel—meaning, those who accept God's rule and live by the Torah.

R. Hanina bar Pappa, and some say, R. Simlai, gave the following exposition [of the verse, "They that fashion a graven image are all of them vanity, and their delectable things shall not profit, and their own witnesses see not nor know" (Is. 44:9)]: "In the age to come the Holy One, blessed be He, will bring a scroll of the Torah and hold it in His bosom and say, 'Let him who has kept himself busy with it come and take his reward.' Then all the gentiles will crowd together: 'All of the nations are gathered together' (Is. 43:9). The Holy One, blessed

be He, will say to them, 'Do not crowd together before Me in a mob.
But let each nation enter together with its scribes, 'and let the peoples be gathered together' (Is. 43:9), and the word 'people' means 'kingdom': 'and one kingdom shall be stronger than the other' (Gen. 25:23)."

Israel contends with the great empires, Rome and Persia, as the
principals of world politics in the time of the Rabbinic sages. Rome
comes first:

> "The Holy One, blessed be He, will say to them, 'How have you
> defined your chief occupation?'
> "They will say before Him, 'Lord of the world, a vast number of
> marketplaces have we set up, a vast number of bathhouses we have
> made, a vast amount of silver and gold have we accumulated. And
> all of these things we have done only in behalf of Israel, so that they
> may define as their chief occupation the study of the Torah.'
> "The Holy One, blessed be He, will say to them, 'You complete
> idiots! Whatever you have done has been for your own convenience.
> You have set up a vast number of marketplaces to be sure, but that
> was so as to set up whorehouses in them. The bathhouses were for
> your own pleasure. Silver and gold belong to me anyhow: "Mine is
> the silver and mine is the gold, says the Lord of hosts" (Hag. 2:8).
> Are there any among you who have been telling of "this," and "this"
> is only the Torah: "And this is the Torah that Moses set before the
> children of Israel' (Dt. 4:44). So they will make their exit, humiliated."

Now come the Persians, with the same case:

> "When the kingdom of Rome has made its exit, the kingdom of Persia
> enters afterward.
> "The Holy One, blessed be He, will say to them, 'How have you
> defined your chief occupation?'
> "They will say before Him, 'Lord of the world, We have thrown
> up a vast number of bridges, we have conquered a vast number of
> towns, we have made a vast number of wars, and all of them we did
> only for Israel, so that they may define as their chief occupation the
> study of the Torah.'
> "The Holy One, blessed be He, will say to them, 'Whatever you
> have done has been for your own convenience. You have thrown up
> a vast number of bridges, to collect tolls, you have conquered a vast
> number of towns, to collect the corvée, and, as to making a vast num-
> ber of wars, I am the one who makes wars: "The Lord is a man of
> war" (Ex. 19:17). Are there any among you who have been telling of
> "*this*," and in context the word "this" refers only to the Torah, as
> shown in the following analogous usage: "And *this* is the Torah that

Moses set before the children of Israel" (Dt. 4:44).' So they will make their exit, humiliated.

"And so it will go with each and every nation."

But God had shown special favor to Israel, by forcing Israel to accept the Torah. The nations point to the fact that, when God offered the Torah to Israel at Sinai, he held Mount Sinai over their heads and offered them the choice of the Torah or the mountain:

> "They will say to him, 'Lord of the world, did You hold a mountain over us like a cask and when they refused to accept the Torah you held the mountain over Israel like a cask and said to them, 'If you accept the Torah, well and good, and if not, then there is where your grave will be.'"

Now comes a counterthrust. God points out that the nations of the world all descend from Noah—the story of Genesis always forms the Judaic anthropology, and also Noah's. Now while Israel got the Torah, Noah too, and therefore also his heirs, were vouchsafed commandments. But, God points out, they did not keep the seven commandments assigned to them:

> "Then the Holy One, blessed be He, will say to them, 'Let us make known what happened first: "Let them announce to us former things" (Is. 43:9). As to the seven religious duties that you did accept, where have you actually carried them out?"
>
> "This is what the gentiles say before him, 'Lord of the world, Israel, who accepted it—where in the world have they actually carried it out?'

"If we have failed, so has Israel," the nations claim. And who is to testify otherwise? Certainly not God, who is biased in their favor:

> "The Holy One, blessed be He, will say to them, 'I shall bear witness concerning them, that they have carried out the whole of the Torah!'
>
> "They will say before Him, 'Lord of the world, is there a father who is permitted to give testimony concerning his son? For it is written, "Israel is my son, my firstborn" (Ex. 4:22).'
>
> "The Holy One, blessed be He, will say to them, 'The Heaven and the earth will give testimony in their behalf that they have carried out the entirety of the Torah.'
>
> "They will say before him, 'Lord of the world, the Heaven and earth have a selfish interest in the testimony that they give: 'If not for my covenant with day and with night, I should not have appointed the ordinances of Heaven and earth' (Jer. 33:25).'"

Israel's enemies will testify concerning them: Nimrod, Laban, Potiphar, Nebuchadnezzar, and the rest:

> "The Holy One, blessed be He, will say to them, 'Some of them may well come and give testimony concerning Israel that they have observed the entirety of the Torah. Let Nimrod come and give testimony in behalf of Abraham that he never worshipped idols. Let Laban come and give testimony in behalf of Jacob, that he never was suspect of thievery. Let the wife of Potiphar come and give testimony in behalf of Joseph, that he was never suspect of 'sin.' Let Nebuchadnessar come and give testimony in behalf of Hananiah, Mishael, and Azariah, that they never bowed down to the idol. Let Darius come and give testimony in behalf of Daniel, that he did not neglect even the optional prayers. Let Bildad the Shuhite and Zophar the Naamatite and Eliphaz the Temanite and Elihu son of Barachel the Buzite come and testify in behalf of Israel that they have observed the entirety of the Torah: "Let the nations bring their own witnesses, that they may be justified" (Is. 43:9).'"

Now the nations ask for another chance:

> "They will say before Him, 'Lord of the world, Give it to us to begin with, and let us carry it out.'
> "The Holy One, blessed be He, will say to them, 'World-class idiots! He who took the trouble to prepare on the eve of the Sabbath [Friday] will eat on the Sabbath, but he who took no trouble on the even of the Sabbath—what in the world is he going to eat on the Sabbath! Still, [I'll give you another chance.] I have a rather simple religious duty, which is called "the tabernacle." Go and do that one.'"
> "They will make themselves appear to be converts, and they will put on phylacteries on their heads and arms and fringes on their garments and a mezuzah on their doors. But when they witness the war of Gog and Magog, He will say to them, 'How come you have come?' They will say, '"Against the Lord and against His Messiah."' For so it is said, 'Why are the nations in an uproar and why do the peoples mutter in vain' (Ps. 2:1). Then each one of them will rid himself of his religious duty and go his way: 'Let us break their bands asunder' (Ps. 2:3). Then the Holy One, blessed be He, goes into session and laughs at them: 'He who sits in Heaven laughs' (Ps. 2:4)."
> Bavli Abodah Zarah 2a–b

What is important in the colloquy is the basic theological view, that the gentiles are what they are by reason of their own decision, an act of will. And so too is Israel. Then Israel's task is to keep separate from the nations, whom God will judge in the end of days. Israel by definition differs from the nations, not on ethnic grounds at all. The difference comes about solely by reason of God's decision and God's action. God responds to the character of the nations' response to the Torah, where God is made manifest and God's will is made known. That explains who and what is "Israel": Israel is Israel by reason of the Torah—that alone. Hence there can be no "children after the promise" who also are not "children after the flesh," since by keeping the covenant, gentiles become that "Israel after the flesh" that stands perpetually at Sinai.

How then is Israel to relate to the gentiles; that is, how are the faithful to deal with the unbelievers? The theology of Judaism emerges from both law, Halakhah, and lore, Aggadah, as we noted in chapter one. The Halakhah in its norms of behavior treats gentiles as undifferentiated, but as individuals. The Aggadah in its norms of belief treats gentiles as "the nations" and takes no interest in individuals or in transactions between private persons. In the theology of the Oral Torah, the category—the gentiles or the nations, without elaborate differentiation—encompasses all who are not-Israelites, that is, who do not belong to Israel and therefore do not know and serve God. That category takes on meaning only as complement and opposite to its generative counterpart, having no standing—self-defining characteristics—on its own. That is, since Israel encompasses the sector of humanity that knows and serves God by reason of God's self-manifestation in the Torah, the gentiles are comprised by everybody else: those placed by their own intention and active decision beyond the limits of God's revelation. Guided by the Torah Israel worships God; without its illumination, gentiles worship idols. At the outset, therefore, the main point registers: by "gentiles" sages understand God's enemies, and by Israel sages understand those who know God as God has made himself known, which is, through the Torah. In no way do we deal with secular categories, but with theological ones.

The Halakhah then serves as the means for the translation of theological conviction into social policy. Gentiles are assumed to be ready to murder any Israelite they can get their hands on, rape any Israelite women, commit bestiality with any Israelite cow. The Oral Torah cites few cases to indicate that that conviction responds to ordinary, everyday events; the hostility to gentiles flows from a theory of idolatry, not the facts of everyday social intercourse, which, as we have seen, sages recognize is full of neighborly cordiality. Then why take for granted that gentiles routinely commit the mortal sins of not merely idolatry but bestiality, fornication, and murder? That is because the Halakhah takes as its task the realization of the theological principle that those who hate Israel hate God, those who hate God hate Israel, and God will ultimately vanquish Israel's enemies as his own—just as God too was redeemed from Egypt. So the theory of idolatry, involving alienation from God, accounts for the wicked conduct imputed to idolaters, without regard to whether, in fact, that is how idolaters conduct themselves. That matter of logic is stated in so many words in Sifré to Numbers LXXXIV:IV:

> 1. A. "and let them that hate you flee before you":
>   B. And do those who hate [come before] Him Who spoke and brought the world into being?
>   C. The purpose of the verse at hand is to say that whoever hates Israel is as if he hates Him Who spoke and by His word brought the world into being.

The same proposition is reworked. God can have no adversaries, but gentile enemies of Israel act as though they were his enemies:

> D. Along these same lines: "In the greatness of Your majesty You overthrow Your adversaries" (Ex. 15:7).
> E. And are there really adversaries before Him Who spoke and by His word brought the world into being? But Scripture thus indicates that whoever rose up against Israel is as if he rose up against the Omnipresent.
> F. Along these same lines: "Do not forget the clamor of your foes, the uproar of your adversaries, which goes up continually" (Ps. 74:23).
> G. "For lo, Your enemies, O Lord" (Ps. 92:10).
> H. "For those who are far from You shall perish, You put an end to those who are false to You" (Ps. 73:27).
> I. "For lo, Your enemies are in tumult, those who hate You have raised their heads" (Ps. 83:2). On what account? "They lay crafty plans against Your people, they consult together against Your protected ones" (Ps. 83:3).

Israel hates God's enemies, and Israel is hated because of its loyalty to God (a matter to which we shall return presently):

> J. "Do I not hate those who hate You, O Lord? And do I not loathe them that rise up against You? I hate them with perfect hatred, I count them my enemies" (Ps. 139:21–22).

K. And so too Scripture says, "For whoever lays hands on You is as if he lays hands on the apple of his eye" (Zech. 2:12).

L. R. Judah says, "What is written is not, 'the apple of an eye' but 'the apple of *his* eye,' it is as if Scripture speaks of Him above, but Scripture has used an euphemism."

Now the consequences of these propositions are drawn:

V. And whoever gives help to Israel is as if he gives help to Him Who spoke and by His word brought the world into being, as it is said, "Curse Meroz, says the angel of the Lord, curse bitterly its inhabitants, because they came not to the help of the Lord, to the help of the Lord against the mighty" (Judges 5:23).

W. R. Simeon b. Eleazar says, "You have no more prized part of the body than the eye and Israel has been compared to it. A further comparison: if a man is hit on his head, only his eyes feel it. Accordingly, you have no more prized part of the body than the eye, and Israel has been compared to it."

X. So Scripture says, "What, my son, what, son of my womb? what, son of my vows" (Prov. 31:2).

Y. And it says, "When I was a son with my father, tender, the only one in the sight of my mother, he taught me and said to me, 'Let your heart hold fast my words'" (Prov. 4:3–4).

The proposition announced at the outset is fully articulated—those who hate Israel hate God, those who are enemies of Israel are enemies of God, those who help Israel help God—and then systematically instantiated by facts set forth in Scripture. The systematic proof extends beyond verses of Scripture, with a catalogue of the archetypal enemies assembled: Pharaoh, Sisera, Sennacherib, Nebuchadnezzar, Haman. So the paradigm reinforces the initial allegation and repertoire of texts. The context then of all thought on Israel and the gentiles finds definition in supernatural issues and context in theology. In the Oral Torah sages at no point deem as merely secular the category, "the gentiles."

Now let us see how the gentiles are characterized in this-worldly terms, as we have noted how "being Israel" is assumed to mean that a given set of virtues will mark the Israelite individual. When God blesses gentile nations, they do not acknowledge him but blaspheme, but when he blesses Israel, they glorify him and bless him; these judgments elaborate the basic principle that the gentiles do not know God, and Israel does. But what emerges here is that even when the gentiles ought to recognize God's hand in their affairs, even when God blesses them, they still deny him, turning ignorance into willfulness. What is striking is the exact balance of three gentiles as against three Israelites, all of the status of world-rulers, the common cluster, Pharaoh, Sennacherib, Nebuchadnezzar, vs. the standard cluster, David, Solomon, and Daniel in Pesiqta deRab Kahana XXVIII:I.1:

> A. "On the eighth day you shall have a solemn assembly. [You shall do no laborious work, but you shall offer a burnt-offering, an offering by Fire, a pleasing odor to the Lord . . . These you shall offer to the Lord at your appointed feasts in addition to your votive-offerings and your freewill-offerings, for your burnt-offerings and for your cereal-offerings and for your drink-offerings and for your peace-offerings]" (Numbers 29:35–9).
> B. But you have increased the nation, "O Lord, you have increased the nation; [You are glorified; You have enlarged all the borders of the land]" (Is. 17:25).

The proposition having been stated, the composer proceeds to amass evidence for the two contrasting propositions, first gentile rulers:

> C. You gave security to the wicked Pharaoh. Did he then call You "Lord"? Was it not with blasphemies and curses that he said, "Who is the Lord, that I should listen to His voice" (Ex. 5:2)!
> D. You gave security to the wicked Sennacherib. Did he then call You "Lord"? Was it not with blasphemies and curses that he said, "Who is there among all the gods of the lands" (2 Kgs. 18:35).
> E. You gave security to the wicked Nebuchadnezzar. Did he then call You "Lord"? Was it not with blasphemies and curses that he said, "And who is God to save you from my power" (Dan. 3:15).

Now, nicely balanced, come Israelite counterparts:

> F. "You have increased the nation; You are glorified":
> G. You gave security to David and so he blessed You: "David blessed the Lord before all the congregation" (1 Chr. 29:10).
> H. You gave security to his son, Solomon, and so he blessed You: "Blessed is the Lord Who has given rest to His people Israel" (1 Kgs. 8:56).
> I. You gave security to Daniel and so he blessed You: "Daniel answered and said, Blessed be the name of God" (Dan. 2:20).

Here is another set of opposites—three enemies, three saints, a fair match. In each case, the Israelite responded to God's favor with blessings, and the gentile with blasphemy. In this way the gentiles show the price they pay for not knowing God but serving no-gods instead. Like philosophers, the sages in the documents of the Oral Torah appeal to a single cause to account for diverse phenomena; the same factor that explains Israel has also to account for the opposite, that is, the gentiles; what Israel has, gentiles lack, and that common point has made all the difference. Idolatry is what angers God and turns him against the gentiles, stated in so many words at Bavli Abodah Zarah 1:1 I.23/4b: "That time at which God gets angry comes when the kings put their crowns on their heads and prostrate themselves to the sun. Forthwith the Holy One, blessed be He, grows angry." That is why it is absolutely forbidden to conduct any sort of commerce with gentiles in connection with occasions of idolatrous worship, e.g., festivals and the like.

When we come to the Halakhah's treatment of the laws governing interaction with gentiles/idolaters, our question must be, Why do the Rabbinic sages treat gentiles as a major consideration and therefore define a principal category of the Halakhah in this wise? It is because sages must devote a considerable account to the challenge to that justice represented by gentile power and prosperity, Israel's subordination and penury. These challenge the conviction that the omnipotent and only God governs with justice and mercy. For if the story of the moral order tells about justice that encompasses all creation, the chapter of gentile rule vastly disrupts the account. Gentile rule forms the point of tension, the source of conflict, attracting attention and demanding explanation. For the critical problematic inherent in the category, Israel, is that its anti-category, the gentiles, dominate. And that explains why the systemic problematic focuses upon the question, how can justice be thought to order the world if the gentiles rule? That formulation furthermore forms the public counterpart to the private perplexity: how is it that the wicked prosper and the righteous suffer? The two challenges to the conviction of the rule of moral rationality—gentile hegemony and the prosperity of wicked persons—match.

Yet here the Halakhah turns out to make its own point, one that we ought not to miss. The Halakhah presupposes not gentile hegemony—legitimate rule—but only gentile power; and it further takes for granted that Israelites may make choices, may specifically refrain from trading in what gentiles value in the service of their gods, and may hold back from gentiles what gentiles require for that service.

Focused upon interiorities that prove real and tangible, not matters of theological theory at all, the Halakhah of the tractate on idolatry, Abodah Zarah, legislates for a world in which Israelites, while subordinate in some ways, control their own conduct and govern their own destiny. Israelites may live in a world governed by gentiles, but they form intentions and carry them out. They may decide what to sell and what not to sell, whom to hire for what particular act of labor and to whom not to sell their own labor.

The Halakhah therefore makes a formidable statement of Israel's freedom to make choices, its opportunity within the context of everyday life to preserve a territory free of idolatrous contamination, much as Israel in entering the Land was to create a territory free of the worship of idols and their presence. In the setting of world order Israel may find itself subject to the will of others, but in the house of Israel, Israelites can and should establish a realm for God's rule and presence, free of idolatry.

Accordingly, the religious problem of the Halakhah therefore focuses on the inner world of Israel in command of itself. The religious problem of the Aggadah, by contrast, explains, rationalizes as best it can, gentile hegemony. The Halakhah sees as within Israel's dominion that world for which Israel bears responsibility; there sages legislate. The Aggadah forms a different perspective upon the world subject to gentile rule, that is, the world beyond the limits of Israel's own power. The Halakhah speaks of Israel at the heart of matters, the Aggadah, of Israel within humanity.

To see the contrast between the Halakhah and the Aggadah on gentiles, let me briefly reprise the Aggadic account of the matter. Who, speaking categorically not historically, indeed are these "non-Israelites," called gentiles ("the nations," "the peoples," and the like)? The answer is dictated by the form of the question: Who exactly is a "non-Israelite"? Then the answer concerning the signified is always relative to its signifier, Israel? Within humanity-other-than-Israel, differentiation articulates itself along gross, political lines, always in relationship to Israel. If humanity is differentiated politically, then, it is a differentiation imposed by what has happened between a differentiated portion of humanity and Israel. It is, then, that segment of humanity that under given circumstances has interacted with Israel: (1) Israel arising at the end and climax of the class of world empires, Babylonia, Media, Greece, Rome; or (2) Israel against Egypt;

or (3) Israel against Canaan. That is the point at which Babylonia, Media, Greece, Rome, Egypt, or Canaan take a place in the narrative, become actors for the moment, but never givens, never enduring native categories. Then, when politics do not impose their structure of power-relationships, humanity is divided between Israel and everyone else.

In the story of the moral plan for creation, the nations find their proportionate position in relationship to Israel. If the nations acquire importance by reason of their dealings with Israel, the monarchies that enjoy prominence benefit because they ruled Israel:

5. A. "the mind of Pharaoh and his servants was changed toward the people":
   B. This indicates that when the Israelites went out of Egypt, the monarchy of the Egyptians came to an end,
   C. as it is said, "Who are our servants?"
6. A. "[and they said, 'What is this that we have done, that we have let Israel go] from serving us?'"
   B. "Who are our servants?"] They said, "Now all the nations of the world will be chiming in against us like a bell, saying, 'Now these, who were in their domain, they let go to leave them!'
   C. "Now how are *we* going to send to Aram Naharaim and Aram Soba officers and task-masters to bring us slave-boys and slave girls?"
   D. This indicates that Pharaoh ruled from one end of the world to the other, having governors from one end of the world to the other.
   E. This was for the sake of the honor of Israel.
   F. Of Pharaoh it is said, "The king sent and loosed him, even the ruler of peoples, and set him free' (Ps. 105:20).

We now recapitulate the matter, moving through the sequence, Assyria, then the recurring cluster of four, Babylonia, Media, Greece, and Rome, the last four standing for the world-empires to that time, the first six centuries c.e., so far as sages' memories reconstructed history:

7. A. And so you find that every nation and language that subjugated Israel ruled from one end of the world to the other, for the sake of the honor of Israel.
   B. What does Scripture say in connection with Assyria? "And my hand has found as a nest the riches of the peoples, and as one gathers lost eggs have I gathered all the earth, and there was

none that moved the wing or opened the mouth or chirped"
(Is. 10:14).

C. What does Scripture say of Babylonia? "And it shall come to
pass that the nation and kingdom that will not serve this same
Nebuchadnezzar, king of Babylonia" (Jer. 27:8).

D. What does Scripture say of Media? "Then king Darius wrote
to all the peoples" (Dan. 6:26).

E. What does Scripture say of Greece? "The beast had also four
heads and dominion was given to it" (Dan. 7:6).

F. What does Scripture say of the fourth kingdom [Rome]? "And
it shall devour the whole earth and shall tread it down and
break it in pieces" (Dan. 7:23).

G. So you learn that every nation and language that subjugated
Israel ruled from one end of the world to the other, for the
sake of the honor of Israel.

Mekilta Attributed to R. Ishmael XX:II.5–7

A nation is distinguished by its interaction with Israel, and that interaction brings about the magnification of the name of that nation. It
would be difficult to express with greater power the proposition that
Israel then forms the center and heart of humanity, and the gentiles circle in their orbits round about. Little in the Halakhic repertoire recapitulates these convictions, which the Halakhah in no way
acknowledges. For the Halakhah matters are very different, as we
have seen.

What then is the difference between the gentile and the Israelite,
individually and collectively (there being no distinction in Judaism
between the private person, Israel the Israelite, and the public, social
and political entity, Israel God's people)? A picture in cartographic
form of the theological anthropology of the Oral Torah would portray a many-colored Israel at the center of the circle, with the perimeter comprised by all-white gentiles. The perimeter would be an
undifferentiated white, the color of death, since, in the *Halakhah*, gentiles like their idols, as we have seen, are a source of uncleanness
of the same virulence as corpse-uncleanness. The law of uncleanness
bears its theological counterpart in the lore of death and resurrection,
a single theology animating both. Gentile-idolaters and Israelite worshippers of the one and only God part company at death. For the
moment Israelites die but rise from the grave, gentiles die and remain
there. The roads intersect at the grave, each component of humanity taking its own path beyond. Israelites—meaning, those possessed

of right conviction—will rise from the grave, stand in judgment, but then enter upon eternal life, to which no one else will enjoy access. So, in substance, humanity viewed whole is divided between those who get a share in the world to come and who will stand when subject to divine judgment—Israel—and those who will not.

Clearly, the moral ordering of the world encompasses all humanity. But God does not neglect the gentiles or fail to exercise dominion over them. For even now, gentiles are subject to a number of commandments or religious obligations. God cares for gentiles as for Israel, he wants gentiles as much as Israel to enter the kingdom of Heaven, and he assigns to gentiles opportunities to evince their acceptance of his rule. One of these commandments is not to curse God's name, so Bavli Sanhedrin 7:5 I.2/56a: "Any man who curses his God shall bear his sin" (Lev. 24:15): It would have been clear had the text simply said, "A man." Why does it specify, "Any"? It serves to encompass idolaters, who are admonished not to curse the Name, just as Israelites are so admonished. Not cursing God, even while worshipping idols, seems a minimal expectation.

But in fact there are seven such religious obligations that apply to the children of Noah. It is not surprising—indeed, it is predictable—that the definition of the matter should find its place in the Halakhah of Abodah Zarah (8:4–6):

> T. 8:4 A. Concerning seven religious requirements were the children of Noah admonished:
>
> B. setting up courts of justice, idolatry, blasphemy [cursing the Name of God], fornication, bloodshed, and thievery.

We now proceed to show how each of these religious obligations is represented as applying to gentiles as much as to Israelites:

> C. Concerning setting up courts of justice—how so [how does Scripture or reason validate the claim that gentiles are to set up courts of justice]?
>
> D. Just as Israelites are commanded to call into session in their towns courts of justice.
>
> E. Concerning idolatry and blasphemy—how so? . . .
>
> F. Concerning fornication—how so?
>
> G. "On account of any form of prohibited sexual relationship on account of which an Israelite court inflicts the death-penalty, the children of Noah are subject to warning," the words of R. Meir.

H. And sages say, "There are many prohibited relationships, on account of which an Israelite court does not inflict the death-penalty and the children of Noah are [not] warned. In regard to these forbidden relationships the nations are judged in accord with the laws governing the nations.

I. "And you have only the prohibitions of sexual relations with a betrothed maiden alone."

The systemization of Scripture's evidence for the stated proposition continues:

T. 8:5 A. For bloodshed—how so?

B. A gentile [who kills] a gentile and a gentile who kills an Israelite are liable. An Israelite [who kills] a gentile is exempt.

C. Concerning thievery?

D. [If] one has stolen, or robbed, and so too in the case of finding a beautiful captive [woman], and in similar cases:

E. a gentile in regard to a gentile, or a gentile in regard to an Israelite—it is prohibited. And an Israelite in regard to a gentile—it is permitted.

T. 8:6 A. Concerning a limb cut from a living beast—how so?

B. A dangling limb on a beast, [which] is not [so connected] as to bring about healing,

C. is forbidden for use by the children of Noah, and, it goes without saying, for Israelites.

D. But if there is [in the connecting flesh] sufficient [blood supply] to bring about healing,

E. it is permitted to Israelites, and, it goes without saying, to the children of Noah.

As in the case of Israelites, so the death penalty applies to a child of Noah, so Bavli Sanhedrin 7:5 I.4–5/57a: "On account of violating three religious duties are children of Noah put to death: on account of adultery, murder, and blasphemy." R. Huna, R. Judah, and all the disciples of Rab say, "On account of seven commandments a son of Noah is put to death. The All-Merciful revealed that fact of one of them, and the same rule applies to all of them." But just as Israelites, educated in the Torah, are assumed to exhibit certain uniform virtues, e.g., forbearance, so gentiles, lacking that same education, are assumed to conform to a different model.

Gentiles, by reason of their condition outside of the Torah, are characterized by certain traits natural to their situation, and these are worldly. Not only so, but the sages' theology of gentiles shapes the normative law in how to relate to them. If an Israelite is by nature forbearing and forgiving, the gentile by nature is ferocious. That explains why in the Halakhah as much as in the Aggadah gentiles are always suspect of the cardinal sins, bestiality, fornication, and bloodshed, as well as constant idolatry. That view of matters is embodied in normative law, as we have seen. The law of the Mishnah corresponds to the lore of scriptural exegesis; the theory of the gentiles governs in both. Beyond the Torah there not only is no salvation from death, there is not even the possibility of a common decency. The Torah makes all the difference. The upshot may be stated very simply. Israel and the gentiles form the two divisions of humanity. The one will die but rise from the grave to eternal life with God. When the other dies, it perishes; that is the end. Moses said it very well: Choose life. The gentiles sustain comparison and contrast with Israel, the point of ultimate division being death for the one, eternal life for the other.

If Israel and the gentiles are deemed comparable, the gentiles do not acknowledge or know God; therefore, while they are like Israelites in sharing a common humanity by reason of mythic genealogy—deriving from Noah—the gentiles do not receive in a meritorious manner the blessings that God bestows upon them. So much for the points of stress of the Aggadah. When it comes to the Halakhah, as we have seen, the religious problematic focuses not upon the gentiles but upon Israel: what, given the world as it is, can Israel do in the dominion subject to Israel's own will and intention? That is the question that, as we now see, the Halakhah fully answers. For the Halakhah constructs, indeed defines, the interiority of an Israel sustaining God's service in a world of idolatry: life against death in the two concrete and tangible dimensions by which life is sustained: trade and the production of food, the foci of the Halakhah. No wonder Israel must refrain from engaging with idolatry on days of the festivals for idols that the great fairs embody—then especially.

C. CONVERTING JUDAISM (AND ALL THE REST): CHRISTIANITY

Christianity has had to deal with many "others" during its history. Some of those have been "significant others," who have turned out to teach us about ourselves. That has been the case internationally in the instances of Judaism, Islam, Hinduism, and Buddhism; and

locally in the instances of such movements as Marxism, Rastafarianism
and New Age spirituality. The capacity to fashion a separate identity while remaining in dialogue with others has characterized Christian thought, even during periods when prejudice has also been a
powerful factor.

The principal reason for that is that Christianity deploys two powerful conceptions to understand itself in relation to others. The first
is the metaphor of the body of Christ, embracing both the faithful
and the entire cosmos, as discussed in Chapter Three. The second
is the theology of the "Word" (the *logos*, see Chapter Two)—the
source of all human understanding, the power of creation—which
Jesus personally embodied. Both those conceptions were framed as
Christianity defined itself in respect of Israel. It is in that sense that
the relationship between Christianity and Judaism uniquely reveals
Christian identity. In this section, we will focus on the theology of
the *logos* and its vital antecedent: the Christian appropriation of the
Scriptures of Israel. Paul is the best guide to those hermeneutics,
just as Justin is the clearest theologian of the *logos*, whose debt to
Pauline thinking is manifest.

Paul's understanding of the body of Christ comports well with his
definition of faith. Just as he argued in Galatians that to believe in
Christ was to fulfill the faith of Abraham, so he argued in 1 Corinthians
that such faith made believers one body in Christ. The idiom of
Galatians, written around the year 53 c.e., is biblical; that of 1 Corinthians, written around the year 56 c.e., is philosophical, developing idioms of thought popularized by Stoicism. But both letters in
their differing ways implicitly raise the question of Israel as commonly defined in the Roman Empire. If faith (*pistis*) fulfills the vocation of Abraham and incorporates the believer into Christ, what
further value can be attached to what the Scriptures call Israel? That
is a question which Paul himself addresses at length in his letter to
the Romans.

Paul is never more himself than in Romans chapters 9–11, which
is just where he frames the issue of Israel in a way which became
classic for Christianity. Romans itself is the most mature of the genuinely Pauline letters, written around the year 57 c.e. to a community which he had not personally founded. His letter to Rome
is, in effect, a fulsome introduction to his own thinking, and the

main lines of Paul's argument seem reasonably clear. But the form of his argumentation, with its many references to Scripture and deductions from Scripture, strike many readers as both foreign and convoluted. Why is a basically simple idea wrapped up in an esoteric package? As we shall see, that question will itself require refinement as we encounter Paul's thinking, but it will serve us well as we first approach our text.

An observant student could sketch out a précis of Paul's thought in Romans 9–11, without reference to the Scriptures he cites. The result would be a reasonable, self-contained address, which could be delivered succinctly:

> Although I am distressed that my people have not accepted the gospel (9:1–5), their failure is not God's: it is just that He has, as always, chosen freely whom He wills (9:6–13). That might seem hard, but God is sovereign in the matter of choice (9:14–23), and He has simply decided to call both Jews and gentiles (9:24–33).
>
> There is now no distinction between Jew and Greek in the matter of salvation: if you confess the Lord Jesus and believe God raised him from the dead, you will be saved (10:1–21, v. 9). Those who are believers must not, however, imagine that God has rejected His people. After all, there are some Jews who do believe in Jesus (11:1–10), and even those who do not believe have, in their lack of faith, provided an opportunity for gentiles (11:11–24). Once the fullness of the gentiles is accomplished, all Israel, including both Jews and gentiles, will be seen to be saved (11:25–36).

There are, of course, crucial facets within each of the statements in the above précis, but they are subsidiary to the main lines of the argument. What becomes unmistakably clear, when we boil Paul's ornate speech down to its essentials, is that he is making a cogent case for a particular view of how God's saving activity in Christ Jesus is consistent with his election of Israel. Once it is clear that Israel is elected, not sovereign, so that divine choice, rather than divine right, is operative, Paul's observations follow logically.

Paul's design at this point comports well with the purpose of his letter to the Romans as a whole, and makes sense within the Hellenistic environment in which he functioned. Stanley Stowers has explained that the writing of letters, whether at the common level of incidental discourse, or with a refined standard of rhetoric, was conventional within the culture of the Mediterranean Basin and is a natural context in which to understand much of the New Testament.[1] As Stowers shows,[2] that convention also influenced ancient Judaism, which—despite the impression of an isolated phenomenon which some writers give—was itself a lively constituent within the cultural life of its time. But Stowers is well within the scholarly consensus when he concludes that Judaism did not actively appropriate the convention and transmit it directly to Christianity.

Specifically, Paul in Romans appears to be writing a "protreptic letter," by which Stowers means a work designed to convert the reader to Paul's set of teachings. Stowers is able on the basis of a comparison with Greco-Roman convention to argue that the entire letter is designed to present Paul's gospel of salvation for gentiles and to defend it against the charge that it means the loss of Israel's salvation. The analysis of Romans according to its function within its most plausible social setting therefore helps us to resolve the main lines of its purpose.

Indeed, the clarity of function which emerges from such an approach may appear to be at odds with the convoluted character of Paul's argument. Even if Romans be a "protreptic letter," the involved argument from Scripture in chapters 9–11 is obviously the result of a dynamic not evidenced by the letter as a whole. Of course, Scripture does play a crucial role in Romans generally (as it does normally in Pauline thought), but the consistency of recourse to textual argument makes these chapters appear distinctive.

Before we consider why Paul's form of argumentation in Romans 9–11 is exegetical in a way most of the letter is not, we must first appreciate how the simple, discursive case Paul makes is enhanced by means of reference to Scripture. At each major point in the argument, well known passages of Scripture are cited.

A crucial bridge is provided by narratives concerning Isaac. In Romans 9:7, Paul quotes Genesis 21:12, "After Isaac shall your seed

---

[1] *Letter Writing in Greco-Roman Antiquity*: Library of Early Christianity (Philadelphia: Westminster, 1986), 25.

[2] Pp. 41–42. See 2 Samuel 11:14–15; 1 Kings 21:8–10; 2 Kings 10:1–6; 19:9–14; Ezra 4–6:12, as well as to the more frequent references in Philo, Josephus, and 1, 2 Maccabees. Cf. also J. A. Fitzmyer, "Aramaic Epistolography," *A Wandering Aramean: Collected Aramaic Essays*: SBL Monograph Series 25 (Chicago: Scholars Press, 1979), 183–204; W. A. Meeks and R. L. Wilken, *Jews and Christians in Antioch in the First Four Centuries of the Common Era*: SBL Sources for Biblical Study 13 (Ann Arbor: Scholars Press, 1978).

be named." Now that reference may appear simply to be an instance of using a "proof-text," chosen pretty much at random from a much larger number of those that might have been cited. But the quotation comes at the climax of a story in which God tells Abraham to accede to Sarah's demand, and cast out Hagar and Ishmael, "for the son of this slave woman shall not inherit with my son Isaac" (Genesis 21:10).

The analogy with the situation Paul believes he addresses is striking. He spells the analogy out in Romans 9:8, "That is, these children of the flesh are not children of God, but children of the promise are reckoned as the seed." Of course, that finding requires that Isaac correspond to the promise, and Paul makes just that correspondence. In Romans 9:9, he quotes Genesis 18:14 (or perhaps v. 10), "At this time (next year) I will come, and Sarah will have a son." That verse, of course, is resonant, since it caps the story of God's visitation at Mamre: Sarah laughs (v. 12), and is blessed with Isaac, whose name means "he laughs," because it is God's joke in the end. In Paul's argument, what may seem to be the frivolity of God's sovereign choice is a serious principle, attested in Scripture.

The pattern established in Romans 9:6–9 is followed consistently in the chapters we are concerned with. At first, Paul does not cite a specific Scripture in what follows, but he does invoke the general case of Rebecca and Isaac (9:10, 11). She conceived twins, and before they did anything, or were even born, Rebecca was told, "The greater will serve the lesser" (Romans 9:12 and Genesis 25:23). At issue, of course, is the rivalry between Esau and Jacob, which is a major motif of Genesis. Paul sums it all up with a quotation from Malachi, "I loved Jacob and hated Esau" (Romans 9:13 and Malachi 1:2, 3). That Paul can draw upon Malachi's appropriation of the motif in Genesis is especially compelling: he implicitly claims that his analogy has prophetic warrant. The fundamentals of his scriptural reasoning are drawn from the Torah, but the nature of his reasoning, he claims, is in line with that of the prophets.[3]

---

[3] One possible source for this contention within Paul's thinking is offered by the prophetic Targumim, where *meturgemanin* commonly spoke on behalf of the Prophets of Israel, sometimes in an innovative fashion; see Chilton, *The Glory of Israel: The Theology and Provenience of the Isaiah Targum,* Journal for the Study of the Old Testament Supplement Series, 23 (Sheffield: JSOT, 1982), 52–56.

Paul appears to have operated with the conventional categorization of the Hebrew Bible in Judaism. That categorization recognized divisions of the canon into the Torah (the Pentateuch), the Prophets (including the Former Prophets, from Joshua through 2 Kings, and the Latter Prophets, more familiarly considered prophetic in English), and the Writings (an essentially miscellaneous category). The coherence and consistency of the canon is simply one of Paul's assumptions. Likewise, the words of Scripture are for him practically identical with the emerging Septuagint, if one allows for the occasional influence of the Hebrew text and Targumic interpretations.

It is indicative of the consistency of Pauline rhetoric that he now moves from Genesis to Exodus. That shift in scriptural foundation, at 9:14–15, corresponds precisely to the development of Paul's argument (see the précis): having rejoiced in God's sovereign choice as the fulfillment of promise, Paul now defends God's sovereignty against the charge that it is unjust or arbitrary (9:14). God said to Moses, "I will have mercy on whom I have mercy, and I will show compassion to whom I will show compassion" (Exodus 33:19; Romans 9:15). In Exodus, God speaks of his mercy and compassion just as he is revealing his goodness to Moses; Paul's point is that God's choices are consistent with his just revelation to Moses.

In the statement to Moses in Exodus 33:19, the narrative setting connects the definition of God's people with his revelation of his name and glory (Exodus 33:12–23): what is at issue is the very nature of God and nature of his people together. A particular case in Exodus of God deciding not to have mercy, as Paul says (9:18), is that of Pharaoh, of whom Scripture says, "For this purpose I have raised you up, that I might display my power over you, and that my name might be announced in all the earth" (Romans 9:17; Exodus 9:16). God's "name" is at issue in both passages in Exodus which have been cited (33:19 and 9:16), and their association betrays Paul's almost midrashic logic, in which Scripture is held in different places and contexts to address the same issues coherently.

The assumption of that coherence is carried over to the prophets: Isaiah (29:16; 45:9, in Romans 9:20) and Jeremiah (18:6, in Romans 9:21) are used to demonstrate that it is misguided for a vessel of punishment to answer back to its maker. Consideration of Isaiah 29:16; 45:9; and Jeremiah 18:6 within their literary contexts shows that Paul is still attending carefully to the sense of the passages he cites. In all, the paramount issue is the fate of Israel, as determined by a sovereign God.

The next development of Paul's argument, at 9:24–25 (again, cf. the précis) corresponds to a shift in canonical focus. It is demonstrated by citing Hosea and Isaiah that those who are called by God are from both Jews and gentiles (9:24). First, Hosea shows—at least, to Paul's satisfaction—that gentiles are to be included among God's people (9:25, 26). Paul garbles the quotation from Hosea, drawing first from 2:23, and then from 1:10, and here is stretching to make a point. Hosea is contextually concerned with the restoration of Israel, not the inclusion of gentiles; Paul reads what he takes to be a general truth of Scripture into a passage in which that meaning has no literary place.

He returns to his usual, more acute interpretation in 9:27–29 when he cites passages from Isaiah by way of arguing that Jews as such are not chosen, but that a remnant from their ranks is to be saved (Isaiah 10:22; 28:22 and Isaiah 1:9). Moreover, he cites a curious and creative mixture of Isaiah 28:16 and 8:14 in Romans 9:33, in order to show that the principle of selecting from the elect places a stone of stumbling and a rock of offense in the midst of Israel (Romans 9:30–32).

Paul's exegetical method is never more complex than in Romans 9, and we need to pause for breath before proceeding further. Although the details of the Pauline execution may dazzle us (as they were no doubt intended to), the fact is that certain characteristic traits are plain. Paul argues from the Torah that (1) God operates by fulfilling promises (9:1–13), and that (2) those promises are kept for those chosen by God (9:14–23). He then purports to demonstrate from the Prophets that God has chosen his people from among Jews and gentiles (9:24–33). On the whole, but for two exceptions, Paul cites his passages with care and contextual sensitivity, which means that any reader will better appreciate the argument if he or she is familiar with the Scriptures of Israel.

The two exceptions to Paul's care and sensitivity are instructive. As we have seen, he reads gentiles into Hosea (9:25, 26), and splices together two verses of Isaiah (9:33). These are not mere lapses on Paul's part. To his mind, the entry of gentiles among the ranks of God's chosen, and the coming of Christ as a rock of offense to many in Israel, are facts of experience which co-exist with and interpret facts of Scripture. Paul's "text" is not only the Scripture, but the revelation that Jesus is God's Son.

Once these interpretative characteristics of Paul's argument are appreciated, Romans 10 and 11 may more briefly be summarized from the point of view of their reference to Scripture. In chapter 10, Paul makes his famous, daring assertion that, in Deuteronomy 30:11–14, when Moses refers to the nearness of the commandment, he means not any precise instruction, but the presence of Christ, who can neither be brought down from Heaven, nor brought up from the abyss, except by God's power (Romans 10:6–8).

How does Paul know the Scriptures, properly understood, adduce Christ? He has just told us in v. 4, "Christ is the point (*telos*) of the law, for the righteousness of every believer." By again citing Isaiah 28:16, in v. 11, Paul may betray his own awareness that he is invoking Christ, rather than deducing Christ, at this point. The other usages in chapter 10—of Leviticus 18:5 in 10:5, of Joel 3:5 in 10:13, of Isaiah 52:7 in 10:15, of Isaiah 53:1 in 10:16, of Psalm 19:4 in 10:18, and of Isaiah 65:1, 2 in 10:20, 21—fall within the more usual Pauline range of texts which illustrate a coherent principle.

Chapter 11 may be surveyed even more summarily, because the usages of Scripture are all illustrative. There are no special invocations of Christ or of the motif of the inclusion of the gentiles. Until this point, the bulk of Paul's references have come from the Torah and the Latter Prophets. Now he brings balance to his case scripturally, by citing the instance of Elijah from the Former Prophets. Again, attention to the contexts of the Scriptures Paul cites richly rewards itself. The assertion that God has not rejected his people in 11:2, is drawn from 1 Samuel 12:22 and a context in which the prophet Samuel assures Israel that, despite their wickedness, God's choice is constant (1 Samuel 12:19–25). The closing portion of that passage, however, does threaten, "But if you act wickedly, you shall be swept away, both you and your king" (1 Samuel 12:25). Wickedness does not revoke God's choice, but it does alter its scope.

In other words, the thought of the remnant, which has been an explicit part of the argument since 9:27, 28 (by means of the citation of Isaiah 10:22, 23), has remained with Paul throughout. For that reason, the reference to Elijah in 11:2b–5 (cf. 1 Kings 19:1–18, and vv. 10, 14 & 18 in particular) is apposite: there is a prophetic analogy of the circumstances Paul finds himself in, where only a radical minority has kept faith. Once it is established that the residue of the remnant can be deliberately hardened in their rebellion (cf. Deuteronomy 29:3 in 11:8 and Psalm 69:22, 23 in 11:9), there is no further need of scriptural warrant for what Paul argues.

He does, however, offer a final citation of Isaiah (59:20, 21 and 27:9) in 11:26, 27, by way of making his comprehensive assertion that "all Israel"—but a chastened, forgiven Israel, not a claimant as of right—is to be saved. At this crucial moment, he must again splice Scriptures, not merely cite them, to achieve the dual stress on deliverance and forgiveness which is the apogee of his argument.

We may set out mentally, as it were side by side, two analyses of Romans 9–11. Followed along one track, the chapters instance protreptic discourse, in which Paul appeals to his readers to follow his way of thinking. He wishes to convince them that God's inclusion of believing gentiles with Jews who accept Jesus as Christ represents a fulfillment of the promise to Israel. Followed along the second track, the same chapters represent a carefully orchestrated argument from all the main sections of the Hebrew canon, cited in translation, which is designed to sweep readers up in the promise that all Israel—forgiven Jews and gentiles—are to be saved (11:26, 27).

It is obvious that the two tracks of analysis are complementary, and neither alone would adequately account for the chapters generally. But it is equally obvious that the chapters are crafted as a whole: the references to Scripture are not only keyed to major developments of the argument but contribute those developments. It is not a matter of discursive thought merely being illustrated scripturally (although illustration is one function of Scripture in Romans). Rather, logic and interpretation here interpenetrate to a remarkable degree, and give Romans 9–11 a unique character within the Pauline corpus. The questions therefore emerge, What is Paul doing here, which makes the chapters distinctive, and Why does he do it? Answers are forthcoming, when the purpose of Paul's argument is appreciated.

We would quickly decide that we understood what Paul is doing within this text and why he is doing it, were we able to accept the suggestion—developed in much recent scholarship—that Paul is here providing his readers with a midrash.[4] It has become conventional

---

[4] See, for example, W. R. Stegner, "Romans 9:6–29—A Midrash," *Journal for the Study of the New Testament* 22 (1984), 37–52.

to observe that the noun "midrash" is derived from the verbal form
darash (to "seek" or to "search" in Hebrew), and therefore to infer
that "midrash" refers to any "searching out" of meaning on the basis
of Scripture within Judaism. It is fairly obvious that, if one is willing to work with such a free-wheeling definition, Romans 9–11 is
indeed "midrash." But such a description obscures more than it
discloses.

When the rabbis produced the documents known collectively as
midrashim, the formal aim was—on the whole—to produce commentaries on Scripture. But the "commentary" was not, as in modern usage, an attempt strictly (and historically) to explain the meaning
of a given document. Rather, the sense that the rabbis explored in
their midrashim was the meaning of Scripture within their practice
and liturgy and teaching, which were understood as of a piece with
the Torah revealed to Moses on Sinai. That is, midrash represents
a synthesis of written text and Rabbinic sensibility, in which both
are accorded the status of revelation.

Jacob Neusner has shown that a given midrash may be composed
of four distinct orders of interpretation:[5]

(1) close exegesis, or discussion by each word or phrase of Scripture;
(2) amplification of the meaning of a passage;
(3) illustration of a particular theme by various passages;
(4) anthological collection around a general topic.

The result of the compilations of varying readings, involving different
categories of interpretation, was the eleven distinct midrashim (on
various books of the Bible) which emerged by the end of the sixth
century.

When one sets out the midrashim systematically, and provides precise examples (as Neusner does), the distance from Paul's activity in
Romans in striking. His focus is no single biblical book, so that the
general form of midrash is not at issue. The first two categories, exegesis and amplification, which Neusner shows were most prominent
in the earliest midrashim (of the second century C.E.) simply do not
obtain in the case of Paul. It might be said—at a stretch—that the
third and fourth categories, illustration and amplification, do char-

---

[5] *Midrash in Context: Exegesis in Formative Judaism*: The Foundations of Judaism 1
(Philadelphia: Fortress, 1983), 82, 83.

acterize Pauline interpretation. But the stretch is considerable, because Paul does not merely illustrate by means of Scripture (although illustration is among his techniques); he argues through it and with it towards a conclusion which Scripture itself does not draw, but—at best—is generally consistent with. And, of course, his over-arching theme, of Jesus Christ's completion of the Torah, the Prophets, and the Writings, could never be described as Rabbinic. For all those reasons, to style Paul's interpretation as "midrash" is misleading.

Having called attention to the inadequacy of any direct identification of Paul's method with the Rabbis', a certain analogy remains. Both proceed synthetically, and the synthesis moves in two directions at once. First, both take Scripture as a whole, as making a harmonious, common claim upon the mind. Indeed, it should be pointed out that Paul specifies Torah first, and then the Prophets (by name) and the Writings, more punctiliously than the Rabbis usually do. It appears that Paul wishes to make the point of Scripture's unity, and also that he is making an inherently convoluted argument easier to follow than it would be if he were addressing genuine experts. Second, both Paul and the Rabbis also synthesize Scripture with their own sensibilities, their grasp of what Scripture as a whole means.

The last point is perhaps best illustrated by how the Rabbis of Leviticus Rabbah took the reference to Isaac in Genesis 21:12, which Paul in Romans 9:7–8 interpreted to mean that the "children of promise" were the true "children of God." In Leviticus Rabbah, by contrast, Abraham's seed is defined, without justification, as those who believe in the world to come. What was for Paul obviously Christological was for the rabbis (of a much later period) self-evidently a Halakhah of eschatological faith. Just when Rabbinic and Pauline interpretation seem analogous, they prove they are antipodal.

Paul has also been compared to the sectarians of Qumran and to Philo, in respect of his interpretation of Scripture. But the famous *pesharim* of Qumran are designed to relate Scripture exactly to the history of the community, and Philo is concerned to comment systematically on Scripture, so as to elucidate its allegedly philosophical truth.[6] Both the pesharim and the Philonic corpus represent

---

[6] See Bruce Chilton, "Commenting on the Old Testament (with Particular Reference to the Pesharim, Philo, and the Mekilta)," *It is Written: Scripture Citing Scripture:*

different activities and settings from Paul's: his scriptural interpretation strictly serves the protreptic function of Romans. He shows no sustained interest in historicizing Scripture (as in the *pesharim*) or in philosophizing with it (as in Philo). Paul is driven by other motives, which is why Romans 9–11 is neither midrash, pesher, nor philosophical commentary.

Paul is arguing with all the Christians of Rome, both Jews and gentiles, in an attempt to promote unity. It is true that Paul had no direct, personal acquaintance with the community at Rome; to that extent, there is an abstract quality about the letter to the Romans which sets it apart from other Pauline letters. Writing at a distance from a church known only at second hand, Paul approximates, more nearly than he ever does, to the presentation of his theology in a systematic fashion.

Nonetheless, the central, social issue in the church at Rome was known to Paul: there had been disturbances involving Jews in the city, and probably Christians as well, that resulted in their being expelled in 49 c.e. under the Emperor Claudius.[7] Their gradual reintegration into a single church with gentiles, which is Paul's goal, could only be accomplished by means of conveying a coherent vision in which both Jews and gentiles had a place.

The letter to the Romans offers just such a vision, which is summed up under the slogan which appears here—and only here—within the Pauline corpus: salvation is for the Jew first, and then for the Greek (1:16; 2:9, 10 cf. 3:9, 29; 9:24; 10:12). Salvation is the possession of neither, but it is offered and granted to both as children of promise, provided it is accepted by means of a willingness to be forgiven.

His letter to the Galatians presents Paul in such heated controversy with Jews who were also Christians, and with those who demanded that the conditions of Judaism be fulfilled by all followers of Christ (whether Jew or Gentile), that one might have expected Paul to have used the occasion of his letter to the Romans finally to argue that the gospel of Christ could rightly be severed from its

---

Essays in Honour of Barnabas Lindars, S.S.F. (ed. D. A. Carson and H. G. M. Williamson; Cambridge: Cambridge University Press, 1988), 122–140.

[7] See Wolfgang Wiefel, "The Jewish Community in Ancient Rome and the Origins of Roman Christianity," *The Romans Debate* (ed. K. Donfried; Peabody: Hendrickson, 1991), 100–119.

Judaic roots. Yet having written to the Galatians ca. 53 C.E., Paul went on in his Corinthian correspondence (ca. 55–56 C.E.) himself to appropriate scriptural stories of Israel's salvation directly for the church (see, for example, 1 Corinthians 10:1–4), and even to put believing Christians in the role of teachers comparable to—if greater than!—Moses (cf. 2 Corinthians 3:7–18).[8]

Here, in Rome (ca. 57 C.E.), was a case in which Judaism had been weakened, to the point that gentiles in the church were tempted to imagine that the divine right of Israel had been usurped definitively by the non-Jewish church (cf. Romans 11:13–24). Paul's response is unequivocal: the rejection of many in Israel does not give late comers any special privilege. Indeed, the implication of the remnant is that the essential promise to Israel is confirmed, although the rebellion of some in Israel demonstrates that no one, Jewish or not, can presume upon God's gracious election. When Paul insists throughout Romans that salvation is to Jews first, and then to Greeks, the implication is that the same dynamics of redemption, initially worked out in the case of Israel, are now available to all humanity by means of Jesus Christ.

Romans 9–11 embody that leitmotif in the letter generally. The salvation effected in Christ is uniquely comprehended by means of Scripture, where "Scripture" refers to the canon of Israel. When Paul turns to his Gentile readers alone in 11:13–24, he momentarily drops any reference to Scripture, and argues from an agricultural image. His message is clear: however weak the Jewish component may appear, they are root and you are branch. And it is all Israel, root and branch, which God is determined to save. Paul's purpose, once identified, explains both the nature and the form of his argument. The body of Christ is indeed the single definition of the church, but the presence within it of some in Israel who believe is crucial even to Paul.

Only from the second century do we find a literature which engages in a spirited, intellectual defense of Christianity across the range of other religious and philosophical options. That defense was principally conducted in the midst of the religious and philosophical pluralism

---

[8] Still, Paul's position in Romans may be regarded as adumbrated in 1 Corinthians 1:21–25; 9:20–23; 10:32–33; 12:13; Galatians 3:28.

of the second century. In that environment, in which adherents of various groups were attracted to Christianity, it was imperative to develop an account of the intellectual integrity of faith, an "apology" in the philosophical sense. Such literature developed the paradigmatic attitude of Christianity towards faiths other than Judaism.

Christianity's apologists crafted a distinctive view of the divine "Word" (*logos*) which conveys the truth of God to humanity. That Logos was Jesus Christ, understood as the human teacher who at last fully incarnated what philosophers and prophets had been searching for and had partially seen. Gnostic Christians were inclined to see that "Word" as a uniquely divine, ahistoric revelation of the truth. That contention only underlines by comparison how central the Logos-doctrine had become to Christianity generally.

Justin Martyr was the theologian who articulated that doctrine most clearly, on the basis of the Gospel according to John. In 151 c.e. he addressed his *Apology* to the Emperor himself, Antonius Pius. Such was his confidence that the "true philosophy" represented by Christ, attested in the Hebrew Scriptures, would triumph among the other options available at the time. Justin himself had been trained within some of those traditions, and by his Samaritan birth he could claim to represent something of the wisdom of the East. Somewhere between 162 and 168, however, Justin was martyred in Rome, a victim of the increasing hostility to Christianity under the reign of Marcus Aurelius.[9]

Justin argued that the light of reason in people is put there by God and is to be equated with the word of God incarnate in Jesus. His belief in the salvation of people as they actually are is attested by his attachment to millenarianism, the conviction that Christ would return to reign with his saints for a thousand years. That conviction, derived from Revelation 20, was fervently maintained by many Christians during the second century, in opposition to the abstract view of salvation which Gnosticism preferred.

In strictly religious terms, Christianity did not compete well within the second century. Greco-Roman preferences were for ancient faiths, and the movement centered on Jesus was incontrovertibly recent. Moreover, it could and often did appear to be subversive of the

[9] See Henry Chadwick, *The Early Church* (London: Penguin, 1993), 29, 74–79.

authority of the Emperor. After all, Christians did not accept the imperial title of *divi filius*, and they actually applied it to their criminal rabbi. And he was a rabbi who was not a rabbi, because the recognized authorities of Judaism did not accept Christians as among their numbers. For such reasons, the persecution of Christianity had been an established policy of state for nearly a century by the time Justin wrote.

The Christianity which Justin defended, however, was as much a philosophy as it was a religion. His claim was that the light of reason in humanity, which had already been indirectly available, actually became fully manifest in the case of Jesus Christ. Jesus, therefore, was the perfect sage, and Socrates as much as Isaiah was his prophet. In that sense, Christianity was as old as humanity; it was only its open manifestation that was recent.

In order to make his case, Justin used arguments which had been employed before by Philo of Alexandria (Jesus' older contemporary), but on behalf of Judaism. Philo had also identified the *logos*, the prophetic word articulated in Scripture, as the reason by which God created the world and animates humanity. Philo even makes out the historical case that Moses influenced the Greek philosophers directly,[10] so that the extent to which Greek philosophy illuminates God's wisdom is derivative. Justin is bolder in his Platonism, in that his argument does not rely on such an historical argument, but on the contention that in Jesus the primordial archetype of humanity and of the world itself, the *logos*, became accessible and knowable in a way it was not before.

One can easily imagine a debate between Philo and Justin. Had it occurred, that would have been the only encounter between Judaism and Christianity on philosophical terrain that they both claimed and were comfortable with. Philo's case, argued in his brilliant continuous commentary on the Pentateuch in Greek, identified the creative *logos* behind our world and in our minds as the Torah that God revealed perfectly to Moses. Justin, in a less voluminous way, more as the essayist than as the scholar, insisted that our knowledge of

---

[10] For a discussion of this motif (in *Quaestiones et Solutiones in Genesin* iv. 152, for example), see Harry Austryn Wolfson, *Philo: Foundations of Religious Philosophy in Judaism, Christianity, and Islam* (Cambridge, Mass.: Harvard University Press, 1947), 141–143, 160–163.

the *logos* implies that it is eternally human, and that its human instance is Jesus.

The comparison between Philo and Justin shows the extent to which Judaism in the first century and Christianity in the second century relied upon the revival of Platonism to provide them with a way of expressing how their respective religions were philosophically the most appropriate. The Platonic picture of perfect intellectual models or types was their common axiom, invoked in Philo's rounded, elegant Greek, and in Justin's controversial, rhetorical Greek. Had they met and disputed, Judaism and Christianity would have been represented for the only time in their history as approximate equals, and on a level playing field.

Justin sets his *Dialogue with Trypho, A Jew* in the period after the revolt under Simon called Bar Kokhba (*Dialogue*, chapter 1), which occurred between 132 and 135. Thematically, Justin disputes Trypho's conception of the permanent obligation of the law (chapters 1–47), and sees the purpose of Scriptures in their witness to Christ's divinity (chapters 48–108), which justifies the acceptance of non-Jews within the church (chapters 109–136). Trypho is portrayed as arguing that the systemic meaning of the Scriptures is the law, while Justin argues that their meaning is Christ.

Justin describes his own development from Platonism to Christianity as a result of a conversation with an old man. The sage convinced him that the highest good which Platonism can attain, the human soul, should not be confused with God himself, since the soul depends upon God for life (chapter 6). Knowledge of God depends rather upon the revelation of God's Spirit (chapter 7):

> Long ago, he replied, there lived men more ancient than all the so-called philosophers, men righteous and beloved of God, who spoke by the divine spirit and foretold things to come, that even now are taking place. These men were called prophets. They alone both saw the truth and proclaimed it to men, without awe or fear of anyone, moved by no desire for glory, but speaking only those things which they saw and heard when filled with the Holy Spirit. Their writings are still with us, and whoever will may read them and, if he believes them, gain much knowledge of the beginning and end of things, and all else a philosopher ought to know. For they did not employ logic to prove their statements, seeing they were witnesses to the truth. . . . They glorified the creator of all things, as God and Father, and proclaimed the Christ sent by him as his Son. . . . But pray that, before all else,

the gates of light may be opened to you. For not everyone can see or understand these things, but only he to whom God and his Christ have granted wisdom.

Here is a self-conscious Christianity, which distinguishes itself from Judaism and proclaims itself the true and only adequate philosophy. Justin's account of the truth of the *logos* depends upon two sources of revelation, resonant with one another: the prophetic Scriptures which attest the Spirit and the wise reader who has been inspired by the Spirit.

Justin is quite clear, then, that his concern is not with the immediate reference of Scripture, what we would call its historical meaning. That has also come to be known (rather confusingly) as its literal meaning. I prefer the description of "immediate reference": the meaning of Scripture within the conditions in which it was produced. In his *Dialogue*, Justin portrays Trypho as being limited to the immediate reference of Scripture, enslaved by its specification of laws.

Justin is committed to a typological reading of Scripture, the Christian norm during the second century. The prophets were understood to represent "types" of Christ, impressions on their minds of the heavenly reality, God's own Son. Isaac, for example, was taken to be a type of Jesus; where Isaac was nearly offered on Mount Moriah in Genesis 22, Jesus was actually offered on Golgotha. That typology, which Paul had initiated in the first century, became a typical motif during the second century. Trypho, by contrast, is portrayed as becoming lost in the immediate minutiae of the prophetic text. So prevalent was this understanding of Judaism, by the end of the century, Christians such as Clement of Alexandria (*Paidagogos* I.5 [34]) and Tertullian (*Apology* 20–21) referred to any limitation to the immediate reference of Scripture (its "literal meaning") as its Jewish sense.

Anyone familiar with the development of Judaism from the second century onward will see the irony of this understanding of Judaic interpretation. The second century was just the period when Scripture was being interpreted in terms of its eternal meaning, when any limitation to its immediate reference came to be overridden by an appeal to the significance of the eternal Torah. Genesis 22 is a case in point: from the second century, it came to be asserted that Isaac was slain on Moriah, that he accepted his fate as a fully grown adult, and that God raised him from the dead. In other words, Isaac was a type in Judaism, as well, but of a different truth: an emblem of a martyr's obedience to the Torah rather than of a prophet's vision of Christ.[11]

So what is presented by Justin as a meeting of minds is in fact a missing of minds. Both Justin and Trypho actually make the immediate reference of Scripture ancillary to its systemic significance. But because Christianity is now committed to the *logos* as its systemic center, and Judaism is now committed to the Torah as its systemic center, the two cannot understand one another. Any objection from one side to the other seems silly: it misses the systemic point.

The genius of Justin certainly does not reside in his confrontation with Trypho, but in his account of how Christianity works as the discovery of meaning. The recognition of God's Spirit in the text on the basis of God's spirit within the reader is a classic formulation, an articulate development of Paul's teaching (see 1 Corinthians 2). Indeed, Justin first makes a principle unmistakably plain that was already implicit in Paul's thought. Justin's motif of the *logos* could be applied to any philosophical system, as well as to Judaism. Indeed, part of Justin's argument is that Christ is the truth of the Prophets and of the philosophers at one and the same time. The intrinsic link between Israel's truth and any truth worthy of the name was intimated by Paul, when he referred to the gentiles as having law inscribed in their hearts (Romans 2:14–16). For Justin, that link is fully specifiable. It is the *logos* which became incarnate in the case of Jesus. For that reason, the relationship of Christianity to Judaism turns out to be paradigmatic of Christianity's relationship to every other religious and philosophical system.

D. THE FAITHFUL AND THE UNFAITHFUL: ISLAM

The Qur'ān itself offers a developed interpretation of God's dealing with successive peoples through a series of His chosen messengers (sing. *rasūl*, "apostle, emissary, messenger, envoy") or prophets (sing. *nabī*), from Adam to Muhammad, as we have seen above (esp. chap-

---

[11] See Bruce Chilton, "Isaac and the Second Night: A Consideration," *Biblica* 61 (1980), 78–88.

ter three).[12] The salvation history, or *Heilsgeschichte*, that emerges in the qur'ānic text and which is developed in subsequent Muslim tradition, rests upon several premises: that God has given humankind from its inception clear signs of His sovereignty over creation. These signs are all around in the wonders and beauties of the natural world, and these natural "signs" (*āyāt*) are supplemented by the direct revelations that God has provided successive peoples and generations through His messengers and prophets. The final, culminating revelation that He has sent down is that of the verses (lit. "signs," *āyāt*), of the Qur'ān, wherein His guidance for the faithful is contained. In the case of past communities that received God's revelation through one of His messengers, each failed in certain crucial ways to preserve and live by their revelation. They thereby failed in their obligation to continue as "believers," true worshipers of the one God. Each either rejected God's emissary and revelation or, having accepted them, failed with the passage of time to protect the verbal integrity of God's word and to practice faithfully the worship and way of life taught them by revelation and the preaching of their special apostle, or messenger.

Islām thus does not begin with Muhammad ibn 'Abdullāh of Mecca; he is rather the last in a long series of emissaries sent by God to call human beings to true submission to the Lord of created beings. Symbolically, the first historical Muslim was Abraham (more literally, as later tradition would develop the story of God's dealings with humankind, the first Muslim, as well as God's first emissary, was the first man, Adam. Abraham is thus not technically the first prophet or envoy of God since the creation). He stands in the qur'ānic, as in Jewish and Christian, tradition, as the paradigm of human faith in the One God, the prototypical monotheist. Both for his willingness to leave behind his idolatrous father and family and homeland in Ur and for his willingness to sacrifice his only (and divinely

---

[12] The distinction between *rasūl* and *nabī* is not spelled out in the Qur'ān or early Islamic tradition, but the general distinction seems to be that the apostles are the smaller, more select group, each of whom is associated with a specific community, or *ummah*, as a bearer of a divine revelation to that community, whereas the prophets are a larger group of God's representatives among humankind. While not explicitly stated, it would appear from Qur'ān and early sources that all apostles are also prophets (as in the case of Muhammad), but not all prophets are apostles. See article "Rasūl," *EI*[2] 8:454.

promised) son at God's command, Abraham stands for Muslims as
for Christians and Jews as the emblem of unconditional faith in the
Living God. He is described in the Qur'ān as a *ḥanīf* (a pre-Islamic
monotheist [or possibly a word meaning "gentile" originally]: S. 2:135,
3:67, etc.; also applied twice in the Qur'ān to Muhammad), as the
"friend" of God (S. 4:125), and as "a submitting (*muslim*) *ḥanīf*, not
one of the idolaters" (S. 3:67). Muhammad's life and mission and
faith recapitulate above all the life and mission of Abraham, who
also was given a Scripture by God, and who, like Muhammad, had
to fight adversity and exile and have his faith repeatedly tested.

Since God has provided guidance to each community (*ummah*),
culminating with His sending of Muhammad as a prophetic emissary to the Arabs, human beings have little excuse for their refusal
to have faith in the one Lord of creation. In the classical Islamic
view there is thus a kind of perversity to unbelief, since each community has received not only the signs of revelation all around them
in the natural world, but also explicit verbal guidance in revelation.
However, with time each has either rejected, tampered with or otherwise neglected God's merciful guidance toward the proper worship and service of Himself. Thus the *kāfirs* (sing. *kāfir*, Arabic plur.
kuffār, "those who are ungrateful to, or ungratefully reject [God]")
are not only unbelievers, but willful unbelievers who have been shown
the truth but refuse to accept it. Such "rejectors" or "unbelievers"
included eventually the Christians and Jews and Muslim apostates
as well as the outright polytheists who were the first to be labeled
kāfirs in the qur'ānic revelations. The faithful (*mu'minūn*; sing. *mu'min*)
on the other hand are those who have heard, had faith in, and
obeyed God's will as revealed in His Scripture (*kitāb*, lit. "book, writing, what is laid down or prescribed"). This *kitāb* is understood both
as God's eternal Scripture residing with Him and as the separate
manifestations of it in human history, the culminating instance of
which is the Qur'ān, which is accordingly also referred to as *al-kitāb*,
"the Book," or "the Scripture," as Sūrah 6:114 shows clearly:

> Shall I search for someone other than God as judge, when He it is
> who sent down to you the *kitāb* in distinct segments?[13] Those to whom

---

[13] *Mufassalan*, which can also mean "clearly explained" instead of "in divided/dis-
tinct segments."

We have [already] given the *kitāb* know that it is sent down in truth from Your Lord, so do not be one of those who is doubting.

This understanding of the history of revelation contains also a general interpretation of the wider history of religion and the place of Muhammad and his community in it—something that neither the Hebrew scriptures nor the Christian scriptures offer in the same degree. The former tell of the history of the religion of Israel against the backdrop of creation, the flood, other patriarchal narratives, and the heathen peoples in contact with the Israelites. The latter tell of the coming of Jesus the Christ or Messiah and interpret this as the culmination and fulfillment of Israelite and Jewish tradition, with relatively little reference to religious life beyond that of Israel and the Jews. The qur'ānic narrative, on the other hand, assumes the general outlines of the biblical narratives, designates the Patriarchs, Moses, and Jesus as earlier Apostles or Prophets. It further expands the biblical horizon to include other prophetic or apostolic figures outside the biblical tradition. These include such Arabian figures as Sālih, Shu'ayb, and Hūd; later Islamic tradition would even expand the hypothetical number of messengers or apostle to over three hundred.[14] Indeed, the very indeterminacy of the number of divine emissaries and prophets has offered through the centuries the possibility of making the notion of pre-Islamic revelations and divine representatives on earth expandable to include virtually any pre-Muhammad nation as their recipients.

Still, it is above all the religion of the Abrahamic tradition to which Muslims are clearly called, as these words to Muhammad make explicit:

> Say, "We have faith in God and in what was revealed to us, and in that which was revealed to Abraham, Ishmael, Isaac, Jacob, and the tribes, and in that which was brought to Moses, Jesus, and the prophets from their Lord. We do not distinguish among any of them, and to Him we have submitted." (S. 3:84)

---

[14] "Rasūl," *EI*[2] 8:455.

The Other "Scriptured" Monotheists

Other passages reflect the qur'ānic recognition of the piety and faith in God of other monotheists known to the Arabian world in which the Qur'ān was revealed and in which the early Muslims were well aware of other religious communities apart from the pagan tribes. The text links "those who have faith [presumably the Muslims],[15] the Christians, the Jews, and the Sabians (*Sābi'ūn*)"[16] (mentioned alongside the first three in S. 5:69, 2:62; cf. 22:17) and identifies all of these as "those who have faith in God and the Last Day, and who do good." All of these are clearly accorded special status on account of their submission to the one true God. As Sūrah 2:62 puts it, "they will have their reward with their Lord, and no fear will be upon them, nor will they grieve." Specifically, the non-Muslims referred to in such passages are all those identified as "people of Scripture" (*ahl al-kitāb*): those communities to whom God has vouchsafed a scriptural revelation from His heavenly *kitāb* as guidance. They include Jews and Christians in the first instance, but also other groups who have had a "book" as well. In later times, these other groups were identified with new communities that Muslims encountered over the centuries (both as minorities and as majorities) and with whom they had to live. These were peoples or religious groups such as the star-worshippers of Harrān in the early third/ninth cen-

---

[15] This verse is said by many Muslim exegetes to have been abrogated by later verses according salvation only to Muslims. Some interpreters also take the first phrase to refer to the hypocrites among the Muslims; others take it to refer to all of the three specified groups that follow here. Possibly it was an early revelation that was later deemed problematic as a statement of salvation being possible for Muslims and other monotheists alike.

[16] S. 2:62. The *Sābi'ūn* are mentioned alongside the first three categories of worshippers of God in S. 5:69, 2:62; cf. 22:17). It would appear that relatively soon after the lifetime of Muhammad, whatever he and his contemporaries understood under *Sābi'ūn* was lost to the young Islamic community (for example, the early exegete Ibn 'Abbās says that they were a Christian splinter group; Tabarī says that the word refers to anyone who has left one religion for another). This proved a boon to various groups in subsequent history who wanted to claim inclusion in the *ahl al-kitāb* under this rubric.Islamics scholarship has tried to identify the qur'ānic *Sābi'ūn* as possibly Mandaeans, more recent scholarship denies this in favor of Manichaeans. Islamic scholarship has variously identified them as Iraqi Mandaeans (D. Chwolson, J. Horovitz, H. H. Schaeder, R. Bell), pre-Islamic monotheists otherwise referred to in the Qur'ān as *Hanīfs* (A. Sprenger; J. Pedersen), or Manichaeans—later termed *zindīks* by classical Muslim Arab writers (F. C. de Blois).

tury, Zoroastrians (Parsis) at various points, and even Hindus later on in the Muslim-ruled states of South Asia.

Nevertheless, in the earliest Arabian community especially, along with the pagans of Mecca, Medina, and the wider peninsula, it was the formally recognized "people of Scripture" who were the primary religious "others" for Muslims. These consisted in, first, the Arab Jews and Christians in the Arabian peninsula and then the less well-known Jewish and Christian communities of the Levant, Egypt, and Abyssinia. From the period of the last decade of Muhammad's life in Medina, when the Muslim community first became a reality, the Jews and Christians were the two religious communities with which the first Muslims had most explicitly and consciously to deal—largely because they were communities with identifiable and prominent scriptures and monotheistic notions of God. Of course, with the pagans there was little to deal about: either these converted and became part of the Muslim *Ummah*, or they were considered the enemies of God because of their idolatry and refusal to abandon it once they had received His message. The qur'ānic revelations from this time are not all easy to reconcile with each other, as we shall see below. However, it does appear that both irenic tendencies and impulses to violence toward the two monotheist communities were encouraged at different times by the qur'ānic word, probably according to the particular situation that a given revelation addressed.

Thus we read the following words addressed to the Muslims in Sūrah 29:46, calling on them to approach the other "Scripture folk" kindly, as persons of kindred faith:

> Do not dispute other than in a good way with the people of Scripture, except for those of them who do evil; and say: "We have faith in that which has been revealed to us and revealed to you. Our God and your God are One, and to Him we submit [ourselves]."

There are also passages like the following two, which seem to distinguish some of the "Scripture folk" who fall short of a true and pure faith in God because of their impiety and rejection of Him. These are in implicit contrast to others in their particular community who are presumably persons of genuine piety and faith:

> There is a group among the people of Scripture who desire to make you go astray, and they make no one to go astray except themselves, but they do not realize it. (S. 3:69)

> Truly, those among the people of Scripture and the idolaters who
> reject [God] ungratefully will be in the Fire of Gehenna forever. Those
> are the most evil of [all] created beings. (S. 98:6)

As one might expect from these statements about the unbelievers of
the people of Scripture, in other passages those members of these
communities who are faithful servants of God are praised in very
positive terms, as in Sūrah 3:199:

> Truly, among the people of Scripture there are some who have faith
> in God and what was revealed to you [Muslims], and what was revealed
> to them, submissive to God. They do not sell the *āyāt* [signs, verses]
> of God for a paltry price. Those are they for whom their reward is
> with their Lord. Truly God is quick to reckon.

There are also passages that seem to look with approbation upon
the Christians while condemning the Jews along with the polytheists:

> You [Muhammad] will find the Jews and those who associate other
> gods [with God] the strongest in hostility to the faithful. And you will
> find the closest of them in friendship to the faithful to be those who
> say, "Truly, we are Christians." That is because among them are
> priests and monks, and because they are not arrogant. (S. 5:82)

Finally, there are also segments in the Qur'ān that are sharp in their
criticism of all the people of Scripture who do not recognize Islam
as the path fulfilling their own traditions:

> Say, "O people of Scripture! Why do you deny God's signs/revela-
> tions, when God is witness to what you do?" Say, "O people of
> Scripture! Why do you bar from the way of God those who have faith,
> desiring to make it crooked, when you yourselves are witnesses to it,
> and God is not unaware of what you do?" (S. 3:98–9)

Such passages, probably revealed at different times and to different
ends during Muhammad's career, indicate how easy it has been for
later generations to find justification for either rapprochement and
toleration of Christians and Jews or antagonism and belligerence
towards them. Taking all the diverse qur'ānic statements about the
people of Scripture together, it is impossible to ascertain a single
clear "line" regarding their proper treatment at the hands of Muslims.
The historical trajectory of the early Islamic empire led to actions
of violence and discrimination on occasion, but also, and more typically, to acts of charity, understanding, and often remarkable toler-

ation vis-à-vis Jews and Christians in particular. Sadly, the later experiences of the Christian Crusades, the Ottoman-Christian state rivalries, and then European global imperialism and colonialism in the modern age did much to replace the more irenic Muslim approach to Jews and Christians with more belligerent and intolerant responses to perceived threats. Indeed, these factors would lead to an increase in the late 20th century in attitudes of enmity and postures of conflict rather than reconciliation and toleration. Nevertheless, these developments are far removed from the world of early Islam, and even much of the medieval world as well: Jews and Christians were not only generally left alone so long as they did not present problems for Muslim rule, but individual Jews and Christians were able to reach high positions of governmental trust and power in the early and middle periods. Even conflict between Muslims and "Scripture folk" on the battlefield was minor compared to other kinds of interaction in the early Islamic centuries.

What is particularly important to remember is that so long as Muslims were dealing with other religious minorities (apart from overt polytheists) *within* their own Muslim-ruled states, legal toleration was the norm and communal strife remained minimal. This is especially true if one compares the situation of Jews and Christians in Muslim states with that of Jews and Muslims in Christian states in the same periods. Of course, border areas were a special case. In these, Muslim populations were typically threatened by non-Muslim states close by, and warfare with these non-Muslim states was frequent. As a result, toleration had a harder time flourishing in these contexts, as one would expect in any similar situation anywhere.

In the early Islamic state, the legal status of such "tolerated" groups of scripture-folk was established formally as that of *ahl al-dhimmah*, "people of the covenant," those who were given promise of protection (and freedom from military service) by Muslim ruling institutions in exchange for the payment of a poll tax (*jizyah*). This status was only available to those people of Scripture who did not continue to fight Muslim political authority—a practice based on Sūrah 9:29:

> From among those given Scripture, fight those who do not have faith in God or in the Last Day, and who do not forbid what God and His messenger have forbidden and do not practice the religion of truth, until they, brought low [subdued], pay the poll tax by their own hand [or: willingly?].

The toleration of "people of Scripture" as "covenant" groups was one that allowed tolerated non-Muslims to continue to follow their own religious traditions while living under (and often serving as ranking representatives of) Muslim governmental authority. In theory, this toleration did not extend to polytheists, but as noted above, even adherents of the many Hindu and other Indian religious traditions, most of whom would not be described as strict monotheists by usual standard, were extended toleration as covenant people and people of Scripture under Muslim states in the Subcontinent from at least the 13th century onward.

The Idolatrous Polytheists

Peoples identified as overt, non-scriptural polytheists, however, were seldom if every accorded such tolerated status. The prototypical poly-theists were the pagan Arab tribes who resisted submission to the One God preached by Muhammad and the Qur'ān, and who were fought until they submitted, and idolatry was officially ended in the Arabian Peninsula. In the Muslim view (as in that of Judaic tradi-tion, as we have seen above), the most heinous sin against God that a human can commit is that of *shirk*, "associating" some other thing or being with the Almighty and Omnipotent himself. Thus idolatry, or any kind of polytheism, is abhorred above all forms of false reli-gion in Islam and is accordingly proscribed.

> Truly, God does not forgive that one ascribes partners to Him, although He forgives whatever is short of this to whomever He will. Whoever ascribes partners to God has incurred a massive guilt. (S. 4:48)

This abhorrence of *shirk* is rooted in the Qur'ān and its relentless preaching against those who would set up partners to God (see Chapter Two above). The idolaters or polytheists (*mushrikūn*, "those who associate [partners with God]") are enemies of God and to be fought wherever they are encountered if they refuse to renounce their false gods and worship the One Lord of all Being. As in Judaism, the idolater or polytheist is unclean: "O you who are faithful! Truly, the polytheists are unclean, so let them not draw near the holy mosque after this present year. . . ." (S. 9:28, in reference to the poly-theists who wanted to continue to make pilgrimage to the Holy

Shrine in Mecca). This is not, however, an attitude extended generally to apply also to Jews and Christians.

Therefore, with the large exception of the prescribed toleration of "people of Scripture" as worshippers of the one God of Abraham, Isaac, and Jacob, traditional Muslim attitudes towards non-Muslims who worship false gods have much in common with Judaism. Just as idolatry defines the boundary between Israel and everybody else (see above, pp. 209 ff.), so too does it mark in traditional Islam the boundary between Muslims and all others besides Christians, Jews and those others accepted also as possessors of a scripture. For Muslims, the other scriptural monotheists are, to be sure, flawed worshippers of God, since they have not accepted the qur'ānic preaching after it has come. Nevertheless, even though they can be termed "unbelievers" or "deniers [of God]" (*kāfirūn*), they are not in the view of the Qur'ān and earliest Muslims to be considered polytheists (*mushrikūn*) and summarily forced to give up their own religious faith and practice—something held to be right and proper to enforce with the polytheists.

Jihād. The question of *jihād* and its interpretation as actual warfare against the enemies of Islam is one that has continued to vex non-Muslims' understanding of, and attitudes toward, Islam and Muslims down to the present moment. It has also many times divided Muslims themselves, since there has always been a division of Muslim opinion concerning the legitimacy of "striving in God's way" through actual hostile action against unbelievers.

Alongside the tradition of *jihād* as physical fighting, there has existed from the earliest period the equally venerable tradition of true *jihād* being the internal religious battle of each Muslim against his or her baser nature and actions. This kind of personal, internal struggle is what the classical scholarly tradition in Islam came to label "the greater *jihād*," as opposed to physically fighting "in God's way," which they labeled "the lesser *jihād*." Indeed, it appears from the Qur'ān that in the earliest period of the revelations in Mecca, the faithful were urged not to fight back at all against their enemies and detractors, despite the provocations and persecution visited upon them by the latter. Once the new community was constituted in Medina, however, the Muslims had to go over to a more activist, belligerent policy in order first to survive, then to bring Islam to

Mecca and defeat the idolaters there. A fine recent study of the origins of the notion of actual warfare being a licit means to defend or secure the Muslim community provides a persuasive picture of the diversity of ideas in the earliest Muslim community about the validity of fighting on behalf of Islam and the Muslims.[17] This study shows clearly that it is a major anachronistic mistake to project back onto the earliest period the later Muslim interpretations of *jihād* as legitimate warfare against non-Muslim groups or even other Muslim states.

We do find in the Qur'ān passages such as the following that endorse fighting (*qitāl, muhārabah*) "in the way of God." But even here, there is frequent emphasis upon this as a defensive or reactive measure against those who have attacked Muhammad and the Muslims first. The following passage explicitly forbids ruthless fighting:

> Fight in the way of God those who fight you, but do not transgress [normal limits]. God has no love for those who transgress [limits]. Kill them wherever you find them, and drive them out from where they have driven you out; truly, civil strife is worse than slaughter. (S. 2:190–91)

It is, however, evident in some passages that there existed in the qur'ānic worldview a clear distinction between warfare or fighting in God's cause and that done on behalf of an evil cause:

> What is [wrong] with you, that you do not fight in the way of God and of the oppressed—men, women, and children, who say, "Our Lord, bring us out of this city of evildoing people, and give us from Your own side a guardian. Give us from Your own side a helper!" Those who have faith fight in the way of God, and those who have ungratefully denied [God] fight in the way of idols. So fight the friends of Satan. (S. 4:75–76)

There is also distinct indication in the Qur'ān that dying while fighting for God's cause is to be considered a blessed thing that might earn one paradise. Even the verse (4:74) preceding the text just quoted says that ". . . on him who fights in the way of God, whether he be killed or victorious, shall We bestow a great recompense." Others also make this point:

---

[17] Reuven Firestone, *Jihād: The Origin of Holy War in Islam* (New York and Oxford: Oxford University Press, 1999).

Truly, God has bought from the faithful their persons and their possessions [in payment] for the Garden that will be theirs. They fight in the way of God so that they kill and are killed. This is a promise binding upon Him in the Torah, the Gospel and the Qur'ān. Who is more reliable in fulfilling his covenant than God? So rejoice in the bargain you have made, for that is the ultimate happiness. (S. 9:111)

When one comes to the Hadīth literature, a portion of which is certainly later—at least in its compilation, if not its composition—than the 'Uthmanic text of the Qur'ān, *jihād* appears more prominently and clearly as physical warfare that is not only licit but meritorious. The major collections (e.g., Bukhārī, Muslim, Mālik's *Muwattā'*) have typically a separate chapter devoted to *jihād* or "*jihād* and expeditions." Here there are varied traditions that reflect efforts, most often probably well after the Prophet's death, but still ascribed to him, to affirm the importance of fighting on behalf of the faith and even becoming a martyr for it. Thus Muhammad is cited as having said that "Paradise lies in the shadows of swords" (al-Bukhārī 56[*Jihād*]:22:1), and Abū Hurayrah quotes Muhammad as saying:

I have been commanded to fight people until they say, "There is no god but God." And whoever says "there is no god but God," his life and his property shall be kept inviolate by me, save for his lawful due, and his accounting will be with God." (ibid., 56:102:5)

The traditions that bolster *jihād*, however, still reflect the mainstream view that the baseline of piety is the performance of daily worship and the other obligations laid on all Muslims—so much so that one of the hadīths that Mālik's *Muwattā'* offers is the following:

He who struggles (*al-mujāhid*) in the way of God is like one who fasts and performs the *ṣalāt* constantly. He does not tire of the *ṣalāt* nor of fasting until he returns [from the struggle (*jihād*)]. (*Muwattā'* 21(*Jihād*):1)

Yet another report emphasizes the blessings of martyrdom in God's cause:

Anas b. Mālik reported that the Prophet said: "No servant [of God] who dies and is well received by God would be happy to return to this world, even were he given the world and what is in it, save only the martyr. For he sees the excellence of martyrdom to the extent that he would be happy to return to the world and be killed yet another time." (al-Bukhārī 56[*Jihād*]:6:1)

The danger in focusing upon ideas of militant *jihād* and martyrdom is that a reader may come away with the mistaken impression that both of these were central elements in the preaching and practice of early Islam. In actuality, they were not. But they were still realities that emerged first in Muhammad's struggle with the Meccans after the *Hijrah*, in his eventual conflicts with the Jewish Arab tribes in Medina that opposed the Muslims or even sided with the Meccans, and in his confrontations with the pagan clans of the Hijāz and the wider world of the Peninsula. In the early caliphal period of the first two centuries, *jihād* and martyrdom were used by the central power to justify their own expansion at the expense of Byzantine or other states in the region. They were also used by groups like the Khārijites and some of the proto-Shī'ites to justify their opposition to what they saw as illegitimate and unjust rule under the Umayyads and their 'Abbasid successors. This fact raises one last important question faced by the Muslims in their formative age: Who is a Muslim?

Who Are the Faithful?

In the time of the Prophet, it was relatively clear who was considered a believer, or faithful member of the new community, and who was not. Still, even in the Qur'ān, some of the early converts or potential converts from among Jews and Christians were charged with dissent from, or hypocrisy in, the practice of the new faith. These "dissenters," or "hypocrites" (as the term *munāfiqūn* came to mean in the post-qur'ānic period),[18] seem to have been treated at least some of the time effectively as unbelievers, no better, and perhaps even worse (since some of them could be termed renegades from the faith, or apostates). This possibility of judging some of one's nominally fellow Muslims to be effectively unbelievers became a reality for the first time in the contested caliphate of 'Alī (656–661) not even thirty years after Muhammad's death. Out of the divisions that emerged in this period of civil conflict, the "Seceders," or Khārijites, developed as a splinter group that tended to consider all who did not come to their camp as non-Muslims, unbelievers. They also argued that major sin cut off the perpetrator from the community—

---

[18] See A. Brockett, "al-Munāfikūn," *EI*[2] 7:562.

a position that the majority of Muslims felt was an arrogation of God's prerogative to judge who is and who is not one of His faithful worshippers. The other group that had its origins in the turmoil of 'Alī's caliphate was that of the Shī'ah, the "partisans" of 'Alī (and his descendants in the only male lineage from the Prophet's family). While Shī'īs and the larger, "mainstream" Muslims who eventually called themselves "the people of the Sunnah [of the Prophet] and the Community" (hence their later appellation as "Sunnīs") have never fully excluded each other from the category of "Muslim," at various times each has treated the other as so misguided as to be effectively "unbelievers" (see above, pp. 106–110). Similarly, even though *jihād* as a legal category was resolutely described from early on to be valid only with respect to non-Muslims who fought or oppressed the members of the *Ummah*, it was on occasion, especially in later periods and even today, applied to wars with other Muslim states as well. Thus, as in the case of every religious tradition, it is very hard to generalize about Muslim practice on the basis of particular segments of legal or religious scholarly theory.

In conclusion, we may note that the general tendency in Islam has been to consider a person who claims to be a Muslim a Muslim, leaving his or her judgment to God alone. Beyond this, there is a deeply rooted tradition in Islam, going back to a family of famous sayings ascribed to the Prophet, that says that every person is born *muslim*, submissive to God. Thus there is considered to be in the naïve human psyche a natural predisposition, or *fitrah*, to true faith in and worship of God: "Every infant is born according to the *fitrah*; then his parents make him a Jew or a Christian or a Magian [Zoroastrian]" (see above, pp. 102–103). This can be taken as offering an answer to the question (i) as to whether infants are saved or damned by their faith if they die young, (ii) as speaking to the issue of inheritance (since the general position of the law schools was that Muslims cannot inherit from non-Muslims, and vice-versa), or (iii) as simply recognizing that every infant is born in a sound state and able to grow up a Muslim or become an unbeliever later on. This bears upon the general Muslim tendency to see all unbelievers as potentially reclaimable monotheists, so long as they do not ungratefully reject the clear signs of God in the world around them and the clear revelations from God in His final Scripture, the Qur'ān. Hence the recurring theme of *da'wah*, or "calling" to repentance and true faith—a calling directed not only to polytheists and "people of Scripture," but also to Muslims who have strayed or whose faith has flagged. Potentially all humankind is *muslim* in the deepest sense of that word: "submissive" to the One God, the God of Abraham, Isaac, Jacob, Jesus, and, finally, Muhammad.

CHAPTER SIX

THE END OF DAYS

A. The Issue

The concurrence of Judaism, Christianity, and Islam on the direction of human existence on earth to one beyond the grave marks them as a single genus among religions. All three traditions agree that to be human is to be responsible for one's deeds and answerable to the one and omnipotent, just and merciful God. They share the conviction that the deeds one does in this world bear consequences for one's situation in the world to come, and the merit attained through this-worldly-deeds, e.g., of generosity or piety, persists, determining one's status through eternity. It is in the vital details where the three differ on the story of the end-time, the resurrection of the dead for judgment and eternal life. Judaism focuses upon Israel—we cannot overstress that Israel means those who know the one true God and keep his will—and its critical role in bringing about the end of days. Christianity commits itself to the theory of a comprehensive shift of the human constitution, from the medium of flesh and soul to the medium of spirit, in its argument that the promises to Israel are in fact to be worked out for humanity at large. The Islamic focus is on the individual's responsibility at the end of days for his or her actions in this world. Those actions will be judged at the hour of resurrection, when God calls all of His creation back to himself; in accordance with that ultimate judgment, each resurrected being will be ushered into either everlasting salvation or everlasting punishment.

B. Sanctification Now, for Salvation Then: Judaism

Judaism's position on life beyond the grave at the end of days in history is captured by a single doctrine: God's justice and mercy require him to accord life beyond the grave to all who qualify, otherwise man will not bear responsibility for what he does. Since life continues beyond the grave, what we do in the initial life goes to our account, one way or the other, upon which we draw when we rise from death to eternal life. Scripture itself is explicit that benefits accrue both now and in the age to come:

> A. A man should not take a dam with the young, and even to purify a person afflicted with the skin ailment [as is required at Lev. 14] [M. Hul. 12:5A] therewith,
>
> B. because a transgression will have been committed therewith.
>
> C. R. Jacob says, "You find no [other] commandment in the Torah, the specification of the reward for which is (not) located by its side,
>
> D. "and the [promise of the] resurrection of the dead is written alongside it [as well],
>
> E. "as it is said, 'If along the road you find a bird's nest . . . with fledglings or eggs and the mother sitting over the fledglings or on the eggs, to not take the mother together with her young. Let the mother go and take only the young, in order that you may be well and have a long life' (Dt. 22:6–7).
>
> F. "If this one went up to the top of a tree and fell and died, or to the top of a building and fell and died, where has the good of this one gone, and where is the prolonging of his life?
>
> G. "One must therefore conclude: 'So that it will be good for you'— in this world. 'And so that your days may be prolonged'—in the world of endless time."

Tosefta-tractate Hullin 10:16

The Rabbinic sages in this way identify a case in which one's conduct in this age affects his standing in the age to come. And that captures the entire matter.

But the topic is not a simple one. The authoritative sources of classical Judaism encompass a variety of opinion on what will happen at the end of days, which Judaism calls "the world to come." But a general picture to which all opinion concurs is readily gained. Three components are primary. First comes the resurrection of the dead. At the end of a time of upheaval, the Messiah will bring the dead out of their graves and restore Israel to the Land of Israel. There the dead will come under God's judgment, at which the deeds they did in life are weighed in the balance, good against bad. Nearly all Israel will gain a portion in the world to come, which will restore the eternal perfection of the Garden of Eden as the story of man runs its course. The age that is coming will find Adam's successor, Israel, in Eden's replacement, the Land of Israel. Resurrected, judged,

and justified Israel—comprising nearly all Israelites who ever lived—
Israel will now be gathered into and eternally rooted in the Land
of Israel: Paradise regained.

The absolute given, a logical necessity of a theology revealing
God's justice, maintains that individual life goes forward from this
world, past the grave, to the world to come, where people are both
judged and promised eternal life. That is a necessary doctrine for a
system that insists upon the rationality and order of the universe
under God's rule. Without judgment and eternal life for the righteous, this world's imbalance cannot be righted, nor can God's justice be revealed. Monotheism without an eschatology of judgment
and the world to come leaves unresolved the tensions inherent in
the starting point: God is one, God is just. That is why the starting point of the theology dictates its conclusion: the deeds one does
in this world bear consequences for one's situation in the world to
come, and the merit attained through this-worldly-deeds, e.g., generosity, persists; individuals retain their status as such through all
time to come.

What logic within monotheism as set forth by Judaism, Christianity,
and Islam operates within the Judaic and, later, Christian and Muslim,
doctrine of the resurrection of the dead? Within the framework of
the theology of a just and merciful God, man must survive the grave,
or justice cannot be done. This world on its own hardly serves, for
the wicked prosper and the righteous suffer. Then, to begin with,
the righteous, who will stand in judgment and enter the world to
come, must by definition encompass in their number not only those
alive at the very final moment of humanity's life beyond Eden, but
also all those who have ever lived. Otherwise where is the order,
whence the justice, for the unnumbered ranks of the humble and
virtuous who perished in poverty, knowing full well that the arrogant and wicked died after enjoying a long, satisfying, and nasty life?
The promise of renewed life, forever, systematically accounted for
the ultimate justice of existence, even for private lives. Now, by
definition, the world to come cannot commence without the presence of all who belong to the party of life. And that requirement
explains why we follow the logical sequence, first, resurrection and
judgment, then, the world or the age to come and life eternal. There
is no reversing the order, for obvious reasons built into the logic of
the theology's basic premise and purpose. Let me state the matter

negatively. Only with a complete loss of sense—omission of all those who have died before the end of days—can the world to come and life eternal take place prior to the resurrection of the dead. But then world order proves manifestly unjust. So the very explanation of the justice of world order dictates that matters be just so.

That is why, throughout the Torah the main point of the theological eschatology—the theory of last things—registers both negatively and affirmatively. Death does not mark the end of the individual human life, nor exile the last stop in the journey of Holy Israel. Israelites will live in the age or the world to come, all Israel in the Land of Israel; and Israel will comprehend all who know the one true God. The restoration of world order that completes the demonstration of God's justice encompasses both private life and the domain of all Israel. For both, restorationist theology provides eternal life; to be Israel means to live. As far as the individual is concerned, beyond the grave, at a determinate moment, he or she (1) rises from the grave in resurrection, (2) is judged, and (3) enjoys the world to come. For the entirety of Israel, congruently: all Israel participates in the resurrection, which takes place in the Land of Israel, and enters the world to come.

A single sentence captures the story of the world to come: *When Israel returns to God, God will restore their fortunes.* The sentence remains brief enough with the added adjectival clause, *in the model of Adam and Eve in Eden.* Everything else amplifies details. That simple sentence is explicitly built on the verb-root for return, encompassing restore, *shub,* yielding *teshubah,* repentance as well as the causative form of the verb, *hashib,* thus return or restore. It thereby defines the condition, (intransitive) return or repentance, for the advent of the age to come, which encompasses the action, (transitively) to return matters to their original condition.

How, exactly, do sages envisage restoration? Predictably, because they think paradigmatically and not in historical (let alone cyclical) sequences, sages find models of the end in beginnings. That is why in this context they cluster, and systematically review, the two principal ones, liberation and restoration. First is the account of Israel's liberation from Egypt, the initial act of redemption, which will be recapitulated in the end. Second comes the story of Adam and Eden for their picture of the world to come, the return of Adam to Eden, now in the form of Israel to Zion. (A secondary motif in the latter paradigm contains the complementary category, Gehenna, to which gentiles—meaning, those who deny God—and Israelites who sufficiently sin are consigned when they are denied life.) In the latter case the important point for paradigmatic thinking is that there is no meaningful difference between the world to come and "the Garden of Eden." We go over, once more in so many words, an explicit statement that the two are not to be distinguished:

A. He who performs mostly good deeds inherits the Garden of Eden, but he who performs mostly transgression inherits Gehenna.
Yerushalmi-tractate *Pe'ah* 1:1 XXXII.1

The Garden of Eden is the opposite of Gehenna, and the context—Mishnah *Pe'ah*'s picture of how good deeds store up merit for the world to come—explains the rest. Since Mishnah-tractate *Pe'ah* at the outset speaks of the world to come, so inheriting the Garden of Eden in context bears precisely the meaning of inheriting the world to come; there is no difference, and the two, Eden and the world to come, are interchangeable when sages speak of what happens after death or after resurrection and judgment. For man, entering the world to come, on the other side of resurrection and judgment, marks a homecoming. At the moment of return to Eden, entry into the world to come, man returns to his original condition, in God's image, after God's likeness, complement and conclusion of creation. Here is the ultimate complementarity, the final point of correspondence.

Return, restoration, and renewal mark the end of days for Israel, a process that to begin with depends upon Israel's own repentance:

A. "Restore us to Yourself, O Lord, that we may be restored!":
B. Said the Community of Israel before the Holy One, blessed be He, "Lord of the world, it all depends on You: 'Restore us to Yourself, O Lord.'"
C. 'Return to me and I will return to you, says the Lord of hosts' (Mal. 3:7)."
D. Said the Community of Israel before the Holy One, blessed be He, "Lord of the world, it all depends on You: 'Restore us, O God of our salvation' (Ps. 85:5)."
E. Thus it says, "Restore us to Yourself, O Lord, that we may be restored!"
Lamentations Rabbati CXLIII:i.1ff.

Israel insists that restoration depends on God, but God repays the compliment, and the exchange then is equal: God restores Israel when Israel returns to God, just as we learned when we examined the category of repentance and atonement.

Now we see a sequence of models of redemption. First, as anticipated, comes the explicit comparison of Adam's Eden with the coming restoration, part of a sequence of recapitulated paradigms, which continue the foregoing:

> 2. A. "Renew our days as of old":
>   B. As in the days of the first Adam: "So He drove out the man and He placed at the east of the garden of Eden the cherubim" (Gen. 3:24). [The word for "east" and the word for "of old" using the same letters, the sense, is this: "Renew our days like those of him in connection with whom *kedem* is stated." After being driven out, Adam repented of his sin.]

The restoration involves the Temple offerings as well, which later on are defined in particular; this is here too "as in the days of old":

> 3. A. Another interpretation of the phrase, "Renew our days as of old":
>   B. That is in line with this verse: "Then shall the offering of Judah and Jerusalem be pleasant to the Lord as in the days of old and as in ancient years" (Mal. 3:4).

But the restoration is multidimensional, since it involves, also, the figures of Moses and Solomon:

> B. "as in the days of old": this refers to Moses: "Then his people remembered the days of old, the days of Moses" (Is. 63:11).
> C. "and as in ancient years": this refers to the time of Solomon.

Noah and Abel, for reasons that are specified, now are introduced; they are necessary for the reason given at the end:

> 4. A. [Another interpretation of the phrase, "Renew our days as of old":]
>   B. Rabbi says, "'as in the days of old' refers to the time of Noah: 'For this is as the waters of Noah unto me' (Is. 54:9).
>   "'and as in ancient years' refers to the time of Abel, prior to whose time there was no idolatry in the world."
>   Lamentations Rabbati CXLIII:i.1ff.

Noah represents the moment at which God made his peace with man, even in man's flawed condition. Of intense interest for this analysis, within the restorationist pattern, Abel stands for the time before idolatry, thus explicitly excluding idolaters from the world to come. While Noah, representing all of humanity, and Abel, standing even for antediluvian humanity, make their appearance, the upshot remains exclusionary. The restoration to perfection involves the exclusion of imperfection, and so idolaters cannot enter the new Eden.

By "last things," therefore, the Rabbinic sages' theology means the model of things that applies at the last, from now on, for eternity. By that, in the sages' case, they mean to say, *the last, the final realization or recapitulation of the ever-present and enduring paradigm(s)*, creation and exodus, for instance. A paradigm organizes and classifies relationships, treats concrete events as merely exemplary. So the actualities of this one's conduct with, and attitude toward, that One are restated in generalizations, laws, or rules. "Love God" defines a relationship, and actions and attitudes that express that relationship then may be exemplified by incidents that show what happens when Israel loves God, or what happens when Israel does not love God.

Creation therefore reaches its complement and completion in redemption, which forms a somewhat jarring match. Here, when sages speak of "the world to come" they refer to the realization of a paradigm that is established "of old," restoring the original condition of humanity: living forever in Paradise. That means the redemption of Israel is built into the very structure of creation. That is why God himself not only participated in Israel's affairs, going into exile, as we noted in connection with God's abandoning the Temple, but also participates in the return to the Land:

> B. R. Simeon ben Yohai says, "Come and see how dear [the nation of] Israel is before The Holy One, Blessed Be He, for wherever they were exiled, the divine Presence was with them.
> C. "[When] they were exiled to Egypt, the divine Presence was with them, as is said, 'was I not exiled to your father's house when they were in Egypt (1 Sam. 2:27).
> D. "[When] they were exiled to Babylonia, the divine Presence was with them, as is said, 'for your sake I was sent to Babylonia' (Is. 43:14).
> E. 'And also when they will be redeemed [in the future], the divine Presence will be with them, as is said, 'and the Lord your God will return your return' (Deut. 30:3).
> F. "It does not say 'and He will cause to return' (ve-heshib) but 'and He will return' (ve-shab). This teaches that The Holy One, Blessed Be He, will return with them from among the places of exile.'
> Bavli Megillah 4:4/I.10/29a

Specifically, God redeems Israel and saves the individual Israelite, and *when* that act of redemption or salvation takes place bears no consequence for the meaning of the act or the consequences thereof. It is an act that embodies a relationship, and relationships take place unmediated by time or circumstance. That, sum and substance, embodies the result of paradigmatic thinking, extending beginnings to endings, creation to the world to come.

So much for the definition of the world to come in the paradigmatic—that is, the other-than-temporal-historical—terms that are required. The world to come marks the final condition of world order. It signifies the realization of correct and perfect relationships between God and man, God and Israel in particular. Those who reject God having been disposed of, the age to come finds its definition in the time of total reconciliation between God and man. It is the age when man loves God and accepts his dominion and completes the work of repentance and atonement for acts of rebellion. While, clearly, that reconciliation of God and man takes place in individual life, in which case, as already instantiated, we may use the language of salvation, it also governs the public life of Israel, in which case we may speak of redemption. That leads us to wonder what is at stake in the location of the theology's final chapter in what is clearly not a historical-eschatological setting but one that finds definition in intangibles of relationship: reconciliation, return, renewal, right attitude.

So we reasonably ask: What indeed do sages have in mind when they speak of the world to come—concrete actualities, or intangible feelings and attitudes, impalpable matters of the spirit? May we suppose that we deal with a mere narration, in mythic form, of what in fact represents an inner, other-worldly, intangible, and spiritual encounter? That is to say, if all that is at stake is abstract patterns of relationships that happen to come to expression in tales of the eschaton, one might suppose that the conception, "the world to come," simply serves as another way of saying, "man reconciled with God." Then, through paradigmatic thinking, sages should be represented as finding in the myth a vivid and palpable way of speaking of the inner life of intentionality and attitude. That is a possible reading of the character of the discourse at hand. But that would drastically misrepresent the worldly reality, the concrete actuality, of sages' account of matters, their intent to speak to the here and now. That is stated in a powerful story, that ends: the Messiah will come, the dead will be raised, "today, if you will it"! We contemplate what is palpable and real in an ordinary, everyday sense, not what is intangible or merely "spiritual," in the vulgar sense.

First, while their Israel is the holy people, living in the plane of transcendence, their Israel truly lives in the trenchant world of marketplace and farm, and engages in the material and physical transactions of farming and love. Sages found no cause to differentiate an "Israel after the spirit" from their "Israel after the flesh," since when they referred to Israel, they meant all those who know God as God made himself manifest, meaning, in the Torah, and at the end, that Israel, shorn of the handful of aliens (those who deny God, the resurrection of the dead, the resurrection of the dead as a fact set forth by God in the Torah, and so on), all together, in the flesh, sees God and enters onto eternal life.

Second, their Israel does constitute a political entity—this world's embodiment of the locus of God's rule—and as we have already noted, God's intervention at the very least will bring about a radical change in the politics of world order, Rome giving way to Israel. Sages put forth a theology of intentionality that governs only by appeal to theoretical politics. Sages, like philosophers, were public intellectuals, undertaking the work of the community of holy Israel (sages) or the polis (philosophers). They thought about concrete, practical things, and at no point can we identify an area of the law or lore of the Oral Torah that has no bearing upon the everyday world of the here and now. That, indeed, is the very upshot of the point-by-point match of *Halakhah* and *Aggadah*, law and lore, that we have had occasion to review here and there.

Third, when they speak of the world to come, the sages mean a world that is public and shared, not private and inner-facing, and certainly not personal as distinct from public. It is not a world of relativities and relationships as these intangibles are concretely symbolized, but a world of real encounter. Sages know a palpable God who punishes arrogance and rewards humility, in both instances in worldly ways. Prayers are answered with rain or healing, virtue responded to with grace bearing material benefit, acts of generosity with miracles. Heaven intervenes in matters of health and sickness, in the abundance or scarcity of crops, in good fortune and ill. Sages insist upon an exact correspondence between practicalities and transcendent relationships.

Accordingly, since man corresponds to God and in important ways serves God's purpose, the spiritualization of matters earthly would seriously misinterpret what is at stake here. When sages see the world to come as the climax and conclusion of the processes of creation that commenced with Eden, they envisage the world that comes within their everyday gaze, the people they see out there, in the street, not only imagined inside, in the heart. Take the resurrection for instance. When the dead are raised from the grave, they will stink and need new clothes:

> A. Raba contrasted [these two verses]: "It is written, 'I kill and I make alive' (Deut. 32:39) and it is written, 'I wound and I heal' (Deut. 32:39). [The former implies that one is resurrected just as he was at death, thus with blemishes, and the other implies that at the resurrection all wounds are healed].
> B. "Said the Holy One, blessed be He, 'What I kill I bring to life,' and then, 'What I have wounded I heal.'"
>
> Bavli Sanhedrin 11:1–2 I.25.91b

That humble fact captures the dialectic of paradigmatic, as against historical, thinking. History produces the dialectic of past against present, resolved in the future (thesis, antithesis, synthesis). Paradigms set the past within the present, Abraham or Moses consorting with the here and now and Jacob shaping public policy today—a considerable tension not to be resolved at all. On the one hand, the advent of the world to come is represented as part of an ordinal sequence, though, for reasons fully exposed, that sequence should not be treated as identical with temporal, historical happenings. On the other hand, the paradigm is fully as palpable in its shaping of the everyday world and workaday experience as history. So at the resurrection, the corpse will need a bath. A theology that does not "spiritualize," that is, that does not represent as intangible God in Heaven any more than man on earth, will insist upon the material and physical character of resurrection and the life of the Garden of Eden that is the world to come. That theology will have no motive to treat the transformation of relationships represented by the resurrection of the dead and the judgment and the world or age to

come as other than consubstantial with the experienced world of the
moment—if also marvelously different.

In sages' vision the world to come will mark an age of illumination, celebration, eating, drinking, and dancing—bliss forever. Take
lavish lighting, for example. Living in a time long before street lighting, when the stars and the moon alone illuminated the darkness,
when sages promised that, in the world to come people will go out
at night by the light of God, it meant something:

A. R. Samuel bar Nahman: "While in this age people go by day in
the light of the sun and by night in the light of the moon, in the
coming age, they will undertake to go only by the light of the sun
by day, and not by the light of the moon by night.
B. "What verse of Scripture indicates it? 'The sun shall no longer be
your light by day, nor the moon shine on you when evening falls;
[the Lord shall be your everlasting light, your God shall be your
glory. Never again shall your sun set, nor your moon withdraw
her light; but the Lord shall be your everlasting light and the days
of your mourning shall be ended]' (Is. 60:19–20).
C. "By what light will they walk? By the light of the Holy One, blessed
be He, in line with the passage: 'the Lord shall be your everlasting light.'"

Pesiqta deRab Kahana XXI:V.2

In a moment we shall see that other sources of supernatural light
will defeat the darkness. Further, in the world to come or the time
of the Messiah, there will be celebrations for the righteous. God will
preside over a banquet for the righteous; he will lead the dancing; he
will prepare a tabernacle for the righteous to provide shade by day:

Rabbah said R. Yohanan said, "The Holy One, blessed be He, is destined to make a banquet for the righteous out of the meat of Leviathan:
'Companions will make a banquet of it' (Job 40:30). The meaning of
'banquet' derives from the usage of the same word in the verse, 'And
He prepared for them a great banquet and they ate and drank'
(2 Kgs. 6:23)."

The banquet will be for the disciples of sages in particular.

"'Companions' can refer only to disciples of sages, in line with this
usage: 'You that dwells in the gardens, the Companions hearken for
your voice, cause me to hear it' (Song 8:13). The rest of the creature
will be cut up and sold in the markets of Jerusalem: 'They will part
him among the Canaanites' (Job 40:30), and 'Canaanites' must be

merchants, in line with this usage: 'As for the Canaanite, the balances of deceit are in his hand, he loves to oppress' (Hos. 12:8). If you prefer: 'Whose merchants are princes, whose traffickers are the honorable of the earth' (Is. 23:8).'"

Bavli Baba Batra 5:1A–D IV.28ff./75a

The main point, then, is that the righteous, in general, will be given shelter from the sun and rain, constructed out of the hide of Leviathan.

Nearly everybody who knows the one true God gets to the world to come, but, when there, some are treated better than others, once more in response to their conduct in life. So even beyond resurrection and judgment, what people did in life determines how they will spend even the joys of eternity. This point is critical in the ultimate balancing of the scales of justice, and we shall dwell on the matter:

IV.38 A. And said Rabbah said R. Yohanan, "The righteous are destined to be called by the name of the Holy One, blessed be He: 'Every one that is called by My name, and whom I have created for My glory, I have formed him, yes, I have made him' (Is. 43:7)."

IV.39 A. Said R. Samuel bar Nahmani said R. Yohanan, "There are three who are called by the name of the Holy One, blessed be He, and these are they: the righteous, the Messiah, and Jerusalem.

B. "The righteous, as we have just said.

C. "The Messiah: 'And this is the name whereby He shall be called, the Lord is our righteousness' (Jer. 23:6).

D. "Jerusalem: 'It shall be eighteen thousand reeds round about, and the name of the city from that day shall be, "the Lord is there"' (Ezek. 48:35). Do not read 'there' but 'its name.'"

The righteous then will be called holy, and Jerusalem will be exalted as well:

IV.40 A. Said R. Eleazar, "The time will come when 'holy' will be said before the name of the righteous as it is said before the name of the Holy One, blessed be He: 'And it shall come to pass that he that is left in Zion and he that remains in Jerusalem shall be called holy' (Is. 4:3)."

IV.41 A. And said Rabbah said R. Yohanan, "The Holy One, blessed be He, is destined to lift up Jerusalem to a height of three parasangs: 'And she shall be lifted up and be settled in her place' (Is. 4:3). '. . . In her place' means 'like her place' [Jerusalem will be lifted up to a height equal to the extent of the space it occupies]."

Bavli Baba Batra 5:1A–D IV.38–41

The righteous, the Messiah, and Jerusalem now form a single category of complements, united by the common trait that all will be called "holy" as God now is called holy. The model of anticipation then reaches a daring position, which is that, in time to come, the righteous, the Messiah, and Jerusalem all enter into the category of God himself. That explains why they will have a banquet that God will make for them, that God will make a tabernacle for the righteous much as Moses made a tabernacle for the Lord in the wilderness, and Jerusalem will enlighten the world.

People enjoy a continuous existence both in this world, past the grave, and in the world to come, so that what they do in this world affects their situation in the world to come. We need not review what has already been said about the logical necessity of resurrection and judgment. We recall how resurrection solves the problem of inequity in private life, the imbalance of virtue and prosperity such as a fully-realized, this-worldly justice would effect. It suffices to note that, once judgment has taken place, and the balance is righted, then the world to come defines the place and time for the reward of virtue to come to realization. Acts of loving kindness bear their own reward, and for certain actions of that kind, there is no limit to the reward in both this world and the next. Transgressions also bear their punishments, if not here, then there. These are familiar ideas, predictable in a system of stasis and balance.

Here it suffices to deal only with the relationship between this world and the world to come as sages complete their account of the perfect justice of world order. The most important point comes first. Suffering in this world for the Torah brings reward in the world to come. Here we clearly refer to disciples of sages, but that is only right, in context, for we want to know how, in the world to come, they will receive recompense for the sacrifices that, in this world, they make for Torah study:

> III.5 A. R. Judah b. R. Simon interpreted, "Whoever blackens his face [in fasting] on account of teachings of Torah in this world will find that the Holy One, blessed be He, polishes his luster in the world to come.
> B. "For it is said, 'His countenance shall be as the Lebanon, excellent as the cedars' (Song 5:15)."
> Bavli Sanhedrin 11:1–2 III.5/100a

Now we proceed to the reward for accepting poverty:

> C. R. Tanhum bar Hanilai said, "Whoever starves himself for words of Torah in his world will the Holy One, blessed be He, feed to satisfaction in the world to come,
>
> D. "as it is said, 'They shall be abundantly satisfied with the fatness of Your house, and You shall make them drink of the river of Your pleasures' (Ps. 36:9)."

From disciples, we turn to every righteous person:

> E. When R. Dimi came, he said, "The Holy One, blessed be He, is destined to give to every righteous person his full packload, as it is said, 'Blessed be the Lord, day by day, Who loads us with benefits, even the God of our salvation, Selah' (Ps. 68:20)."
>
> F. Said Abbayye to him, "And is it possible to say so? Is it not said, 'Who has measured the waters in the hollow of His hand and measured out Heaven with the span' (Is. 40:12)?"
>
> G. He said to him, "What is the reason that you are not at home in matters of lore [but only in matters of law and legal analysis]. They say in the West in the name of Raba bar Mari, 'The Holy One, blessed be He, is destined to give each righteous person three hundred and ten worlds, as it is said, "That I may cause those who love Me to inherit substance and I will fill their treasures," (Prov. 8:21), and the numerical value of the word for substance is three hundred ten.'"
>
> Bavli Sanhedrin 11:1–2 III.5/100a

The position throughout is the familiar one that a balance governs all things, so that if one suffers now, in this world, then one will rejoice in a reward in the world to come. That principle of balance, proportion, and commensurability comes to expression in diverse ways. People mourn now, but will rejoice later on. Mourning now is appropriate, but must be kept in due proportion; it must not descend into sheer despair. This same conception then applies to Torah study. One sacrifices for Torah study in this world, but one will get a reward in the world to come.

So much for Israelites and for all Israel. As we realize full well, gentiles, meaning, all those who practice idolatry, along with their idolatry simply will cease to exist; some will perish, just as Israelites will perish, just as the Generation of the Flood, the Generation of the Dispersion, the men of Sodom, and certain Israelites will perish. But some—a great many—will give up idolatry and thereby accept God's self-manifestation in the Torah and become part of Israel. The gentiles as such are not subject to redemption; they have no choice at the advent of the world to come but to accept God or become extinct. But that is not the precise formulation that the system will set forth. Rather, the correct language is not that the gentiles will cease to exist, but rather that the category "gentiles with their idolatry" will cease to function. Idolatry having come to an end, God having been recognized by all mankind, everyone will enter the category Israel.

When, therefore, does the end come, and what will bring it? When Israel really wants the Messiah to come, he will come. But special weight attaches to the word "want" or "will." What Israel on its own, as an act of free will, must *want* is only what God wants. What Israel must do is give up any notion of accomplishing on its own, by its own act of will, the work of redemption. It is only through the self-abnegation of repentance that Israel can accomplish its goal. Specifically, when Israel's will conforms to the will of God, then God will respond to the act of repentance by bringing about the time of restoration and eternal life. This is expressed in a colloquy that announces that the Messiah will come when all Israel keeps a single Sabbath. And that will take place when Israel wants it to take place. It requires only an act of will on the part of Israel to accept one of the Ten Commandments. Then in a broader restatement of matters, the entire redemptive process is made to depend upon Israel's repentance as is seen in Yerushalmi Taanit 1:1 II:5:

G. The Israelites said to Isaiah, "O our Rabbi, Isaiah, What will come for us out of this night?"
H. He said to them, "Wait for me, until I can present the question."
I. Once he had asked the question, he came back to them.
J. They said to him, "Watchman, what of the night? What did the Guardian of the ages say [a play on 'of the night' and 'say']?"
K. He said to them, "The watchman says: 'Morning comes; and also the night. [If you will inquire, inquire; come back again]'" (Is. 21:12).
L. They said to him, "Also the night?"
M. He said to them, "It is not what you are thinking. But there will be morning for the righteous, and night for the wicked, morning for Israel, and night for idolaters."

Now comes the main point in the exchange: when will this happen? It will happen when Israel wants. And what is standing in the way is Israel's arrogance, to be atoned for by Israel's remorseful repentance:

N. They said to him, "When?"

O. He said to them, "Whenever you want, He too wants [it to be]—
if you want it, he wants it."

P. They said to him, "What is standing in the way?"

Q. He said to them, "Repentance: 'come back again'" (Is. 21:12).

This is stated in the clearest possible way: one day will do it.

R. R. Aha in the name of R. Tanhum b. R. Hiyya, "If Israel repents
for one day, forthwith the son of David will come.

S. "What is the scriptural basis? 'O that today you would hearken to
His voice!'" (Ps. 95:7).

Now comes the introduction of the Sabbath as a test case:

T. Said R. Levi, "If Israel would keep a single Sabbath in the proper
way, forthwith the son of David will come.

U. "What is the scriptural basis for this view? 'Moses said, Eat it today,
for today is a Sabbath to the Lord; [today you will not find it in
the field]' (Ex. 16:25).

V. "And it says [For thus said the Lord God, the Holy One of Israel],
'In returning and rest you shall be saved; [in quietness and in trust
shall be your strength.' And you would not]'" (Is. 30:15). By means
of returning and [Sabbath] rest you will be redeemed.

The main point, then, is the linkage of repentance to the coming
restoration of Israel to the Land, the dead to life, by the Messiah.
But the advent of the Messiah depends wholly upon Israel's will. If
Israel will subordinate its will to God's, all else will follow. That is
what Scripture says, and that is what Judaism, resting squarely on
Scripture, teaches too.

C. RESURRECTION AS METAMORPHOSIS: CHRISTIANITY

Jesus held that, at the end of time, God would change human life
so radically that ordinary human relationships would no longer prevail. That conviction of a radical change brought with it a commitment to the language of eschatology, of the ultimate transformation
God both promised and threatened. Although Jesus' eschatology was
sophisticated, his commitment to that idiom of discourse is evident.[1]

---

[1] See Bruce Chilton, *Pure Kingdom: Jesus' Vision of God*: Studying the Historical
Jesus 1 (Eerdmans: Grand Rapids, 1996).

Some efforts have been made recently to discount the eschatological dimension of Jesus' teaching; they have not prevailed. Periodically,
theologians in the West have attempted to convert Jesus' perspective into their own sense that the world is a static and changeless
entity, but that appears to have been far from his own orientation.[2]

In respect of the discussion of the general orientation of Jesus'
theology, few scholars would take exception to what has been asserted
so far. Consensus is much more difficult to come by, when it concerns Jesus' understanding of what is to occur *to particular human beings*
within God's disclosure of his kingdom. Resurrection, as usually
defined, promises actual life to individual persons within God's global
transformation of all things. Because Jesus, on a straightforward reading of the Gospels, does not say much about resurrection as such,
there has been a lively dispute over whether he had any distinctive
(or even emphatic) teaching in that regard.

Still, when Jesus does address the issue, his contribution seems to
be unequivocal. Sadducees are portrayed as asking a mocking question of Jesus, designed to disprove the possibility of resurrection:[3]
Moses commanded that, were a man to die childless, his brother
should raise up a seed for him. Suppose there were seven brothers,
the first of whom was married. If they all died childless in sequence,
whose wife would the woman be in the resurrection (see Matthew
22:23–28; Mark 12:18–23; Luke 20:27–33)?

Jesus' response is categorical and direct (following Mark 12:24–27,
compare Matthew 22:29–32; Luke 20:34–38):

> You completely deceive yourselves, knowing neither the Scriptures nor
> the power of God! Because when they arise from the dead, they neither

---

[2] See Bruce Chilton, *The Kingdom of God in the Teaching of Jesus* (London: SPCK,
1984). For discussion since that time, and particularly the contribution of Marcus
Borg, see *Pure Kingdom*.

[3] Acts 23:8 makes out that the Sadducees deny resurrection altogether, and that
is also the judgment of Josephus. I have argued that, despite their unequivocal statements (or rather, precisely because they are so unequivocal), we should be cautious
about what the Sadducees denied; *The Temple of Jesus: His Sacrificial Program within a
Cultural History of Sacrifice* (University Park: Pennsylvania State University Press, 1992),
82. The Sadducees' position is attributed to them only by unsympathetic observers,
Josephus (War 2§165–166) and various Christians (Mark 12:18–27; Matthew 22:23–
33; Luke 20:27–38; Acts 23:6–8). And Targumic texts as late as the Middle Ages
continue to refer to the denial of resurrection within the dispute between Cain and
Abel which is developed at Genesis 4:8.

marry nor are given in marriage, but are as angels in the Heavens. But concerning the dead, that they rise, have you not read in the book of Moses about the bush, when God said to him, I am the God of Abraham and the God of Isaac and the God or Jacob? He is not God of the dead but of the living. You deceive yourselves greatly.

Of the two arguments, the one from Scripture is the more immediately fitting, an appeal both to the nature of God and to the evaluation of the patriarchs in early Judaism. If God identifies himself with Abraham, Isaac, and Jacob, it must be that in his sight, they live. And those three patriarchs—once we join in this analogical reflection—are indeed living principles of Judaism itself; they are Israel as chosen in the case of Abraham (see Genesis 15), as redeemed in the case of Isaac (see Genesis 22), and as struggling to identity in the case of Jacob (see Genesis 32). That evocation of patriarchal identity is implied, rather than demonstrated; but the assumption is that the hearer is able to make such connections between the text of Scripture and the fulfillment of that Scripture within present experience.[4] But that implicit logic of the argument from Scripture only makes the other argument seem all the bolder by comparison.

The direct comparison between people in the resurrection and angels is consonant with the thought that the patriarchs must live in the sight of God, since angels are normally associated with God's throne (so, for example, Daniel 7:9–14). So once the patriarchs are held to be alive before God, the comparison with angels is feasible. But Jesus' statement is not only a theoretical assertion of the majesty of God, a majesty which includes the patriarchs (and, by extension, the patriarchs comparability to the angels); it is also an emphatic claim of what we might call divine anthropology. Jesus asserts that human relations are radically altered in the resurrection, because sexual identity changes.[5] That claim of substantial regeneration and

---

[4] For Jesus' characteristic attitude towards Scripture, see Bruce Chilton, *A Galilean Rabbi and His Bible: Jesus' Use of the Interpreted Scripture of His Time* (Wilmington: Glazier, 1984); also published with the subtitle, *Jesus' own interpretation of Isaiah* (London: SPCK, 1984).

[5] It is commonly asserted that Jesus accorded with accepted understandings of resurrection within Judaism; see Pheme Perkins, *Resurrection: New Testament Witness and Contemporary Reflection* (London: Chapman, 1984), 75. That is an unobjectionable finding, but it leads to an odd conclusion: "Nor can one presume that Jesus makes any significant contribution to or elaboration of these common modes of speaking."

transcendence became a major theme among the more theological thinkers who followed Jesus, beginning with Paul.

But how is it that Jesus' position in regard to the resurrection is only spelled out in one passage within the Gospels? There is a general explanation that might be offered in this regard, but it is only partially satisfactory. The intent of the Synoptic Gospels, on the one hand, and that of the Fourth Gospel, on the other, are quite different. The Synoptics are designed in the interests of catechesis, for the preparation of proselytes for baptism, while the Gospel according to John is homiletic. What was in all probability the original ending of John states the purpose as maintaining the faith of believers so that they might go on to have life in the name of Christ (John 20:31), while the introduction to Luke speaks of the things which the reader has only recently learned (Luke 1:1–4, and the verb is *katecheo*).[6] In between the initial preparation of catechumens and the advanced interpretation offered to those well beyond that point, a great deal of instruction naturally took place.

The Lord's Prayer provides a stunning example of the kind of teaching that may have fallen in between initial catechesis and homiletics in some communities. John's Gospel contains no version of the prayer, presumably because it is assumed as elementary knowledge. But then, Mark's Gospel also omits it, but for a different reason: the assumption is that oral instruction, apart from public catechesis, is to *complement* what the catechumen learns from the Gospel. The prayer is by no means advanced knowledge; after all, the catechumen will have to learn to say *'Abbā* at baptism (see Galatians 4:6; Romans 8:15), and to know what that means. Yet were our knowledge of Jesus and early Christianity limited to Mark and John among

---

Perkins is not clear about what she means here, or the basis of her assertion. Does warning the reader against presuming that Jesus had something original to say imply that he in fact said nothing original? Why speak of presumption at all, when there is an actual saying to hand? But the analysis of the saying is also confused, because Perkins speaks of it as invented by Mark when it has anything new to say, and as routine insofar as it may be attributed to Jesus. The discussion typifies the ill-defined program of trivializing the place of Jesus within the tradition of the New Testament by critics who once tended to exaggerate the literary aspirations of those who composed the documents.

[6] For further discussion of the relationship between John and the Synoptics in terms of their social functions, see Bruce Chilton, *Profiles of a Rabbi: Synoptic Opportunities in Reading about Jesus*, Brown Judaic Studies 177 (Atlanta: Scholars Press, 1989).

the Gospels, we would not be aware of the prayer or of its importance within the teaching of Jesus and the practice of his movement.

Teaching in regard to the resurrection may be held to belong more to an intermediate level of instruction within early Christianity than to a preparatory or advanced level. After all, Mark's Gospel relates no story of the appearance of the risen Jesus, but only the narrative of the women at the tomb (Mark 16:1–8). The silence of the women is the last word in the Gospel—and it is an approving word. The Markan community is thereby instructed to maintain reserve in the face of persecution. But it is very clear what that reserve is about: the angelic young man at the tomb (Mark 16:6, 7) and Jesus himself at an earlier stage (Mark 8:31; 9:9, 31; 10:33, 34) leave no doubt that the full disclosure of Jesus' identity lies in his resurrection. As the Markan catechumen approaches the paschal mystery, when baptism will occur and full access to Eucharist extended for the first time, the door to the truth of Jesus' resurrection is opened in the Gospel, but actual entry to that truth awaits further (perhaps private) instruction.[7]

But the analogy between the handling of the resurrection of Jesus in the Gospels and the handling of the Lord's Prayer is only partial. First, the apparent lack of Mark is made up by Matthew (6:9–13) and Luke (11:2–4), and together those Gospels provide a cogent representation of the model of prayer which Jesus taught, a model which is not without echo in the Gospels according to Mark and John.[8] Second, the resurrection of Jesus is actually introduced as a topic in Mark, only then to be omitted at the end of the Gospel. When that lacuna is made up in Matthew, Luke, and John (as well as in the artificial ending provided Mark itself in many manuscripts), the result is a series of stories whose cogency does not approach that of the Lord's Prayer in Matthew and Luke.

---

[7] To this extent, the so-called Secret Gospel of Mark which Morton Smith identified and popularized may provide an insight into the post-catechetical moment in early Christianity. But of course, the controversy concerning that work does not permit any conclusions to be drawn on the basis of Smith's contribution alone. See James H. Charlesworth and Craig A. Evans, "Jesus in the Agrapha and Apocryphal Gospels," *Studying the Historical Jesus: Evaluations of the State of Current Research*, New Testament Tools and Studies XIX (ed. B. Chilton and C. A. Evans; Leiden: Brill, 1994), 479–533, 526–532.

[8] See Chilton, *Jesus' Prayer and Jesus' Eucharist: His Personal Practice of Spirituality* (Valley Forge: Trinity Press International, 1997).

So it will not do to try to invoke a general explanation, in terms of the level of instruction involved, to account for the absence or the discordance of stories of Jesus' resurrection and for the relative paucity of Jesus' own teaching regarding resurrection within the Gospels. Rather, there seems to have been a deliberate policy of esotericism in this regard. To some extent, the silence of the women in Mark is an index of this policy, and the atmospheric possibility of persecution for belief in the name of Jesus is which their silence doubtless reflects offers (once again) a partial explanation for the counsel of silence. But all of these explanations which involve the happenstance of history—the educational pitch of the Gospels, the esoteric practice of early Christianity, the pressures exerted by the possibility of persecution for belief in Jesus' resurrection—do not account for the qualitative difference in the manner of handling the resurrection as compared, say, to the Lord's Prayer. And after all: the resurrection of Jesus is on any known reading the most obviously distinctive element in Christian teaching: How can there be a lack of cogency in providing for instruction on this point within the Gospels?

Together with those explanations, which may be characterized in terms of their reference to extrinsic circumstances, we must consider the *intrinsic structure of belief in Jesus' resurrection* as received and practiced within early Christianity. Something about the way belief in the resurrection was structured, within the social and historical environment which has already been described, produced the apparent lacuna and the evident discrepancies we have referred to within the textual tradition and what produced that tradition. Mark is a good initial guide to the complexity of that structure. The young man at the tomb instructs the women to tell the disciples and Peter that Jesus goes before them into Galilee, and that they will see Jesus there (Mark 16:7). That is, Peter is identified as the central named witness of Jesus' resurrection; but then no actual story of an appearance to Peter is conveyed. Instead, this Gospel ends with the women turned away from a tomb they do not even inspect thoroughly.

"The Lord has risen, and has appeared to Simon" (Luke 24:34) is the acclamation—widely recognized as primitive (compare 1 Corinthians 15:5)—which Luke alone relates; but here again, no actual story is attached to this statement. Instead, Luke then gives us, in addition to a recognizable but distinctive narrative of the tomb (now

specified as empty in Luke 24:1–12), the story of Jesus' appearance
to the two disciples who were on their way to Emmaus (Luke
24:13–35). That story emphasizes that Jesus was not instantly recognizable to the disciples, and he disappears once they finally do
recognize him during a meal; the theme is explicitly given as Jesus'
manifestation in the breaking of bread (v. 35), which occurs in the
evidently liturgical context of the reminiscence of Jesus and the interpretation of Scripture (vv. 18–27). So alongside the narrative of the
empty tomb, which anticipates that Jesus' resurrection involves the
physical body that was buried (especially in its Lukan form, see v. 3
within vv. 1–12), there is a story which portrays the resurrection in
straightforwardly visionary and eucharistic terms: Jesus is seen, but
not recognized, then recognized, and no longer seen. The conflict
with the story of the empty tomb is manifest, and all the more so
as it is actually referred to by Kleopas in what he says to the stranger
who turns out to be the risen Jesus (vv. 22–23).

Luke's Gospel is designed to resolve that conflict to some extent.
That design is reflected in the way the Gospel smoothes out the
problem which would have been caused by telling the disciples to
go to Galilee (as in Mark), since the risen Jesus appears only in the
vicinity of Jerusalem in Luke. Instead, Luke's two men (rather than
one young man) remind the women of what Jesus said *when he was
in Galilee* (Luke 24:4–8). That enables the focus to remain Jerusalem,
where the appearance to Simon occurred, and in whose vicinity the
disclosure of the risen Jesus was experienced in the breaking of bread.
In that same Jerusalem itself, finally (never Galilee in Luke) Jesus
appears in the midst of the disciples in the context of another meal
(also associated with the interpretation of Scripture and the recollection of Jesus) and shows them that he is flesh and bone, not spirit.
He commissions them, instructing them to remain in Jerusalem until
the power to become witnesses comes upon them. Leading them out
to Bethany, he is taken up to Heaven while he is in the act of blessing them (Luke 24:36–52). This final appearance in Luke fulfills the
expectations raised by the empty tomb, and it is a triumph of harmoni-
zation: Jesus not only says he is flesh and bone, he shows his hands
and his feet, offers to be touched, asks for food and eats it (vv. 38–
43). Yet this physical emphasis is also synthesized with the visionary
and liturgical idiom of what happened near and at Emmaus. But in
all of this, interestingly, there is silence regarding Peter's experience.

Matthew returns the focus to Galilee, *and to Galilee alone*, as the locus of the risen Jesus. Here Jesus himself actually encounters the women as they run to tell the disciples what the angel has said, and he tells them to instruct his brothers to go to Galilee (Matthew 28:10). The reference to "brothers" at this point, rather than to "disciples" (cf. 28:7), is apparently deliberate; the angel speaks to the women as disciples, while Jesus is adding an injunction for a distinct group. After the story about the guard and the high priests (Matthew 28:11–15), however, the last passage in the Gospel according to Matthew, the appearance of Jesus in Galilee, concerns only the eleven disciples. They see, worship (and doubt), receiving the commission to baptize all nations in the knowledge that Jesus is always with them. In its own way, and centered in Galilee rather than in Jerusalem, Matthew achieves what Luke achieves: the appearances of the risen Jesus are visionary (and almost abstract), but the explanation of that vision is that his body was raised. The guards' experience of the earthquake and the angel—and their willingness to broadcast the lie (concocted by high priests and elders) that Jesus' body had been stolen (Matthew 28:2–4, 11–15)—underscores that explanation. What remains startling about Matthew is the complete absence of direct reference to Peter in this context (compare Matthew 28:7 to Mark 16:7), although Peter is singled out for special treatment in the same Gospel (see Matthew 16:17–19).

Matthew's silence regarding Peter and Luke's laconic reference to the tradition that he was the first to have the Lord appear to him call attention to the structural oddity in testimony to Jesus' resurrection in the New Testament. Simon Kephas/Peter is held to be the fountainhead of this faith (as in 1 Corinthians 15:5), but the Synoptic Gospels have no tradition of the appearance to Peter in particular. John's Gospel puts Peter and the other disciple whom Jesus loved at the site of the empty tomb.[9] The other disciple is said

---

[9] Luke 24:12 puts Peter alone there. For a defense of that tradition as historical, see Pierre Benoit, *Passion et résurrection du Seigneur* (Paris: Cerf, 1985), 288–290. But Benoit's attempt to make John's Gospel the nearest point to the fountainhead of such traditions is not convincing. John rather seems to aggregate the elements already present within the Synoptic Gospels. Mark's young man becomes the other disciple, Luke's reference to Peter's presence at the tomb is expanded, Matthew's description of Jesus' manifestation to the women is turned into a private appearance to Mary Magdalene, Luke's tradition of appearances to the disciples in Jerusalem

to have seen the tomb and to have believed, but Peter only sees it
(John 20:1–10). Mary Magdalene then sees two angels and Jesus,
but does not recognize him at first and is forbidden to touch him:
her commission is to tell the brothers that he goes to the Father
(John 20:11–18). Likewise, Jesus' commission at this point is simply
to go to the Father, which presupposes—as Benoit points out—that
in what follows any descent from the Father is only for the purpose
of appearing to the disciples.[10] Commissioning is the purpose of Jesus
in what follows. He appears among the disciples when the doors
were shut for fear of the Jews, and provides Holy Spirit for forgiving and confirming sins (John 20:19–23).[11] During the appearance,
he shows his hands and his side in order to be recognized (20:20),
which he does again in a second appearance, this time for the benefit
of Thomas, and with the offer to touch his hands and his side (John
20:24–29). Obviously, the coalescing of the empty tomb and the
visionary appearances has continued in John, but the problem of
Simon Peter has not so far been resolved.

That resolution comes in the close of the present text of John,
which is widely considered an addendum or annex (John 21).[12] Here,
Peter and six other disciples are fishing on the Sea of Galilee, and
Jesus appears on the shore unrecognized, asking if they have anything to eat. They have not caught anything all night, but at Jesus'
command they cast their net, and catch more fish than they can
pull up. The disciple whom Jesus loves recognizes Jesus, and informs
Peter who the stranger is. Peter leaps into the water, and swims to
shore, followed by the others in the boat. Jesus, whose identity none

---

during meals is honored with a cognate emphasis on both visionary and physical
aspects, and Matthew's localization (together with Mark's promise) of such an event,
also with much less physical emphasis and in Galilee, is also respected.

[10] Benoit, p. 291. He goes on to suggest that the return of Jesus after this point
must be "totally spiritualized, in particular in the Eucharist." That suggests the
extent to which the Gospel has shifted idioms within its presentation of the resurrection. He deals with the story of what happened near Emmaus in much the same
way, pp. 297–325.

[11] An evident echo of Matthew 16:17–19, the placement of which here serves to
highlight Peter's importance within the tradition of the resurrection, without actually solving the problem that, by the implication of John 20:6–9, Peter saw the
empty tomb, but did not believe as the other disciple did. John 21 will return to
the question of Peter, reflecting an awareness that his place within what has been
said has not yet been resolved.

[12] See Benoit, 327–353.

dares to ask, directs the preparation of breakfast from the 153 large fish that were caught. Finally, Peter himself is commissioned to shepherd the flock of Jesus.

Although this third appearance of the risen Jesus in John is the only appearance which features Peter,[13] the allusions to baptism and the direction of the church make it clear that it is far from the sort of tradition which would have been formed in any immediate proximity to Peter's experience. Still, one feature stands out. As in the story of what happened near and at Emmaus (which holds the place of an appearance to Peter in Luke), Jesus is not immediately known; his identity is a matter of inference (see John 21:7, 12 and Luke 24:16, 31). This, of course, is just the direction in which all of the Gospels are *not headed* in their structuring of traditions. They anticipate an instantly recognizable Jesus, fully continuous with the man who was buried: that is the point of the story of the empty tomb as it is developed in all four Gospels.

Their insistence on the physical continuity of the buried and risen Jesus is reflected in the way they present other stories. Jesus raises to life the son of the widow of Nain (Luke 7:11–17), the daughter of Jairus (Matthew 9:18–19, 23–26; Mark 5:21–24, 35–43; Luke 8:40–42, 49–56), and Lazarus (11:1–46). An excellent study has shown that all of these stories represent the conviction that Jesus' resurrection promised the resurrection of the faithful.[14] But that connection also worked the other way: expectations of how the resurrection was to happen generally influenced the presentation of how the risen Jesus appeared. When Paul insisted that "flesh and blood can not inherit the kingdom of God" (1 Corinthians 15:50), he was not opposing an abstract proposition.[15] Indeed, it would seem on the face of

---

[13] It has been argued that the *Gospel of Peter* represents a more primitive tradition, but the fact is that the text incorporates elements from the canonical Gospels. It appears to be a pastiche, much in the vein of the longer ending of Mark. See Charlesworth and Evans, pp. 503–514.

[14] See Gérard Rochais, *Les récits de résurrection des mort dans le Nouveau Testament*, Society for New Testament Studies Monograph Series 40 (Cambridge: Cambridge University Press, 1981).

[15] In this case, Paul is stating something with which his readers would have agreed. The disagreement with some in Corinth is not over whether there is to be a resurrection, but what resurrection is to involve. See A. J. M. Wedderburn, *Baptism and Resurrection: Studies in Pauline Theology against Its Graeco-Roman Background*, Wissenschaftliche Untersuchungen zum Neuen Testament 44 (Tübingen: Mohr, 1987),

the matter to contradict the statement in 1 Thessalonians 4:13–18
that the dead will be raised and presented with the living, snatched
up into the air for that purpose, so as always to be with the Lord.
That literally physical belief in the general resurrection, which has
been styled apocalyptic,[16] influenced the portrayal of Jesus' resurrection, and is most manifest in the story of the empty tomb.

Within his discussion of 1 Corinthians 15:50 in its wider context,
Peter Carnley concludes with a telling insight:

> It is clear that Paul is struggling imaginatively to explain the nature
> of the resurrection body. This suggests that, whatever his Damascus
> road experience was, it was sufficiently ambiguous and unclear as not
> to be of real help in explaining the detailed nature of the body of the
> resurrection. The evidence thus leads us back to the view that his ini-
> tial experiential encounter with the raised Christ was in the nature of
> some kind of "heavenly vision." The fact that the nature of the body
> of the resurrection seems to have been open to speculation indicates
> that this was indeed a speculative matter that was brought up rather
> than settled by the encounter with the raised Jesus on the Damascus
> road.[17]

Carnley goes on to analyze the appearance of Jesus in Matthew in
similar terms, and he points out that Acts 26:19 formally describes
Paul's encounter with the risen Jesus as a "heavenly vision."[18] Carnley
does not observe that Paul himself claimed he had "seen our Lord
Jesus" (1 Corinthians 9:1) and included himself in the record of those
to whom the Jesus "appeared" (1 Corinthians 15:8, cf. v. 5). But
those citations only strengthen Carnley's overall point, that vision is
the fundamental category within which the initial experience of Jesus
as risen was apprehended (p. 245).[19] The narrative of the empty
tomb, a relatively late tradition within the Gospels as embellished in
Luke and John (as the consensus of scholarship would have it), functions to explain the theophany of the risen Jesus, although in itself

---

35–36. Given Paul's form of words in 1 Corinthians 15:29, the tendency to make
any disagreement about resurrection into a denial is evident (cf. n. 3 above).
  [16] Rochais, 187. See also Kenneth Grayston, *Dying, We Live: A New Enquiry into
the Death of Christ in the New Testament* (New York: Oxford University Press, 1990), 13.
  [17] Peter Carnley, *The Structure of Resurrection Belief* (Oxford: Clarendon, 1987), 233.
  [18] Carnley, pp. 237–238.
  [19] Similarly, see Francis Schüssler Fiorenza, *Foundational Theology: Jesus and the
Church* (New York: Crossroad, 1984), 35–37.

it is not a theophany.[20] That is why John 20:6–9 can put Simon Peter on the site of the empty tomb and yet not attribute belief in the resurrection of Jesus to him.

Care should be taken, however, not to use the language of vision in a reductionist way to describe what Paul did or did not see on the road to Damascus. In chapter 9, those around Paul hear the voice, but see nothing (Acts 9:7): the light blinds Paul, which is what brings him to Ananias and baptism (Acts 9:3–18). In chapter 22, Paul is quoted as saying his Companions saw the light, but did not hear the voice (22:9), and that may be consistent with the sense of what he says later (Acts 26:12–18). A hasty reference to the visionary passages in Acts has led to the suggestion that the resurrection was simply an experience of a heavenly light (*Lichtglanz*).[21] The portrayal of Paul's vision of the risen Jesus in Acts surely warns us away from reducing the experience to a single sensation, and rather emphasizes the importance of being in the presence of one identified as Jesus who commissions the recipient of the vision to a divine purpose. The "vision" or "appearance," so designated because the verbal usage "he was seen" (*ophthe*) is preferred in the New Testament, involves the awareness—mediated by a variety of senses and apprehensions—that Jesus is indeed present to one, and present so as to convey a divine imperative.

Those twin emphases, the identity of Jesus and the commissioning, underlie all stories of the actual appearance of the risen Jesus (and are not present in the later narrative of the empty tomb). In his recent study, Francis Schüssler Fiorenza has shown that the appearances of Jesus in the New Testament serve neither to console people generally about immortality nor to make an abstract point about God's eschatological victory.[22] Rather, "in almost all the stories the identity motif is present because even in appearances to the group he is either not recognized or recognized only with doubt and

---

[20] That statement is only accurate, of course, if the qualifying statement ("in itself") is observed. As soon as the young man or men are taken as angels, and more especially when the risen Jesus himself appears on the scene, the story of the empty tomb becomes theophanic. But the bulk of scholarship, and simple common sense, evaluates those elements as embellishments.

[21] For a suitably cautious assessment, see Carnley, 240–242.

[22] *Foundational Theology*, 45.

suspicion, so that he must confirm his identify before commissioning them."[23]

That insight, which conforms with the analysis here, comports
with Paul's capacity to claim that he has seen the Lord (1 Corinthians 9:1) and at the same time to refer to that moment as when
it pleased God to reveal His son "in" him (Galatians 1:15–16). The
conviction of divine presence, identified with Jesus and inciting to a
commission, defines the content of the experience that he had been
raised from the dead. That definition does justice to the narratives
of Jesus' appearance in the Gospels, to Paul's experience, and to the
appearance to James as given in the *Gospel to the Hebrews*.[24] In the
last case, James is informed by Jesus that he, as the son of man (of
Daniel 7), has risen from the dead. In that case as well as in the
others, the language of effective personal presence more accurately
conveys the scene than does the language of vision. "Vision," we
might conclude, is the overall category of experience in which our
sources would place the resurrection of Jesus; but the experience was
of his effectively divine and personal presence after his death.

Jesus' own teaching of resurrection involved a refusal to grant an
assumption of physical survival or the continuation of sexual relationships, and in so doing disappointed the expectations raised by the
story of the empty tomb, as well as the stories of the raisings of
the son of the widow of Nain, of Jairus' daughter, and of Lazarus.
The increasingly physical terms of reference of early Christian teaching, as in 1 Thessalonians 4:13–18, complicated the structure of the
traditions of Jesus' resurrection and of his teaching concerning the
resurrection. There is little of Jesus' teaching preserved, for the same
reason that there is only an echo of Peter's experience of the risen
Jesus: in both cases, the challenge to the assumptions of the embellishments of the story of the empty tomb was too great to be incorporated into the tradition of the Gospels.

Paul's discussion of the issue of the resurrection in 1 Corinthians
15 clearly represents his continuing commitment to the categorical
understanding of the resurrection that Jesus initiated. The particular occasion of his teaching is the apparent denial of the resurrec-

---

[23] *Foundational Theology*, 37.
[24] Cited in Jerome's *Famous Men*, 2; see Edgar Hennecke and Wilhelm Schneemel-
cher (tr. R. McL. Wilson), *New Testament Apocrypha* (London: SCM, 1973).

tion on the part of some people in Corinth (1 Corinthians 15:12b): "how can some of you say that there is no resurrection of the dead?"[25] His response to that denial is first of all on the basis of the integrity of apostolic preaching. Indeed, Paul prefaces his question with the earliest extant catalog of the traditions regarding Jesus' resurrection (1 Corinthians 15:1–11). That record makes it plain why so much variety within stories of the appearance of the risen Jesus in the Gospels was possible: reference is made to a separate appearance to Cephas, then to the Twelve, then to more than five hundred "brothers" (cf. Matthew 28:10!), then to James, then to "all the apostles," and then finally to Paul himself (vv. 5–8). The depth and range of that catalog is what enables Paul to press on to his first argument against the Corinthian denial of the resurrection (15:13–14): "But if there is no resurrection of the dead, neither has Christ been raised; and if Christ has not been raised, then our preaching is empty and your faith is empty!"

Paul expands on this argument in what follows (1 Corinthians 15:15–19), but the gist of what he says in that section is as simple as what he says at first: faith in Jesus' resurrection logically requires our affirmation of the reality of resurrection generally. That may seem to be an argument entirely from hypothesis, until we remember that Paul sees the moment when belief in Jesus occurs as the occasion of our reception of the Spirit of God (so Galatians 4:4–6):

When the fullness of time came, God sent forth His Son, born from woman, born under law, so that He might redeem those under law, in order that we might obtain Sonship. And because you are sons, God sent the Spirit of His Son into your hearts, crying, "Abba! Father!"

Because the Spirit in baptism is nothing other than the living Spirit of God's Son, Jesus' resurrection is attested by the very fact of the primordially Christian experience of faith. The availability of his Spirit shows that he has been raised from the dead. In addition, the preaching in his name formally claims his resurrection, so that to

---

[25] For a survey of attempts to explain this statement, see Wedderburn, pp. 6–37. He comes to no finding regarding what view Paul meant to attribute to some Corinthians, but he seems correct in affirming that a simple denial on their part (despite the form of words Paul uses) is unlikely (cf. nn. 3, 13 above). More likely, Paul was dealing with people who did not agree with his teaching of a bodily resurrection.

deny resurrection as a whole is to make the apostolic preaching into a lie: empty preaching, as Paul says, and therefore empty faith.

Paul's emphasis in this context on the spiritual integrity of the apostolic preaching, attested in baptismal experience, is consonant with Jesus' earlier claim that the Scriptures warrant the resurrection (since God is God of the living, rather than of the dead). Implicitly, apostolic preaching is accorded the same sort of authority which Jesus attributed to the Scriptures of Israel. Paul also proceeds—in a manner comparable to Jesus' argument (but in the reverse order)— to an argument on the basis of *the category of humanity* that the resurrection involves: he portrays Jesus as the first of those raised from the dead. His resurrection is what provides hope for the resurrection of the dead as a whole (1 Corinthians 15:20–28).

That hope, Paul goes on to argue, is what permits the Corinthians themselves to engage in the practice of being baptized on behalf of the dead (15:29).[26] The practice assumes that, when the dead come to be raised, even if they have not been baptized during life, baptism on their behalf after their death will confer benefit. Similarly, Paul takes his own courage as an example of the hopeful attitude which must assume the resurrection of the dead as its ground: why else would Christians encounter the dangers that they do (15:30–32a)?

The claim of resurrection, then, does not only involve a hope based upon a reception of Spirit and the promise of Scripture (whether in the form of the Scriptures of Israel or the apostolic preaching). Resurrection as an actual hope impinges directly upon what we conceive becomes of persons as we presently know them after they have died. (And that, of course, will immediately influence our conception of people as they are now perceived and how we might engage with them.) Paul's argument therefore cannot and does not rest solely on assertions of the spiritual integrity of the biblical witness and the apostolic preaching. He must also spell out an anthropology of resurrection, such that the spiritual hope and the scriptural witness are worked out within the terms of reference of human experience.

---

[26] For a discussion of the practice in relation to Judaic custom (cf. 2 Maccabees 12:40–45), see Ethelbert Stauffer (tr. J. Marsh), *New Testament Theology* (New York: Macmillan, 1955), 299 n. 544. C. K. Barrett also comes to the conclusion that the vicarious effect of baptism is at issue, *A Commentary on the First Epistle to the Corinthians* (London: Black, 1968), 362–364, although he is somewhat skeptical of Stauffer's analysis.

Precisely when he does that in 1 Corinthians 15, Paul develops a Christian metaphysics. He does so by comparing people in the resurrection, not to angels, as Jesus himself had done, but *to the resurrected Jesus*. And that comparison functions for Paul both (as we have already seen) because Jesus is preached as raised from the dead and because, within the experience of baptism, Jesus is known as the living source of the Spirit of God.[27] Jesus as raised from the dead is the point of departure for Paul's thinking about the resurrection, and because his focus is a human being, his analysis of the resurrection is much more systematic than Jesus'.

When Paul thinks of a person, he conceives of a body as composed of flesh, physical substance which varies from one created thing to another (for example, people, animals, birds, and fish; 1 Corinthians 15:35–39). But in addition to being physical bodies, people are also what Paul calls a "psychic body," that is bodies with souls (1 Corinthians 15:44). Unfortunately, the phrase is wrongly translated in many modern versions, but its dependence on the noun for "soul" [*psyche*] is obvious. The adjective does not mean "physical" as we use that word.[28] In other words, people as bodies are not just lumps of flesh, but they are self-aware. That self-awareness is precisely what makes them "psychic body."

Now in addition to being physical body and psychic body, Paul says we are (or can be, within the power of resurrection, since the issue is no longer natural endowment) "spiritual body" (1 Corinthians 15:44): "it is sown a psychic body, it is raised a spiritual body." Spirit in Paul's understanding (see below) is the medium in which we can relate thoughts and feelings to one another and to God. The explanation of how spirit may be the medium of God's communication is developed earlier in 1 Corinthians (2:10–11). Paul develops his position by quoting a passage from Isaiah 64:4 (in 2:9), which speaks of things beyond human understanding which God has readied for those who love him, and Paul then goes on to say (2:10–11):

---

[27] As Perkins (p. 227) puts it, "These associations make it clear that the resurrection of Jesus had been understood from an early time as the eschatological turning point of the ages and not merely as the reward for Jesus as a righteous individual."

[28] Although that is a simple point, it apparently requires some emphasis. Scholars of Paul routinely assert that Paul is speaking of some sort of physical resurrection, when that is exactly what Paul denies. See Tom Wright, *What Did Paul Really Say?* (Grand Rapids: Eerdmans, 1997), 50.

> God has revealed them to us through the Spirit; for the Spirit searches all things, even the depths of God. For who knows a person's affairs except the person's spirit within? So also no one has known God's affairs except the Spirit of God.

As Paul sees human relations, one person can only know what another thinks and feels on the basis of their shared "spirit." "Spirit" is the name for what links one person with another, and by means of that link we can also know what God thinks and feels. The Spirit at issue in the case of God, Paul goes on to say, is not "the spirit of the world," but "the Spirit of God" (1 Corinthians 2:12): the medium of ordinary, human exchange becomes in baptism the vehicle of divine revelation.

Paul's remark in 1 Corinthians 2 is part of a complete anthropology, which is now spelled out further in 1 Corinthians 15. Jesus on the basis of the resurrection is the last Adam, a life-giving spirit (1 Corinthians 15:45) just as the first Adam was a living "being" or "soul" (the two words are the same in Greek, *psyche*). Jesus is the basis on which we can realize our identities as God's children, the brothers and sisters of Christ, and know the power of the resurrection. In so saying, Paul defines a distinctive Christology as well as a characteristic spirituality. The metaphysics of both, which relate Christ to creation and believers to God, is predicated upon a regeneration of human nature. "Flesh" and "soul" become, not ends in themselves, but way stations on the course to "Spirit."

In his treatment of the resurrection, Origen shows himself a brilliant exegete and a profound theologian. He sees clearly that, in 1 Corinthians 15, Paul insists that the resurrection from the dead must be a bodily one. And Origen provides the logical grounding of Paul's claim (*On First Principles* 2.10.1):

> If it is certain that we are to be possessed of bodies, and if those bodies that have fallen are declared to rise again—and the expression "rise again" could not properly be used except of that which had previously fallen—then there can be no doubt that these bodies rise again in order that at the resurrection we may once more be clothed with them.

But Origen equally insists upon Paul's assertion that "flesh and blood cannot inherit the kingdom of God" (1 Corinthians 15:50). There must be a radical transition from flesh to spirit, as God fashions a body that can dwell in the heavens (*On First Principles* 2.10.3).

Origen pursues the point of this transition into a debate with fellow Christians (*On First Principles* 2.10.3):

> We now direct the discussion to some of our own people, who either from want of intellect or from lack of instruction introduce an exceedingly low and mean idea of the resurrection of the body. We ask these men in what manner they think that the "psychic body" will, by the grace of the resurrection be changed and become "spiritual;" and in what manner they think that what is sown "in dishonor" is to "rise in glory," and what is sown "in corruption" is to be transformed into "incorruption." Certainly if they believe the Apostle, who says that the body, when it rises in glory and in power and in incorruptibility, has already become spiritual, it seems absurd and contrary to the meaning of the apostle to say that it is still entangled in the passions of flesh and blood.

Origen's emphatic denial of a physical understanding of the resurrection is especially interesting for two reasons.

First, his confidence in this denial attests the strength of his conviction that such an understanding is "low and mean": the problem is not that physical resurrection is unbelievable, but that the conception is unworthy of the hope that faith speaks of. Origen's argument presupposes, of course, that a physical understanding of the resurrection was current in Christian Alexandria. But he insists, again following Paul's analysis, that the body which is raised in resurrection is continuous with the physical body in principle, but different from it in substance (*On First Principles* 2.10.3):

> So our bodies should be supposed to fall like a grain of wheat into the earth, but implanted in them is the cause that maintains the essence of the body. Although the bodies die and are corrupted and scattered, nevertheless by the word of God that same cause that has all along been safe in the essence of the body raises them up from the earth and restores and refashions them, just as the power that exists in a grain of wheat refashions and restores the grain, after its corruption and death, into a body with stalk and ear. And so in the case of those who shall be counted worthy of obtaining an inheritance in the kingdom of Heaven, the cause before mentioned, by which the body is refashioned, at the order of God refashions out of the earthly and animate body a spiritual body, which can dwell in Heaven.

The direction and orientation of Origen's analysis is defined by his concern to describe what in humanity may be regarded as ultimately compatible with the divine. For that reason, physical survival is rejected as an adequate category for explaining the resurrection. Instead, he emphasizes the change of substance that must be involved.

Second, the force behind Origen's assertion is categorical. The resolution of the stated contradictions—"psychic" as distinct from "spiritual," "dishonor" as distinct from "glory," "corruption" as distinct from "incorruption"—involve taking Paul's language as directly applicable to the human condition. In the case of each contradiction, the first item in the pair needs to yield to the spiritual progression of the second item in the pair. That is the progressive logic of Origen's thought, now applied comprehensively to human experience.

In Origen's articulation, progressive thinking insists upon the radical transition which resurrection involves. Although his discussion is a brilliant exegesis of Paul's argument, Origen also elevates the progressive principle above any other consideration which Paul introduces. What had been in Paul a method for understanding Scripture (see Galatians 4:21–31) that was applicable outside that field becomes in Origen the fundamental principle of global spiritual revolution. Only that, in his mind, can do justice to the promise of being raised from the dead.

For all that the transition from flesh to spirit is radical, Origen is also clear that personal continuity is involved. To put the matter positively, one is clothed bodily with one's own body, as we have already seen. To put the matter negatively, sins borne by the body of flesh may be thought of as visited upon the body that is raised from the dead (*On First Principles* 2.10.8):

> just as the saints will receive back the very bodies in which they have lived in holiness and purity during their stay in the habitations of this life, but bright and glorious as a result of the resurrection, so, too, the impious, who in this life have loved the darkness of error and the night of ignorance will after the resurrection be clothed with murky and black bodies, in order that this very gloom of ignorance, which in the present world has taken possession of the inner parts of their mind, may in the world to come be revealed through the garment of their outward body.

Although Origen is quite consciously engaging in speculation at this point, he firmly rejects the notion that the flesh is involved in the resurrection, even when biblical promises appear to envisage earthly joys (*On First Principles* 2.11.2):

Now some men, who reject the labor of thinking and seek after the outward and literal meaning of the law, or rather give way to their own desires and lusts, disciples of the mere letter, consider that the promises of the future are to be looked for in the form of pleasure and bodily luxury. And chiefly on this account they desire after the resurrection to have flesh of such a sort that they will never lack the power to eat and drink and to do all things that pertain to flesh and blood, not following the teaching of the apostle Paul about the resurrection of a "spiritual body."

His reasons for rejecting such a millenarian view are both exegetical and theological.

Paul is the ground of the apostolic authority he invokes, in a reading we have already seen. He uses that perspective to consider the Scriptures generally (*On First Principles* 2.11.3). But Origen deepens his argument from interpretation with a deeply theological argument. He maintains that the most urgent longing is the desire "to learn the design of those things which we perceive to have been made by God." This longing is as basic to our minds as the eye is the body: constitutionally, we long for the vision of God (*On First Principles* 2.11.4).

The manner in which Origen develops his own thought is complex, involving a notion of education in paradise prior to one's entry into the realm of Heaven proper (*On First Principles* 2.11.6):

I think that the saints when they depart from this life will remain in some place situated on the earth, which the divine Scripture calls "paradise." This will be a place of learning and, so to speak, a lecture room or school for souls, in which they may be taught about all that they had seen on earth and may also receive some indication of what is to follow in the future. Just as when placed in this life they had obtained certain indications of the future, see indeed "through a glass darkly," and yet truly seen "in part," they are revealed more openly and clearly to the saints in the proper places and times. If anyone is of truly pure heart and of clean mind and well-trained understanding he will make swifter progress and quickly ascend to the region of the air,[29] until he reaches the Kingdom of Heaven, passing through the

---

[29] At this point, Origen is reading 1 Thessalonians 4 through the lens of 1 Corinthians 15, just as later in the passage he incorporates the language of "mansions" from John 14:2.

series of those "mansions," if I may so call them, which the Greeks
have termed spheres—that is, globes—but which the divine Scripture
calls Heavens.

Even this brief excerpt from a convoluted description represents the
complexity of Origen's vision, but two factors remain plain and simple. First, the vision of God is the moving element through the entire
discussion. Second, Origen clearly represents and develops a construction of the Christian faith in which eschatology has been swal-
lowed up in an emphasis upon transcendence. The only time which
truly matters is that time until a person's death, which determines
one's experience in paradise and in the resurrection. "Heaven" as
cosmographic place now occupies the central position once occupied by the eschatological kingdom of God in Jesus' teaching. That,
too, occurs on the authority of progressive dialectics, the refinement
of Pauline metaphysics which gave Christianity its science of the
afterlife.

D. LIVING FOR RESURRECTION AND JUDGMENT: ISLAM

O People, if you are in doubt about the Resurrection, truly We have
created you from dust, then from a drop, then from a clot, then from
a bit of flesh, formed or unformed, so that We may make it clear to
you; We cause what We will to remain in the wombs until a set time;
then We draw you forth as infants. . . . And one sees the earth dried
up, but if We send down upon it water, it stirs and swells and causes
all beautiful kinds [of plant] to burgeon. That is because God is the
Truth, and brings alive the dead, and has power over all things; and
because the Hour will come—there is no doubt of it; and because
God will resurrect those who are in the graves. (S. 22:5–7)

Islam shares with its Jewish and Christian sister traditions a thoroughly linear, unidirectional, and teleological understanding of history. It begins when God in eternity created the universe and the
earth, upon which he placed humankind with their special responsibilities. For Muslims, the Qur'ān tells of what became in later
Islamic tradition an event said to have taken place before God's creation of the world—a primordial covenant that God sealed with
human beings while they were as yet unborn souls:

> Recall when your Lord drew forth from the children of Adam, from
> their loins, their posterity and caused them to bear witness on their
> own behalf: "Am I not your Lord?" And they said: "Yes, we bear wit-
> ness [to it]!" [That was] lest you say on the Day of Resurrection, "We
> were unaware of this," or lest you say, "Our fathers associated part-
> ners with God before; and we are their posterity after them; will You
> cause us to perish because of what the purveyors of falsehood did?"
> (S. 7:171–2)

Just as God created humankind in the beginning and charged them
with recognition of His sovereignty as their Lord, so at some future
point known only to Him, He will reclaim his own in a final Day
of Judgment or Reckoning. Its timing is known only to Him: "and
with Him is the knowledge of the Hour, and to Him you shall
return" (S. 43:85). Thus history will end, and the reality that we
know will cease to be—this is inevitable, no matter the timing.

Human beings live as it were between two eternities, but also
share in eternity, for God has promised that according to the quality of their lives in the world, they shall be rewarded or punished
in the hereafter, and that will be for eternity: they will be brought
"home" (ma'ād, lit. "place of return," as in Sūrah 28:85: "He who
has made the Qur'ān a duty for you will surely bring you home
again"). The reasoning and responsible beings whom God brought
forth into time from eternity in the creation of the world are destined to be gathered by Him after their trials in earthly existence
back into eternity, for "unto Him is the return" (S. 96:8). More than
this: God has created this world and the next as places of testing
and concomitant reward, respectively:

> Blessed be He in Whose hand is sovereignty, and Who has power
> over everything—He Who has created life and death in order to test
> you, which of you is best in works. He is the Exalted, the Forgiving.
> (S. 67:1–2)

This moral testing of human beings in their works is the tempering
process that prepares them for eternal life with God, beyond life and
death. Both the eternal happiness promised the righteous and god-
fearing, and the eternal punishment promised the evildoers and godless, are depicted in terms of earthly analogies, the first as life in an
eternal Eden, gardens of pleasure, rest, and refreshment; and the
second in terms of suffering in endless Fires of torment.

Eschatology

Human beings thus live in a teleological reality in which birth, life, and death in this "nearer [world]" (*al-dunyā*) is directed towards resurrection to, and eternal existence in, that "other" existence ([*al-dār*] *al-ākhirah*, "the last [abode]," the "end," "the hereafter"). In a teleologically oriented world such as that of the traditional Muslim worldview, eschatological matters are necessarily of primary importance. Resurrection and life beyond the grave are the logical corollaries of the sovereignty and justice of God and of the responsibility (for choosing obedience and service to God) that was bestowed upon human beings alone among all God's creatures. However strongly Islamic theology went on later to affirm God's absolute power and predestinarian control of His creation—in order to safeguard His omnipotence, omniscience, and transcendence—even in the Qur'ān itself it is clear that human beings are considered to be responsible for their separate destinies in the hereafter. As with Calvinist predestination in Christianity, Muslim predestination in no way entails the possibility of some kind of abdication of the personal responsibility to choose good and eschew evil.[30]

In a very concrete sense, this life is directed towards the next: "He it is Who made the earth subservient to you, so walk in its byways and eat of what He has provided; and unto Him is the resurrection" (S. 67:15). Every person's destiny at the time of resurrection will be the result of his or her choices and actions in "the life of this world." In other words, resurrection entails a reckoning for each human soul of what it earned in its time on earth. This whole process of resurrection and judgment is presented as a single, great, culminating event of worldly existence and history. It is termed variously the Day of Resurrection (*yawm al-qiyāmah*, S. 2:85; *yawm al-baʿth*, S. 30:56), the Last Day (*al-yawm al-ākhirah*, S. 2:8), the Day of Judgment (*yawm al-dīn*, S. 1:4), the Day of Reckoning (*yawm al-*

---

[30] The later Ashʿarite theological formula that became, for the Sunni theological mainstream, a scholastic solution of the problem of the apparent contradiction between divine predestination on the one hand and human responsibility and freedom to choose good or evil on the other, resorted to a notion of the "acquisition" of one's acts by each human actor as he or she fulfills his/her God-given destiny. But this was a development that came only late in the classical period, in the fourth–tenth century, as a result of ongoing theological disputes among the scholars about the nature of God and of the problems of theodicy and justice.

Ḥisāb, S. 40:27), the Day of Decision (*yawm al-faṣl*, S. 37:21) and the Hour (*al-sāʿah*, S. 22:7). The Hour stands as the telos, the final point towards which human history is directed, where one is returned to one's creator, and a person's actions and intentions are reckoned according to God's justice (albeit tempered by His infinite mercy). At this time, one's existence is transformed into a new, eternal being subject to either God's lasting pleasure or His lasting punishment. In what follows we shall trace the steps that lead, in traditional Muslim thought, from life through death to resurrection, judgment, and eternal life.

Between Death and Resurrection

Given the idea of a culminating Day of Resurrection or Day of Judgment at the end of history, one obvious question had first to be dealt with: What happens to the dead in the period from their individual deaths until the coming of the Hour? After all, human beings die at vastly different points in the historical movement from creation to resurrection and judgment. Some notion of what happens between the hour of death and the last hour, when the trumpet sounds to announce the judgment, had to be gleaned from the qur'ānic word and Muhammad's preaching. In the Qur'ān no significant attention or definitive explanation is given to this issue, but there are a few passages upon which classical and later Islamic thinkers based their interpretations.

Two fundamental ideas about the period between death and resurrection can be seen in, or at least extrapolated from, the Qur'ān and classical sources. At death, (i) the individual soul will be called forth by angels (S. 6:93; 25:21–2) to pass over from this world (*al-dunyā*) into the grave, (ii) into a state known as the *barzakh*, or "barrier" (S. 23:100: "and behind them is a barrier until the day they are resurrected") that separates life from death, and death from the final resurrection on the Day of Reckoning. As one of the earliest extant interpretive texts on the Qur'ān puts it, "the *barzakh* is the grave [lit., "graves"] that lies between you and the hereafter" (Mujāhid, *Tafsīr*, p. 488). The notion of the *barzakh* as a kind of limbo between each individual death (and a first or preliminary judgment) and the collective resurrection and final judgment developed out of these and other qur'ānic passages.

With respect to a preliminary judgment of a dead soul's life, there are varied references in the Hadīth to "the punishment in the grave," which would seem to indicate that sinners can expect judgment and retribution even before Judgment Day, once they enter their graves. Various traditions report Muhammad to have prayed regularly that he be spared the "punishment in the grave" (al-Bukhārī 23:89:5). This notion is supported by al-Bukhārī (23:89) in his citation of Sūrah 9:101, in which God says, "We shall punish them twice, and then they will be brought back to a mighty punishment," and in his further citation of Sūrah 6:93 in which the angels are said to call for the dead person's soul. Two other qur'ānic passages mention angels that take the life of the sinner and, in one instance, strike him at death (S. 8:52; 47:29). There is also mention in the Tradition literature of the coming of one or two angels (in later tradition given the names Nakīr and Munkar) to interrogate the newly deceased soul in the grave about his or her deeds in life (e.g. Muslim 1:163; al-Bukhārī 23:89:1; Musnad 3:233). Thus arose the idea that a person of faith can expect a comfortable experience in the grave, or in the *barzakh*, but an unbeliever only pain and punishment, until the Hour comes.

The Judgment Preaching

While the theme of the *barzakh* does not get much elaboration in the earliest sources, the theme of the Last Day, Resurrection, Judgment and the ensuing consignment of every human being to eternal bliss with God or eternal suffering without God looms large in both Qur'ān and *hadīth*. This theme is indisputably important, although its overemphasis by many modern scholars, especially in the qur'ānic context, has come at the expense of other significant core themes of the earliest Islamic preaching. These themes are primarily three: the signs of God in nature, the high moral standards by which God wants human beings to live, and the long history of God's efforts to give guidance to previous peoples and communities. Rightly seen, the Judgment Day theme is, however, a corollary of, and therefore inextricably intertwined with, these other three themes, each of which is also key to the qur'ānic worldview and that of most later Islamic tradition.

Consequently, a more integrated picture of the judgment preaching of Qur'ān and Sunnah and these three themes yields the following basic messages: (i) God's many signs in the natural world are to be seen as proofs that resurrection, judgment, and the transformation of this world on the Last Day are parts of a divine activity that parallels and recapitulates creation; (ii) the coherence of the moral universe (as depicted in and attested to by Qur'ān and Tradition) demands a final, just reckoning of earthly accounts on the Last Day, and (iii) the coming Judgment is the culmination of the long history of God's interactions with successive peoples through revelation and prophetic activity. These three elements in the qur'ānic and traditional Muslim understanding of eschatology reflect that fact that, as in Jewish and Christian piety, the teleological orientation of human striving in this world is fundamental to the Islamic *Heilsgeschichte*, or salvation-history. This history points towards the fulfillment of God's promises of justice to His creatures and the fulfillment in eternity of all that is imperfect and incomplete in this contingent, temporal world of striving in which we as human beings are caught up here.

The first theme, God's natural signs, involves the argument that God's creative work, so dramatically visible in the natural world around us, is a close parallel to, and indeed a promise of, His promised creative work of resurrection at the end of the created world:

> O People, if you are in doubt about the Resurrection (*ba'th*), truly We have created you from dust, then from a drop, then from a clot, then from a bit of flesh, formed or unformed, so that We may make it clear to you; We cause what we will to remain in the wombs until a set time; then we draw you forth as infants. . . . And you see the earth dried up, but if We send down upon it water, it stirs and swells and causes all beautiful kinds [of plant] to burgeon. That is because God is the Truth, and gives life to the dead, and has power over all things; and because the Hour (*as-sā'ah*) will come—there is no doubt of it; and because God will resurrect (*yab'athu*) those who are in the graves. (S. 2:5–7)

In particular, the constant revival of the earth with rain is taken as an earthly emblem or type of the coming Resurrection:

> And We have sent down from the sky blessed water with which We make burgeon gardens, the seed of the grain, and the tall date-palms with clustered fruit, as a provision for [Our] servants. And with this [water] we have revived a dead land; thus will be the coming forth [from the grave]. (S. 50:9–11)

In these and other qur'ānic passages (e.g., 23:12–22; 23:78–90; 67:14–26; and 71:15–20) God's creative power, exemplified in the creation of the earth, of human beings, and of new plant life (and in the ongoing re-creation and sustenance of each) is clearly connected to, and suggests, His power to bring back to life at "the Hour" what He has originally created in the world of natural growth and decay, birth and death. He who has created human beings from a drop of sperm or from clay can also recreate them from the moldering remains of the grave. He who revivifies living things with life-giving rains can also revivify those who have died. The resurrection parallels and recapitulates the creation and sustenance of humankind in the natural world:

> To Him is your return, all of you—the true promise of God. Surely He produces creation and then repeats it in order to reward those who are faithful and do good works justly, while as for those who reject faith, theirs is a boiling drink and agonizing punishment because they denied [God]. (S. 10:4)

Here it is not obvious that Paradise and the Fire are considered to lie in some remote location; rather there is the implication that "a new creation" (S. 50:15) simply replaces the old. Thus it is possible, as others have cogently argued,[31] to understand the Qur'ān to be saying that the world will be transformed rather than eradicated. For example, Sūrah 14:48 speaks of "a day when the earth will be transformed into other than the earth, and the Heavens [likewise], and they will come forth to God, the One, the All-Powerful." Similarly, the use of "renew" (*yu'īdu*) after mention of God's original creation refers to the end of days and emphasizes that the first creation will be recapitulated in new form (e.g., S. 56:60–62).[32]

As regards the second major theme, that of the inherent connection between how one lives in this world and what happens on the Day of Judgment, the Qur'ān's overriding emphasis throughout is moralistic in content and tone. A preponderant number of its verses are devoted to admonition and exhortation to humankind regarding

---

[31] For example, Fazlur Rahman, *Major Themes of the Qur'ān* (Minneapolis and Chicago, 1980), ch. 6, and Muhammad Abdel Haleem, *Understanding the Qur'ān: Themes and Style* (London and New York, 1999), ch. 7.

[32] On this, and for further references, see Rahman, 111.

the living of upright lives, doing good deeds, thinking pure thoughts, caring for one's fellows, and subordinating all of life to the will of God. Such are those who shall be rewarded with God's pleasure and the blessings of paradise:

> Truly, the god-fearing shall be amidst gardens and springs, receiving what their Lord has given them; for before that they had been doers of good. They slept but little of the night [because of their attention to prayer], and at dawn they sought [God's] forgiveness. From their wealth a share went to the beggar and the outcast. Surely, in the earth are signs for those of conviction, and in yourselves; do you not clearly see? And in the Heaven is your sustenance and that which you are promised. By the Lord of Heaven and earth, it is the truth, as true as your own speech! (S. 51:15–23)

Such persons' destinies will contrast sharply with the fates of those who have rejected God and His messengers and scriptures and followed their own willful desires. The latter are those who have been proud and heedless of their fellows, unwilling to follow the difficult path of moral rectitude and piety in this world, and their end will be a painful one in the punishment of the Fire:

> Truly, We created humankind subject to affliction! Does he imagine that none has power over him? [When] he says, "I have expended untold wealth," does he think that none has seen him? Did We not give him two eyes, a tongue, and two lips, and guide him to the two paths? But he did not attempt the steep way—and what will tell you what the steep way is? The freeing of a slave, or on a day of hunger feeding an orphan from one's kin or a needy one in misery! And then to be of those who have faith and encourage one another to endure and encourage one another to be compassionate. These are the Companions of the right hand; but as for those who refuse to have faith in Our signs [or "verses," "revelations": $\bar{a}y\bar{a}t$], they are the Companions of the left hand. Over them is a cloaking Fire. (S. 90:4–20)

The theme of the coming Judgment as the culmination of God's dealings with previous peoples (and now the Arabs), constitutes the third major, recurring element of the qur'ānic preaching. It is essentially a reassurance that in a history directed at a future reckoning, God has never left His creatures without help or preparation for that final accounting. On the Last Day, God will remind those who are ultimately consigned to the Fire that they were sent warnings and guidance, which they ignored:

> Those who reject faith are driven into Hell (Gehenna) in companies until, once they reach it and its gates are opened, its guardians will say to them: "Did not messengers of your own come to you, reciting to you God's signs [or: revelations, *āyāt*] and warning you of the meeting [with God] on this your day?" They will say, "Yes, indeed." But the word of punishment falls upon those who reject [God]. It is said, "Enter the gates of Hell (Gehenna), to abide forever therein. How evil is the resting place of the arrogant." (S. 39:71)

Thus a fundamental given of the Muslim worldview is that no nation has been left without guidance. Nonetheless, most have ungratefully rejected that guidance and frivolously squandered their earthly existence, seizing the pleasures of the present, fleeting world at the high risk of eternal punishment. On the last day, their accounts will be reckoned up and payment will be demanded. Still, despite clear warnings, they do not recognize this basic truth:

> Their reckoning draws near for people, and they turn aside heedlessly. No new reminder from their Lord comes to them except they listen to it yet go on playing, their hearts diverted. (S. 39:1–3)

In other words (S. 3:77), "those who, at the price of God's promise and their oaths, purchase a small profit will have no share in the Hereafter (*al-ākhirah*)." Moral life in the here and now is the prerequisite for eternal life in the enjoyment of God's pleasure in the next life, and the Qur'ān, like every other previous revelation, has this as its core salvific message. It is an explicit reminder that there is a real moral economy, like those of the Jewish and Christian traditions, which is fulfilled in the hereafter: what you earn in this world ("that which your hands have prepared in advance [for you before the Hour]": S. 3:182, 8:51, etc.) will be requited in the next world, good for good, evil for evil. Previous peoples have had their opportunities to heed earlier messengers and prophets, and Muslims are now called upon to seize their opportunity to be faithful and thus win eternal life in God's everlasting Gardens, or Paradise. The call to faith and obedience in both earlier revelations and in the qur'ānic message sent through Muhammad is a call to prepare for eternity.

The Last Things

The scenario for this coming of the end-time of resurrection, judgment, and entrance into eternity is a dramatic one, both in the resounding words of the Qur'ān and in their elaboration in the *hadīth* with myriad colorful additions that flesh out the qur'ānic narrative in vivid, often literal detail. Two major elements stand out: (i) the presaging of the Hour by cataclysmic earthly portents of the End, and (ii) the sequence of events on the Day of Reckoning itself.

Signs or portents of the imminent arrival of the eschaton—the Day of Judgment (*yaum al-dīn*) or Day of Decision (*yaum al-fasl*)— are suggested in a variety of qur'ānic passages. The gist of those passages that deal with the signs presaging the event itself is that there will be a cosmic cataclysm of unnatural events, involving natural disasters and other strange occurrences at the mundane level. All these are the explicit signs of the coming Hour or Eschaton:

> When the sky is split open, when the planets are scattered, when the seas boil forth, when the graves are torn up, a soul will realize what [deeds] it put forward and what it held back. (S. 82:1–5)

> When the earth trembles in earthquake, and the earth brings forth its burdens, and the person asks, "What is wrong with it?" On that day it will tell its stories to which Your Lord has inspired it. On that day, people will come forth separately to be shown their works, and whoever has done a grain's weight of good shall see it; whoever has done a grain's weight of evil shall see it. (S. 99)

The sky will become "like molten metal" (S. 70:8), the mountains will be "blown away" (S. 77:10) "like tufts of wool" (S. 70:9; 101:5), the moon will be eclipsed, the sun and moon will come together (S. 75:8–9), and the stars will be "extinguished" (S. 77:8). The sun will be veiled, mountains will move, seas will flood, the sky will be ripped away (S. 81:1, 3, 6, 11), and the stars will be extinguished (S. 77:8). Nursing mothers will abandon their suckling babes and pregnant women will miscarry (S. 22:2), children will turn gray (as if aged: S. 73–17), one's sight will be blotted out (S. 75:7, and sepulchres will be overturned (S. 82:4). It is a time when "the camels pregnant with young will be abandoned, and the wild beasts will be collected together." (S. 81:4–5). In brief, chaos will prevail.

To these vivid images, the *hadīth* add many additional examples and details of the signs of the Hour. The events both preceding and following the coming of the end-time are alluded to in various books of the *hadīth* collections, especially those books entitled "Fitan," or "Trials," which treat things related to the judgment. One refrain of

such traditions ascribed to the Prophet is that of violence and intra-
communal strife: "The Hour will not come until two great [Mus-
lim] parties fight one another and there is a huge slaughter between
them, while the claim of each is the same."[33] Another prophetic tradition warns,

> Just before the Hour, there will be days in which ignorance will descend,
> knowledge will be taken away, and *harj* will multiply—and "*harj*" means
> "killing." (al-Bukhārī 88:5:1–4)

Some accounts forecast conflict with the Byzantines and even the
conquest of their territory. Others speak of the subsequent appearance of the so-called "Antichrist," al-Dajjāl, to bring final tyranny,
suffering, and injustice, followed by the descent of Jesus for a final
victory of righteousness—all as tokens of the eschaton (*Muslim* 52:34;
cf. 52:37).

Some *hadīths* offer different lists of the signs of the coming of the
Last Day ascribed to the Prophet, such as the following:

> The Hour will not come before you see ten signs: smoke, al-Dajjāl,
> the Beast [of the earth], the rising of the sun in the west, the descent
> of Jesus son of Mary, Gog and Magog, and three landslides—in the
> east, in the west, and in the Arabian peninsula—, and the end of that
> will be a Fire that comes forth from the Yemen and drives humankind
> to their place of assembly [for Judgment]. (*Muslim* 52)

Other reports have the Prophet say that the Hour will not come
until a Fire from the land of the Hijāz illumines the necks of the
camels of Busra [in Syria]" (ibid. 52:42; al-Bukhārī 88:25:1), the living will want to be in their graves, and idols will be worshipped
again as before Islām (al-Bukhārī 88:23:1, 24:2). Turmoil, famine,
and idol worship are mentioned in other traditions, and in one even
the appearance of "nearly thirty lying *Dajjāl*s, each of whom claims
to be the apostle of God" (ibid. 52:79; al-Bukhārī 88:26:2). According
to the various traditions, the Dajjāl seems to be a type of the older
figure of the Antichrist, a horrible, one-eyed rejector of God (*kāfir*)
whose brief sway on earth will be the time of evil and unholy ter-
rors before the coming of the Hour, or before Jesus (who in some

---

[33] *Muslim* 52:17, 18; cf. 52:52–56; cf. *Íaḥīfat Hammām b. Munabbih*, ed. Rif'at
Fawzī 'Abd al-Muṭṭalib (Cairo, 1985), 23–24, *hadīths* 23–26.

accounts will kill the Dajjāl) comes again and reestablishes peace
prior to the Hour.

Still other traditions, many of them clearly created well after the
time of the Prophet and ascribed to him, add to the aforementioned
events that presage the Hour the coming (apart from that of Jesus)
of a "rightly guided one," or *mahdī*. This figure, in the more developed traditions, is expected as a deliverer who will do away with
the Dajjāl and usher in a reign of peace until the judgment itself.
Some traditions speak of *al-mahdī* as a prince from the house of
Muhammad whose rule will fill the earth with justice (*Musnad* 1:99,
376–77; al-Tirmidhi 31:52). His reign will last for seven, or up to
nine, years (Abu Dawud 35:7–9; *Musnad* 3:21, 26). It appears that
in Umayyad times (to 750), the tendency was to apply the name *al-
mahdī* to various persons who were expected to usher in better times,
the famously pious caliph 'Umar II (717–720) being the clearest
example. However, most typically, the figures identified as *al-mahdī*
were related to the Prophet or 'Alī and were persons in whose names
revolutions were raised. Gradually, 'Alid sympathizers focused ever
more on a future *mahdī* figure who would redeem things in a most
imperfect world by his reign at the end of time. These ideas led
eventually to the elaboration of the Twelver Shī'ite doctrine of the
"occultation," or concealment of the twelfth imam in descent from
the Prophet until the end of days when his ultimate "return" as the
awaited *mahdī* will result in an apocalyptic battle with the Dajjāl and
his forces of evil, the outcome of which will be the latters' defeat
and the redemption of those who have been faithful to the true
imams.[34]

In all these accounts, especially those of the *hadīth*, it is possible
to see the implication that the Hour is very near. In other words,
one might conclude that these traditions indicate that there was
strong expectation of actually experiencing in their lifetimes the end-
time, or eschaton, among the early Muslims, possibly even as early
as the time of the Prophet. But such judgment preaching as we find
in Qur'ān and *hadīth*, like that in other traditions, is by definition
aimed at bringing a sharp awareness of mortality and the brevity of

---

[34] See the article "al-Mahdī" by Wilferd Madelung, *EI*²; Moojan Momen, *An
Introduction to Shī'ī Islam* (New Haven, Conn.: Yale University Press), 161–171. Cf.
Mahmoud Ayoub, *Redemptive Suffering in Islam* (The Hague: Mouton, 1978), 216–229.

time and even history in the face of eternity, thus emphasizing the
imminence of judgment and the passing of temporality. This kind
of awareness of judgment and the burden it puts upon whomever
would not be found wanting came to be a strong theme of early
Muslim asceticism and some Sufi piety as well as more puritanical
strands of later Islam. It emphasizes the transience of this world in
the face of the abiding reality of the next (and of the punishments
that await the evildoers there). This is evident in the *hadīth* ascribed
to Muhammad in which he says, "If you knew what I know, you
would surely cry more and laugh less!"[35] It is also suggested by the
stories of early Muslim ascetics sometimes known as the "Weepers"
(*bakkā'ūn*), who, overcome with the fear of God, lamented their sins,
the uncertainty of salvation (given their human failings), and the
threat of eternal punishment. The textual basis for weeping as a sign
of piety is either Sūrah 19:58 ("when the signs of the All-Merciful
were recited to them, they fell down, prostrating and weeping") or
Sūrah 17:109 ("They fall down on their chins, weeping").[36]

Thus there is a way in which the strong stress in the classical
sources upon moral action vis-à-vis one's fellows and pure and true
worship and service of God alone necessarily places every human
being who pays heed to the message squarely before his or her ultimate destiny in every conscious moment of this life: judgment is
always imminent, eternity always just before one. Whether or not
Muhammad and the earliest Muslims considered the end of the world
close at hand even in their lifetimes, the early Islamic preaching is
aimed at preparing everyone among the faithful for the Hour, were
it to come this very instant:

> That is the Day of Truth, and whoever wants to do so should take
> recourse in his Lord. Truly, We are warning you of a retribution close
> at hand, a day in which man will see that which his hand has ear-
> lier prepared: and the unbeliever will say, "How I wish that I were
> dust!" (S. 78:39–40)

Insofar as the human perspective is concerned, every day is potentially the Day of Judgment, and the moral imperative is to be ready
to render an account of one's deeds at every moment.

---

[35] *Ṣaḥīfat Hammām*, 22, *hadīth* 12.
[36] On "weeping" in early Islam, see Fritz Meier, "Bakkā'," *EI*², *s.v.*

The events that will take place at the judgment itself are equally vivid and can be taken either literally or metaphorically. To begin with, according to the Qur'ān, God will take up His whole creation at the final reckoning and effectively suspend it, then pass judgment on His creatures:

> And they have not reckoned God's power rightly, and the earth will be entirely within the grip of His hand on the Day of Resurrection, and the Heavens will be rolled up in His right hand. Praised be He and exalted be He above that which they ascribe to Him [in the way of partners]. The trumpet is blown and whoever is in the Heavens and the earth blacks out save those whom God wills. Then it is blown another time and lo, they stand waiting. And the earth shines with the light of its Lord, and the Book is placed, and the prophets and witnesses are brought in, and judgment by the truth is made among them, and they are not wronged. Each soul is paid full measure for what it has wrought, and He is All-knowing about that which they do. And those who have denied [God] are driven in companies into Gehenna. (S. 39:67–71)

What we see here is echoed in many other passages. All still living will die: "every soul will taste death, then unto Us you will be returned" (S. 29:57).

From the Qur'ān we can reconstruct the onset of the Hour. The resurrection of bodies begins with the blowing of a trumpet (cf. S. 74:8; 78:18), mentioned above, or with two trumpet blasts according to Sūrah 79:6–7 (the word used here literally means "shaking" rather than trumpeting and could refer to the shuddering of the earth)—one to awaken the dead and the second to gather them for judgment. In any case, after the clarion's call God will gather all beings together, the faithful and the unbelievers, men and djinn, angels and demons (S. 20:102; 19:68, 85; 6:128–30; 34:40).

The *hadīth* offers further details about what will ensue when the trumpet has sounded. First will come the gathering of all humans on a vast plain of judgment under the brilliant light of the sun, where the only shade will be that of the divine throne of judgment. Then the wicked, who are facing consignment to the Fire, will be caught in the blazing heat of the Last Day with no recourse and no protection. The righteous Muslims meanwhile will come to meet the Prophet and quench their thirst at a great water basin or pool, although those among them who have made changes in Islam after the Prophet's death will be pulled back and denied access (al-Bukhārī

88:1:1–3; Muslim 43:33ff.; *Musnad* 1:334f.). Shīʿite hadiths place not only Muhammad, but also his cousin and son-in-law, ʿAlī, at the basin, offering water to the righteous followers of the true imams as relief from the burning heat of the plain of judgment.[37]

Once all are gathered, each person will have to face what he or she has done on earth, and each will have to do so alone, on "a day when no one will have any power at all to help another. Full disposition that day belongs to God" (S. 82:19; cf. 6:94; 19:80; 81:34–7). It would appear that the fate of each individual is already very clear: "Truly, the human being is a clear witness against himself" (S. 75:14). One early *hadīth* says that the miser's wealth shall meet him at the Hour in the form of a large snake, which will devour him.[38] In a more general example, the Qurʾān says of the judgment of the wicked: "Today we seal their mouths, and their hands will speak and their feet will bear witness to that which they have earned." (S. 36:65).

However, according to several passages in the Qurʾān, the deeds of each person will also have been recorded in Heaven in a book of deeds, or *kitāb*. At the reckoning this book appears either as a single heavenly ledger (S. 23:62; 45:29), or a separate, personal book that each receives and in which one's earthly deeds are tallied:

> And every person's bird [of augury] We have fastened to his neck, and We shall bring forth for him on the Day of Resurrection a book that he will find spread open. [It will be said to him,] "Read your book. Your soul is sufficient as a reckoning against you today." (S. 17:13–14)

According to Sūrah 69:19–37 and 56:27–56, those on the right (the pious) will receive their records in their right hands, those on the left (the impious) will receive theirs in their left, thus marking the verdict on each:

> As for the one given his record (*kitāb*) in his right hand, he will say, 'take and read my book. I knew I would be held to account.' And he will be in a blissful state. . . . While as for him who is given his book in his left, he will say, 'Would only that I had not be been given my book and did not know my accounting.' (S. 69:19–21, 25–26)

---

[37] See examples cited by Ayoub, 205–209.
[38] *Ṣaḥīfat Hammām*, 33, *hadīth* 73.

Another image used in the Qur'ān is that of the scales on which each person's deeds will be weighed to determine his or her fate:

> So they whose scales are heavy, those are the ones who prosper; and they whose scales are light, those and they who lose their souls in Gehenna eternally. (S. 23:102–103; cf. 7:8–9; 21:47, etc.)

After the reckoning of deeds, it appears that the righteous will proceed to their happy fate, while the ungodly will find their punishment. Tradition takes up here the motif of a crossing of the bridge, or *sirāt*, which is referred to in the Qur'ān in rather ambiguous terms (albeit traditionally taken as eschatological), in Sūrah 37:23–4 and 36:66. These are interpreted as referring to a bridge over the Fire that all must cross over; later tradition elaborates this in various ways, seeing the *sirāt* as a sorting device for the righteous, who pass over with ease (as if it were a wide way), and the evildoers, who fall into the Fire (because it is for them as narrow as a blade), or as a bridge leading to the Garden, across which the Prophet as intercessor will lead his people.

The issue of intercession by the Prophet for his community on the Last Day is not a simple one. The Qur'ān has conflicting statements about the possibility of intercession of any kind, whether by angels for the faithful or by anyone for the unbelievers. However, the *hadīth* has many examples of the intercession on behalf of the faithful by the Prophet at judgment (and in Shī'ite *hadīth*s, by Fātimah and the imams, especially 'Alī and his martyred son Husayn). For example, one tradition has Muhammad say that God grants every prophet one request, and he will ask that this be deferred to the Resurrection, when he will use his boon to intercede for his people.[39] There is even a tradition in which the faithful who have been marked for Paradise are said to be able to intercede with God for their sinful brethren and sisters who are otherwise designated for the eternal Fire:

> On the Day of Resurrection, the people of [Paradise] will be drawn up in line, and when one of the people of the Fire passes them one of them [the people of the Fire] will say, "So and so, do you not remember the day you asked me for drink, and I gave you something

---

[39] Ibid., 23, *hadīth* 20.

to drink?" And he [one of the people of Paradise] will intercede for him. And [another] man will pass by and say, "Do you not remember the day I gave you [water] for ritual purification?" And thereupon he will intercede for him. (Ibn Majah 33:8:2)

How early such traditions are is always a question, but the very fact of the qur'ānic stress upon God's great mercy, which is expanded substantially in the traditions, would suggest that intercession would not be rejected by all Muslims at any time. This is reinforced in one hadith, which has Muhammad say that God will say at the Last Judgment, "The angels have interceded, the prophets have interceded, and the faithful have interceded; there remains only the Most Merciful of the merciful" (*Muslim* 1:302; al-Bukhārī 97:24:5; *Musnad* 3:94–95).

The Hereafter

The Qur'ān at points makes clear that the concepts of the Garden and the Fire are earthly concepts or similitudes for the unknowable realities of eternal salvation and eternal damnation, respectively. Thus Sūrah 13:35 reads,

> The similitude of the Garden that is promised to the godfearing [is a place] underneath which flow rivers; its food and its shade are everlasting. That is the reward of those who are godfearing, while the reward of the ungrateful deniers [of God] is the Fire.

The nature of the Fire and the Garden, Hell and Paradise could be treated at great length. In the context of our focus on the end of days, suffice it here to close by remarking only three things: (i) the bliss of paradise and the agony of hell are emphasized from the Qur'ān forward in Islamic tradition; (ii) whichever of these two destinations one receives is the inexorable result of one's moral or immoral life and one's faith in and worship of, or lack of faith in, and failure to worship exclusively, God the Lord of creation; and (iii) the joys of Paradise and torments of Hell are described in often physical terms, but usually ones that admit as logically of figurative as of literal interpretation.

What is understood to be real is the fact of ultimate retribution for evil deeds and unbelief, and ultimate recompense for good deeds and faith. The details of the Garden and of the Fire, of Paradise and Hell, are vividly portrayed in Islamic tradition, as they are (albeit in somewhat less detail) in the Qur'ān itself, but it is not the details so much as the ultimate reality of eternal salvation or eternal punishment as the dual choice of human fates that is at issue. And the way to inherit a blessed eternity is to pay heed to God and His messengers and books and not give in to the temptation to invest ourselves in our present, transient lives—something that the Qur'ān warns about constantly:

> But you prefer the life of this world, when the Hereafter is better and more enduring. Truly, this is in the scrolls of old, The scrolls of Abraham and Moses. (S. 87:16–19)

This is the ultimate import of the judgment preaching of the Qur'ān and classical Islamic tradition: that it matters eternally what choices we make in the here and now. In both possible ends of human existence, the overarching fact is that each is finally in God's hands, as is everything in existence: "Do not all things reach God at last?" (S. 42:53)—a suitable conclusion for not only our treatment of Islamic eschatology, but also of this entire book on the classical formulations of the three great monotheistic faiths.

INDEX OF SCRIPTURE AND ANCIENT SOURCES

Note: All works cited in this index are arranged alphabetically within their tradition's categorization.

| 2.11.4 | 289 |
| 2.11.6 | 289 |

Philo
De specialibus legibus
| 3.131 | 137 |

Plato
Republic
| 462C–D | 137 |

Seneca
De clementia
| 1.5.1 | 137 |

Tertullian
Apology
| 20–21 | 239 |

CREEDAL STATEMENTS, ISLAMIC

Fiqh Akbar I
| 1–5 | 109 |
| 7 | 109 |

HADĪTH

Ibn Majah
| 33:8:2 | 306 |

Malik's Muwatta
| 18:58 | 201 |
| 21:1 | 251 |

Musnad of Ibn Hanbal
1:99	301
1:334f.	304
1:376–77	301
2:18	107
2:187	197
3:5	201
3:21	301
3:26	301
3:94–95	306
3:233	294

Sahih al-Bukhārī
3:10	195
10:62:1	199
23:89	294
23:89:1	294
23:89:5	294
30:2	201
35:7	205
46:3	113
56:6:1	251
56:22:1	251
56:102:5	251
59:1:4	97
60:8:5	111
60:8:14	111
60:19:1	111
61:1:5	111
61:1:6	111

81:18	205
81:53:1	98
82:1:2	87
82:1:3	87
82:3:5	89
88:1:1–3	303–304
88:5:1–4	300
88:23:1	300
88:24:2	300
88:25:1	300
88:26:2	300
97:12	82
97:24:5	306

Sahih Muslim b. al-Hajjāj
1:163	294
1:302	306
2.6	199
3:5	206
13:165	201
30:15	197
43:33ff.	304
43:168	111
44:199	111
46:3	87
46:7	88
46:22	103
46:23–26	103
49:14	97
49:15	97
51:40	98
52	300
52:17	300
52:18	300
52:34	300

OLD TESTAMENT PSEUDEPIGRAPHA

PROPHETIC BIOGRAPHY

QUR'ĀN

82:4	299	99:6–8	88, 299
82:19	304	99:7–8	88
87:16–19	307	101:5	299
90:4–20	297	112	93
92:5–10	88	112:3	92
96:8	96, 291	112:4	91
98:6	246		

QUR'ĀNIC COMMENTARY

Tafsīr of Mujāhid
488   293

TALMUD OF BABYLONIA (BAVLI)

Abodah Zarah		Menahot	
2a–b	212	29b	76
4b	217	53b	75
Arakhin		Sanhedrin	
15a–b	74	56a	221
Baba Batra		57a	222
75a	266	91b	264
Berakhot		100a	267, 268
6a–b	72	111a–b	69
7a70, 73		Shabbat	
Makkot		31a	77, 168, 174
23b–24a	174		
Megillah		89a	71
29a	261	133b	78

TALMUD OF THE LAND OF ISRAEL (YERUSHALMI)

Abodah Zarah		1:9.II.S	66
3:1.II.AA	65	Sanhedrin	
Bekharot		1:1.IV.Q	65
9:1.VII.E	67	1:4.V.FF–GG	65
Horayot		2:1.III.O	65
3:5.III.PP	65	5:1.IV.E	66
Nedarim		10:1.IX	64
6:9.III.CCCCf	66	Ta'anit	
Pe'ah		1:1.II:5	269
1:1.XXXII.1	259	1:1.X.Eff	65
Qiddushin			
1:7.IX.B	66		

TOSEFTA

Abodah Zarah		Hullin	
8:4–6	221	10:16	256

INDEX OF SUBJECTS

hadīth, 24–25, 32–34, 205–206
hāfiz, 30
hajj, 198, 201–202
Halakhah, 8, 161–163, 167–172,
  213–218
Hexapla (Origen), 21
Hillel, 174
History of the Church (Eusebius), 20–21
Holy Spirit
  Paul's teachings on, 176, 285–286
  as source of Christian theology, 13,
  19
Holy Things, 162, 170
Hosea, 229
households
  as fundamental social unit, 141
  halakhah concerning, 163
Hullin, 162
humility, 71
al-Husayn, 108, 305

ʿibādāt, 198–202
idolatry/idolaters
  as act of will, 209–213
  at end of days, 268–269
  and Islam, 245, 248–252
  as like death, 220
  relations between Israel and,
  213–219
  religious obligations of, 221–222
al-ilāh, 81
Incarnation, 13, 18–19, 49
intentionality, 206–207
intercession, 305–306
Irenaeus, 16–20
Isaac, 227, 239–240
Isaiah, 229
Islam
  acts of worship, 198–202
  authoritative writings of, 28–35, 197
  centrist position in *aqīdah* (creed),
  109–110
  community of the faithful in,
  100–114
  diversity of traditions, 1, 23
  eschatology in, 292–293, 298–307
  faithful and unfaithful, 240–254
  islām defined, 23, 190–191
  mahdist movements, 108
  naming God, 80–84
  "pillars," 198–202
  Qurʾān as preeminent document of,
  23–25, 29–32

and relation to Arabs, 105–106
as religion of Abraham, 102–103
resurrection and judgment in,
  290–307
sharīʿa, 110, 113, 192–193, 196
Shīʿī and Sunnī differences in
  Hadīth, 25
Shīʿism, 108, 253
Shīʿites and imams, 107–108
social relations in, 198, 202–207
Sūfī practice, 203
Sunnī ascendency, 108–110
texts from early, 25
theology of, 26–28
as universal religion, 99
way of life, 190–207
Islamic civil war, first, 107, 252–253
Israel
  community in early Christian circles,
  114–127
  community in Synoptic Gospels,
  127–138
  confrontation of Judaism and
  Christianity over, 151, 152,
  155–156
  ethnicity of, examined, 139–146
  favored by God over Nations,
  209–213
  holiness of, over time, 169–170
  in Judaism, 3, 4
  as metaphor for family, 152–156
  in Mishnah, 147–149
  restoration of at end of days,
  258–270
  as sui generis, 150–151, 157–159
  in Yerushalmi, 150–152

Jacob, 227
jamāʿah, 101
James the Just, and Israel, 116–121,
  126
Jerusalem, 115–116, 117, 125
Jesus
  called Christ, 38–39
  as central mediator of knowledge of
  God, 177–178
  eschatological teachings of, 270–273
  and Eucharistic practice, 132–138
  as God Incarnate, 18–19, 36–38,
  49–50, 56–59
  identity and titles of, 39–44
  as *logos* and light of reason, 236–240
  Muslim conception of, 92

INDEX OF MODERN AUTHORS